Trial by Jury

Trial by Jury

The Seventh Amendment and Anglo-American Special Juries

James Oldham

NEW YORK UNIVERSITY PRESS
New York and London

NEW YORK UNIVERSITY PRESS
New York and London
www.nyupress.org

Library of Congress Cataloging-in-Publication Data
Oldham, James.
Trial by jury : the Seventh Amendment and
Anglo-American special juries / James Oldham.
p. cm.
Includes bibliographical references and index.
ISBN–13: 978–0–8147–6204–2 (cloth : alk. paper)
ISBN–10: 0–8147–6204–2 (cloth : alk. paper)
1. United States. Constitution. 7th Amendment.
2. Jury—UnitedStates—History. 3. Jury—England—History.
4. Constitutional law—United States. I. Title.
KF8972.O415 2006
347.73'752—dc22 2005036696

New York University Press books are printed on acid-free paper,
and their binding materials are chosen for strength and durability.

Manufactured in the United States of America
10 9 8 7 6 5 4 3 2 1

Contents

Preface

Over the past twenty years, I have studied and written about aspects of the history of trial by jury in England and America. Most of these studies were published, although in diverse journals and books, both English and American. They were never designed to be parts of a coordinated history, but they nonetheless fell into two broad categories. One was the historical use of juries of experts, and the other was the preservation of the civil jury in the United States by the Seventh Amendment to the Constitution. This book brings together in a single volume edited and updated versions of these prior writings, augmented by new material.

What prompted my initial interest in jury history was the popular use in English common-law courts in the eighteenth and nineteenth centuries of what was called the "special jury." By the late eighteenth century, the most common form of the special jury was a jury of merchants impaneled to decide a commercial case, and the merchants customarily relied on their own commercial expertise as much as on the evidence produced in court. These were clearly juries of experts, but also they were juries of peers whenever, as was typical, the parties to the litigation were businessmen.

The Chief Justice of England's leading common-law court in the late eighteenth century (the Court of King's Bench) was Lord Mansfield, a judge of formidable intelligence and influence. Mansfield was famous for his instrumental use of special juries in articulating and developing principles of commercial law. In the early stages of my research on Lord Mansfield's judicial career, I became curious to know the origins of the special jury, and this led to a long article on the subject. Later I looked ahead to the nineteenth century and wrote about the continuing popularity of the special jury into and beyond the reform era, after which it fell subject to abuse and was largely abandoned. The third and last part of the work that I have done on the history of the special jury was an examination of its trajectory in the United States, where in a number of states variations of the special jury—or, as it is sometimes called, the "struck jury"—yet survive.

Two additional examples of juries composed of jurors with particular knowledge or expertise were the so-called self-informing jury and the jury of matrons. Edited and updated versions of published studies of these types of juries, together with the special jury articles, make up chapters 5 through 9 in this book.

The first four chapters address the scope of the civil jury-trial guarantee embodied in the Seventh Amendment to the U.S. Constitution. Chapters 1 and 2 first appeared in a *festschrift* for Brian Simpson, and part of chapter 3 was published in a review essay of Tom Green's book, *Verdict According to Conscience.* The remainder of chapter 3 and all of chapter 4 are new.

I am grateful to the following publishers and journals for permission to present in this book edited, updated, and reconfigured versions of the various earlier studies:

- Oxford University Press (chapters 1 and 2, adapted from "The Seventh Amendment Right to Jury Trial: Late Eighteenth-Century Practice Reconsidered," in Katherine O'Donovan and Gerry R. Rubin, eds., *Human Rights and Legal History: Essays in Honour of Brian Simpson,* Oxford University Press [2000]).
- Greenwood Publishing Group (part of chapter 3, from "The Jury: Perspectives on Thomas Andrew Green's *Verdict According to Conscience,*" VIII *Criminal Justice History* 163 (1987); chapter 5 from "On Pleading the Belly: A History of the Jury of Matrons," VI *Criminal Justice History* 1 [1985]).
- The Selden Society (chapter 6, part of the pamphlet version of my lecture at the Annual General Meeting in London in July 2004, "The Varied Life of the Self-Informing Jury" [2005]).
- *University of Chicago Law Review* (chapter 7, from "The Origins of the Special Jury," 50 University of *Chicago Law Review* 137 [1983]).
- *Journal of Legal History* (part of chapter 8, from "Special Juries in England: Nineteenth Century Usage and Reform," 8 *Journal of Legal History* (London) 148 [1987]).

- Hart Publishing (part of chapter 8, from "Jury Research in the English Reports in CD-ROM," in John Cairns and Grant McLeod, eds., *"The Dearest Birth Right of the People of England": The Jury in the History of the Common Law,* Hart Publishing [2002]).
- *William and Mary Bill of Rights Journal* (chapter 9, from "The History of the Special (Struck) Jury in the United States and Its Relationship to Voir-dire Practices, the Reasonable Cross-Section Requirement, and Peremptory Challenges," 5 *William and Mary Bill of Rights Journal* 623 [1998]).

Certain editorial conventions have been followed in the preparation of this book. The general citation format for primary and secondary printed sources corresponds to *The Chicago Manual of Style,* except that I follow the New York University Press convention of not naming publishers of books published before the twentieth century. For printed case reports, I use the standard "Bluebook" citation form for American cases, and for English cases, I follow the standard conventions and abbreviations for citations to the nominative reports, as reflected in the full reprint of the *English Reports.* Parallel citations to the nominative reports and to the *English Reports* reprints are given. When original documentary sources are quoted, I modernize spelling, capitalization, and punctuation to the extent necessary for comprehension or clarity.

I am indebted to my institution, Georgetown University Law Center, for research grants that facilitated archival work in London for several of the previous studies, as well as for chapter 4. In the task of editing the prior publications and conforming them to the guidelines followed by the Press, I have had indispensable help from Faculty Assistant Diane Hedgecock and Faculty Manuscript Editor Anna Selden. For library and bibliographical queries, Special Collections Librarian Laura Bédard, as always, has provided invaluable help. With meticulous care, Barbara Wilcie Kern provided the detailed index, the tables of statutes and cases, and essential proofreading. Finally, I am grateful to Deborah Gershenowitz, at New York University Press, for her strong support of the concept of this book and for her patience and guidance.

Introduction

This book explores the colorful and varied history of trial by jury as established in England, transplanted to America, and preserved in the U.S. Constitution. Special attention is given to the scope of the Seventh Amendment guarantee of trial by jury and to the emergence and spread of the philosophy that juries must be formed from a jury pool that reflects a reasonable cross-section of the local population. That philosophy is compared to, and contrasted with, past experience in the history of trial by jury that featured juries of experts, such as juries of merchants in commercial cases and juries of women (matrons) impaneled to assess a female litigant's claim of pregnancy.

The civil jury in federal courts is protected in the U.S. Constitution by the declaration in the Seventh Amendment that, "In suits at common law, where the value in controversy shall exceed twenty dollars, the right to trial by jury shall be preserved." What does this simple expression mean? As is explained in chapter 1, the U.S. Supreme Court informed us, early in the nineteenth century, that the expression meant the right to trial by jury as determined by the practices and rules of the common law of England ("the grand reservoir of all our jurisprudence") as of 1791, when the Seventh Amendment took effect. This has become known as "the historical test." Superimposing a template of 1791 English practices onto modern American lawsuits is often no easy task—indeed, in the view of many critics, the formula makes little sense. Sensible or not, the Supreme Court adheres steadfastly to the historical test, and in application it poses a number of difficult questions.

Consider, for example, the English common-law practice in 1791 that featured the widespread use of the "special jury," usually a jury of experts. Frequently merchant jurors were impaneled to allow them to apply their expertise in deciding commercial disputes. Does the historical test preserve the special jury? Special juries were in fact used extensively in the

United States for nearly two centuries, but selecting juries from exclusive classes of people is not in keeping with the pervasively egalitarian spirit of late-twentieth- and twenty-first-century America. Indeed, the Supreme Court has ruled that in criminal cases, the Sixth Amendment demands that jurors be chosen from a jury pool that profiles a reasonable cross-section of the local population. As is obvious, the "reasonable cross-section" requirement and the special jury are fundamentally incompatible. These developments, including the English experience with special juries, are explored in detail in chapters 7, 8, and 9.

If juries of experts in federal civil cases are no longer palatable, could the jury be dispensed with altogether whenever factual issues become so complicated, scientific, or specialized that they exceed the grasp of the average citizen found in the jury pools? This question—often described as whether there can be a "complexity exception" to the Seventh Amendment—has been explored in academic scholarship but never squarely faced by the Supreme Court. In light of late-eighteenth-century decisions by the English Court of Chancery, a strong argument can be made that such an exception would be valid under the historical test. This is discussed in chapter 2.

Since the Seventh Amendment governs only civil cases in the federal courts, there is still room for debate about whether, as a matter of state law, impaneling jurors with special qualifications remains viable. One juror qualification from the England of 1791, however, is clearly impermissible today—the requirement that jurors be male. Women were not given the formal right to be jurors until the twentieth century, yet there is a fascinating and surprising history of the use of juries of women from at least the fifteenth to the nineteenth centuries in England, as well as in early America. In an era when the all-male community of medical doctors remained in deep ignorance about the mysteries of pregnancy, juries of women were impaneled to determine whether female parties to litigation were "quick with child." The reason for the practice, of course, was that the female jurors were the experts. Who better could tell whether a woman was pregnant than other women who had experience with childbirth? Usually the female litigant who claimed to be pregnant was a woman who had been convicted of a capital offense. The full story is told in chapter 5.

Especially with respect to civil juries, an issue that once was fiercely controversial in England and early America was whether the jury had the power to decide the law as well as the facts. In some measure, this issue derives from the early era of the jury in England, when the jury was said to be "self-informing." That is, the jurors came from the neighborhood, and some of them, at least, were expected to know or to find out the facts of the dispute in litigation, rather than to reach a verdict based exclusively on evidence introduced in court. This early phase of trial by jury is summarized in chapter 6.

Once the modern model of trial by jury arrived (probably during the 1500s) and the jury was to base its deliberations and verdict only on evidence introduced in court, the familiar maxim emerged that juries were to find the facts but judges were to declare the law. Inevitably, however, the question arose whether the jury had the power to ignore the law when not to do so would lead to a result that the jury thought unjust. At various times in history, juries have ignored the law, and the behavior has come to be known as "jury nullification." This occurred in the early eighteenth century in England when the criminal statutes constituted what has been termed "the bloody code" because so many offenses were punishable by death. Theft of something worth at least forty shillings was a common example, and juries often balked at sending petty thieves to the gallows, especially when the defendants told convincing stories of sympathetic or unfortunate circumstances. At times, juries were openly invited by the judges to return a verdict of "guilty of the theft of thirty-nine shillings," even when the proof of much higher value was evident.

Another widely known phase of the contest over jury power erupted in the eighteenth century in seditious libel prosecutions, where, by traditional legal rules established in the late seventeenth and early eighteenth centuries in England, the role of the jury was severely limited. In a number of notorious cases associated with popular clamor for freedom of the press, juries refused to cooperate, and a campaign emerged to change the law. By Fox's Libel Act of 1792, 32 G.3, c.60, it was established that in seditious libel cases, the jury could determine "the whole matter"—not only the facts about a challenged publication but also whether the publication was libelous.

As can readily be imagined, there have been and remain many contexts in which juries have been tempted to ignore the law, and not always in the name of mercy. Notorious examples in the United States occurred in the Reconstruction Era after the Civil War. Yet the notion of validating the law-finding power of juries continues to have powerful popular appeal. Indeed, an organization exists in the United States called the Fully Informed Jury Association that, among other things, lobbies state legislatures to enact statutes that would require judges to instruct juries that they have the right to determine law as well as fact. There is a large recent literature on jury nullification. Although the topic is not a central focus of this book, jury nullification is addressed in chapter 3.

Even if juries are to be kept to fact determinations, issues arise about what is factual and what is not. The problem of differentiating law from fact is also addressed in chapter 3. A related question is whether determinations of damages are invariably "findings of fact" and therefore always the responsibility of the jury. Prompted by recent Supreme Court decisions, an exploration of two aspects of this question is found in chapter 4: first, whether juries are essential (unless waived) to determine compensatory damages when the defendant's liability is admitted, for example, after default judgments are entered, and, second, whether jury determinations of punitive damages fall under any Seventh Amendment protection.

In England, the civil jury trial is largely extinct, and there are persistent efforts to scale back trial by jury even in criminal cases.[1] In the United States, the number of jury trials is decreasing (the result of a number of factors, such as plea bargaining in criminal cases, settlement of civil cases, and the use of alternative methods of dispute resolution), yet the constitutional protection of trial by jury continues to receive strong endorsement from the Supreme Court. This is demonstrated most recently in cases dealing with "sentencing factors," discussed in chapter 3.

1

The Scope of the Seventh Amendment Guarantee

Trial by jury in the United States, however controversial in application, remains a treasured part of most citizens' concept of liberty. Everyone is familiar with the safeguards that trial by jury supplies to criminal defendants. Nearly everyone knows that the right to a jury trial also applies to civil cases, although it can be waived. The source of the right in civil cases in federal courts is the Seventh Amendment, and in state courts the right is preserved by comparable provisions of state constitutions.

The Seventh Amendment provides that "in suits at common law" involving more than twenty dollars, "the right to jury trial shall be preserved." This seems simple and straightforward, but what does it mean? What right to jury trial? What did the framers have in mind by their simple formulation? One possibility is that they intended to preserve the jury trial practices that existed in suits at common law in the United States when the Seventh Amendment became effective. But, as Edith Henderson observed in her study of the background of the Seventh Amendment, there were enormous and unsystematic variations among the original thirteen states, and, although "a general guarantee of the civil jury as an institution was widely desired, . . . there was no consensus on the precise extent of its power."[1] Indeed, the Seventh Amendment can be viewed as a formulation that was deliberately imprecise in order to cover divergent practices.

Unavoidably, it fell to the Supreme Court to fashion a test that could be used to measure the scope of the protection embodied in the Seventh Amendment, or in state imitations. The Court did so in 1812 in the case of *United States v. Wonson,* in which Justice Joseph Story wrote: "Beyond all question, the common law here alluded to [in the Seventh Amendment] is not the common law of any individual state, (for it probably differs in all), but it is the common law of England, the grand reservoir of all our jurisprudence."[2] Story added that his proposition must be so obvious "to every person acquainted with the history of the law" that it needed no explanation.[3] He did not peg the test to 1791, the year when the Seventh Amendment took effect; this feature was clarified in a later opinion by the Court.[4]

The rule thus fashioned by the Supreme Court came to be called "the historical test." A commonly quoted, succinct version of the test is the following 1935 formulation in the case of *Dimick v. Schiedt:* "In order to ascertain the scope and meaning of the Seventh Amendment, resort must be had to the appropriate rules of the common law established at the time of the adoption of that constitutional provision in 1791."[5]

This test survives to the present day, despite unrelenting criticism from those who favor flexibility in constitutional interpretation. Illustrative is the following summary by Martin Redish:

> Blind adherence to history would seem to place modern judicial administration in an historical straight jacket, controlled by the policies of a society of 200 years ago. Traditional constitutional analysis has never been so limited. Ever since Chief Justice Marshall admonished that it "is a constitution we are expounding," courts generally have been willing to read the broad language of the Constitution to account for changing social conditions.[6]

In the past decade, the Supreme Court had several opportunities to revisit the historical test for the scope of the Seventh Amendment right to jury trial.[7] In 1996, in *Markman v. Westview Instruments, Inc.,* the Court emphatically declined the opportunity, unanimously reaffirming the historical test but finding no jury trial necessity on applying the test to the facts of the case. On the basis of my understanding of English trial practice in the late eighteenth century, the Court's application of the historical test to the facts of *Markman* seems to me to be wrong. In reaching this conclusion I rely mainly on manuscript sources, both judges' notes and original court documents.[8]

The discussion to follow is in two parts. The first summarizes the Court's application of the historical test in *Markman v. Westview Instruments, Inc.* The second invokes the eighteenth-century English manuscript sources to assess whether the historical test was soundly applied in Justice David Souter's unanimous opinion for the Court in *Markman.*

The Markman Decision

In *Markman,* the plaintiff owned a patent on a method for tracking inventory in dry-cleaning establishments. He sued Westview Instruments for patent infringement and won a jury verdict. Central to the dispute was the meaning of the term "inventory" in the patent claim, as to which plaintiff presented his own testimony and that of an independent expert witness. The trial judge, however, granted a deferred motion for judgment on a matter of law, concluding that the term "inventory" could not support the meaning contended for by plaintiff. Markman appealed, claiming that the trial judge had improperly supplanted the jury. The U.S. Court of Appeals for the Federal Circuit affirmed the trial judge, as did the U.S. Supreme Court after a grant of certiorari. Among the issues before the Supreme Court was the application of the historical test for Seventh Amendment rights to the specific facts.

While the Supreme Court's *Markman* decision was pending, Court-watchers commented on the case. One writer expressed hope that the justices would reach beyond narrow patent law "and make some major corrections"; specifically, "the Supreme Court should reject the 1812 holding in *Wonson* requiring federal courts to look to 18th century English law as a constitutional touchstone."[9] The Court, however, did not take that path. After quoting the text of the Seventh Amendment, Justice Souter began his constitutional analysis by declaring that, "Since Justice Story's day, [and] *United States v. Wonson* . . . , we have understood that 'The right of trial by jury thus preserved is the right which existed under the English common law when the Amendment was adopted.'"[10] He noted the Court's "long-standing adherence to this 'historical test'" and explained that if a case is properly regarded as an action at law, "we then ask whether the particular trial decision must fall to the jury in order to preserve the substance of the common-law right as it existed in 1791."[11]

Justice Souter had no trouble with the first step; patent infringement actions were brought at common law in the late eighteenth century.[12] He then posed the fundamental question in a way that foretold the outcome: "Whether a particular issue occurring within a jury trial (here the construction of a patent claim) is itself necessarily a jury issue, the guarantee being essential to preserve the right to a jury's resolution of the ultimate dispute."[13] His answer was no, largely for three reasons. First, late-eighteenth-century English patent law was primitive and did not include the requirement that there be a stated patent "claim." Second, even accepting the point that the patent specification in late-eighteenth-century England could be viewed as closely analogous to the claim in twentieth-century American patent law, there is not much to go on, since the specification itself was relatively new, and "the mere smattering of patent cases that we have from this period shows no established jury practice sufficient to support an argument by analogy that today's construction of a claim should be a guaranteed jury issue."[14] Third, no demonstration was offered the Court that the role of juries in interpreting patents was different from their role with regard to other written instruments, "and we do know that in other kinds of cases during this period judges, not juries, ordinarily construed written documents."[15]

According to eighteenth-century English trial practice, Justice Souter's second reason appears incorrect. There were many more patent cases in England in the second half of the eighteenth century than a "smattering"; indeed, Justice Francis Buller of the Court of King's Bench remarked in *Turner v. Winter* in 1787 that "many patent cases have arisen within our memory,"[16] and Chief Justice James Eyre of the Court of Common Pleas observed in 1795 that "we have had many cases upon patents."[17] It is true that there was not an abundance of *reported* patent cases from the late eighteenth century at the "appellate" level, but this was in no way indicative of the depth of experience at the trial level.[18] Published reports of eighteenth-century trial court proceedings did not exist in England until the late 1790s.[19] But a mere fraction of the cases at the trial level went forward to full court proceedings on motions or on reserved questions of law. There were dozens of patent trials in the English common-law courts during the second half of the eighteenth century. In Lord Chief Justice Mansfield's surviving trial notes (and less than half of the notes that he kept survive), there are nine unreported patent trials, and this was in only one of the three common-law courts, albeit the busiest.[20]

As authority for his third reason, Justice Souter referred to the 1786 decision of the Court of King's Bench in *Macbeath v. Haldimand*[21] because there the construction of written documents and letters was said by Justices Mansfield and Buller to be for the court, not for the jury. Nevertheless, on close inspection, Justice Souter's reliance on *Macbeath* seems misplaced. What was at issue was the legal import of the letters and documents on an agency question—letters and documents about which there was no factual disagreement. Even so, there was a difference of views among the judges. Justice Edward Willes said that since the case came forward after a jury verdict, and since the letters had been before the jury, construction of them was "proper for the consideration of the jury," though he agreed that "construction of deeds is a matter of law." Justice Buller disagreed, saying it depended on whether "they be written in so dubious a manner, as to be capable of different constructions, and can be explained by other transactions," in which case "the whole evidence must be left to the jury to decide upon; for they are to judge of the truth or falsehood of such collateral facts which may vary the sense of the letters themselves." He added that, "if they be not explained by any other circumstances, then, like deeds or other written agreements, the construction of them is a mere matter of law."[22] In *Markman,* plaintiff argued that the term "inventory" was capable of different constructions, so that the whole evidence should have been left to the jury to decide, as was done by the trial judge.

After disposing of the constitutional issue in *Markman,* Justice Souter moved on to other arguments in the case, pointing out that complicated patent issues can be handled better by judges than by lay juries.[23] This "functional" consideration is taken up in the next chapter, but in order to understand more fully the historical test, it is first necessary to consider what cases customarily went to juries in eighteenth-century English trial practice.

Eighteenth-Century English Trial Practice

In the overwhelming majority of civil cases in the common-law courts in eighteenth-century England, the plaintiffs sought damages in jury trials. The forms of action were varied. Although actions were still brought on ancient writs such as Debt, Assault and False Imprisonment, or Trespass *vi et armis,* the most popular form of action by the 1770s was Trespass on the Case.[24] This catch-all category encompassed all contract and quasi-contract actions, as well as a host of other private civil actions. This can readily be seen in Lord Mansfield's trial notes[25] and in a sampling of the plea rolls for the Court of Common Pleas in the 1770s.[26] The latter contain two types of entries of particular relevance to jury practice: (1)

default judgments with unascertained damages to be determined by a writ of inquiry;[27] and (2) actions in which the defendant "puts himself upon the country," that is, denies the plaintiff's claim and requests a jury trial. There are examples of pleadings that show a demurrer and joinder on a question of law, in which case there would be no jury trial, but these are quite rare. For example, in the plea rolls for Trinity Term 1770, there is only one case on demurrer, compared with 181 cases sent to jury trial.[28] Yet, in the late eighteenth century, the demurrer was virtually the only pretrial method in the common-law courts for taking a case forward for decision without calling a jury.[29]

In other words, almost all cases in the common-law courts were tried before juries. There was no pretrial discovery,[30] nor was there any pretrial conference or procedure (other than the demurrer) that would allow a judge to determine before trial that a case presented no issue to be decided by a jury or that an issue in a case should be withheld from the jury.

Once the jury was convened and the trial began, however, the picture changed. It was open to the judge to enter a nonsuit against the plaintiff. The jury could be requested to give a special verdict.[31] Also, it was common to allow the jury to give a verdict for the plaintiff that would be subject to a "case stated," that is, the verdict would stand or fall according to the judgment given by the full court on a reserved question of law after argument the following term. And, after the trial concluded, motions for new trials could be argued, as could motions in arrest of judgment.

There is no need to go through these devices in detail.[32] I will, however, give some examples out of Lord Mansfield's trial notes of late-eighteenth-century trial practice, which can then be used in considering the Seventh Amendment's historical test. Three aspects of Lord Mansfield's trial notes are of interest: the frequent entry of a nonsuit, the jury verdicts subject to a case stated, and what happened in cases where Mansfield indicated that he was dissatisfied with the verdict.

In legal literature, the eighteenth-century nonsuit is described as a technical procedure requiring that the plaintiff's name be called at the end of his evidence when that evidence seemed inadequate; a nonsuit would be entered only if he failed to answer.[33] The plaintiff could decide whether to be present or not, and this fact led Austin Scott to state, mistakenly, that "At common law nonsuits were wholly voluntary."[34]

Edith Henderson, in her influential Seventh Amendment study, claimed that "If the plaintiff should somehow obtain a verdict in a case proper for nonsuit, defendant could move, before the judges *en banc,* to have the verdict set aside and judgment of nonsuit entered."[35] One of Henderson's authorities is a Mansfield case, and it demonstrates the technique. In *Abbot v. Plumbe,*[36] plaintiff obtained a verdict, and Mansfield "saved the question of the sufficiency of the evidence."[37] The following term, counsel for defendant obtained a rule (that is, an order) for plaintiff to show cause why a nonsuit should not be granted. On argument, plaintiff's evidence proved insufficient, and the rule was made absolute (that is, the nonsuit was granted). In practical effect, this case works out to be identical to the "case stated," in which a verdict for plaintiff is made subject to argument and decision on a reserved question of law.

Lord Mansfield's trial notes show a much less technical, much more free-floating use of the nonsuit than the procedure described by Henderson and illustrated by *Abbot v. Plumbe.* In many cases, it became clear as the plaintiff's evidence unfolded that his claim was factually groundless, and a nonsuit was entered with plaintiff's consent. For example, in *Sharpe v. Maidman,*[38] Mansfield wrote at the end of his notes of the case: "They could not prove delivery. Plaintiff nonsuited, of themselves. I said nothing." We should remember, of course, that there was very little pretrial preparation in these cases and that the barristers and parties were often uncertain about what directions the evidence would take.

In other actions, Lord Mansfield perceived that, as a matter of law, plaintiff had no case. In *Trinder v. Smith,*[39] the *London Chronicle* reported that "the action was based on the supposition that the defendant was liable to pay the tradesmen for the costs of the expenditures for the voyages because the defendant had insured his money lent on the mortgage," but after Mansfield observed "that there was not the least pretence for such action, Mr. Trinder very genteely gave it up."[40] Whether or not there was always genteel acquiescence, Mansfield would declare a nonsuit in such cases. Thus, in a suit by a creditor for payment for necessaries supplied to defendant's wife, the plaintiff was nonsuited because, according to the *London Chronicle,* it appeared to the court that defendant and his wife "had been many years separated, and that separation notoriously known."[41] In another action by the payee against the acceptor of a bill of exchange, Mansfield, according to his own notes, "nonsuited the Plaintiff by reason of the indorsement on the back, which I thought discharged the Acceptor."[42] Later, on a motion for new trial, the judges determined that, "instead of a nonsuit, the question should have been left to the jury, it being a question of intention arising out of the circumstances," but, as two of the three judges hearing the motion thought the jury should have received strong directions to find for the defendant, and in view of the small amount involved, a new trial was denied.[43]

As may have been true in the previous case, Mansfield occasionally noted that, in declaring a nonsuit, he also invited the plaintiff to move for a new trial in order to argue the case before the full Court of King's Bench. In *Luke v. Edwards,*[44] for example, an overseer of the poor sued for false imprisonment, and Mansfield wrote: "Plaintiff [was] nonsuited, because I thought the evidence proved a legal imprisonment. Liberty to move for a new trial without costs."[45] Furthermore, although the nonsuit was usually declared at the close of plaintiff's evidence, there are examples of nonsuits after both parties presented testimony, or even after argument (at trial) on a point of law.[46]

Two additional relevant trial practices exhibited in Lord Mansfield's trial notes are the directed verdict and the "case stated." Edith Henderson reached conclusions about English trial practice by researching printed sources, and while most of her description is correct, the trial notes suggest some differences. She states that the English cases "do not sustain" the view that the directed verdict as practiced in the late eighteenth century was not binding on the jury.[47] The only authority she gives for her claim is the *Macbeath* case, discussed earlier.[48] But, in that case, the motion for new trial failed because a majority of the judges thought, as was noted, that the construction of the uncontested written documents in the case was for the court, not the jury. I do not see how the case stands for the proposition that the trial judge's directed verdict was binding. That this was not so is clearly demonstrated in Lord Mansfield's trial notes. In *Brammall v. Jones,*[49] for instance, plaintiff recovered a verdict of more than £337 for his claim to part of the proceeds from the condemnation of a ship, and Mansfield wrote at the end of his notes: "Verdict against my direction, but as Defendant had a bond [of] indemnity I doubt whether it should be set aside." Mansfield's comment, of course, implies that he had the power to set aside the verdict, but this would have been done by the full court on a motion for new trial.[50] This is what happened in an action to collect on an insurance policy, *Shirley v. Wilkinson.*[51] At the first trial, Mansfield noted: "I thought the suppression of what the Captain wrote in his letter of the 20th of July material and that the policy was void, but the Jury, nine of whom I know, found otherwise." Despite Mansfield's view of the case, the jury verdict awarded plaintiff substantial damages at the second trial, as well as at the first.

At times, Mansfield noted his dissatisfaction with the verdict but apparently let the verdict stand without any invitation to move for a new trial. Thus, in *Olney v. Allen*,[52] a suit for payment for taking care of defendant's cattle, Mansfield noted: "Damages contrary to my directions," adding that "I looked at Plaintiff's books, though I made no mention of it," and then explaining why he thought the verdict wrong. Yet, the verdict stood. So did the verdict in *Harris v. Worsley*,[53] a medical malpractice action, where, after recording a verdict for plaintiff for two guineas, Mansfield wrote: "To the astonishment of every body. [It was] clear Defendant had treated her right upon a suspicion of a fracture & Plaintiff had not suffered."

In several cases, Mansfield not only declared the verdict wrong but expressly ruled out a new trial. This could occur when there had already been one or two new trials,[54] but not always. Thus, in *Walnutt v. Pomfret*,[55] plaintiff won a verdict of £111 in an action for wages owed to his wife, and Mansfield wrote: "I directed the Jury from the injustice of the demand upon the state of it to find against Plaintiff, but they found for the wages & then named the sum. There can be no new trial."

I do not agree with another of Henderson's claims—that the "case stated" device, "Used only when there was no substantial factual controversy, . . . reduced the jury's role to a formality," so that "the jury scarcely participated at all."[56] This is not even remotely shown in Lord Mansfield's trial notes, and Mansfield was a great believer in the case stated.[57] There are dozens of examples of the procedure in the trial notes. In them, the testimony is as full and the role of the jury is as substantial as in other cases. The verdicts are as realistic an assessment of plaintiff's damages as they ever are. Well-known illustrative cases in the trial notes include *Luke v. Lyde*[58] and *Moses v. Macferlan*.[59] In almost all cases, the verdict for plaintiff is quantified and entered, subject to the case stated; only in one instance did Mansfield note: "The verdict [is] to be entered according to the opinion of the court."[60]

Variations on the "case stated" procedure appear in the trial notes. The counterpart when the verdict was for defendant was to argue the question of law on a motion for new trial. Thus, in *Evans v. Saunders*,[61] a tenant was sued for, among other things, taking away fixtures, and after the verdict for defendants, Mansfield wrote: "I was of opinion [that] the tenant might [take] away the frame [&] plate glass of the hothouse. I told Mr. Howarth [plaintiff's counsel] if he found reason, he might move the court [for a new trial], instead of a case."

With these trial practices in mind, let us now return to the historical test of the Seventh Amendment and to Justice Souter's opinion in the *Markman* case. Recall that Justice Souter put his second question as whether a specific issue can be removed from the jury when the basic structure of the jury trial remains in place. How would this have worked had *Markman* come before Mansfield in the Court of King's Bench in, say, 1785?[62]

In *Markman,* the trial judge granted a motion for judgment as a matter of law, but only after a jury verdict for plaintiff had been given. *Markman* was thus comparable in form to some of the nonsuits ordered by Lord Mansfield, described earlier. Yet, I suggest that the motion in *Markman* was improperly granted by the trial judge, since there was conflicting testimony about the meaning of the term "inventory," and in late-eighteenth-century England, this conflict would almost certainly have been sent to the jury for resolution. It might have been sent with strong instructions, but, except for one theoretical possibility (discussed later), it would have been sent. It was customary to send "the whole matter" to the jury. If the jury disregarded the trial judge's directions, a new trial might be granted, but, as we have seen, this did not necessarily happen.

On the specific question in *Markman,* I have no doubt that the issue of the patent claim construction would have gone to the jury. As has been noted, the issue was not like that in *Macbeath,* where there were uncontested written documents in evidence that had to be construed. The issue was much closer to that in an influential late-eighteenth-century patent infringement action tried before Lord Mansfield in 1778, *Liardet v. Johnson.*[63] In *Liardet,* plaintiff had patented a method of making stucco, and defendant claimed that he was not guilty of infringement since the patent specification did not properly describe how to make the stucco. Justice Buller's notes of the case (when it came on for argument on a motion for new trial) survive at Lincoln's Inn, and Buller noted that Lord Mansfield "left to the jury . . . all objections made to exactness, certainty and propriety of the Specification, & whether any workman could make it by [the Specification]."[64]

The *Liardet* case was relied on by Markman in argument to the Supreme Court, but Justice Souter was not persuaded. He concluded that *Liardet* "does not show that juries construed disputed terms in a patent" and that "From its ambiguous references" (in the earlier quotation from Justice Buller's notes) "we cannot infer the existence of an established practice."[65]

The one theory that might lead to a different conclusion about the issue in *Markman* is the possibility that the evidence on what is ostensibly a fact question (the meaning of "inventory") was so clear that, in the opinion of the judges, reasonable minds could not differ, so that the question thereby became one of law rather than fact. This notion is familiar to the modern lawyer. It was also recognized in eighteenth-century England, but only rarely, and controversially.[66] Lord Mansfield generally avoided the issue by leaving things to his juries, while at the same time giving strong instructions to the juries to come out the way he thought the verdicts should go.

There were situations, nonetheless, in which the judges would take possession of an ostensibly factual issue and convert it into a legal issue. They did so when certainty was desirable, and because of their conviction that any reasonable person assessing the evidence in the cases could come to but one conclusion.

In *Markman,* then, a conclusion that reasonable minds could not differ on what "inventory" meant in the patent claim would have been a legitimate resolution, both under modern law and within the English legal framework of 1791. Although there is some suggestion of this view in the majority opinion by the Federal Circuit in *Markman,* the opinion seized the opportunity to paint on a larger canvas and to appropriate to the court the construction of the patent claim. The broader issues were also those dealt with by the Supreme Court.

Conclusion

The Seventh Amendment historical test has become an American legal fiction in application, since many more things were lodged with juries in England in 1791 than modern American courts, including the Supreme Court, are prepared to acknowledge. It is easy to appreciate the appeal of the historical test to the Court, in that it permits what many would regard as constructive change while maintaining the appearance of certainty, maintaining as well the stability and reassurance that come from appearing to stay in touch with the historical past. *Markman* is the proof. In a unanimous opinion, the Court removed a complex patent issue—one that arises in nearly every patent infringement suit—from the province of the jury. The Court did so by claiming and appearing to comply with Justice Story's now venerable historical test.

The *Markman* opinion, whether right or wrong on historical grounds, might have become (and might have been intended by Justice Souter to become) a platform from which to address the "complexity exception" in a future case, emphasizing the third prong of the *Markman* formulation—functional considerations such as the relative "skills of judges and juries."[67] Yet in post-*Markman* decisions, the Supreme Court has reaffirmed the broad scope of the Seventh Amendment's jury-trial guarantee; indeed, in *City of Monterey v. Del Monte Dunes at Monterey, Ltd.*,[68] Justice Anthony Kennedy, in his plurality opinion, used "considerations of process and function," invoking *Markman*, to *require* a jury trial in the inverse condemnation proceeding before the Court.[69]

In the next chapter, I demonstrate how a complexity exception can be viewed as compatible with eighteenth-century English trial practice. This would allow the Supreme Court to establish such an exception directly and without the manipulation of the historical test that appears to inhabit Justice Souter's opinion in *Markman.* The Seventh Amendment landscape now described by federal court precedent could be said to be almost upside down. Juries continue to be required in many complex actions for damages, no matter how unrealistic it may be for a common jury to function effectively. Special juries, which might function effectively, are no longer available.[70] Yet, in construing patent claims, something juries frequently did in the late eighteenth century in England, no juries are allowed, and a new layer called a "*Markman* hearing" is inserted in patent proceedings, an innovation not necessarily welcomed in practice as an improvement in case-handling efficiency.[71] Recently, Chief Judge Haldane Robert Mayer of the Federal Circuit asserted that "Nearly a decade of confusion has resulted from the fiction that [patent] claim construction is a matter of law," and "To pretend otherwise inspires cynicism."[72]

2

The "Complexity Exception"

In the 1995 decision of the Federal Circuit in *Markman v. Westview Instruments, Inc.,* Judge Mayer declared in his opinion concurring in the judgment: "Today's decision . . . threatens to do indirectly what we have declined to do directly, that is, create a 'complexity exception' to the Seventh Amendment for patent cases."[1] Judge Mayer's remark relates to a larger debate in Seventh Amendment cases, inspired by a footnote in a 1970 Supreme Court decision, *Ross v. Bernhard,*[2] a shareholder derivative suit in which the Court held that the shareholder plaintiffs did have a right to a jury trial. *Ross* involved a strand of the historical test for Seventh Amendment coverage different from that presented in *Markman*—whether a suit should be called predominantly equitable or legal, which is to be determined mainly by the nature of the remedy sought. If equitable, the case will be aligned with suits tried in the Court of Chancery in the eighteenth century in England, and no jury will be required. If legal, a jury will be a matter of right, assuming the case resembles sufficiently jury trials in the English common law of 1791 (as *Markman* did not, according to the Supreme Court).[3] The law-versus-equity line of cases decided by the Supreme Court has been criticized as being overinclusive and ahistorical, extending jury trial to new causes of action (mainly those created by statute) unnecessarily.[4]

In deciding that a jury trial was required in *Ross,* the Supreme Court observed in a footnote: "As our cases indicate, the 'legal' nature of an issue is determined by considering, first, the pre-merger (of law and equity) custom with reference to such questions; second, the remedy sought; and, third, the practical abilities and limitations of juries."[5] The third criterion was an open invitation for a claim that cases that are too complex need not be subjected to jury trial.[6] That claim was made before the U.S. Court of Appeals for the Third Circuit in 1980 in *In re. Japanese Electronic Products Litigation,*[7] and, in gathering ammunition for the case, the parties commissioned the legal historians Morris Arnold and Patrick Devlin on opposing sides to study the question. Parts of these studies were published in the *Pennsylvania Law Review* and the *Columbia Law Review*.[8] Lord Devlin followed up with another article in the *Michigan Law Review* several years later.[9]

The argument for a generalized complexity exception to the Seventh Amendment jury-trial guarantee was built upon Chancery cases. The ordinary course when a factual dispute arose in a case before the Court of Chancery was for the Lord Chancellor to refer the question to one of the common-law courts for jury-trial resolution, suspending the Chancery case to await the verdict, afterward continuing the case "on the equity reserved." Lord Devlin claimed, however, that long before 1791 it was well established that factual issues that arose in a Chancery case need not be sent to the law courts for jury-trial resolution if the questions were too complicated, for example, in cases seeking an accounting. This practice, viewed as part of the overarching authority of the Chancellor to prevent injustice, validated the complexity exception without the necessity of showing that the Chancellor actively prevented common-law jury cases from going forward because the subject matter was beyond the jury's grasp. Nevertheless, Devlin argued that two pre-1791 cases showed that the Chancellor did indeed occasionally enjoin the common-law courts in this way. Devlin's interpretation of those two cases—*Clench v. Tomley* and *Blad v. Bamfield*[10]—was the principal focus of Arnold's opposing article. Arnold argued that *Clench,* when fully understood from manuscript sources, did not support what Devlin claimed, and Arnold discounted *Blad* as standing "for the simple proposition that suits involving foreign relations ought to be tried in prerogative courts."[11]

The Third Circuit Court of Appeals was not persuaded "that complexity alone ever was an established basis of equitable jurisdiction."[12] On the court's analysis, this would have to be proved by establishing "the authority of a chancellor to remove difficult issues from juries in suits at law," and there was but "meager support" for such authority (one possible reading of *Clench*). The suits in equity seeking an accounting were inconclusive ("We are aware of no case . . . in which a chancellor ordered an accounting in a suit involving nothing more than liability for money damages in trespass or tort"),[13] and the cases sent by Chancery to the law courts for advisory jury verdicts were brushed aside as "irrelevant to our inquiry" ("These cases say nothing about the chancellor's authority to provide for nonjury trials in suits at common law").[14]

The court also declined to adopt the broader argument advanced on the basis of Lord Devlin's research—that the Chancellor, "aware of the limited capabilities of juries and, as evidenced by his practices in accounting and advisory jury cases, often viewed these limitations as an impediment to justice"; thus, he "would have exercised his control over his jurisdiction to decide the [complex] case in chancery."[15] Observing that this approach had not been taken in any previous federal court decision, the court chose "not to pioneer in this use of history."[16] Yet, in effect, the court did just that, using the due process clause of the Fifth Amendment instead of the historical exercise of the Chancellor's jurisdiction under the Seventh Amendment. On the premise that "the law presumes that a jury will . . . resolve each disputed issue on the basis of a fair and reasonable assessment of the evidence and a fair and reasonable application of relevant legal rules," the court concluded that "due process precludes trial by jury when a jury is unable to perform this task with a reasonable understanding of the evidence and the legal rules."[17]

In his later article, Lord Devlin celebrated the Court of Appeals's due process decision, and he elaborated on the similarities between equity as practiced in the Court of Chancery and due process. He also placed heavy emphasis on an 1804 Irish Chancery case, *O'Connor v. Spaight,*[18] decided by Lord Redesdale, who in his pretitled life as John Mitford had written *A Treatise on the Pleadings in Suits in the Court of Chancery,* first published in London in 1780 and substantially revised for a 1789 edition.[19] In the treatise, Mitford explained that courts of equity had assumed jurisdiction "in a variety of complicated cases of account [and other matters]" and "seem by degrees to have been considered as having on these subjects a concurrent jurisdiction with the courts of common law."[20] In *O'Connor,* Lord Redesdale (Mitford) stated: "The ground on which I think this is a proper case for equity, is, that the account has become so complicated that a court of law would be incompetent to examine it upon a trial at *Nisi Prius,* with all necessary accuracy. . . . This is a principle upon which courts of equity constantly act."[21]

In his *Columbia Law Review* article, Devlin dealt briefly with *Gyles v. Wilcox,*[22] decided by Lord Chancellor Hardwicke in 1740, a case that seems to me to have more persuasive force than is shown by the one-half page that Devlin devoted to it.[23] Devlin mentioned only one of the two published reports and omitted any reference to the arbitration feature of the case.[24] *Gyles* was a copyright infringement case brought for injunctive relief under the Statute of Queen Anne.[25] Fletcher Gyles was a bookseller who published an edition of Matthew Hale's *Pleas of the Crown.* Wilcox then published a volume called *Modern Crown Law,* which Gyles claimed was nothing but his book with a few obsolete statutes omitted and with all the Latin and French quotations translated into English. Lord Hardwicke, in Atkyns's report, observed that the question was whether Wilcox's work was a fair abridgement, which it would not be if merely "colourably shortened." This was a factual inquiry, and when the attorney general, Dudley Ryder, suggested that it be sent to a jury, Hardwicke said, "The court is not under an indispensable obligation to send all facts to a jury, but may refer them to a master, to state them, where it is a question of nicety and difficulty, and more fit for men of learning to inquire into, than a common jury." He added that "The House of Lords very often, in matters of account which are extremely perplexed and intricate, refer it to two merchants named by the parties, to consider the case, and report their opinions upon it, rather than leave it to a jury" and he decided to follow that course in the case before him.[26] Accordingly, a reference to arbitration was agreed to.[27]

The *Gyles* opinion, of course, is not dispositive of whether there was, in equity, a generalized "complexity exception" to the practice of sending factual questions to the law counts for jury trial. In an 1803 case involving tithes owing on land, Lord Chancellor Eldon observed that, "Beyond all question, it belongs to the constitution of a Court of Equity to decide upon matters of fact, if they think proper," but he added that "Courts of Equity have for a great number of years, where questions of fact have been disputable, thought it a more proper exercise of their jurisdiction, to have them determined by a jury."[28] Nevertheless, Lord Hardwicke's language in *Gyles,* the preeminence of Hardwicke (whose decisions both as Chief Justice of the Court of King's Bench and as Lord Chancellor were much respected), and the fact that the *Gyles* case was *not* the typical problem of accounts combine to make the case a strong precedent. Also forceful is the version of Hardwicke's opinion in Barnardiston's report of *Gyles.* According to Barnardiston, Hardwicke said that "Whether the second Book is the same Book with the former is a Matter of Fact, and a Fact of Difficulty to be determined," but "the Court is not confined to send all Matters of Fact to be tried [before a jury]." Where "the Facts are of an extensive nature, as matters of account, or the like" the court customarily referred them to the Master of the Rolls[29] and might direct "that the Master should be attended by two Persons skilled in the Profession of the Law, to assist him." Hardwicke explained that "Directions of this Sort have been made in Mathematical and Algebraical Inquiries."[30]

One could take the view, as did the Third Circuit Court of Appeals, that, as an exercise of the Chancellor's discretion not to send the case to an advisory jury, *Gyles* is not of much weight in relation to the Seventh Amendment inquiry. Instead of an action brought at common law for damages, as in *Markman,* the bill in *Gyles* was in Chancery for an injunction, and a factual issue arose. *No* case in late-eighteenth-century England is known where the plaintiff sued at common law for damages, as in *Markman,* yet the common-law court decided the factual issues were beyond the jury's capacity, causing the court to send the case to Chancery.

There would, however, be responses to such a viewpoint. One could return to Lord Devlin's argument that, just as the Chancellor refrained from sending complex factual issues out for advisory jury verdicts, he was willing to enjoin common-law proceedings when the issues were too specialized or too complex for effective jury handling. The fact that few examples of this can be found in the printed reports may result from the simple explanation that the Chancellor was rarely asked. As Morris Arnold observed in his "Modest Replication," "the plaintiff is the master of his cause of action; once it is characterized as legal by him, the ordinary attributes of a trial at law, including the availability of a jury, necessarily follow."[31] In responding to a plaintiff's declaration,[32] the defendant was required either to demur or plead, specially or generally, and, as was shown earlier with Common Pleas records, demurrers were rarely entered.[33] By the late eighteenth century, general pleas were common,[34] but if a special plea was entered by defendant, plaintiff would file a replication, and in either case the dispute would proceed to jury trial,[35] propelled by standard fees and filings required of plaintiff's attorney.[36] It would be hard to imagine that a defendant, after putting himself upon the country with a general plea, would appeal to Chancery to enjoin that very process. Possibly such a request would be made by a defendant who, instead of demurring, had entered a special plea to plaintiff's declaration. Yet, if the special plea raised factual claims, the defendant would expect that the plaintiff would deny them by replication and request a jury trial.[37]

To return our focus to the possibility of a complexity exception to the Seventh Amendment, if an eighteenth-century barrister had been asked for an example of complex civil litigation of his day, one answer would undoubtedly have been the accounting case that went to Chancery to begin with. Other cases that raised difficult questions of fact, such as construction or engineering disputes, were commonly referred to arbitration, as indeed the *Gyles* case was. This allowed the parties to have the benefit of arbitrators with specialized knowledge, training, or expertise. In the last quarter of the eighteenth century, literally *thousands* of cases in the English common-law courts were resolved in this way, without jury trial.[38] Arbitration referrals were done with consent of the parties, to be sure, and, although occasionally a party resisted,[39] resistance was quite rare.[40] It cannot be said that every case referred to arbitration by the common-law courts involved technical or complicated facts, but many clearly did.[41]

There is, moreover, another basic point. As is shown in chapter 7, most business cases tried in the common-law courts in England by 1791 were tried by special juries, not common juries, and typically the special jurors were merchants who were encouraged to use their own familiarity with relevant mercantile customs and practices in deciding upon their verdicts. The special jury exists no more in England and is a rarity in the United States.[42] This major difference between modern jury-trial practices and those that prevailed in 1791 has not been identified by the Supreme Court or the lower federal courts as relevant to the ongoing application of the historical test in measuring the scope of the Seventh Amendment guarantee. Yet, the special jury was available to either party in England in 1791 as a matter of *right.* As stated by Baker John Sellon in *The Practice of the Courts of King's Bench and Common Pleas* (1793), the special jury section of "An Act for the better Regulation of Juries" (1730)[43] "gives the subject a liberty of having a special jury in all cases whatsoever, which before that statute was only granted in certain circumstances."[44]

The composite picture of how business litigation was handled in late-eighteenth-century England argues against the proposition that the Seventh Amendment requires juries in twenty-first-century America in complex civil cases. Many eighteenth-century business disputes called for a financial accounting, and this equitable remedy would be sought in Chancery. If factual questions arose, the Court of Chancery was under no compulsion to send the factual questions to a jury. The same was true of claims that sought other equitable relief, such as the injunction in *Gyles.* If a business dispute was begun in the law courts, the virtually automatic response by the defendant was to put himself "upon the country," but relatively few of these cases would be tried by a common jury. The defendant could demand a special jury, and ordinarily the defendant did so in such a case. Alternatively, the case could be referred to arbitration, bypassing the jury altogether. There is also the undeniable fact that *nothing* in the eighteenth-century English legal landscape remotely approached the sheer proportions of today's complex antitrust and mass tort cases.[45] This was recognized by the Third Circuit Court of Appeals in the *In re. Japanese Electronic Products* case[46] in holding that a jury was not required for the case before it—an antitrust conspiracy case that had been in discovery for nine years, with more than 100,000 pages of depositions and thousands of different product models in evidence. As noted earlier, the court relied on the theory that when a case reaches a deeply complex level, the jury can no longer perform its task effectively and that if the case were forced to go before a jury, due process under the Fifth Amendment would be denied.[47]

The Third Circuit's Fifth Amendment trump of the Seventh Amendment jury-trial guarantee did not become established in other circuits. Neither this nor a more direct complexity exception to the Seventh Amendment is likely to gain a real purchase in the federal courts until a clearer endorsement emerges from the Supreme Court. In a 1990 decision extending jury trial to suits by union members for back pay, *Chauffeurs, Teamsters and Helpers, Local No. 391 v. Terry*,[48] Justice John Paul Stevens in his concurring opinion argued for a "functional" approach to Seventh Amendment coverage ("whether 'the issues [presented by the claim] are typical grist for the jury's judgment'"), but in the plurality opinion, Justice Thurgood Marshall stated, "This Court has never relied on this consideration 'as an independent basis for extending the right to a jury trial under the Seventh Amendment.'"[49]

Justice Souter in *Markman* recognized the limitations of juries in complex cases, but he did so as a matter of common sense and judicial administration, not as a matter of constitutional mandate. He wrote that, "Since evidence of common-law practice at the time of the framing does not entail application of the Seventh Amendment's jury guarantee to the construction of the claim document, we must look elsewhere . . . in order to allocate it as between court or jury."[50] He later added, "Where history and precedent provide no clear answers, functional considerations also play their part in the choice between judge and jury to define terms of art."[51] Justice Souter explained that "The construction of written instruments is one of those things that judges often do and are likely to do better than jurors unburdened by training in exegesis."[52] Plaintiff protested that a jury "should decide a question of meaning peculiar to a trade or profession . . . because the question is a subject of testimony requiring credibility determinations, which are the jury's forte."[53] Justice Souter agreed that sometimes there is a need for credibility determinations of expert testimony in patent cases, but he thought this rare, stating that "a jury's capabilities to evaluate demeanor" or "to reflect community standards" is "much less significant than a trained ability to evaluate the testimony in relation to the overall structure of the patent." Accordingly, he concluded, "there is sufficient reason to treat construction of terms of art like many other responsibilities that we cede to a judge in the normal course of trial, notwithstanding its evidentiary underpinnings."[54]

It is unclear whether, if squarely put to it, Justice Souter would elevate these functional considerations to the constitutional level. My guess is that he would interpret the constitutional history in a way that would not require a jury in cases of extreme complexity, and were he to do so, perhaps the *Gyles* precedent would be helpful. It is doubtful, however, that the other justices would be in full agreement. As is shown in chapter 4, the unanimity displayed in *Markman* no longer describes the Supreme Court's Seventh Amendment decision-making.

Conclusion

A complexity exception to the Seventh Amendment would not be inconsistent with late-eighteenth-century trial procedures in the English courts. Such an exception could be questioned by those who insist that the drafters of the Seventh Amendment meant to preserve every inch of the theoretical right to a jury trial that a civil litigant would have had in England in 1791. Yet, as we have seen, this absolutist approach has not been the path taken by the Supreme Court. If the goal of the Seventh Amendment, as embodied in the historical test, was to preserve the right to trial by jury in civil cases as that right was known in actual practice in England in 1791, the complexity exception can be justified.

3

Law versus Fact

Three questions are examined in this chapter: first, when, if ever, does the jury have the right to decide the law as well as the facts, in which case there would be no need to worry about the law-fact distinction?; second, if the jury is to be limited to facts but the jury reaches a wrong verdict, what can the court do about it?; and third, what is "fact," and how stationary over time has the law-fact boundary been?

Jury Nullification

In *Dimick v. Schiedt,*[1] the Supreme Court stated the following familiar proposition: "The controlling distinction between the power of the court and that of the jury is that the former is the power to determine the law and the latter to determine the facts."[2] This division of power, even if true, has not always been peaceable. In earlier times, both in England and in America, the power issue was caught up in popular protests about freedom of the press, as played out in politically charged libel prosecutions. Recently in America, the issue has been rekindled by those who believe the jury should have the power to decide the law by ignoring it—that is, by what has come to be called "jury nullification."

To understand nineteenth-century developments, the place to start is with an assessment of how things stood in England and America in the late eighteenth century on the jury's law-finding authority. A very different power alignment between judge and jury from that given by the U.S. Supreme Court in 1935 in the *Dimick* case was displayed in Supreme Court Justice John Jay's instructions to the jury in the 1794 case of *Georgia v. Brailsford.*[3] Jay reminded the jury "of the good old rule, that on questions of fact, it is the province of the jury, on questions of law, it is the province of the court to decide," but he then observed that "You have

Medallions commemorating the 1794 acquittals of Thomas Hardy, John Horne Tooke, and others, prosecuted for a treasonous conspiracy as leaders of popular societies that were said to advocate the overthrow of the government in England, in sympathy with France. The medallions celebrate trial by jury and the role of counsel in the case, Thomas Erskine and Vicary Gibbs. Courtesy of Professor Sir John Baker.

nevertheless a right to take upon yourselves to judge of both, and to determine the law as well as the facts in controversy."[4] Both facts and law, he told the jury, were "lawfully within your power of decision." Jay said also that he was confident the jury would "pay that respect which is due to the opinion of the court" since presumptively "juries are the best judges of facts" and "the court are the best judges of the law."[5]

John Jay's instructions corresponded to the understanding in many state courts in the postrevolutionary era. As William E. Nelson observes of Massachusetts in the late eighteenth century, "the jury's power to find law was virtually unlimited."[6] This condition appears not to have been true in all states,[7] but in Massachusetts and other jurisdictions it was shaped by a combination of procedural rules and "a deeply ingrained and increasingly 'patriotic' distrust of the independence of the British Judiciary."[8]

In England, the "law-finding" controversy dates back to the seventeenth century, to *Bushell's Case* (1670)[9] and its antecedents. *Bushell's Case* was the landmark decision that established the principle that jurors could not be fined for perjury for issuing a verdict against the evidence. The background and the influence of this decision are fully explored by Thomas Green in *Verdict According to Conscience.*[10] Green points out that seventeenth-century attitudes about jury functions had been to some degree handed down from the self-informing era when jurors were expected to have independent knowledge of the incident being tried and to employ that knowledge however they thought best.[11] This meant that the jury played an openly instrumental part in shaping the substantive law of the time. This heritage of liberal jury discretion, Green observes, actually slowed the development of the substantive law by forestalling the bench

John Jay (1745–1829), first Chief Justice of the United States. Courtesy of the Georgetown University Law Center.

from coming to grips with hard questions that would emerge in the inevitable "close cases" encountered in "free flow of fact situations."[12] As for *Bushell's Case,* Green explains how Justice Vaughan's unremarkable opinion was transformed by tract writers Sir John Hawles, Henry Care, and others into an expansive interpretation of the jury's law-finding capacity—an interpretation central to the eighteenth-century seditious libel debates.[13] Green also shows how advocates of law-finding in seditious libel cases were backed into the position that the jury must be allowed to find law generally, opening them to challenge over the competency of jurors to do so.[14]

The English law and procedure applicable to seditious libel cases were shaped substantially by Chief Justice Holt of the Court of King's Bench at the turn of the eighteenth century.[15] The importance of the seditious libel cases to the law-fact distinction was the explicit rule that the question of law—whether the publication in question was libelous—was not given to the jury. If there was proof that the defendant participated in printing or publishing the controverted writing, and if there was no issue of innuendo about the content of the writing, the jury was instructed to bring in a guilty verdict. Thereafter, the court would say whether the publication was seditious (and the court almost always found that it was). This was in principle galling to jurors, but especially so in cases where the jurors thought the publication inoffensive.

The contest between judge and jury during the eighteenth century was fueled by the public agitation for freedom of the press that, during Mansfield's time, surrounded John Wilkes and his publication, *The North Briton,* and the published letters of the anonymous writer called Junius.[16] As is well known, Lord Mansfield was excoriated in the public press for his traditionalist view of the restricted role of the jury in seditious libel cases. This became the battleground for the Wilkites, who thought it absurd and repressive to force a jury that found nothing objectionable in the content of a publication nevertheless to return a guilty verdict. For example, Serjeant John Glynn, defense counsel in many of the libel cases during the late 1760s and early 1770s, was reported in connection with the trial of the publisher John Almon to have "observed the ridicule of calling together a *Special* jury, to determine only whether a man printed and *published* a certain paper; for where there are no *blanks* [innuendoes], that is all which the doctrine leaves them to consider."[17]

In the printed report of the last important seditious libel case tried before Lord Mansfield, the *Dean of St. Asaph's Case (Rex v. Shipley),*[18] Edward Bearcroft, lead counsel for the crown, stated "that it is the right of the jury, if they please, on the plea of not guilty, to take upon themselves the decision of every question of law necessary to the acquittal of the defendant," to which Lord Mansfield responded "that he should call it the power, not the right."[19] The report in *The London Chronicle* gave the exchange slightly differently—Bearcroft "admitted . . . that juries could determine upon law and fact, in all cases where the general issue was pleaded," and Mansfield stated: "Nobody had ever any doubt on that, no one doubts their *power* to decide, but their *right.*"[20] This exchange contrasts with the view of those favoring jury law-finding, as given by Green in the following quotation from Thomas Leach:

> In the institutions of civil government, power and right are, and must be, convertible terms. Civil power, and civil right, are the mere creatures of the law and know no other limits, than the law imposes upon them. The law speaks the language of prohibition, not of admonition. What it permits to be done, uncensured, and confirms, when it is done, it has delegated the power to do, and the exercise of that power, is of right.[21]

For his part, Mansfield took it to be a matter of admonition. In the trial of John Miller in 1770 for publishing the letters of Junius, Mansfield was reported to have included in his instructions to the jury the following: "If you choose to *determine* the *point of law,* you should be very clear for your consciences' sake, that your determination is law; but if the law was, in every case, to be determined by juries, we should be in a miserable condition, as nothing could be more uncertain, from the different opinions of mankind."[22] Several juries in the Wilkes and Junius prosecutions refused to return guilty verdicts despite clear proof of publication and the absence of any question of innuendo. With apparently comfortable consciences, these jurors took the law into their own hands.

In America, the most famous comparable example of jury behavior was the early (1735) *Zenger* case.[23] John Peter Zenger was publisher of the *New York Weekly Journal,* a tabloid devoted to aggressive opposition to Governor William Cosby, of New York. According to Stanley Katz, the *Journal* clearly and consistently favored an expanded jury role in seditious libel prosecutions.[24] Soon Zenger had the personal opportunity to seek that expanded jury role when his seditious libel prosecution was begun in 1734. Zenger was represented by Andrew Hamilton, reputedly "the best lawyer in America."[25] Katz states that Hamilton produced a

Andrew Hamilton making his famous argument to the jury in the trial of John Peter Zenger (1735). Part of the jury is in view on the left, and the caption reads: "By no means," exclaimed Hamilton in his clear, thrilling, silvery voice. "It is not the bare printing and publishing of a paper that will make it a libel. The words themselves must be libelous, that is, false, scandalous, and seditious, else my client is not guilty." Courtesy of the Library of Congress.

"masterpiece of early American legal argument," but "neither history nor law justified his glorification of the jury's role in libel cases."[26] In his instructions to the jury, Chief Justice James De Lancey remarked on "the great pains Mr. Hamilton has taken to show how little regard juries are to pay to the opinion of the judges." De Lancey observed that "the facts or words in the information are confessed" and then gave the following timid instruction: "The only thing that can come in question before you is whether the words as set forth in the information make a libel. And that is a matter of law, no doubt, and which you may leave to the Court."[27] Hamilton's eloquence prevailed, and Zenger was acquitted.

In a manner analogous to the strategic exploitation of *Bushell's Case* by "friends of liberty,"[28] the *Zenger* case became a rallying cry for those who argued for the power of the jury to decide the law as well as the facts.

That argument continues to the present in the United States, most prominently under the banner of the Fully Informed Jury Association ("FIJA").[29] Throughout the 1990s and continuing to the present, FIJA has lobbied for state legislation requiring judges to instruct juries about their power to nullify. Thus far, the effort has not succeeded, but in 2003, FIJA came close in New Hampshire. The New Hampshire House of Representatives passed a bill that would have affirmed the jury's "inalienable right to judge both the law and the facts in controversy" by adding the following new section to the New Hampshire Revised Statutes: "519:23-a. Right of Accused: In all criminal proceedings the court shall instruct the jury of its inherent right to judge the law as well as the facts and to nullify."[30] Against expectations, however, the state Senate Judiciary Committee voted against the bill, and it was not enacted.[31]

Several states have language comparable to that attempted in New Hampshire in early statutes or in their constitutions. Article ten, section five, of the Maryland constitution of 1851, for example, declares that, "In the trial of all criminal cases, the jury shall be the judges of law as well as fact." This provision had little effect, since only a few years after the Maryland constitution was adopted, the Maryland Supreme Court called the section "merely declaratory," observing that it had "not altered the preexisting law regulating the powers the court and jury in criminal cases."[32] A similar process occurred in Indiana, although the Indiana Supreme Court's interpretative emasculation of its mid-nineteenth-century constitutional provision did not happen until the mid-twentieth century.[33]

The extent to which the jury nullification debate continues in the courts is shown in the recent *en banc* decision of the Ninth Circuit in *United States v. Navarro-Vargas*.[34] Appellants argued that their indictments should be dismissed because the trial court had wrongly instructed the jury about its constitutional role. By a vote of six to five, the Ninth Circuit Court of Appeals ruled that grand jurors need not be informed of their nullification power. The dissent scornfully observed that, according to the majority, the constitutional protection embodied in the grand jury "must give way to the unbridled exercise of prosecutorial discretion" and that "The majority arrives at this remarkable conclusion by relying principally upon British history and the use of the grand jury in England prior to King George III."[35] The majority, however, noted that the courts have uniformly rejected the idea that "*petit* juries should be informed of their nullification power" and then observed:

> While we celebrate grand jury independence in defense of the First Amendment in the case of Peter Zenger and those accused of violating the Alien and Sedition Acts, and we praise grand jury resistance to the morally obnoxious fugitive slave laws, we must acknowledge as well that grand juries have also refused to enforce lawful and wise legislation, including some of the most important legislation in American history: the Reconstruction laws implementing the Thirteenth, Fourteenth, and Fifteenth Amendments. Grand jury independence, evidently, has historically served causes both good and ill.[36]

Granting New Trials

Avoidance of the "miserable condition" to which Mansfield referred in *Rex v. Miller*[37] was, of course, the rationale behind the traditional view in civil cases that questions of law were for the court and questions of fact for the jury. When the jury got it wrong—either on the evidence or on the law—the remedy was to order a new trial.

By the eighteenth century, new trials had long been granted upon a finding of an improper verdict. During the seventeenth and early eighteenth centuries, it was believed that the first instance of such a new trial was in 1665 as recorded in *Style,* but this idea was later discarded. In *Bright v. Enyon,*[38] Mansfield cited references to earlier new trials in a 1648 case and then added, "The reason why this matter cannot be traced further back is, that the old report-books do not give any accounts of determinations made by the Court upon motions."[39]

One context for the debate was the question whether a new trial could be granted after a trial before a full court, the "trial at bar." Mansfield, in *Bright v. Enyon,* could not understand this, stating: "It is at least equally reasonable to do it after trials at bar, as after trials at nisi prius . . . or indeed, rather more so, as the latter must be done upon what could have actually and personally appeared to a single judge only; whereas the former is grounded upon what must have manifestly and fully appeared to the whole court."[40] Earlier in the century, however, there was much uncertainty about a new trial after a trial at bar, and the arguments in those cases provide a counterpoint in civil cases to the law-finding debate in the criminal-trial setting.

In principle, the worry over the new trial after the trial at bar was no different from the general question of granting new trials in the

The Court of King's Bench conducting a trial at bar in Westminster Hall, London, 1804. Courtesy of Professor Sir John Baker.

post–*Bushell's Case* era. When the assertion was made that the first jury went against the evidence or the trial judge's instructions, the rights of the jury came under scrutiny, and if the jury were the sole judge of the facts, how was a new trial feasible?[41] This was thought especially problematical after a trial at bar, when the jury would have had the benefit of guidance from all of the judges and when the same judges who instructed the jury were being called upon to grant a new trial. In the unreported case of *Rex v. Guardian,*[42] for example, Chief Justice Holt stated "that he would not affirm that a new trial could not be after a Tryal at Bar but that it ought not to be pushed but upon very good reason."

The question was taken up more fully in the 1739 decision of *Smith v. Parkhurst,*[43] an ejectment action in which a special verdict was given in favor of the plaintiff. Two of the three points argued were that a new trial should not be granted after a trial at bar and that it should not be given when the jury had returned a special verdict. Chief Justice William Lee observed that the courts had been granting new trials for at least eighty years (since the first reported case in *Style*) and then stated the following:

> There is no foundation for what was said at the Bar that the Court by granting a new Trial would accuse the jury of Perjury, for Perjury is a willfull Act, & therefore if the jury give a Verdict to the Court of their judgment upon the Matter of fact, tho' they are mistaken yet they are not guilty of Perjury, as a judge may be guilty of an Error in a point of Law, yet there is no Perjury in that. Bract. 289. The only Remedy at Common Law in case of a false Verdict was an Attaint which was attended with great difficulties, & the jury were hardly ever convicted by reason of the Sworn judgment in Attaint, & that was the Reason why the Courts were willing to have things examined again upon a new Trial.[44]

Lee disposed of the argument concerning the trial at bar without trouble, finding no obstacle to granting a new trial in such cases under strong circumstances. He did not find it necessary to resolve the special verdict argument, but he observed nevertheless: "There is a great deal of . . . learning in *Bushell's Case,* & Vaughan says a great deal of a general Verdict & a Special Verdict, for every general Verdict includes matter of Law, but a Special Verdict finds only facts to which the judge if he was asked could not answer, for the jury are confessedly judges of the Fact."[45]

In an echo of the self-informing jury from centuries earlier, one of the points noticed by Vaughan in *Bushell's Case* was that jurors might have "personal knowledge" that conflicted with the evidence brought out in court, thus reinforcing the need to respect the jurors' determination. In *Smith v. Parkhurst,* counsel for the plaintiff urged that "the evidence of one or two witnesses ought not to overturn the finding of twelve gentlemen of figure and fortune, who might too be governed by their own knowledge."[46] To this, counsel for defendants rejoined:

> As to the objection, that the jury might perhaps go upon their own knowledge; this, if allowed, will put an end to the granting a new trial in any case whatsoever, because on such a supposition no verdict can be said to be found against evidence. A jury are by their oaths obliged to go according to evidence, i.e. the evidence given in Court: and if a jury-man be prepossessed, it is a good cause of challenge; which seems to be a

> proof that a juror ought not to go by his own knowledge. If a juror does indeed know anything material in the cause, he ought to acquaint the Court therewith, and be sworn as a witness, that he may be cross-examined.[47]

Although Chief Justice Lee found no need to respond to this point in *Smith,* an earlier, unreported decision of the Court of King's Bench under Chief Justice Raymond speaks squarely to the point. In *Constable v. Nichols* (1726), the Chief Justice stated that "If a Jury Man knows anything of his own knowledge He ought not to acquaint his fellows with it privately, but must be sworn in open Court, for He is a Witness; as in this Case a jury Man was sworn, & gave Evidence."[48]

What Is "Fact"?

Notwithstanding John Jay's instructions to the jury in *Georgia v. Brailsford,*[49] and notwithstanding the persistence of the jury nullification debate, the occasions for jury nullification have been and likely will continue to be few. In the main stream of jury trials, both past and present, the governing rule has been and will remain that juries find the facts and judges declare the law. This, however, begs another question: What is "fact"?

One step removed from seditious libel prosecutions were private libel and defamation actions. Here, what words were actionable was a question of law, but how was this decided? What criteria were used, for example, to apply the *mitior sensus* doctrine—that if the words were capable of an innocuous construction, they were not actionable?[50] Was the possibility of an innocuous construction a question of law or fact? Richard Helmholz speculates in his introduction to *Select Cases in Defamation to 1600* that lawyers may have found certain of the sixteenth-century cases he discusses worth reporting "because they were themselves uncertain about why the words were actionable."[51]

Uncertainty about what words were actionable continued in the eighteenth century, as is shown by two unreported cases that highlight the vagueness of the law-fact distinction. In *Davy v. Jones* (1716),[52] a motion in arrest of judgment was granted after a jury verdict for the plaintiff. The reasons given for granting the motion were that the temporal damages alleged were not special enough and that the words charged ("Thou art an Whore to Parson Perry") "in themselves were not Actionable." There was no elaboration, but if the question turned on how in common understanding the words would be interpreted, why was the jury determination not accepted? This question was more distinctly put in the action for *scandalum magnatum, Duke of Richmond v. Costelo*.[53] There, the duke sued for damages for words, in several variations, that referred to him as "an old Rogue." At the first trial, in 1710, Chief Justice Holt "told the jury that as they ought to consider the honour of his Grace, so also the circumstances of the Man [defendant], that they ought to give Damages to correct him but not ruin him." The jury gave a general verdict for the plaintiff. After Holt's death, the case was argued before the full Court of King's Bench on a motion in arrest of judgment. At the first argument, Chief Justice Parker observed that "Rogue is no word of heat among Noble men," and at the second argument he observed that "Rogue" was not a legal word, that the action might lie if "in common understanding [it] imported scandal," and that "if a man is entrusted with a particular matter & breaks his trust he is said to be a Rogue." Who is to say how the word "rogue" is to be regarded among noblemen or whether it imported scandal in common understanding? Do common jurors know about this? Would special jurors?

Ultimately, the Court of King's Bench in the *Duke of Richmond* case upheld the jury verdict. Chief Justice Parker ruled that "there is no case in the Books that Words of Great Men shall be measured in *mitiori sensu* . . . but they shall be taken in the worst sense"; further, "The taking Words in a mild or severe sense is a mistake, the true rule is to take them according to the natural meaning of & agreeable to Common Understanding."[54] He then declared what was agreeable to common understanding as if exclusively a matter of law: "To say a man is a Rogue is to say he is vitious and corrupt"; "something shocking & attended with Baseness" is "the most essential Ingredient to make a Rogue"; and so forth. This interpretation entitled the plaintiff to damages since "Every Peer Is a Great Officer & of Great Dignity," and, although words of heat are common among private persons (who can return them in kind), "where respect is due by Law these words of contempt which produce Great Men's Revenge are an Injury."

The defamation examples show how hard it is to sort out the law-finding character of the jury in cases governed by a vague, fact-intensive legal standard.[55] Put another way, they illustrate a type of case in which questions of law and questions of fact are so closely intertwined that juries often engage in some amount of law-finding and judges engage in some amount of fact-finding.

In a scholarly late-nineteenth-century essay, "'Law and Fact' in Jury Trials," James Bradley Thayer addressed the question of the line between law and fact and did so with the eye of the realist. He pointed out that, historically, the judges "settled a great many questions of fact for themselves" and that the maxim (that matters of law are for the court and matters of fact are for the jury) "was never meant to be taken absolutely."[56] Thayer observed, however, that the judges' practice of answering questions of fact involved in the issues before them had "often been disguised by calling them questions of law."[57] He quoted an 1879 letter by the English Chief Justice Sir Alexander Cockburn in which that jurist asserted that "The right mode of dealing with a question of fact which is thought desirable to withdraw from the jury is to say that it shall, though a question of fact, be determined by the judge."[58] Thayer explained that, for policy reasons, many questions of fact were "taken possession of by the judges"—for example, the construction of writings, especially in early days, when, "to be sure, the jury could not read."[59] As another potent example, he cited the judges' "power of fixing the definition of legal terms," such as "reasonable notice."[60] "In this way," Thayer stated, "what is reasonable notice of the dishonor of a bill grew to be fixed," and "ordinary notice is sufficient if given on the following day."[61] For this proposition, Thayer cited the case of *Tindal v. Brown*.[62]

Tindal was a 1786 decision of the Court of King's Bench, and the story of the struggle in that court over whether to take the "reasonable notice" question away from the jury is instructive. It began in 1782 with the cases of *Medcalf v. Hall*[63] and *Appleton v. Sweetapple*.[64] There, special juries (different ones) stubbornly rejected the weight of the evidence on what was a reasonable time after receipt for merchants to deliver drafts to their banks for payment. After the first trial in *Medcalf*, Lord Mansfield granted a new one, and a manuscript report of the case includes the following comments by Mansfield during argument on the motion for a new trial: "I have taken some trouble in informing myself as to the sense of mankind upon it. All the Merchants I have talked to are against the Verdict and I am told the majority of the Bankers are so likewise. In a Case therfore of this consequence, without saying the verdict is wrong, I think it should undergo another consideration."[65] And, according to *The London Chronicle,* July 4, 1782:

> Lord Mansfield declared it was a question of great commercial consequence and since the last trial had been the subject of much talk in the city. The Court had therefore taken deliberation on it and there was not a case in print or manuscript which had not been searched in. His Lordship gave his opinion the same as on the former trial, that the next morning was a reasonable time. But the jury gave a verdict for the defendant.

A rule *nisi* for a third trial was obtained.[66] Lord Mansfield "asked whether there was any instance of a third Trial where the verdict had been twice the same way," and he fretted that he had great doubt about another trial "because it will produce a contest between the Court and jury."[67]

In *Appleton,* two more special juries considered the same issue. Mansfield stated that "it is a Question of law and fact proper for the determination of a jury," and, referring to *Medcalf,* "In another case, a jury have given their opinion, but with too great a latitude." Puisne Judge Buller minced no words; in his view, "It is a question of law, however unpleasant it may be to us, we must not yield to the decision of the jury."[68] A third new trial was moved for in *Appleton* but was denied by Buller, somewhat lamely, because of an incorrect mode of pleading. Then, in *Tindal v. Brown,*[69] another question of the reasonableness of time in connection with commercial paper arose, and the judges reflected on the earlier decisions. The first jury in *Tindal* again found against the evidence, and a new trial was granted. Mansfield stated:

> What is reasonable notice is partly a question of fact, and partly a question of law. It may depend in some measure on facts; such as the distance at which the parties live from each other, the course of the post, &c. But wherever a rule can be laid down with respect to this reasonableness, that should be decided by the court. . . . I cannot form to myself an idea of the ground on which the jury went in giving this verdict. . . . It was well observed by the counsel that the juries were obstinate in the case of

> *Medcalf* and *Hall,* where they struggled so hard, in spite of the opinion of the court.[70]

Again, Buller was more blunt:

> The numerous cases on this subject reflect great discredit on the courts of *Westminster.* They do infinite mischief in the mercantile world; and this evil can only be remedied by doing what the court wished to do in the case of *Medcalf* and *Hall;* by considering the reasonableness of time as a question of law and not of fact. Whether the post goes out this or that day, at what time, &c. are matters of fact: but when those facts are established, it then becomes a question of law on those facts, what notice shall be reasonable.[71]

A new trial was granted, and, unbelievably, the special jury found the same as the first jury (for plaintiff). A *third* new trial was granted, at which point the impasse was solved by a special verdict, allowing the court to give judgment for the defendant.

The issue with which the Court of King's Bench struggled in *Medcalf, Appleton,* and *Tindal* persists. Stephen Weiner points out that throughout the nineteenth and twentieth centuries in commercial cases in the United States, "judicial authority is badly divided concerning the role of judge and jury in applying the reasonable time standard."[72] More recently, Margaret Moses argues that the Uniform Commercial Code legislatively shifts many such questions into the "law" category without any recognition of or concern about the extent to which this trenches upon the Seventh Amendment jury-trial guarantee in civil cases.[73]

On the criminal side, a powerful example of legislative shifting of the line between law and fact has recently been addressed by the Supreme Court. In the late twentieth century, state legislatures began to tack onto selected criminal statutes "sentencing factors." The statutes authorized the trial judge to assess whether any "sentencing factor" was present in the case being decided and, if one was indeed present, to increase a convicted defendant's sentence up to a specified amount. A common example would be to permit the trial judge to take into account as a "sentencing factor" the defendant's prior criminal record.

As the sentencing factor methodology caught on, factors were added that seemed distinctly factual in nature. Thus, in a prosecution that eventually became a seminal Supreme Court decision (*Apprendi v. United States*[74]), a New Jersey statute made possessing a firearm for unlawful purposes a second-degree offense punishable by imprisonment for a term of between five and ten years. A separate statute, however, authorized the trial judge to extend the sentence for any second-degree offense to between ten and twenty years whenever the judge found that the offense constituted a "hate crime," as defined in the statute. The defendant in *Apprendi* fired a gun into the home of an African-American family that had moved into his all-white neighborhood. After he was arrested, his counsel worked out a plea bargain for multiple second-degree firearm offenses that would have had a maximum sentence of twenty years, but with the possibility reserved of a "hate crime" enhancement. At the plea hearing, the trial judge found that the defendant had committed a hate crime and increased the sentence to a maximum of thirty years. No jury had found that the defendant's actions deserved "hate crime" designation because motivated by racial bias, and the Supreme Court held that under the Sixth Amendment, the jury could not be bypassed in this manner. The Court pointed out that "Any possible distinction between an 'element' of a felony offense and a 'sentencing factor' was unknown to the practice of criminal indictment, trial by jury, and judgment by court as it existed during the years surrounding our Nation's founding."[75]

The *Apprendi* decision thus reaffirmed the importance of fact-finding as a jury responsibility, and other cases were to follow. In *Blakely v. Washington*,[76] the defendant was convicted of kidnaping his estranged wife, an offense punishable under applicable Oregon criminal statutes by a maximum of fifty-three months. Another Oregon statute, however, permitted an "exceptional" sentence of up to ninety months on a finding by the trial judge that the defendant had acted with "deliberate cruelty." The trial judge made such a finding and ordered a ninety-month sentence, instead of the forty-nine to fifty-three months that would have been applicable under the defendant's plea bargain. Again the Supreme Court intervened, overturning the judicial enhancement of the sentence because of its unconstitutional invasion of the role of the jury. In the majority opinion, Justice Antonin Scalia observed that the Court's "commitment to *Apprendi* . . . reflects not just respect for longstanding precedent, but the need to give intelligible content to the right of jury trial. That right is no mere procedural formality, but a fundamental reservation of power in our constitutional structure."[77]

Despite the Supreme Court's reaffirmations of the jury's fact-finding role, the cases and state statutes show that, as Thayer argued well over a century ago, the line between law and fact has not been stationary. The question of what is fact is to a significant extent within the control of judges and legislators. At times the process is attended by intermediate labels such as "mixed questions of law and fact" or "legislative facts," but these labels have no normative content. At other times, as in the *Medcalf* series of cases, matters that were once left to juries as fact questions are taken over by the judges because, the judges say, they have become so clear that reasonable minds can no longer differ about them. They have, in other words, become matters of law. Oliver Wendell Holmes, Jr., argued in his classic work, *The Common Law,* that even though facts "do not often repeat themselves in practice," yet "cases with comparatively small variations from each other do," and when this happens, "A judge who has long sat at *nisi prius* ought gradually to acquire a fund of experience which enables him to represent the common sense of the community in ordinary instances far better than an average jury."[78] Thus, "the sphere in which [the judge] is able to rule without taking [the jury's] opinion at all should be continually growing."[79]

The various ways in which common-law judges have always determined, or have appropriated, factual questions are part of a larger inquiry—how the judges took overall control of civil jury trials, predominantly in the nineteenth century. This phenomenon and its constituent elements were recognized by Thayer before the nineteenth century ended, and by others in early-twentieth-century writings.[80] Austin W. Scott divided the elements into questions arising on the pleadings and questions not on the pleadings, and in the latter he counted instructions to the jury, the attaint and the motion for a new trial, the demurrer to evidence, the special verdict, the special case and reserved point, the compulsory nonsuit, the motion to strike out sham pleading, the motion for judgment notwithstanding the verdict, and evidence on appeal.[81] Of these, the motion for new trial proved the most potent.[82] The extent to which the practice of granting new trials had taken root in the early nineteenth century is shown by the 1834 publication in New York of David Graham's six-hundred-page treatise, *An Essay on New Trials.*[83] Graham described the subject of his essay as one that had been "in a great measure overlooked."[84]

The ultimate form of control over the jury, of course, is for the judge simply to discard a jury verdict as against evidence or law and to enter judgment for the party who had lost the verdict. This technique is familiar to modern lawyers as a judgment n.o.v. (*non obstante veredicto,* notwithstanding the verdict), or more recently in the federal courts, a motion m.o.l. (on a matter of law). Prior to statutory authorization in some states in the mid-nineteenth century, however, this was not done. The expression "directed verdict" was used, but if a jury went against the judge's directions, the remedy was always a new trial.[85] Reneé Lettow points out that until the conclusive directed verdict was authorized, "new trial was the only means of dealing with a stubborn jury."[86] As was earlier shown in the case of *Tindal v. Brown,*[87] a special verdict with the parties' consent was also a way around jury stubbornness, but the new trial was far more common. As Lettow observes, the "new trial gave judges substantive control over outcomes while allowing them to claim that they were merely handing on the question to another jury."[88] William E. Nelson gives the summary appraisal that, "by 1804, at the latest, the civil jury had been tamed"; "by that year, the courts were routinely granting new trials in civil cases where the jury had ignored the court's instructions."[89]

A final word about the law-fact distinction concerns the role of special masters in jury trials. We have seen how the Court of Chancery in England in the eighteenth century and earlier was accustomed to deciding complicated factual questions in accounting cases and other actions.[90] Typically in such cases, the Chancery court would refer the fact-finding task to the Master of the Rolls or to one of the Masters in Chancery. This practice was adopted in federal courts in the United States. Writing for the Supreme Court in a 1920 decision, *Ex Parte Peterson,*[91] Justice Louis Brandeis referred to "the power to appoint persons unconnected with the court to aid judges in the performance of specific judicial duties" and observed that, "From the commencement of our Government, [the power] has been exercised by the federal courts, when sitting in equity, by appointing, with or without the consent of the parties, special masters, auditors, examiners, and commissioners."[92] He explained that where, for example, "accounts are complex and intricate . . . it is the better practice to refer the matter to a special master or commissioner than for the judge to undertake to perform the task himself."[93]

Even though Justice Brandeis in *Ex Parte Peterson* referred to the general practice of federal courts sitting in equity, the case before the Court had originated as an action at law for goods sold and delivered, with a counterclaim for an account, and the Court held that it was within the power of the trial court "when necessary to a proper consideration of the case by court and jury, to appoint, without consent of the parties, an auditor to examine books and papers, make computations, and hear testimony."[94] The Court concluded that doing so would not transgress the Seventh Amendment's jury-trial guarantee, since the task of the auditor would function, "in essence, the same as that of pleading." The auditor's report, if admitted at trial, would be treated "at most, as *prima facie* evidence," and the parties would "remain free to call, examine, and cross-examine witnesses as if the report had not been made." For this reason, the trial judge's order appointing the auditor could not "be held unconstitutional as unduly interfering with the jury's determination of issues of fact."[95]

In 1938, the Federal Rules of Civil Procedure were adopted, and, until 2003, Rule 53 expressly permitted federal courts to appoint special masters in jury trials, even over the objection of the parties. Any Seventh Amendment protest could be disposed of by reciting Justice Brandeis's rationale in *Ex Parte Peterson.* Nevertheless, Rule 53 was amended in 2003 to state that a special master cannot be appointed without the parties' consent.[96]

Conclusion

As the device of the new trial, the judgment n.o.v., and the use of special masters in jury trials suggest, the fact-finding role of the jury has been influenced by concepts of procedure. A brief additional example is found in newspaper reports of two insurance cases. In both of them, Lord Mansfield instructed the jury that the facts demonstrated that the insurance policy was *void* from the beginning—that it never took effect. Yet, both cases went to the jury (one a special jury of merchants), resulting in verdicts for defendants.[97] Under modern procedure, there would be no basis for sending such cases to juries, since there was no jury question of fact presented. In the eighteenth century, however, if the conclusive facts were not developed until the defendant's case was put on, the nonsuit would not be appropriate, and the procedure was to give the case to the jury with strong instructions. The jury would be "directed to find for the defendant," but it would not be a "directed verdict" as in the modern sense. In fact, these would be situations in which Mansfield would presumably have said that the jury would have the *power* to find for the plaintiff but would have no *right* to do so.

It would be wrong, however, to leave the impression that judges and juries in the common-law process were constantly at odds. Ordinarily, judges and juries understood each other and cooperatively played their respective parts in fitting together the law, the facts, and the views of society at large.

4

Determining Damages

The Seventh Amendment, the Writ of Inquiry, and Punitive Awards

This chapter explores whether determinations of damages are invariably "findings of fact" that fall within the province of the jury under the jury-trial guarantee of the Seventh Amendment. The chapter revolves around two recent Supreme Court decisions—*City of Monterey v. Del Monte Dunes at Monterey, Ltd.*,[1] and *Cooper Industries, Inc. v. Leatherman Tool Group, Inc.*[2] In *City of Monterey*, an action brought in federal court under 42 U.S.C. §1983, Justice David Souter observed that, in determining damages, "the dollars-and-cents issue is about as 'factual' as one can be."[3] And in *Cooper*, the Court declared that a "jury's award of punitive damages does not constitute a finding of 'fact'" but is rather an expression of moral condemnation.[4]

At issue in *City of Monterey* was whether, under the historical test for the preservation of trial by jury in civil cases under the Seventh Amendment (see chapter 1), a jury was required. The plaintiff claimed that the city of Monterey, by persistently throwing regulatory obstacles in plaintiff-developer's way, had effectively condemned its property without compensation and thus without due process, since plaintiff had done everything the city asked, yet development rights were still refused. The Supreme Court held that a jury was required. There was no majority opinion, but, speaking for a plurality, Justice Kennedy stated that fact questions are typically allocated to the jury[5] and that "whether a landowner has been wholly deprived of all economically viable use of his property is a predominantly factual question."[6] Responding to the city's claim that its actions had been in support of legitimate public interests, Justice Kennedy called this "a mixed question of fact and law," but in the specific case before the Court, it was "essentially fact-bound [in] nature."[7]

It is familiar dogma that juries ascertain facts; judges ascertain and apply the law.[8] Familiar, too, is the notion that "the jury are judges of the damages."[9] The latter proposition is usually stated without adding the implicit rationale: damages are facts. Compensatory damages, at least, are "facts." But, since the Court has now declared (in *Cooper*) that punitive damages are not findings of fact, *de novo* review by federal appellate courts of jury awards of punitive damages does not violate the second clause of the Seventh Amendment—"no fact tried by a jury shall be otherwise re-examined in any Court of the United States, than according to the rules of the common law."[10]

The Court's opinion in *Cooper* was almost unanimous, only Justice Ruth Bader Ginsberg dissenting. In the majority opinion, Justice John Paul Stevens rather casually discarded "the historical material upon which respondent relies so extensively." He observed that "Most of the sources respondent cites merely stand for the proposition that, because it is a fact-sensitive undertaking, determining the amount of punitive damages should be left to the discretion of the jury," but, in any event, "punitive damages have evolved somewhat since the time of respondent's sources."[11]

Merely because a jury's award of punitive damages is no longer characterized by the Supreme Court as a "finding of fact" does not mean that juries will no longer make punitive-damage awards. The Court in *Cooper* implicitly acknowledged that whenever a jury is mandated by the first clause of the Seventh Amendment, setting the amounts of damages in the first instance (both compensatory and punitive) is the jury's responsibility.[12] Punitive-damage awards, however, will be subject to more extensive review than jury determinations of compensatory damages. The *Cooper* case will operate in combination with the Court's earlier holding in *BMW of North America, Inc. v. Gore,*[13] as reaffirmed and refined in *State Farm Mutual Automobile Insurance Co. v. Campbell,*[14] that "grossly excessive" punitive-damage awards constitute a deprivation of property without due process. In assessing whether an award is "grossly excessive," both federal and state courts are to follow three guideposts: the degree of reprehensibility of the offending party's conduct; the disparity between the actual or potential harm suffered by the injured party and the punitive-damages award; and the difference in amount between the award and any civil penalties that might be authorized or imposed in comparable cases.[15]

Thus, when a federal jury returns a substantial award of compensatory and punitive damages and the trial judge allows the award to stand,[16] the defendant can challenge the award on appeal by, first, claiming that the compensatory award is excessive because it is not supported by the evidence, and, in this phase of the review, the appellate court will use the traditional "abuse-of-discretion" standard.[17] Prior to *Cooper,* the same standard would have been applied to the jury's determination of punitive damages. After *Cooper,* if the size of the punitive-damage award is also challenged by defendant, the appellate court must determine whether the punitive-damage award is within constitutional limits, applying *BMW,* and, in making that determination, the court is to review the case *de novo.* If the award is found to be constitutional, then the appellate court "is merely to review the trial court's 'determination under an abuse-of-discretion standard.'"[18]

Only compensatory damages were involved in the *City of Monterey* case, and, as noted earlier, the Court ruled that a jury was required under the historical test. Justice Souter, dissenting, thought that there really was no counterpart in the English common law of 1791 to the American property condemnation cases that have arisen under the due process clause. A further problem for Justice Souter was the logical inconsistency of saying that a jury was constitutionally essential for indirect, or "inverse," condemnation cases, while not essential for direct condemnation cases.[19] Justice Anthony Kennedy acknowledged that, "Because the jury's role in estimating just compensation in condemnation proceedings was inconsistent and unclear at the time the Seventh Amendment was adopted, this Court has said 'that there is no constitutional right to a jury in eminent-domain proceedings.'" Yet, Justice Souter claimed that, "If an emphasis on factual issues vigorously contested were a sufficient criterion for identifying something essential to the preservation of the Seventh Amendment jury right, there ought to be a jury right in direct condemnation cases as well as the inverse ones favored by the plurality."[20]

The rationale of Justice Kennedy's plurality opinion for the line between direct and inverse condemnation cases in applying the Seventh Amendment was that in direct condemnation cases, liability is admitted and the only question is the ascertainment of the amount of the damages, whereas in inverse condemnation situations, both liability and the amount are contested. Although this was unpersuasive to Justice Souter,[21] there is an interesting historical comparison.

For many centuries in England, the writ of inquiry was the standard method for determining the amount of damages when liability was not at issue. The usual situation was the default judgment. The procedure was for the plaintiff to take out a writ of inquiry directing the sheriff to impanel a jury to determine the damages. Customarily, plaintiff would present evidence to support the amount claimed in the complaint (or, in English legal parlance, the "declaration"), which the defendant was at liberty to challenge with evidence of his own.[22]

The writ of inquiry was described in English cases as but a discretionary "inquest of office." This meant, according to oft-repeated language, that the judges could determine the amount of damages themselves. The parallel to the opinion by Justice Kennedy in the *City of Monterey* case now becomes evident. If indeed juries could be dispensed with in England in 1791 whenever damages were sought and liability was not an issue, notwithstanding the "factual" nature of the inquiry into the amount of damages, Kennedy's rationale for the Seventh Amendment line between direct and inverse condemnation has historical support. In the first part of this chapter, I test the strength of this support by examining the English experience with the writ of inquiry and by reflecting on how that experience bears on the historical test used by the Supreme Court for the scope of the Seventh Amendment right to jury trial. In the second part of the chapter, I turn to the implications of *Cooper* and *BMW* after reviewing early common-law cases in which damage awards by juries were rejected by the courts. Long before the Seventh Amendment was adopted, it was established in English common law that jury verdicts could be overturned because the damages fixed by the jury were deemed excessive or inadequate. The cases where this occurred usually involved extraordinary facts or jury behavior, because the strong inclination of the judges, supported by long tradition, was to allow the jury verdict to stand. Among the questions that arise are the following:

- What standards were used to determine whether the damages found by the trial jury were excessive or inadequate?
- When a damage award was overturned as excessive, was the rationale that the award was inappropriately punitive?
- Was the remedy for an excessive or inadequate jury award of damages invariably a new jury trial?
- Historically, where and how did the concepts of *remittitur* and *additur* fit in?

Part I : The Writ of Inquiry and the "Inquest of Office"

Fundamentals

We can obtain the basics from the fifth edition of a leading English practice book published in 1791, the same year the Seventh Amendment was adopted. According to Impey's *New Instructor Clericalis:*

> Generally it is laid down, where damages are to be recovered, a jury must be called in to assess them; unless the defendant, to save charges, will confess the whole damages laid in the declaration; otherwise the entry of the judgment is, *"that the plaintiff ought to recover his damages, because the court know not what damages the plaintiff hath sustained; therefore, the sheriff is commanded by the oaths of twelve honest and lawful men to inquire into the said damages, and return such inquisition into court."* This process is called a *writ of inquiry:* in the execution of which, the sheriff sits as judge, and tries by a jury subject to nearly the same law and conditions as the trial by jury at *nisi prius,* what damages the plaintiff hath really sustained, which must assess some damages.[23]

The writ of inquiry came into play when a plaintiff obtained a judgment but no jury determination of damages had taken place. Overwhelmingly, in terms of numbers of cases, the context was the default judgment. Thousands of examples in eighteenth-century cases can be seen in the Entry Books of Final Judgment at the National Archives in London. Another, much less common context occurred when a plaintiff prevailed after issue had been joined on demurrer.[24]

Writs of inquiry were customarily directed to sheriffs for local handling. A late-eighteenth-century practice book states, for example, that the writ should be delivered to the sheriff in time for him to be able to summon a jury, though in the City of London "a jury is generally sitting at *Guild-hall*—and in *Westminster* at the *Guild-hall Westminster*—if in term, or, if in vacation, at the *Three Tons* in *Brook-Street, Holborn,* between the hours of ten and twelve."[25] Occasionally, concerns were voiced about the lack of quality control in the selection process. In 1751, in *Sparrow v. Reed,* the court observed: "Juries are returned in a better manner at the assizes, than usually, for writs of inquiry. An improper deputy is often appointed to represent the sheriff, sometimes plaintiff's attorney."[26] In 1783, a King's Bench rule was issued that required advance notice for the execution of any writ of inquiry, specifying the nature of the action and the time and place when and where the writ was to be executed, apparently with the objective of upgrading the quality of the jurors. Among other things, the rule stated that the practice had been for writs of inquiry to be brought to the sheriff's office without previous notice, with the result that "standing juries as well in London as in the country (composed of the lowest description of men) have been appointed to try and determine the rights of the parties, by whose ignorance and sometimes influence, great injuries have been done to some of the parties."[27] In important or complicated cases, the writ of inquiry was directed to one of the common-law judges at the assizes or at the sittings during or after term in London.[28] According to Impey, leave to have the writ of inquiry executed before a justice at the sittings or on assize "is seldom granted unless the case is very special, as where the law is mixed with the fact, or it appears to be of too much consequence for the sheriff to undertake."[29] In *Boyfield v. Brown,*[30] a writ of inquiry was executed before Lord Hardwicke, Chief Justice of the Court of King's Bench. According to a manuscript report of the case, a previous writ of inquiry executed before the sheriff had produced a verdict of £200 on an insurance policy, and, after reviewing affidavits received on a motion to set aside the verdict as excessive, Hardwicke said that there appeared to be a reasonable custom of merchants that had not been taken into account, "so that 'tis proper that this should be determined in a more solemn way than on an enquiry before the sheriff."[31] The typical case, however, was heard before the sheriff, and according to Crompton, the procedure was as follows: "When the day of executing the writ comes, the sheriff's deputy and jury are attended by the plaintiff's attorney, with evidence to prove the plaintiff's demand, or the damages sustained by him; and the defendant in mitigation of such damages, may produce witnesses on his part."[32]

The Question of Consent

As earlier noted, if the judges historically could dispense with the writ of inquiry and determine damages themselves, then juries were not essential in the circumstances that normally precipitated the writ (almost always a default judgment). A court could, of course, determine damages if the parties consented, but the meaningful question is whether the judges could do so without that consent. The answer to this question requires consideration of a small group of English cases from the seventeenth and eighteenth centuries, after which the question of consent in U.S. cases can be addressed.

The English Decisions

In *Bruce v. Rawlins,*[33] a 1770 case before the Court of Common Pleas, a writ of inquiry had issued after a default judgment and the jury had awarded £100 damages against defendants, customs-house officers who had (fruitlessly) searched plaintiff's house for uncustomed goods. The motion before the court sought to set aside the inquisition for excessive damages, since the officers were in the house only about an hour and did very little or no damage. Although the court upheld the jury verdict,[34] Chief Justice John Eardley Wilmot began his opinion with the following observation: "This is an inquest of office to inform the conscience of the Court who, if they please, may themselves assess the damages."[35] Probably Chief Justice Wilmot recollected or had a note of a similar remark made by his predecessor in office, Charles Pratt (later Lord Camden), in *Beardmore v. Carrington.*[36] In discussing the rare occasions in which the courts might order a new trial because of excessive damages,[37] Pratt stated that "there is also a difference between a principal verdict of a jury, and a writ of inquiry of damages; the latter being only an inquest of office to inform the conscience of the Court, and which they might have assessed themselves without any inquest at all."[38]

Pratt's and Wilmot's "inquest of office" expression—borrowed, undoubtedly, from the Court of Chancery—was repeated and embellished in later sources. Thus, for example, in John Archbold's nineteenth-century King's Bench practice book, an entire chapter is devoted to the writ of inquiry, and at one point Archbold notes: "As the inquest, however, is merely for the purpose of informing the conscience of the court, the court themselves may, *in all cases,* if they please, assess the damages, *and give final judgment.*"[39] Without more, the Pratt-Wilmot remark, especially as enlarged by Archbold, would suggest that it was open to the court to ascertain damages in lieu of a writ of inquiry whether or not the parties consented.[40] If this were true, historical support for Justice Kennedy's differentiation in the *City of Monterey* case between direct and inverse condemnation cases with regard to the Seventh Amendment right to jury trial would be established.

In fact, however, the authorities are clear that judicial determinations of damages in lieu of a writ of inquiry were always in response to the plaintiff's motion or with the plaintiff's consent. What the judges *never* did was to order a writ of inquiry, receive back a jury verdict of damages, and then, since the verdict "was only to inform the conscience of the court," discard that verdict and determine the damages themselves. By the eighteenth century, the rule that the responsibility for determining damages fell to the jury had become so ingrained that even when the plaintiff requested that the jury be dispensed with, the courts were hesitant to do so. When the judges occasionally did accede to such a plaintiff's request, as in debt cases where there was no dispute about the amount of damages, they still thought it necessary to explain how they could justify taking the job away from the jury. In context, plaintiff's consent was invariably present, and it came to be taken for granted without special mention.

Initially, however, the question of the plaintiff's consent was not taken for granted. It was explicitly dealt with by the Court of King's Bench, on writ of error from the Common Pleas, in a seventeenth-century case, *Holdipp v. Otway.*[41] There, a default judgment for £68 was entered for the plaintiff in an action of debt, and this was followed by a referral to the Prothonotary,[42] who taxed another £50 for interest and damages as compensation for the long delay since the debt had become due. On the writ of error, counsel for the defendant moved to set aside the £50 "because the Court of Common Pleas had taxed damages on occasion of the detention of the debt, where the damages did not appear judicially to the Court, but should have been inquired of by a jury upon a writ of enquiry."[43] The motion was denied because the taxing of the damages and costs had been done "with the assent of the plaintiff, which is always entered upon the record." "But," added the court, "if the plaintiff will not assent to it, then he shall have a writ of enquiry of damages on occasion of the detention of the debt, . . . but it is in the election of the plaintiff and not of the defendant."[44]

Bypassing the Writ of Inquiry On the Plaintiff's Motion

After the entry of a default judgment, it would be up to the plaintiff to move his case to the stage where the judgment could be executed. This would require a determination of damages, ordinarily by means of a writ of inquiry. The plaintiff might, however, seek to save the time and expense of the writ of inquiry and have the amounts determined by the court without a jury. The standard procedure was for the plaintiff to file a motion to show cause why the task of determining damages and costs should not be referred to the appropriate court officer. Undoubtedly, in many cases, defendants also let this motion go by default, but if a defendant attempted to show cause, a ruling by the court would be required.

If there was no question about the amount of the defendant's obligation, so that all that was necessary was the taxation of costs of litigation (and perhaps the computation of interest), the plaintiff's request to bypass the writ of inquiry would likely succeed. Such cases date back at least to the sixteenth century, and the practice reached not only default judgments but also demurrers and other situations where a judgment was reached without the need for a jury. Thus, in 1588, in *Ognell's Case*,[45] Ognell had taken possession of plaintiff's cattle since plaintiff had failed to pay land rent that was due; plaintiff sued in replevin and was nonsuited, and "the question was whether the Court might assess [defendant's] damages, without a writ of inquiry." The Court of King's Bench was of the opinion that it could do so, since the damages were only for the delay in payment of rent. The court noted, however, that had judgment been given for the plaintiff for the taking of his cattle, a writ of inquiry would have been required, since "the damages may be greater or less according to the value of the cattle, and the circumstances of the taking and delaying of them."

The rule stated in *Ognell's Case*—that a jury determination upon a writ of inquiry was essential whenever the damages were uncertain—was consistently followed in later decisions. In 1626, in *Wood v. Brooke*,[46] a determination of damages for plaintiff by the trial court upon demurrer was reversed because, "the damages being uncertain, there ought to issue a writ of inquiry" (otherwise, however, "where the demand is certain, as in debt").[47]

In another early-seventeenth-century case, *Goodwin v. Welsh*,[48] plaintiff obtained judgments against two defendants in trespass actions for goods taken, after the attorney for the defendants pleaded *non sum informatus* ("I am not informed").[49] Writs of inquiry then issued but were contested by the defendants "because the plaintiff at the time of the inquiry did not prove that the goods belonged to him, but only proved the value of the goods." The court rejected defendants' argument "because the writ commands only the value to be inquired and no more, and that alone is the charge of the jury." In passing, the judges observed that they might, if they would, trouble themselves to assess damages in these cases without issuing any writ, "but it is otherwise in the case of *non cul.* [*non culpabilis* (not guilty)] pleaded, for there the trespass is denied, which must be tried by the jury, and there the property and the value also ought to be proved."[50]

Historically, the action of debt required the plaintiff to claim that a sum certain was owed by the defendant, and it became a settled practice, as suggested in *Wood v. Brooke,* for the court to accede to the plaintiff's request in such a case to dispense with the writ of inquiry after a default judgment had entered. Occasional attempts were made as well to dispense with the writ of inquiry in nondebt cases in which it was claimed that the monetary amount owing by the defendant was clear. These met with some success in the Court of Common Pleas but were less well received in King's Bench. In 1791, in *Longman v. Fenn,*[51] plaintiff recovered a default judgment in assumpsit on a promissory note and moved the court to dispense with the writ of inquiry. Counsel for defendant argued that this practice ought to be confined to actions of debt, but the Court of Common Pleas stated that, "as the sum was defined on the face of the note, and as the interest was capable of exact computation by the prothonotary, it was highly reasonable to save the parties the expense of a writ of inquiry."[52]

Some years earlier (1780), in *Thellusson v. Fletcher,*[53] the defendant, an insurance underwriter, suffered a default judgment, and a jury on a writ of inquiry assessed damages at the sum defendant had underwritten, which was challenged by defendant since the jury had done so "without any proof of the amount or value, or any evidence whatever, except of the defendant's handwriting to the policy." The writ of inquiry was upheld by the Court of King's Bench. Justice Francis Buller observed that "Writs of inquiry are often sued out in cases where they are not necessary, as for instance, in actions on covenants for the payment of a sum certain," but he cautioned against assuming "that the amount of the demand is uncertain" merely "because a writ of inquiry has been awarded." He explained:

> In actions upon a bill of exchange, or a promissory note, nothing but the instrument is to be proved before the jury, the sum being thereby ascertained. Though, even in cases where there is no necessity for a writ of inquiry, that proceeding is of use, when the plaintiff goes for interest, which the jury assesses in the name of damages.[54]

In a 1791 case in the Court of King's Bench, *Messin v. Lord Massareene*,[55] plaintiff obtained a default judgment in an action of assumpsit on a foreign judgment and sought to have the damage determination referred to the Master.[56] The court refused plaintiff's request, and Chief Justice Lloyd Kenyon said, "This is an attempt to carry the rule farther than has yet been done: and as there is no instance of the kind, I am not disposed to make a precedent for it." A few years later, in *Nelson v. Sheridan*,[57] another request to dispense with the writ of inquiry came before the Court of King's Bench that involved a default judgment in an action of debt based on a bill of exchange. Counsel for the plaintiff cited many of the authorities already discussed, but, despite those cases and the similarity of the facts to those before the court in *Holdipp v. Otway*, plaintiff's request was refused. Chief Justice Kenyon said it should be left to the jury to consider whether any damages should be given—"perhaps they may think in this case no damages at all ought to be given." Thus, by the 1790s, the Court of King's Bench was inclining against dispensing with the jury for determining damages despite plaintiff's request to do so based on objective facts.

The attitude of the third common-law court, the Court of Exchequer, was explained in 1793 in the case of *Chilton v. Harborn*.[58] There plaintiff had a default judgment on a bill of exchange and, citing the practice in the other courts, moved that the bill might be referred to the Master to compute principal and interest instead of going to a writ of inquiry. Opposing this motion, counsel for defendant argued (incorrectly) "that the practice of the other Courts was so recently adopted, and its effects so little ascertained by practice, that they furnish no example." He claimed that "These cases crept in unperceived." Counsel for plaintiff rejoined that "The principle that the Court is competent to assess the damages, is very ancient," adding that the endorsement of such a practice by eight of the twelve common-law judges (that is, by the judges of the Court of King's Bench and the Court of Common Pleas) "should weigh much in a question of this sort."[59] Nevertheless, the Exchequer judges declined to adopt the practice, at least not in the assumpsit action before the court. Chief Baron Macdonald observed that the cases where the practice had been followed in actions other than debt were "few and straggling," and that in assumpsit the issue was not only what might be due but whether anything was due, whereas in debt it was the sum claimed or nothing. He also noted that there might be little advantage to the plaintiff in going to the Master, stating:

> The saving of expence, or of time, by sending it to the Master, can in no case be considerable, for you can only have, in the first instance, a rule to shew cause, and therefore counsel must be retained. If cause is shewn, that is an additional expense to both parties, of affidavits, &c.; and if the cause shewn is allowed, it goes at last to the jury with this expence superadded. This inconvenience also attends it, that we must in truth try the cause upon affidavits, which is never to be encouraged.[60]

We can now summarize the practice in the English common-law courts. Long before the eighteenth century, language that appeared in the cases declared that the writ of inquiry was but an "inquest of office" to inform the court about damages, though the court could, if it chose, perform that task itself. It is clear, however, that the courts never did this without the consent of the prevailing party, which almost always was the plaintiff seeking execution of a default judgment. And even when the plaintiff sought to dispense with the writ of inquiry, the writ would still be required if there was any uncertainty about the amount of the damages, because resolving that uncertainty required a factual determination, and "the jury are judges of damages."[61]

In the United States

To repeat, the historical test requires the courts to assess the scope of the jury-trial guarantee of the Seventh Amendment according to the practices established in the common law of England as of 1791. The U.S. Supreme Court has never held, or interpreted eighteenth-century English common law as holding, that a plaintiff's request for a writ of inquiry could be denied on the ground that the writ was "but an inquest of office." Perhaps unsurprisingly, the Court has given little attention to the writ of inquiry, but the few references that do exist conform to the English common law as described.

In 1797, in *Brown v. Van Braam,*[62] the plaintiff sued to collect on bills of exchange drawn on London merchants, and, after a default judgment, the Rhode Island trial court ascertained the damages (principal, interest, and "ten percent damages"), plus costs. Neither party had asked for a writ of inquiry, but, on appeal, one of the defendant's arguments was that the damages (not the principal or interest) should have been determined by a jury. Counsel for the plaintiff quoted Justice Wilmot's language from *Bruce v. Rawlins*[63] and also pointed out a Rhode Island statute that specified that damage assessments after default judgments "shall be done by the court, or otherwise, at their discretion."[64] The Supreme Court affirmed without giving any opinion save a remark by Justice Chase that he concurred "on common law principles, and not in compliance with the laws and practice of the state."[65]

In an early-nineteenth-century bill-of-exchange action, *Renner & Bussard v. Marshall*,[66] the District of Columbia trial court determined the damages, and, on appeal to the Supreme Court, one question was "whether judgment could be entered up for the plaintiff for the amount of his damages by the court, without a writ of inquiry."[67] This gave Justice Joseph Story no trouble, as the question "is completely settled by authority in all cases where the action is brought for a sum certain, or which may be made certain by computation."[68] Justice Story said nothing more on the point but cited a number of cases, the first of which was *Holdipp v. Otway*.[69] As earlier stated, *Holdipp* was the case in which the Court of King's Bench explained that the writ of inquiry would not be dispensed with without the plaintiff's assent.[70]

In state courts, writ of inquiry results have been mixed. In the *Van Braam* case, counsel for the plaintiff observed that, influenced by principles of British law, there had been great diversity of theory and practice with writs of inquiry; thus:

> In some of the States, writs of enquiry are executed on every occasion, even to fix a mere computation of interest, but in New England, and especially in Massachusetts and Rhode Island, a writ of enquiry never issues, but at the request of the parties, or by the discretion of the court, in whose presence it is invariably executed.[71]

One explanation for the variations among the states is the controlling effect of a specific state statute, as in Rhode Island. Occasionally, however, Justice Wilmot's remarks in *Bruce v. Rawlins* led state courts to the mistaken conclusion that issuance of a writ of inquiry was wholly a matter of court discretion, regardless of the preferences of the plaintiff. This appears to be what happened in Connecticut. In an 1877 negligence action, the plaintiff obtained a default judgment and then claimed that he had a constitutional right to a jury determination of damages, whereas the defendant argued "that, in accordance with the practice of the state courts in Connecticut, the damages are to be assessed by the court."[72] Speaking for the court, Judge Shipman noted the preservation of trial by jury in state constitutions in a manner akin to that in the Seventh Amendment, reviewed some of the confusing early common-law history of damage determinations after default judgments, and repeated Justice Wilmot's language from *Bruce v. Rawlins,* citing as well *Beardmore v. Carrington.*[73] Shipman observed that the practice in the United States circuit courts had not been uniform—"The more common method has been to assess damages by a jury, upon a writ of inquiry, but it is believed that the practice has conformed to the usages of the state in which the circuit court was held."[74] Shipman concluded that, in the Connecticut case before him, "the assessment of damages by a jury, upon a default, is a matter of practice, and not of right, and that the assessment should be made in this case according to the uniform practice in the state courts. Let the damages be assessed by the court."[75]

Later, the Connecticut Supreme Court decided two default judgment cases in which the plaintiffs claimed that damages should have been determined by juries. In the first of these, the court gave the issue short shrift. Since the practice had always been for the court to determine damages upon a default, the state constitutional provision that "the right to trial by jury shall remain inviolate . . . therefore had no application to the case."[76] The same result was reached in *Lennon v. Rawitzer,*[77] where the court relied on a treatise by Judge Zephaniah Swift ("our most approved text-writer"). The court quoted Judge Swift's explanation of the writ of inquiry procedure, followed by Swift's observation that:

> This mode of proceeding must be productive of expence and delay, and the practice of this state, introduced by our courts, without the authority of a statute, of assessing damages themselves, without the intervention of a jury, is one of the many instances in which we have improved upon the common law of England.[78]

The state decisions, of course, have no bearing on the scope of the Seventh Amendment jury-trial guarantee, which is applicable only in federal courts. Yet they do further illustrate how the English common-law requirement that the plaintiff consent before the writ of inquiry can be dispensed with became obfuscated by Justice Wilmot's remarks in *Bruce v. Rawlins* and then disappeared from view altogether.

At this point we can return to the Supreme Court's *City of Monterey* case. Since the common-law courts in England in 1791 would not determine damages without plaintiff's consent in processing default judgments where liability was admitted but only the quantity of damages needed to be ascertained, the writ of inquiry does not, after all, support Justice Kennedy's rationalization of the Seventh Amendment line between direct condemnation cases (jury not required) and inverse condemnation cases (jury required). Moreover, the emphasis in the eighteenth-century English cases on damage determinations as *factual* determinations leads to Part II of this chapter and *Cooper Industries, Inc. v. Leatherman Tool Group, Inc.*

Part II: Overturning Jury Damage Awards

It is hardly controversial to observe that juries can be unpredictable. There are times when jury verdicts seem inexplicable. When it can be demonstrated on appeal that a jury verdict is unsupported by the evidence introduced at trial, the verdict can be overturned, and when this happens, the customary remedy is to order a new trial. A relatively common application of this process, stretching across many centuries, has been the challenge on appeal to the amount of damages awarded by the jury at trial, either as inadequate or as excessive.

The best-known procedural mechanism for reducing excessive-damages awards is *remittitur.* In such an order, the trial judge concludes that the jury award is excessive, names a lower sum, and gives the plaintiff the option of accepting that lower amount or of having a new trial. Prior to 1935, a comparable procedure existed in federal courts called *additur* in which the trial judge concluded that the jury award was inadequate, named a larger sum, and gave the defendant the option of paying the larger sum or of having a new trial. In *Dimick v. Schiedt,*[79] however, the Supreme Court held *additur* unconstitutional under the Seventh Amendment. The Court concluded that a judicial determination that the damages suffered by the plaintiff were greater than the amount found by the jury would be a re-examination of fact in violation of the second clause of the Seventh Amendment.[80] As the Court put it, "where the verdict is too small, an increase by the court is a bald addition of something which in no sense can be said to be included in the verdict."[81]

Also, as has been stated, the Court later decided that some punitive-damage awards can be unconstitutionally high (*BMW v. Gore; State Farm v. Campbell*), and the Court has declared that a jury's award of punitive damages is not a finding of fact (*Cooper v. Leatherman*). With these Supreme Court decisions in mind, we turn to the English common law as it pertains to inadequate jury awards, followed by the issue of excessive-damage awards.[82]

Inadequate Jury Damages

In the medieval era, the line between judge and jury was not as clear as the distinction that later came to be established. As discussed in chapter 5, the early juries were expected to *know* the facts rather than find them, since the jurors would, in theory at least, come from the neighborhood where the events in litigation took place. In the records of this early era, one can find examples of almost casual increases by the court of jury damages, with no thought of ordering a new trial. Thus, in the prosecution of John Overton in 1403 for ravishing the wife of John London, according to the report of the case, "because it seems to the court that the aforesaid jurors assessed the aforesaid damages on account of the aforesaid ravishment at much too little, the court has increased the aforesaid damages to 100 shillings over and above the aforesaid 50 shillings."[83] Similarly, in a 1405 malpractice case against Nicholas Bradmor for "negligently and foolishly" treating Richard Asser's injured right thumb, having undertaken to heal it, the jury awarded 60 shillings in damages, and "because it seems to the court that the aforesaid jurors have assessed the aforesaid damages at too little, therefore the court increases the aforesaid damages by 20 shillings over and above the aforesaid 60 shillings."[84] In another case, in 1411, the justices increased the damages to the Abbott of Bermondsey for an assault upon his servants.[85] Also, in a case decided in 1404, we can see stirrings of the writ of inquiry procedures described in Part I. John Salage was prosecuted for assaulting Richard Cheddre and was found guilty after demurrer and joinder. The matter was sent to the sheriffs of London "to inquire about the damages and expenses," but the sheriffs took no action. Consequently, Richard Cheddre appeared in court, and, under the circumstances, "it now seems to the court that it is not necessary to make inquiry by the country about the damages the aforesaid Richard Cheddre sustained by reason of the aforesaid beating and wounding but this matter lies better in the discretion of the Justices."[86]

A century later, the role of the jury had changed, and the only instance in the reports of Sir John Spelman that show an increase by the court in damages found by a jury was "in the appeal of mayhem."[87] The judges could do so in these cases "because by the view of the wound the court had as much knowledge as the jurors."[88]

The "mayhem" cases can be thought of as an interesting residual from the bygone era of the self-informing jury. When a defendant "put himself upon the country" in those early days, he was placing himself in the hands of twelve countrymen from the neighborhood, some of whom at least would come into court with personal knowledge of what had happened. The principal advantage in theory that these countrymen had over the judges was this personal knowledge. Therefore, when the issue was something that the judges could see for themselves and evaluate for themselves as well as the jurors could, it was logical for the judges to feel free to intervene by requiring the wounded victim to come into court to be viewed. For a considerable time, the possibility of an increase in damages by this means was entertained only in cases in which the physical effects of the defendant's actions against the plaintiff were evident. In *Davis v. Lord Foliot*,[89] however, the victim was stabbed with a knife, and, although the dagger and the victim were produced in court, counsel for the defendant pointed out that "here the battery is not apparent and the wound is internal, and not to be viewed by the Court"; he argued that, "the Court cannot increase damages upon a view of the party, if he be not maimed, and here is no maiming, but only a battery and wounding." Nevertheless,

> the Court upon view of the party, and examination of the surgeons and witnesses on both sides upon oath, did conclude that they might increase the damages, and that the wound was apparent, and that the damages were too small, and therefore they increased them to £400. And said they would not increase them more, because they could not inquire into all the circumstances of the fact, as the jury might, but they thought fitting to increase them in some proportion, because the offence was great, and such outrageous acts are not to be slightly punished.[90]

Justice Sutherland began his analysis in his opinion for the Supreme Court in *Dimick v. Schiedt* with the mayhem cases. He noted that in these cases, when favorably acted upon, the application for an increase in damages was made by the plaintiff and was "granted absolutely and not as a condition upon which to base a denial of a new trial."[91] He said that the latest case that the Court had been able to find that recognized the rule was *Brown v. Seymour*, decided in 1742.[92] There were, in fact, later instances, although they do not appear in printed sources. In *Hoare v. Crozier,* decided in 1782, a motion was made in the Court of King's Bench to increase damages after a writ of inquiry in an action of assault and battery on a view of the party and an examination of the surgeon (the plaintiff had lost an eye). According to a manuscript report of the case, "The Court did not doubt their power," but Justice Buller said that it did not appear likely that the plaintiff would get much by his motion if it were granted and recommended a settlement, which evidently was accepted.[93]

Justice Sutherland concluded in *Dimick* that the mayhem rule for increasing damages "was obsolete in England at the time of the adoption of the Constitution."[94] While this may not have been strictly true, as the 1782 manuscript case shows, the rule had certainly grown scarce in application, and it is not surprising that the Court did not consider it a "rule of practice" encompassed by the Seventh Amendment historical test.[95]

Apart from the mayhem cases, there was no other instance in the common law in which a court would order that a jury award of damages was inadequate and that the amount should be increased to a specified sum. There were, however, occasional decisions in which the court would overturn an inadequate jury award and order a new trial. This was done sparingly because, as was noted as early as 1588, otherwise "there might be infinite enquiries."[96] The very few cases where a new trial was granted because of inadequate damages appear to have involved jury mistakes or partiality. In *Earl of Peterborough v. Sadler,*[97] defendant was the plaintiff's farmer, and the trial concerned the value of an improvement made by Sadler. According to the report of the case, "a jury of farmers having given two hundred pounds damages, which was thought excessive, and therefore a new trial granted, and a jury of gentlemen ordered, who only gave forty pounds." Thereafter a new trial was sought because of the small sum awarded as damages at the second trial. Chief Justice John Holt thought that "the thing may require a re-examination" and granted the motion. In *Parr v. Purbeck,*[98] plaintiff proved that the defendant owed him £150 for rent, yet the jury on a writ of inquiry awarded but one shilling damages, evidently because the jury "were of the neighbourhood" and knew that the defendant had secured a covenant in the lease to provide him with a flow of water sufficient to run his paper mill, but the commissioner of sewers had made the water course so narrow that the mill could not operate. The King's Bench judges held that it was improper for the jury to take this into account—the lease called for the payment of a sum certain, and the information about the paper mill and the water course was not in evidence. And, in *Woodford v. Eads,*[99] plaintiff sued for the return of a £200 deposit, since defendant had not performed his contract for a stock purchase; after plaintiff received judgment on demurrer, a jury on a writ of inquiry awarded only one pence damages because the jury mistakenly believed that the consent of a third party was required before the money could be paid out. The verdict was set aside.

Absent mistake or partiality, however, and except for the mayhem cases, attempts to have jury verdicts overturned because of inadequate damages were unsuccessful. This was invariably true when the action sounded in tort instead of contract, as in the 1732 King's Bench decision, *Hayward v. Newton,* an action for words (defamation).[100] Four years later, in another King's Bench decision, *Barker v. Dixie,*[101] a malicious prosecution verdict for plaintiff for five shillings damages was upheld despite clear proof that, even apart from intangible harm, the plaintiff had expended £111 in costs. Chief Justice Hardwicke observed that "everyone knows, that it has been taken to be an established distinction, that a new trial may be granted for excessive damages, but may not for small damages."[102] Chief Justice Hardwicke had been the trial judge and was sympathetic to the plaintiff, acknowledging that the court might think differently about the question of inadequate damages "on the reason of the thing" if it were *res integra,* but the principle against granting a new trial in such circumstances was too firmly fixed in the law to be disturbed.[103] He rationalized the result by noting that attaint would lie for a defendant complaining of excessive damages awarded against him by a jury, but the court "would not let the plaintiff come and complain of the verdict given for him."[104] Also, the facts of the case were such that the jury could have gone either way, and "in such cases we will not break in upon the province of the juries who in the language of the law are judges of fact."[105] Chief Justice Hardwicke added, for good measure, that the writ of inquiry "is only an inquest of office, and there are many instances of the courts exercising the same power as juries upon writs of inquiry."[106]

Dating from medieval times, attaint was the theoretical remedy against a jury that brought in a false verdict. The procedure was to impanel a new jury of twenty-four men who would decide whether the first jury had indeed returned a false verdict. The punishment was so severe that the procedure was almost never successfully invoked.[107] Also, after *Bushell's Case,* in 1670,[108] jurors could no longer be fined for a verdict against evidence. Lord Mansfield observed in *Bright v. Enyon,* in 1757,[109] that attaint had been reduced "to a mere sound."[110] Nevertheless, some of the cases that formulated the rules for handling claims that jury awards were inadequate or excessive were worked out while attaint was yet alive.

To summarize: Common-law jury verdicts were overturned because they were too small only in mayhem or grievous-wounding situations where the judges could themselves view the harm or where it could be shown that the trial jurors were improperly prejudiced, had made a mistake of law, or had inappropriately acted upon personal knowledge not in evidence. In the mayhem cases, the remedy was an immediate award of the larger amount of damages that the judges thought justified.

Excessive Damages

Whenever a defendant successfully argued that a jury verdict should be set aside as excessive—because it was "against the evidence"—the unstated subtext was that if the verdict were allowed to stand, it would be unjustifiably punitive. Courts were willing to overturn verdicts in cases involving obligations of fixed or easily calculated value such as contracts or promissory notes, since in such cases the courts could clearly see whether the jury was mistaken.[111] In tort cases, however, the courts almost never intervened. As Chief Justice Wilmot of the Court of Common Pleas stated in *Beardmore v. Carrington,*[112]

> we desire to be understood that this Court does not say, or lay down any rule that there never can happen a case of such excessive damages in tort where the Court may not grant a new trial; but in that case the damages must be monstrous and enormous indeed, and such as all mankind must be ready to exclaim against, at first blush.

Beardmore was one of the cases that followed the seditious libel prosecutions of John Wilkes in the early 1760s. Nathan Carrington was one of the messengers for the Secretary of State, the Earl of Halifax, who had searched the houses and premises of those supposedly involved with the printing or publishing of *The North Briton, No. 45.* Among the homes searched was that of Arthur Beardmore. The only justification for entry into the house was a general warrant, a document that contained neither any factual basis for the search nor the specific name of any suspect. In the best known of the "general warrant" cases, *Entick v. Carrington,*[113] Chief Justice Pratt (later Lord Camden) of the Court of Common Pleas outlawed the use of such warrants. Thereafter, at least fifteen law suits were brought against the Secretary of State and the messengers. Jury verdicts for large damage awards resulted, including an award of £1,000 in *Beardmore*.[114] Although the printed report of the *Beardmore* case published by Wilson gives only a *per curiam* opinion, other sources show that it was Chief Justice Pratt who spoke for the Court.[115] Pratt reviewed prior cases back to the Yearbooks of the 1400s. He acknowledged that in the "ancient cases"—before the practice of granting a new trial had arisen—courts had "corrected damages from evidence laid before them."[116] Only in mayhem cases were damages ever increased. Chief Justice Pratt noted one writ-of-inquiry case from the Yearbook of Henry IV, in which, in what seems an antecedent to *remittitur* as practiced in the United States, the court said, "they would abridge the damages unless the plaintiff would release part thereof."[117] Pratt said this report might be wrong, but also, as has already been noted,[118] "there is . . . a difference between a principal verdict of a jury, and a writ of inquiry of damages; the latter being only an inquest of office to inform the conscience of the Court, and which they might have assessed themselves without any inquest at all."[119]

Later cases in which jury awards of damages were overturned as excessive were explained away by Chief Justice Pratt as due to misbehavior of the jury.[120] One case, *Chambers v. Robinson*,[121] which he said "seems to be the only case where ever a new trial was granted merely for the excessiveness of damages only," was disapproved.[122] Chief Justice Pratt considered the reason given in the case ("to give the defendant a chance of another jury") "a very bad reason; for if it was not, it would be a reason for a third and fourth trial, and would be digging up the Constitution by the roots."[123] Thus, he declared that "we are free to say this case is not law; and that there is not one single case (that is law) in all the books to be found, where the Court has granted a new trial for excessive damages in actions for torts."[124]

Curiously, Chief Justice Pratt failed to mention *Yates v. Swaine*,[125] a 1741 false imprisonment case in which a writ of inquiry verdict for £250 was overturned as excessive. After naming the amount of the verdict, the brief published report states: "No special damages being laid, and it appearing that plaintiff was confined for no longer time than 26 days, and plaintiff himself making no affidavit about the damages or imprisonment, the Court thought the damages excessive, and ordered the inquiry to be set aside, upon payment of costs, and a new writ of inquiry to be executed before a Judge at next assizes."[126] Had Chief Justice Pratt noticed this case, it would have been hard for him to discard it as "not law," since it issued from his own court.

By the late eighteenth century, nevertheless, there was a consensus among the judges that in tort cases, the jury essentially had carte blanche, assuming no jury misbehavior. A good recapitulation of the cases appears in *Duberley v. Gunning,*[127] a 1792 criminal conversation (adultery) case in which the Court of King's Bench upheld a jury verdict for the plaintiff for £5,000, despite evidence that the plaintiff had been grossly inattentive to or negligent about his wife's conduct with the defendant. Chief Justice Kenyon acknowledged that the damages were larger than ought to have been given but "my difficulty arises from being unable to fix any standard by which I can ascertain the excess which, according to my view of the case, I think the jury have run into. . . . Where there is no such standard, how are the errors of the jury to be rectified? What measure can we point out to them, by which they ought to be guided?"[128]

Carte blanche for the jury in determining damages in tort cases has been the common-law tradition in the United States, as well as in England. Indeed, in recent years, a popular impression has taken hold in the United States that jury verdicts often do not represent legitimate compensation for injured tort victims but constitute instead some kind of message about deterrence, vindication, or redistribution.[129] This impression has spread to state legislatures, and, rightly or wrongly, legislative intervention in the shape of tort reform has been robust in recent years.

In this atmosphere, the Supreme Court decided the *Cooper* case. What was *not* at issue in *Cooper* was whether punitive damages could be removed from the jury altogether without offending the Seventh Amendment. Now that the Court has declared (in *Cooper*) that punitive-damage determinations are moral expressions and not findings of fact, it could be argued that it is but a short step to say that the job of determining punitive damages need not be given to juries at all. This argument, in fact, had already been advanced in an article by Paul Mogin entitled, "Why Judges, Not Juries, Should Set Punitive Damages."[130]

Mogin focuses attention on the 1987 Supreme Court's decision in *Tull v. United States.*[131] In *Tull,* plaintiff sued the United States for a civil penalty under the Clean Water Act and the Supreme Court determined that a jury was required to determine liability but not the amount of the penalty; there was "no evidence that the Framers meant to extend the right to a jury to the remedy phase of a civil trial."[132] Mogin thus argues that *Tull* supports his claim that juries need not, under the Seventh Amendment, determine punitive damages.

Mogin wrote before the Supreme Court decided the *Feltner, City of Monterey,* and *Cooper* cases. After these recent decisions, there may be little life left in *Tull.*[133] In *Feltner,* the Court held that, in a copyright infringement action, the Seventh Amendment right to a jury trial "includes the right to have a jury determine the *amount* of statutory damages."[134] Justice Clarence Thomas brushed aside the defendant's claim that "*Tull* demonstrates that a jury determination of the amount of statutory damages is not necessary 'to preserve the substance of the common-law right of trial by jury'" by pointing out that "In *Tull* . . . we were presented with no evidence that juries historically had determined the amount of civil penalties to be paid to the Government."[135] He also noted that *Tull* was "in tension with" prior Court decisions, including *Dimick v. Schiedt.*[136]

Justice William J. Brennan in *Tull* concluded that "Because the nature of the relief authorized by §1319(d) [of the Clean Water Act] was traditionally available only in a court of law, petitioner in this present action is entitled to a jury trial on demand."[137] But, regarding the amount of damages, Justice Brennan stated that "The Seventh Amendment is silent on the question whether a jury must determine the remedy in a trial in which it must determine liability."[138] He then quoted from a 1973 Supreme Court case that in turn quoted from a 1918 article by Austin Scott in which Scott asserted that "Only those incidents which are regarded as fundamental, as inherent in and of the essence of the system of trial by jury, are placed beyond the reach of the legislature."[139] Brennan concluded that "The assessment of a civil penalty is not one of the 'most fundamental elements,'" and, "Since Congress itself may fix the civil penalties, it may delegate that determination to trial judges."[140] Thus, Justice Thomas's holding in *Feltner* that the right to a jury trial "includes the right to have a jury determine the *amount* of statutory damages" seems inconsistent with the Court's earlier accord in *Tull.*[141]

On the broader arguments advanced by Paul Mogin, consider the claim that "whether a party has a right under the Seventh Amendment to have a jury set punitive damages is very much an open question."[142] Again, the guide is the historical test, applying the appropriate rules of the common law operative in England in 1791. What were the English common-law rules of the eighteenth century about punitive damages? Referring to two of the "general warrant" cases, Mogin claims that, in England, "punitive damages were first recognized in 1763"[143] and that "The awards of punitive damages returned in jury trials in a number of cases between 1763 and 1791 hardly made jury determination of such damages one of the most fundamental elements of the jury trial system."[144]

There were, however, other cases both before and after 1763 in which jury awards of damages were unsuccessfully challenged as excessive, and in each such case the jury plainly intended the damages to be punitive, a fact that was understood by the court in allowing the verdict to stand. It was clearly recognized in the English courts prior to 1791 that, in tort cases at least, juries were free to impose, and did impose, punitive damages. Moreover, in a few of the judicial assessments of large jury verdicts, we encounter early versions of the "guideposts" offered by the U.S. Supreme Court in *B.M.W. v. Gore,* especially reprehensibility and proportionality.

Some of the cases that exhibit the courts' attitudes have already been mentioned, such as *Duberley v. Gunning,* the criminal conversation action in 1792 in which a jury verdict for £5,000 was upheld despite suggestions in the evidence of complicity on the part of the plaintiff.[145] An even more extreme example from the prior century (1677) was the case of *Lord Townsend v. Hughes.*[146] There, the Court of Common Pleas upheld a jury verdict for £4,000 in an action of *scandalum magnatum* against the Chancellor of Norwich for having said of the plaintiff, "He is an unworthy man, and acts against law and reason." Chief Justice North of the Court of King's Bench said that "in civil actions the plaintiff is to recover by way of compensation for the damages he hath sustained, and the jury are the proper judges thereof"; also, "as a Judge he could not tell what value to set upon the honour of the plaintiff." Justices Wyndham and Scroggs concurred, but Justice Atkyns dissented, and, in words similar to the Supreme Court's "proportionality" guidepost, stated: "As the Court ought with one eye to look upon the verdict, so with the other they ought to take notice what is contained in the declaration, and then to consider whether the words and damages bear any proportion; if not, then the Court ought to lay their hands upon the verdict."[147]

Returning to the late eighteenth century, the Court of Common Pleas in *Leith v. Pope*[148] upheld a jury verdict of £10,000 for malicious prosecution. Leith, a young Scottish baronet badly in need of money, had borrowed from Pope on exorbitant terms, and when a quarrel broke out between the two men over the security for the loan, Leith initiated two *qui tam* actions for usury against Pope. Subsequently, Pope secured an indictment against Leith accusing Leith of stealing a wagonload of goods and three geldings. The indictment led to a trial at the Old Bailey, and, on cross examination, Pope confessed that the true reason of the prosecution was to get rid of the actions for usury. Leith was acquitted and afterward brought the action for malicious prosecution, tried by a special jury in London before Chief Justice William De Grey. A motion for new trial on the ground of excessiveness of damages was argued to the Court of Common Pleas, and the judges were unanimous in denying the motion. The court stated its opinion "That in cases of tort the Court will not interpose on account of the largeness of damages, unless they are so flagrantly excessive as to afford an internal evidence of the prejudice and the partiality of the jury. That is, unless they are most outrageously disproportionate, either to the wrong received, or to the situation and circumstances of either the plaintiff or the defendant."[149] The court then observed that the prosecution that led to the Old Bailey trial evidenced in defendant "a most depraved and corrupted heart," whereas the plaintiff was a man of family, a baronet, an officer in the army, and a member of Parliament, all of which rendered the value of the injury done to him "adequate to £10,000."[150] Finally, as to the defendant's "circumstances," the court observed that, upon the evidence, he appeared to be "exceedingly wealthy, and well able to sustain such a verdict."[151]

The *Leith* case exhibits, in unrefined form, the entire apparatus erected by the U.S. Supreme Court in *BMW v. Gore* for assessing the constitutionality of punitive damages. All three guideposts—reprehensibility, proportionality, and comparative penalties—were touched upon. For a prosecution so reprehensible, "proceeding from such wicked motives . . . the Court cannot say that any sum assessed by the jury is too much, if the circumstances of the parties will warrant it."[152] The court concluded that the award was not outrageously disproportionate to the wrong received, taking into account the circumstances of the parties. Regarding comparable penalties, the court observed that if the defendant had been working with an associate in orchestrating the false indictment, "both might have been indicted for conspiracy, and have received the most infamous, called emphatically the villainous, judgment."[153] The £10,000 award in *Leith* was not expressly designated as punitive, yet even though the verdict compensated for reputation harm, it is clear that both the jury and the Court of Common Pleas recognized the punitive element.

Chief Justice De Grey's two immediate predecessors in the Court of Common Pleas, John Eardley Wilmot and Charles Pratt, explicitly endorsed the idea of punitive damages in cases that came before them. We have already seen how Pratt upheld a jury verdict for £1,000 in one of the general warrant cases, *Beardmore v. Carrington.*[154] In another such case, *Huckle v. Money,*[155] defendant claimed that "the plaintiff was only a journeyman to . . . the printer at the weekly wages of a guinea, that he was confined but a few hours, and very civilly and well treated by the defendant, so that £300 [the jury verdict] were most outrageous damages."[156] The court unanimously upheld the verdict. Chief Justice Pratt, who had been the trial judge, acknowledged that "if the jury had been confined by their oath to consider the mere personal injury only, perhaps £20 damages would have been thought damages sufficient," but:

> The great point of law touching the liberty of the subject appeared to them [the jury] at the trial; they saw a magistrate over all the King's subjects, exercising arbitrary power, violating *Magna Charta,* and attempting to destroy the liberty of the kingdom, by insisting upon the legality of this general warrant before them; they heard the King's counsel, and saw the Solicitor of the Treasury, endeavouring to support and maintain the legality of the warrant in a tyrannical and severe manner; these are the ideas which struck the jury on the trial, and I think they have done right in giving exemplary damages.[157]

In *Grey v. Grant,*[158] a verdict of £200 was given for "a little assault and battery." The dispute was over a turtle brought to England for plaintiff from the West Indies but mistakenly delivered to defendant. When the defendant, a member of Parliament, refused to return it or pay for it, plaintiff called the defendant a scoundrel, and defendant then struck the plaintiff, producing a black eye. The brief *per curiam* opinion of the Court of Common Pleas upholding the verdict began as follows: "This was a quarrel between two gentlemen, and has been properly tried by a special jury of merchants of London, who are the proper judges of the damages; when a blow is given by one gentleman to another, a challenge and death my ensue, and therefore the jury have done right in giving exemplary damages."[159]

Pratt's successor, Wilmot, was of the same philosophy. In *Tullidge v. Wade,*[160] a trespass action was brought against defendant, claiming that he assaulted plaintiff's daughter "and got her with child, whereby he lost the benefit of her service for a certain space of time, and was put to great charge and expence in her time of lying-in."[161] The jury verdict for £50 was challenged as excessive, and Chief Justice Wilmot began his opinion as follows: "Actions of this sort are brought for example's sake and although the plaintiff's loss in this case may not really amount to the value of 20 shillings, yet the jury have done right in giving liberal damages."[162] In another case decided in the same year, Chief Justice Wilmot upheld a jury verdict of £40 for trespass damages, stating that "he wished they had been 40s. instead of 40£," but they, the jury, "are the constitutional judges as to damages; and there must be some very extraordinary conduct in a Jury to induce the Court to meddle with damages."[163]

The Court of Common Pleas was overshadowed in the late eighteenth century by the Court of King's Bench and its influential chief, Lord Mansfield.[164] Lord Mansfield believed in giving juries a wide latitude in assessing damages, even when some damage awards were acknowledged to be so large as to be punitive. This is clearly shown early in Mansfield's judgeship in the 1758 case of *Wilford v. Buckley.*[165] A jury had awarded £500 in an action for criminal conversation (adultery) against a defendant who was but a clerk with a salary of £50 a year, "which was his whole subsistence,"[166] and the verdict was challenged as excessive. James Burrow's report of the court's opinion is brief, indicating that the court thought criminal conversation actions were "properly and solely under the cognizance of the jury, and fit to be submitted to their decision and estimate."[167] A manuscript report of the same case, however, spells out the court's views in greater detail. According to the manuscript version:

> The Chief Justice having stated the evidence, the Court said they were satisfied with the verdict. . . . *[T]he damages are for public example, as well as private recompence. . . .*
>
> But in matters of tort the jury are the proper judges of the damages, & the court has nothing to do with it. So £1,000, £5,000, & £10,000 have been given in these cases; & in Pennington's Case £1,000 against a footman; & yet no new trial. So on the other side the court will not grant a new trial on the smallness of damages. In Barker & Sir Wolston Dixey for a malicious prosecution the jury gave 5s. damages; & the court would not grant a new trial. In Cibber & Sloper, the husband was consenting, which varys the case; there £10 was given in damages.
>
> In some cases; as in debt on a note of hand of £50, if the jury give £500, the thing is apparent, & the court must see the excess, which is a different thing.[168]

In *Benson v. Frederick,*[169] a jury verdict for £150 damages on a writ of inquiry was challenged as excessive. The defendant, Frederick, a colonel in the Middlesex militia, was annoyed that a major under his command had given Benson a furlough, and "out of mere spite and revenge," Frederick had Benson stripped and flogged. Lord Mansfield "acknowledged that he thought the damages were very great, and beyond the proportion of what the man had suffered," yet he refused to grant a new trial, noting that the defendant could afford to pay the sum.[170]

For truly reprehensible behavior, Lord Mansfield was willing to encourage the jury to return a punitive award. Thus, in a 1779 action brought by a free black named Amissa against a Liverpool slave trader who had hired Amissa as a sailor and then sold him into slavery in Jamaica, Mansfield "summed up the evidence with suitable remarks on the good policy and humanity of such [legal] actions, and recommended to the Jury to give exemplary damages."[171]

A further decision of the Court of King's Bench of significance to the question of punitive damages was *Merest v. Harvey.*[172] Although this was a nineteenth-century decision, the views of the judges correspond to those of the judges of the prior century, especially Pratt and Wilmot. In *Merest,* plaintiff brought a trespass action against defendant and recovered a jury verdict of £500. Plaintiff was described as "a gentleman of fortune" who was shooting on his own estate in a common field contiguous to the highway when the defendant, a banker, magistrate, and member of Parliament, after having dined and drunk freely, passed along in his carriage and stopped, declaring that he would join the plaintiff's shooting party. Plaintiff politely declined to have defendant do so, after which defendant grew intemperate, fired his gun at birds on plaintiff's land, and threatened, as a magistrate, to commit the plaintiff. In upholding the verdict, Chief Justice Gibbs refused to limit the jury to pecuniary damages. He observed that "one can hardly conceive worse conduct" than defendant's and stated: "I wish to know, in a case where a man disregards every principle which actuates the conduct of gentlemen, what is to restrain him except large damages?"[173] Concurring, Justice Heath commented that exemplary damages contributed to the public policy of preventing the practice of dueling.[174]

To summarize: In the late eighteenth century, punitive damages were clearly regarded by the common-law judges as a legitimate jury function. There were, however, instances of proper punitive damages and improper punitive damages. Proper punitive damages were those imposed when the defendant's behavior was very gross and a large damage award, acting as a deterrent, supported public policy. Improper punitive damages were verdicts called "outrageous"—those large enough to shock the judicial conscience and usually involving facts that did not implicate any overriding public interest.[175]

Remittitur and the Question of Remedy

In *Hetzel v. Prince William County, Virginia,*[176] plaintiff sued the defendant for damages under Title VII of the Civil Rights Act of 1964 and obtained a jury verdict for $750,000. The trial court reduced the damages to $500,000, holding that one of the claims supporting the award was legally insufficient. On appeal, the Fourth Circuit held that the $500,000 figure was grossly excessive, in that it was unsupported by the limited evidence of harm presented at trial. On remand, the trial court recalculated the damages and awarded plaintiff $50,000. Plaintiff filed a motion for new trial, declining the $50,000 and characterizing the trial court's order on remand as a *remittitur.* The court granted plaintiff's motion for a new trial, but defendant obtained a writ of mandamus from the Court of Appeals staying the scheduled retrial and stating that the prior appellate decision had ordered the trial court to recalculate the damages "and to enter final judgment thereon." In response, plaintiff claimed that, since it is the jury's role to assess damages, this action violated her Seventh Amendment right to jury trial. The issue reached the Supreme Court on *certiorari.* In a brief 1998 *per curiam* opinion, the Court agreed with the plaintiff and held that she was entitled to a new trial, citing *Dimick v. Schiedt.*[177]

The Court's conclusion in *Hetzel* was fully in accord with eighteenth-century English common law, although this fact requires some explanation. In discussing fifteenth- to seventeenth-century defamation cases, Richard H. Helmholz observes that "the *remittitur* was a significant feature of early slander litigation," even though *remittitur* entries on the plea rolls "did not raise an arguable point of law" and thus "have largely escaped the attention of legal historians."[178] In the English usage, *remittitur* referred to situations in which the plaintiff consented to a sum less than the jury award in order to obtain a bird in hand rather than undergo the expense and uncertainty of appellate proceedings, but the plaintiff was not given the optional alternative of a new trial.[179] This type of *remittitur* might occur where the jury verdict exceeded the amount plaintiff had asked for in his declaration[180] or where the defendant filed a motion to arrest judgment because of excessive damages.[181] Helmholz points out that the *remittitur* required the plaintiff's consent, although the judges could and occasionally did effectively compel that consent by taking the defendant's motion in arrest of judgment under advisement "from one term to the next" until the plaintiff yielded.[182] Nevertheless, the *remittitur,* or *remittitur damna,* referred simply to the entry on the record whereby the plaintiff gave up the excessive damages. Helmholz explains, moreover, that, in a 1622 decision, the King's Bench judges "changed their mind about the wisdom of using the *remittitur* in slander cases."[183] Thereafter, "Discussion of mitigation of damages by use of the *remittitur* disappears from the reports . . . , and when lawyers for dissatisfied defendants in slander actions moved to do something about an excessive award of damages, they invariably asked for the grant of a new trial."[184]

By the late eighteenth century, not only had the motion for new trial become standard procedure for excessive-damages cases, but also the judges spoke disapprovingly of any remedy that would dispense with a new trial. Justice Buller, in *Duberley v. Gunning,*[185] after citing *Beardmore v. Carrington* for the proposition that a court might grant a new trial in a case of excessive damages, stated:

> There are besides many old cases which shew that the instance of the exercise of this power in 1655 [granting a new trial] was not the first. One case is as far back as 7 H. 4, 31 b. [1405–06] though I think the Court there carried their controlling power too far; for the damages in that case being thought by the Court to be excessive, they said they would stay judgment till the plaintiff agreed to relinquish the excess. In that respect indeed they were wrong; because that was taking upon themselves to determine the exact amount, of what the damages ought to have been, which is clearly the province of the jury to decide. The only power which the Courts now claim, is to send the case back to the revision of another jury, when they think that the damages given are enormously disproportionate to the case proved in evidence.[186]

There were, moreover, occasions when a new trial was ordered because of excessive damages and the second jury returned a verdict of damages in the same amount as the first jury. When this happened, the courts neither ordered a third new trial nor declared what the correct damages should be. Instead, the damages returned by the two successive juries stood.[187]

Thus, it is clear that the new trial remedy ordered by the Supreme Court in *Hetzel* corresponded to eighteenth-century English common law. Yet, after *Cooper* (in combination with *B.M.W. v. Gore* and, more recently, *State Farm v. Campbell*), the question of remedy takes on a new aspect. In *Johansen v. Combustion Engineering, Inc.*,[188] the trial court reduced a jury verdict for $45 million in punitive damages to $4.35 million without extending the opportunity to the plaintiff to elect a new trial. As in *Hetzel*, this disposition was argued to be impermissible under the Seventh Amendment. The Eleventh Circuit held, however, that it was the court's responsibility to determine the constitutional upper limit of punitive damages, and that "a constitutionally reduced verdict . . . is really not a remittitur at all." It is, instead, "a determination that the law does not permit the award." Thus, "upon determination of the constitutional limit on a particular award, the District Court may enter a judgment for that amount as a matter of law."[189] The court distinguished *Hetzel* because the Supreme Court there viewed the reduction of the verdict as a traditional *remittitur;* "there was no claim in the case that the Constitution required the reduction."[190] Also, anticipating *Cooper*, the court reviewed the punitive-damage question *de novo*.

A similar result was reached recently by the District of Columbia Court of Appeals in *Daka, Inc. v. McCrae*.[191] The plaintiff recovered a verdict in his sexual harassment action of $5 million, $4,812,500 punitive and $187,500 compensatory, a 26 to 1 ratio. Applying *BMW v. Gore* criteria, as refined in *State Farm v. Campbell*, the court vacated the punitive-damages award and remanded "with directions to reduce the award of punitive damages to a sum consistent with the principles expressed by *State Farm* and in this opinion."[192] The court stated, further:

> Unlike in the usual case where a remittitur is ordered, it will be unnecessary here for the trial judge to give McCrae the option of accepting the remitted amount or a new trial on punitive damages. That is because the amount to be determined by the judge is the constitutional maximum which the jury could properly award, an amount that its actual award has already succeeded.[193]

In the federal courts, there is now a split in the circuits over whether a new trial must be offered when a federal court determines that a jury's punitive-damages award was unconstitutionally high.[194] The issue may require Supreme Court resolution, but after the Court's recent *State Farm* decision, there may be few cases in which juries return extravagant punitive-damages verdicts. Speaking for a six-person majority in *State Farm,* Justice Kennedy gave detailed attention to the *BMW v. Gore* guideposts, and, although he disclaimed any "bright-line ratio" of punitive damages to compensatory, he nevertheless declared: "Our jurisprudence and the principles it has now established demonstrate . . . that, in practice, few awards exceeding a single-digit ratio between punitive and compensatory damages, to a significant degree, will satisfy due process."[195] Further, "When compensatory damages are substantial, then a lesser ratio, perhaps only equal to compensatory damages, can reach the outermost limit of the due process guarantee."[196]

The effect of the *State Farm* decision has been dramatic. In a 2004 study of more than eighty cases in which *State Farm* was applied, more than 80 percent used a single-digit punitive-to-compensatory ratio, and most of those with double-digit ratios had either nominal compensatory damages or unusually reprehensible conduct by the defendants.[197]

There will, nevertheless, be some future cases when juries award punitive damages greater than the due process limits envisioned by the Supreme Court in *BMW v. Gore* and *State Farm v. Campbell.* When this happens, the question of whether to grant a new trial will recur, and the position taken by the circuits dispensing with the new trial option is troubling under the Seventh Amendment historical test. As the cases previously discussed have shown, the "appropriate rules of the common law" as of 1791 establish that it is the jury's function to determine damages, both compensatory and punitive, although, when a reviewing court determines that the amount awarded by the trial jury is excessive, the remedy is a new trial. In its recent *Ross* decision, the Eighth Circuit declared that "plaintiff's consent to a constitutional reduction of a punitive-damages award is 'irrelevant' because the court must decide the issue as a matter of law," citing *Johansen.*[198] Yet, historically, courts that overturned excessive jury awards did so as a matter of law. And, as Justice Buller said in *Duberley* (in 1792), it would be wrong for the court "to determine the exact amount of what the damages ought to have been, which is clearly the province of the jury to decide."[199]

The question here is whether, in carrying out its Fifth Amendment due process responsibility, a federal court is required not only to declare whether a jury award of punitive damages is unconstitutionally high, applying *BMW,* but also, if the award is too high, to name the maximum dollar figure that the Constitution permits. If ten different federal judges were asked individually to apply the *BMW* criteria to the same set of facts and to name the maximum constitutional punitive sum, ten different figures might easily be returned, and it would be hard to declare any of them wrong. In *Ross,* the district court reduced the jury's $750,000 punitive-damages verdict to $120,000, and the Eighth Circuit reduced it again to $60,000, applying the *BMW* guideposts and choosing a 10:1 ratio of punitive to compensatory damages (the ratio struck down in *BMW* was 500:1).[200] Yet it seems foolish to claim that had the jury initially returned punitive damages of $61,000, the award ought to have been declared unconstitutionally high. Surely the better solution—one that effectuates the protections of both the Fifth and the Seventh Amendments—is to refrain from naming a specific dollar figure and to remand for a new trial.[201]

In *Continental Trend Resources,* the Tenth Circuit construed its *BMW* duty as requiring it to ascertain "a precise dollar figure by applying guidelines that contain no absolutes to facts that provide only imprecise potential damage amounts."[202] The court thus declared six million dollars to be "the maximum constitutionally permissible punitive-damage award justified by the facts of this case."[203] The court nevertheless ordered this amount as a *remittitur,* quoting the Ninth Circuit's conclusion in a 1993 case that, "To avoid any conflict with the Seventh Amendment, the preferable choice is to afford the party awarded the grossly excessive punitive damages . . . the option of either accepting the remittitur of the punitive damages award or a new trial on that issue."[204] Presumably if a new trial were conducted, a different factual record could be developed that would support a higher constitutional punitive-damages limit; otherwise, the new trial option would make no practical sense.[205]

In *Johansen,* the Eleventh Circuit saw no reason to follow the "cautious approach" of the new trial remedy, observing: "No new trial need be offered as the Supreme Court itself recognized in *BMW* when it remanded the case to the Alabama Supreme Court to determine 'Whether the appropriate remedy requires a new trial or *merely an independent determination by the Alabama Supreme Court* of the award necessary to vindicate the economic interests of Alabama consumers. . . .' 517 U.S. at 586."[206] The Supreme Court in *BMW,* however, was merely saying that the remedy question was a matter of state law; the Seventh Amendment was inapplicable. Indeed, the Court in *BMW* stated that, "As in Haslip, we are not prepared to draw a bright line marking the limits of a constitutionally acceptable punitive damages award."[207] Thus, the remedy in the federal appellate courts that best responds to the Court's guidance in

BMW and that fulfills the requirements of the Seventh and Fifth Amendments would appear to be a remand for a new trial without naming a specific dollar figure as the constitutional limit of punitive damages.

Conclusion

This chapter explains an obscure but extensive aspect of the history of the jury trial, the writ of inquiry, and examines that history in light of the U.S. Supreme Court's historical test for the scope of the right to jury trial in civil cases guaranteed by the Seventh Amendment. Although many thousands of jury trials were conducted to determine damages by means of writs of inquiry issued after default judgments, the writ of inquiry came to be described as but "an inquest of office to inform the conscience of the court who, if they please, may themselves assess the damages."[208] This expression implies that the court could assess damages without regard to the consent of the parties, yet it is clear that the consent of the plaintiff, in whose favor the default judgment would have been entered, was always essential.[209] For this reason, the writ of inquiry does not represent an historical exception to the right to jury trial practiced in the English common law as of 1791, when the Seventh Amendment was adopted. Nor does it validate the curious line in Supreme Court jurisprudence that dispenses with the jury in eminent-domain, "direct"-condemnation cases, yet requires the jury in indirect, "inverse" condemnation cases, as established in *City of Monterey v. Del Monte Dunes at Monterey, Ltd.*[210]

Damage determinations have historically belonged to juries because they fall within the jury's traditional role of ascertaining facts. The Supreme Court's recent declaration in the context of the re-examination clause of the Seventh Amendment that punitive-damage determinations are moral expressions rather than findings of fact will no doubt be used to argue that the initial setting of punitive damages need not be assigned to the jury.[211] Such attempts could be rebuffed by the simple expedient of pointing out that the first and second clauses of the Seventh Amendment are not coextensive. A more substantive response would be to look to the excessive-damages cases in the common law, which, as has been shown in this chapter, clearly place the right to determine punitive damages in the first instance with the jury.

This analysis admittedly presupposes that the historical test for the scope of the right to jury trial under the Seventh Amendment (the first clause) will continue to be adhered to by the Supreme Court. However anachronistic such adherence might seem, I think it likely, at least for the near future. The Court has had a number of recent chances to jettison the test but instead has steadily affirmed it.

Yet, jury verdicts of punitive damages can now be reexamined *de novo,* and the temptation will be strong for federal reviewing courts, as in the Eleventh and Eighth Circuits, not only to sharply reduce the size of punitive-damages awards under the banner of the Seventh Amendment but also to declare the lower amount as a court order without a new trial. For reasons given earlier, the new trial option required in the Fifth and Tenth Circuits is true to the Supreme Court's historical test for the Seventh Amendment, while at the same time adequately preserving Fifth Amendment due process.

5

The Jury of Matrons

> However it was, this they all agree in, that my mother pleaded her belly, and being found quick with child, she was respited for about seven months; in which time having brought me into the world, and being about again, she was called down, as they term it, to her former judgment, but obtained the favour of being transported to the plantations.
>
> —Daniel Defoe, *Moll Flanders*[1]

It is well known that until the twentieth century, regular jury service in both England and America was exclusively a male preserve.[2] Not so well known is that, for at least seven centuries in England, and also in colonial America, women served on exclusively female special-purpose juries. The special purpose was to determine whether a female party to litigation was pregnant—or, to use the quaint language of the jury charge, whether she was "quick with child of a quick child."[3] To provoke the inquiry, the female party to litigation would, again in the language of the day, "plead her belly."[4] In theory at least, the women chosen to serve on the jury were to be matrons, who were regarded as experts on the subject of pregnancy and childbirth. Ordinarily, the jury of matrons was impaneled in one of two contexts. In civil cases, the matrons decided whether a widow was with child by her late husband, a question that affected the inheritance of the husband's estate. On the criminal side, a stay of execution would be granted to a female defendant who had been sentenced to death but was found to be pregnant. Such a stay could lead to a pardon and was therefore of extreme importance to the prisoner. In both civil and criminal situations, the jury of matrons was required to inspect the woman who claimed to be pregnant and to render a verdict stating whether the woman was or was not with quick child.[5]

In this chapter, I discuss the antiquity of the practice, variations in its civil and criminal usage, procedural questions, late seventeenth- and early-eighteenth-century abuses, and the gradual disappearance of the practice in the nineteenth century as medical knowledge about pregnancy acquired some traces of sophistication. Most of my research has been on the criminal side, an emphasis shaped largely by the nature of the source materials with which I have worked.[6] The sources are predominantly English.

As the discussion to follow illustrates, the jury of matrons constitutes a vivid study of the use, abuse, and obsolescence of a legal mechanism. It is possible to observe the mechanism as it became corrupted and to realize that the corruption became accepted as a makeshift antidote to the harshness of the criminal process. The death of the jury of matrons is independently valuable as a study of the slow, jealous response of the law to the growth of scientific knowledge.

Antiquity

The use of women to inspect a litigant to confirm or reject her claim of pregnancy reaches back to the Romans. In private Roman law, a woman might be examined to establish pregnancy for different reasons. For example, when a husband asserted that his wife was left pregnant by him after divorce but the wife denied it, the Praetor ordered an inspection by three midwives at the house of "a respectable woman."[7] When a woman claimed pregnancy after the death of her husband, however, five free women conducted the examination. The wording of the Praetor's edict is given in *Digest* 25.4.5.10.[8] On the criminal side, no time ordinarily elapsed in the Roman Republic between conviction of a capital offense and execution, but if a condemned woman was pregnant, the execution was delayed until the birth.[9] No independent evidence is known of the method of verifying the pregnancy.

In English law, the earliest known reference to the jury of matrons in civil cases appeared in the early thirteenth century in Bracton. Richardson and Sayles discussed what they term "the curious history of the writ *de ventre inspiciendo.*"[10] They found no evidence of the writ in Glanvill "or in the earliest registers in the time of Henry III,"[11] but Bracton gave two such writs, one of which was "entered on the close roll in February 1220."[12] Richardson and Sayles traced one case in some detail in order to demonstrate the simultaneous availability of the writ out of Chancery and from the justices of the bench.[13] In 1222 and 1223, the writ appeared in several cases, and this fact, plus its appearance on the plea roll in 1223, suggests that it had become established.

It is reasonable to suppose that equally ancient uses of the jury of matrons occurred on the criminal side in England, but the earliest documented case of which I am aware is that recorded by Sayles of Elizabeth Walton's conviction, in 1387, of conspiracy to murder. She was sentenced to death, and "thereupon the said Elizabeth says that she is pregnant and asks the execution of judgement rendered against her be postponed in the meantime."[14] The court impaneled a jury of matrons, which confirmed the pregnancy. Nothing in the report of the case indicates that the procedure was regarded as unusual, again suggesting that the concept was a familiar feature of court practice.

As is later demonstrated,[15] the jury of matrons appeared with regularity in the assize records from the reigns of Elizabeth I and James I transcribed by James Cockburn and in the printed Old Bailey Sessions Papers (hereafter OBSP) that commenced in the late 1600s. Other examples of its use in the seventeenth century have surfaced occasionally in manuscript court records in both England and America. Thus, Margaret Hatch, under sentence to be hanged for manslaughter of her child, pleaded pregnancy, in June 1633, before the governor and the Council of Virginia, and she was found by a jury of matrons not to be with child.[16] Similarly, in January 1611, at the Commissioners of the Peace for Middlesex, Cononia Surbye entered a plea of pregnancy.[17] Further evidence that the use of the jury of matrons was a settled practice throughout England in the sixteenth and seventeenth centuries is the regular reference to it in the leading law books of the time. The practice is described by Edward Coke, Matthew Hale, Staunford, Finch, Lambard, Pulton, and in the principal abridgments.[18]

Applications

Civil Cases

The main use of the jury of matrons in civil cases was to determine questions of inheritance—or, in William Blackstone's cynical language, "when a widow feigns herself with child, in order to exclude the next heir, and a suppositious birth is suspected to be intended."[19] These cases differed in significant ways from the typical criminal cases. For example, the necessity to show a "quickening" appears to have been abandoned in civil cases in the nineteenth century,[20] while this requirement appears, nominally at least, to have persisted in criminal cases as long as the jury of matrons was used.[21] Also, little attention needed to be paid to the criminal defendant after she was declared pregnant—she was simply remanded to prison for the remainder of her normal gestation period (or longer) before being "called down" to her former judgment or pardoned, but the widow in civil cases had further opportunities for deception. If she had erroneously been declared pregnant, or if she suffered a miscarriage or her child was stillborn, how was the court to know? In any of these circumstances, a live infant could easily be borrowed or hired as her supposed newborn. It was thus necessary that the widow be closely watched, as was often ordered by the court.[22]

Another early, if infrequent, use of matrons in civil cases occurred in litigation to obtain a divorce or an annulment of a marriage. In these cases, the wife asserted impotence on the part of the husband as grounds for the divorce or annulment and asserted that, despite cohabitation, she remained a virgin. As stated by Rogers in his 1840 treatise on ecclesiastical law: "Where the woman is the applicant, and was not a widow at her marriage, the court usually expects a certificate, that she is *virgo intacta et apta viro.*"[23] Rogers added that "the certificate of medical persons is required, where possible,"[24] but Rogers was writing at a time when medical knowledge was much advanced. Bishop observed that the inspection "appears formerly to have been performed, as to the woman, in full or in part by matrons and midwives."[25] Professor Richard Helmholz further points out that the inspection by qualified matrons was an accepted method of proof in the canon law.[26] How similar canon and ecclesiastical law procedures for designating and instructing the matrons were to common-law patterns is unclear, but the status of the matrons in canon and ecclesiastical law as presumed experts closely paralleled their use in Anglo-American common law to ascertain a state of pregnancy or recent experience with childbirth.[27]

The most notorious example in English law of an inspection by matrons to ascertain virginity occurred in the Countess of Essex case in 1613. There, a libel was filed by the Countess of Essex alleging that her husband was incapable of consummating their marriage and reciting detailed allegations concerning the earl's inability. In his answer, the Earl acknowledged never having carnally known the countess—nor felt any desire to—but asserted his physical capability. The court was constituted of twelve commissioners appointed by James I,[28] and, according to the report of the case in the *State Trials,* "Notwithstanding the Confessions in the Earl's Answer, the Court thought it necessary to satisfy themselves of the truth by the inspection of midwives and matrons."[29] Thus, "it was decreed by the Court, that six midwives of the best note, and ten other noble matrons, out of which they themselves would chuse two midwives, and four matrons, would inspect the Countess." The women were produced and "sworn *ad inquirend. et inspiciend.* 1. Whether the Lady Frances were a woman fit and apt for carnal copulation without any defect, which might disable her for that purpose. 2. Whether she were a virgin carnally unknown by any man." The women then took the countess to a private room for inspection, and when they returned, the courtroom was cleared except for the Register "that so the ladies and midwives might more fully deliver their secret Reasons, &c. which were not fit to be inserted into the record."[30] They concluded that the countess was physically fit and a virgin.

According to the account of the case by Dr. Daniel Dunn, one of the commissioners, the ten "noble matrons" were to be "women fearing God and mothers of children," and the two midwives chosen from among the six were to be "practised about the delivery of noble women."[31] Dunn described the inspection team as two midwives and three matrons (not four), whom he then named. The midwives were assigned "to see if an obstruction can be observed"; none was found. The divorce was granted by a vote of seven to five.[32] Dr. Dunn voted with the majority. A somewhat different view of the role of the midwives and matrons was stated by the Archbishop of Canterbury in memorials of his dissent. He wrote: "Yet my Lord of *London* told us openly, That he being with them, found that the Ladies knew not well what to make of it; that they had no Skill, nor knew not what was the Truth; but what they said, was upon the Credit of the Midwives, which were but two, and I knew not how tamper'd with."[33] The conclusions of the matrons and midwives raised not a few eyebrows among the polite society that keenly followed the case at the time—indeed, for years afterward. The gossip was fueled by the writings of Arthur Wilson and Sir Anthony Weldon, who asserted that the countess, under pretense of modesty, had gained permission to put on a veil when she was inspected and that another veiled (virginal) young woman of the countess's age and stature, dressed in the countess's clothes, was substituted before the matrons and midwives.[34]

Despite the scandal, the Countess of Essex case confirms the accepted use of matrons in seventeenth-century England to determine delicate questions about the female body. There was a widespread popular awareness of this function of matrons, especially by the close of the seventeenth century and throughout the eighteenth. This awareness is illustrated in the criminal cases discussed in this chapter, and at least once, in 1771, the jury of matrons received lively anecdotal treatment in the popular press. That occasion involved another celebrated figure, the late-eighteenth-century French ambassador (spy?) to England, the Chevalier D'Eon. After accounts began to circulate of appearances by the Chevalier in Europe dressed as a woman, intense speculation developed in England about whether the Chevalier was male or female. This speculation was taken up in the London clubs in the form of wagers, eventually involving, allegedly, well over £120,000.[35] Occasionally, a party to a wager claimed to have sufficient evidence to prove his case and sued to collect, providing high entertainment to the public and considerable annoyance to the courts.[36] Amid this excitement, *Town & Country* magazine published a wonderful engraving entitled "The Trial of M. D'Eon by a Jury of Matrons," depicting twelve sober matrons seated in a jury box, some equipped with spyglasses, inspecting a diminutive Chevalier who stood on a pedestal, draped in nothing but a sheet and his military cross.[37] Accompanying the engraving was a fictitious account of the deliberations of the matrons, who were given the thinly disguised names of wives of prominent political figures of the day.[38]

Criminal Cases

As has been indicated, the customary use of the jury of matrons in criminal cases was to verify or reject the plea of a convicted female under sentence of death that she was pregnant. The jury was given the curious-sounding charge to determine whether the defendant be "quick with child of a quick child." Baron Gurney attempted an explanation of the charge in a nineteenth-century case: "'Quick with child' is having conceived. 'With quick child' is when the child has quickened."[39] There is no evidence of support for the first part of Gurney's explanation,[40] and the "quickening" notion—that the child's life had not begun until the pregnancy reached a sufficiently advanced state to allow the child's movements to be felt—was exploded by the medical advances of the nineteenth century.[41] While it persisted, putting the mother to death before quickening could not constitute the murder of an innocent unborn child, since there was no new life in being.[42] Further, in Blackstone's words, "if she once hath had the benefit of this reprieve, and been delivered, and afterwards becomes pregnant again, she shall not be entitled to the benefit of a further respite for the same cause."[43]

One interesting variation in the criminal cases appears in seventeenth-century archival records for the colonies of Maryland and Massachusetts. These cases involved accusations of murder of newborn infants by their mothers, and juries of matrons were impaneled to ascertain whether the mothers' bodies evidenced any signs of recent childbirth. To illustrate, the following notation appears in the Maryland records for "a Generall Provinciall Court Held at Patuxent September 22th 1656":

> Whereas Judith Catchpole being brought before the Court upon Suspicion of Murdering a Child which She is accused to have brought forth, and denying the fact or that She ever had Child the Court hath ordered that a Jury of able women be Impannelled and to give in their Verdict to the best of their Judgment whether She the Said Judith hath ever had a Child or not.[44]

Later, the names of the jury members are set out and their verdict given (that she "hath not had any Child within the time Charged").[45] In 1662, a jury of twelve women in Kent, Maryland, examined Hannah Jenkins and declared that she was "cleare from child bearing and never had A Child to the best of their knowledge."[46] A similar case occurred in Massachusetts in 1672; five matrons, three of whom were midwives, examined the prisoner and concluded that she had never had a child.[47]

Ordinarily, recent childbirth at full or near term would leave clear marks on the mother's body for the jury to see.[48] Cases of abortion were more difficult, as is illustrated by another Maryland Provincial Court case from the mid-1600s that involved the use of savin, a drug commonly used to induce abortion.[49] In *Proprietary v. Robins,* a jury of six women examined Elizabeth Robins and found her "in a very sad condition." Elizabeth "confessed that she had twice taken savin, once boyled in milk and the other time strayned through a cloath, and at the taking thereof not supposing her self with Child as She Sayeth, takeing it for wormes not knowing the Vertue thereof any other wayes, further confessed that She Supposeth her Self to have a dead Child within her."[50]

Fanciful engraving published in *Town and Country* magazine, 1771, imagining a trial of the Chevelier d'Eon by a jury of matrons to determine whether the Chevalier was male or female. From a private collection.

Whether the jury of matrons was used in England or in other American colonies to inspect the defendant's body for signs of recent childbearing is unsubstantiated, but such a use would not be surprising, since accusations of murder of bastard infants by their mothers represented a significant percentage of the capital cases brought against women in England over the centuries.[51] No such evidence, however, is reflected in the OBSP or the Assize Calendars, even though, as is later discussed, these sources do reflect the frequent, traditional use of the jury of matrons in criminal cases to ascertain the state of pregnancy of convicted female capital offenders.

Witchcraft Trials

Committees of women analogous to the jury of matrons were a common feature of witchcraft trials conducted in Europe and America from the fifteenth to the eighteenth centuries. Describing fifteenth-century procedures for German inquisitions, *The Malleus Maleficarum* (first published in 1486 and said by Edgar Peel to be "the most influential book on witchcraft ever written")[52] stated: "While the officers are preparing for the questioning, let the accused be stripped; or if she is a woman, let her be led to the penal cells and there stripped by honest women of good reputation. And the reason for this is that they should search for any instrument of witchcraft sewn into her clothes."[53]

In England and America, the inspection was for a different purpose—to search the accused's body (usually the genital area) for any "witch's teat" or "witchmark." John Demos noted the widespread belief in "familiars"—"small (sometimes invisible) animals sent here and there to carry out particular projects of *maleficium*"—and explained that "Their connection to their witch-mistress was a very close one: to her they gave their devoted service, from her they received a most intimate form of sustenance. Periodically, she suckled them on 'teats' specially adapted to that purpose."[54] Peel observed that "The conditions medically called 'polymasty'—additional breasts—and 'polythely'—supernumerary nipples—are not quite so uncommon as the layman might think; but failing the discovery of one of these, any wart or sore could be interpreted as a witch's mark."[55] Montague Summers, moreover, emphasized that the witch's mark "was the very sign and seal of Satan upon the actual flesh of his servant and any person who bore such a mark was considered to have been convicted and proven beyond all manner of doubt of being in league with and devoted to the service of the fiend."[56]

Numerous instances of the use in England of women inspectors to discover witchmarks on accused witches have been identified from the sixteenth and seventeenth centuries.[57] Some secondary sources expressly described the inspectors as juries of women or matrons,[58] and it is possible that by the late seventeenth century the use of the jury of matrons to establish pregnancy was common enough to permit ready adoption in witchcraft trials. Notestein termed the absence of such juries in the records of the most important early seventeenth-century witchcraft trials in Lancaster "remarkable," adding (erroneously) that "This method of determining guilt was not yet widely accepted in the courts."[59]

Other sources do not indicate the traditional jury format. For example, one reference is to the "information of 7 women appointed to search [the prisoner] for suspicious witches marks."[60] Indeed, since the search of the accused's body was a *pretrial* procedure, the jury model was inapposite.[61] Ewen endeavored to discover the authority that permitted the bodily inspection of accused witches and concluded that "no written rule or instructions can be found, but it appears that this form of inquiry was carried out by order of justices of the peace, who appointed a body of women for the work."[62] In at least one instance the examination was of sufficient importance to be performed by "midwives specially appointed by the King's [Charles I's] surgeons."[63]

Inspections for witchmarks were also common in witchcraft trials in early Massachusetts. John Demos stated that "Frequently this became an official responsibility of special committees of women appointed by the magistrates 'narrowly and truly to inspect and search [the defendant's] body whether any suspicious signs or marks did appear that were not common or that were preternatural.'"[64] The committee that examined Rebecca Nurse and others in 1692 was nine in number,[65] and it is clear that Starkey's description of this committee as a "jury of women"[66] should not be taken literally. Boyer and Nissenbaum surmised that the nine reputable women were "probably midwives,"[67] but this is unlikely, since, as Starkey related, Rebecca Nurse after her inspection by the women "asked that qualified midwives be allowed to examine the mark on the grounds that it was an injury of childbirth such as any woman might bear and any midwife would recognize."[68]

The fundamental point for purposes of the present study is that the witchcraft trials, both in Europe and America, provide a further illustration of the use of groups or committees of women to inspect the bodies of accused criminals. The ad hoc committees resemble the ecclesiastical and canon law experience previously discussed, although some of the English cases may have used full juries of matrons in a manner analogous to the way that such juries were customarily used in criminal trials. The latter possibility is strongly supported by the evidence of frequent use of juries of matrons in criminal proceedings reflected in Assize Calendars from the late seventeenth and early eighteenth centuries. Several of these were witchcraft trials.[69]

The Assize Calendars

James Cockburn's assiduous production in the 1970s and 1980s of calendars of assize records made available to researchers much information that, in practical terms, had previously been inaccessible. There are ten volumes, five for the reign of Elizabeth I (1558–1603) and five for the reign of James I (1603–1625).[70] A separate volume comprises an analytical introduction to the series. The records all pertain to the Home Circuit (Hertfordshire, Essex, Sussex, Kent, and Surrey). They unequivocally establish the regular use of the jury of matrons throughout the period covered.

In his Introduction, Professor Cockburn writes that "Almost one-half (49.7%) of the women convicted of felony in our period pleaded that they were pregnant, and thirty-eight percent successfully maintained that claim."[71] This does not mean that four out of every five women who pleaded pregnancy were examined by a jury of matrons but rather that four out of five successfully gained a remand to prison upon a plea of pregnancy. According to Cockburn, "There are strong indications that in our period judges frequently reprieved women who pleaded pregnancy, and delayed the physical examination until a subsequent assizes."[72] Cockburn also asserts "that the rules governing pregnancy pleas were in practice manipulated to give assize judges considerable discretion in the punishment of female felons."[73] The discretion often took the form of imprisonment for a term of years instead of hanging—a pattern sufficiently clear in the assize records to be convincing evidence of "penal policy rather than the result of bureaucratic delays or judicial oversight."[74]

The calendars of assize records do not uniformly record the presence or absence of a jury of matrons in pregnancy pleas. This is not surprising, since the calendars span almost seventy years in five different counties. The cases can, however, be grouped into the following general categories:

1. Prisoners remanded "because pregnant" or "on a plea of pregnancy"pursuant to a jury of matrons verdict on the same day as conviction
2. Prisoners remanded "because pregnant" or "on a plea of pregnancy" with no reference to a jury of matrons
3. Prisoners remanded "because pregnant" or "on a plea of pregnancy" with a subsequent examination by a jury of matrons
4. Prisoners found not pregnant by a jury of matrons on the same day as conviction
5. Prisoners "found pregnant" or "found not pregnant" with no explicit reference to a jury of matrons.

The large majority of the cases fall into the first two of these categories. A data summary extracted from the cases is set out in Appendix 3. A surprising revelation from the assize records is the large percentage of cases in which juries of matrons found the defendants *not* pregnant. In all jurisdictions combined for the reign of Elizabeth I, almost three hundred female prisoners (295) are shown pleading pregnancy, of whom half (55 percent) are shown to have been examined by a jury of matrons, either on the day of conviction or subsequently, and, of these, 42 percent were found not pregnant. Comparatively fewer pregnancy cases occurred in the reign of James I; a total of seventy-two women pleaded pregnancy, forty-two of whom (58 percent) are shown to have been examined by a jury of matrons. Only fourteen of those examined (31 percent) were found pregnant.

The assize records establish without question that the jury of matrons was a commonplace feature of the criminal trial in the sixteenth and seventeenth centuries. Since the trials were ordinarily conducted by judges from the central courts in London—judges who also took their turn at the Old Bailey—there is every reason to expect that the London experience at the time with the jury of matrons was equally common. Systematic proof is lacking for the early seventeenth century, but moving forward half a century to the late 1600s brings the Old Bailey Sessions Papers (OBSP) into view, and the OBSP plainly reflect the use of the jury of matrons in a manner suggesting the continuation of a pattern already well established.

The Old Bailey Sessions Papers

To this point, I have surveyed the various applications and historical roots of the jury of matrons as revealed in secondary sources and regular case reports. Most court reporters, however, recorded only appellate stages of litigation and only rarely referred to the jury of matrons, always in civil cases. As has been shown, the assize records reveal the frequent impaneling of juries of matrons in criminal cases in the Home Circuit in the Elizabethan and Jacobean eras. Other transcriptions of manuscript case reports, such as the Selden Society volumes, Professor Helmholz's work on church law, the Maryland and Massachusetts archival records, and the witchcraft trials, supply additional examples, both civil and criminal. The eventual atrophy of the jury of matrons in the nineteenth century can be discerned in writings on medical jurisprudence (discussed later),[75] but without more, little could be said about the ordinary patterns of use or abuse of the jury of matrons in criminal trials. Fortunately, however, there is more—the OBSP.

Starting in the 1670s and continuing long past the period covered by the jury of matrons, the OBSP constitutes a unique resource for information about the criminal trial in London. The papers are best known to modern readers through the work of John Langbein,[76] who describes them as "an early species of periodical journalism, purveying a diet of true-life crime stories for the interest and amusement of a nonlawyer readership."[77] They were "sold on the streets of London within days of the trials they reported" and included all "cases of serious crime (felony) committed in the city of London and the adjacent county of Middlesex."[78] Despite condensation and editorial emphasis designed to promote popular sales, they were largely reliable. According to Professor Langbein: "The generalization that emerges is this: If the OBSP report says something happened, it did; if the OBSP report does not say it happened, it still may have. Legal historical researchers can rely upon the OBSP, but not for negative inferences."[79]

The period most relevant to the jury of matrons runs from the commencement of the OBSP until the mid-1700s. During most of these years, each sessions paper concluded with a summary of the sentences imposed on convicted prisoners, and it is here, if at all, that the jury of matrons is reflected. As an example, at the end of the paper for the fourth session of April 1715,[80] the following statement appears: "The trials being over the Court proceeded to give judgment, as followeth," after which the prisoners sentenced to death (18), to be burned in the hand (23), and to be whipped (17) are named. The report concludes with this sentence:

> Elizabeth Still, Sarah Blanford, Mary Skip, and Sarah Wilmot, severally pleaded their Bellies and a jury of Matrons being impannel'd, found Sarah Wilmot to be with Quick Child, and the other three not.[81]

From such end-of-report summaries, it is possible to develop a reasonably accurate profile of the use of the jury of matrons at the Old Bailey. I have examined the OBSP for the period April 1677 through 1833.[82] Appendix 1 exhibits data from these collections to show the number of sessions covered for each year, the number of females sentenced to death in each year, the number of females who "pleaded their bellies," and the number of the latter group, if any, shown as having been found by a jury of matrons to be with quick child. These statistics tell an interesting tale of abuse that is nicely augmented by popular literature of the early eighteenth century. Before telling that story, however, I will say what I can about how the jury of matrons worked in practice in both civil and criminal cases.

Procedure

Juries of matrons were not like ordinary petit juries. I have found no statutory treatment of them,[83] and they were not encompassed by regular trial jury procedures and requirements. For example, the customary freehold requirements for jurymen would not apply;[84] only in the unusual case would a woman have been a freeholder. Neither does any attempt appear to have been made to ensure that the women resided in the same county as the prisoner.[85] I have discovered nothing to suggest that the customary procedure of returning a panel of twenty-four names in the hope that at least twelve individuals would appear was applied to the jury of matrons in criminal cases,[86] nor have I located any evidence of the need for a "tales" to fill out a jury when less than twelve persons appeared.[87]

Who, then, were the jurors, and how were they obtained for jury service? Some answers can be given that, although incomplete, reveal different patterns in civil and criminal cases.

Civil Cases

The form of the writ *de ventre inspiciendo* contained in the *Registrum Brevium* (register of writs) printed in 1553 is unusual.[88] Richardson and Sayles described it as follows: "On the application of the dead man's brother, the sheriff is directed to accompany certain discreet and law-worthy knights and matrons, who will examine the widow and ascertain whether she is pregnant and, if so, when she conceived and when she is likely to be delivered; the return is to be under the sheriff's seal and is to be brought to the Bench by two of the knights present at the examination."[89]

Literally, the writ directed the sheriff to select twelve law-worthy matrons and twelve law-worthy knights who were to make the examination in the sheriff's presence. The writ remained on the books in this form well into the nineteenth century. This fact put the editors of the *Medical Gazette* in a state of high dudgeon when the writ was requested in Fox's case in the Vice-Chancellor's court in 1835. The indelicacy of requiring the widow "to submit her person to be examined by a mixed jury of men and matrons" was termed "disgustingly indecent," although the editors acknowledged that judicial discretion existed to substitute a less offensive procedure.[90]

The few reports of cases involving the writ *de ventre inspiciendo* suggest that the writ was never enforced in the grossly indecent manner imagined in the *Medical Gazette*. In Willoughby's case in 1597, the widow was "to be *viewed* by twelve knights and *searched* by twelve women in the presence of the twelve knights."[91] These directions indicate only a passive presence by the knights. Some years later, in Theaker's case, details of the inspection were not given, but the report states that the writ "was according to the precedent . . . of the like writ against Lady Willoughby."[92] Further, Francis Hargrave, in his notes to *Coke on Littleton*, wrote that the writ "delicately requires the widow to be inspected by a jury *of her own sex;* and although in subsequent times the sheriff was ordered to summon a jury composed both of men and women, yet still the *search* was to be made by the latter only."[93]

Even though the twelve knights likely never were required to participate in the actual inspection of the woman's body, the writ came to be viewed as a distasteful procedure to be avoided if possible. In *Ex Parte Aiscough* (Chancery, 1730), Dame Elizabeth Chaplin sought the writ, but after her counsel cited Willoughby's and Theaker's cases, the Solicitor General described an unreported case about six years previous in which the Master of the Rolls issued a decree "to appoint two midwives, who should resort to the widow to search her, and see whether she was with child or not."[94] Lord Chancellor King responded: "I take this writ *de ventre inspiciendo* to be of common right, it is in the *register,*" but his order was as follows: "Let the writ *de ventre inspiciendo* issue at Michaelmas, directed to the sheriff of *Middlesex*; in the meanwhile the present heirs may send two women at seasonable times, to see whether she is with child, they giving reasonable notice before hand, so that this may be attended with as little inconvenience as possible to the young lady."[95]

According to Peere Williams's report of the case, two writs were needed—one to see whether the widow be with child, and then a second whereby she would be removed "to a castle where sheriff is to keep her safely." A second report of the case quotes Lord Chancellor King as explaining: "The chief thing is to prevent a suppositious child, but the first writ issues, to see whether she is pregnant or not, because you cannot otherwise come at the second; and if the sheriff returns that she is with child, then the second, which is the material writ, issues out of the Court of King's Bench or Common Pleas."[96] Also, remarking that it would be hard on Lady Chaplin to confine her to the country when she desired to live in town, King said, "you cannot hinder her, for the first [writ] does not confine her, but she may go where she pleases, till the second writ issues, which cannot be had till *Michaelmas* term; and there is no fear of her being brought to bed immediately."[97]

A third report of the case dealt with the second writ in the Court of Common Pleas. After noting that the first writ "was returned that the lady was with child," the report states that the co-heirs moved "for the safe custody of her until her delivery," pointing out that "the lady's mother was likewise with child, and therefore neither she nor any other woman with child were proper persons to be with her."[98] Instead of the relaxed formula suggested by Lord Chancellor King (occasional visits by people of skill), the Court of Common Pleas ordered that a clause be inserted in the writ to prevent other women with child from being with Lady Chaplin, "and ladies were named on the part of the prosecutors or heiresses, to attend the lady during her pregnancy and till her delivery, but they must not name any spinster; and the mother was allowed to visit only."[99]

By the turn of the nineteenth century, the writ appears to have been issued only if insisted upon as a matter of right, no more palatable alternative having been acceptable to the petitioner. Thus, in *Ex Parte Wallop,* Lord Commissioner Eyre "ordered the writ to issue, but to lie in the office for fourteen days; and if, within that time, Mrs. Brown chose to submit to an examination by two midwives . . . whether she is pregnant, then the writ not to go till further orders; otherwise the writ to issue."[100] Six years earlier, in *Ex Parte Bellet,*[101] Master of the Rolls Lloyd Kenyon[102] had been asked to issue the writ, and, according to the reported version of the case, Kenyon announced that he had "a collection of all the applications that have been made on this subject."[103] After debate, Kenyon granted the writ. Among the manuscripts held by the Inner Temple Library is John Mitford's manuscript version of Kenyon's decision, which is much fuller than the printed report. According to Mitford's version, Kenyon observed:

> The Writ de ventre inspiciendo has so rarely issued especially of late times, that it is difficult to discover what is the proper mode of proceeding upon it. The writ itself, as it appears in the register, for it is not in Fitzherbert's Natura Brevium, merely directs an enquiry whether the woman is pregnant or not, and if pregnant at what time it is probable she will be delivered, and it is returnable to the Court of Common Pleas.[104]

Kenyon then discussed differences between the accounts of the writ in early authorities and ordered the sheriff to take the twelve knights and the twelve women to the allegedly pregnant woman's house, adding that it would be decent (though not necessary) to give her notice. He stated his own view that the sheriff could use force if needed, but he did not advise it, since he could find no authority for using force.

Subsequently, the writ was returned to Common Pleas and the inquisition was ordered; the sheriff was commanded to take "twelve discreet and lawful Knights and twelve discreet and lawful women of your county" and "go in person to the said Grace [Baron] and . . . cause her to be viewed and strictly examined and to be handled by her breasts and her belly in all manner by which you may be assured whether or not she is pregnant."[105] This the sheriff did and returned a verdict that the twelve named women say, under oath, and in the presence of the twelve named knights, "that Grace Baron is pregnant and that they believe she will be delivered on or about 6 weeks from the date of this Inquisition."[106] The court then ordered that Grace be confined in a place approved by the sheriff until the birth and that she be visited each day by at least one of the women of the jury of matrons. At the end of the manuscript report of the case, Mitford wrote the following:

> After Grace Baron had been some time under the restraint imposed upon her by this writ, she confessed she was not with child; and it was believed that she had intended to pretend that a child of one of her sisters was her child, two of her sisters being pregnant, and delivered nearly about same time when she pretended her time would be up.[107]

The latest reported English case to show issuance of the writ *de ventre inspiciendo* was brought before the Vice-Chancellor Knight Bruce in 1845. In *Blakemore v. Blakemore,*[108] a gentleman described as "of dissolute and intemperate habits" but worth some money had married a barmaid of an inn in Wales. In time, he left her in the country and returned to the city, where he died. The widow claimed to have been left pregnant by her late husband, even though she had been living with her husband's groom since before the husband died. At the Chancery hearing, Vice-Chancellor Knight Bruce blandly inquired, "The subsisting connection is one of sin?" He was told, "there has been no second marriage." The Vice-Chancellor's ruling was: "Let the ordinary course be followed. The jury is a jury of women."

Criminal Cases

Blackstone, Hale, and other authorities state that in criminal cases the jury was to be made up of matrons or "discreet women,"[109] and one early OBSP refers to a "jury of women."[110] Virtually all of the cases, however, refer simply to "matrons." It is unlikely that any uniform definition of "matron" existed, or, even if it did, that it was adhered to in the process of impaneling juries.[111] *The Oxford English Dictionary* provides a retrospective definition of "matron": "A married woman considered as having expert knowledge in matters of childbirth, pregnancy, etc.; now only in jury of matrons."[112] In the mid-eighteenth century, Dr. Samuel Johnson's two definitions of "matron" were "an elderly lady" and "an old woman."[113] But, in 1708, John Kersey defined "matron" as "a prudent and virtuous, motherly woman, also one of the grave women that have the over-sight of children in an Hospital."[114] It is fair to assume that the term "matron" was meant to exclude young single women and perhaps women who had never been married.[115]

It is also clear that the pattern in ecclesiastical and canon law of regularly including midwives on the inspection team did not take place at common law. Why this was so is less clear. As in many professions, there were complaints about unqualified or incompetent practitioners,[116] but for many centuries midwives were the recognized experts on childbirth. According to Ackerknecht, "the learned physician became the helper of the masses and therefore an obstetrician-gynecologist only during the 19th century."[117] Other researchers claim that "the British man-midwife displaced the traditional female practitioner during the eighteenth century," especially during and after the 1740s.[118] Even by the 1740s, however, the practice of impaneling juries of matrons had long been established. One could imagine a sixteenth-century "midwives book" analogous to the freeholders book for ordinary jurymen, from which some or all of the members of the juries of matrons would be taken, but there is no evidence of any such practice, perhaps for the simple reason that there was an insufficient supply of midwives.[119]

There is no evidence, in fact, of any repository whatever of names from which matrons would be summoned and virtually no evidence of the use of customary forms associated with the summoning of jurymen.[120] In the late-seventeenth-century work *The Office of the Clerk of Assize,* the clerk is directed, upon a plea of pregnancy, to "command the Sheriff to retorn an Enquest of 12 Women for the justices; and when the Sheriff hath retorned them, the *Clerk of Assize* shall call over their names [and swear them in]."[121] This raises the possibility of some delay between the command to the sheriff and the return of matrons, as would be normal jury practice. But the suggestion is undercut by the many cases in the Assize Calendars in which the jury of matrons was impaneled on the same day as conviction.[122] Since the plea of pregnancy would not be made before conviction, these cases demonstrate that it was feasible for the sheriff to produce matrons almost instantly. The easiest and most logical explanation for this is that the matrons were obtained "*de circumstantibus*"—that is, from among the audience in the courtroom or from bystanders in the courthouse. The only delay was that required to round up the twelve "matrons." It is improbable that, in such a slapdash impaneling process, particular care was taken to ensure that the women chosen had genuine experience with pregnancy or childbirth. The sheriff's request for jury members must have been verbal, and he may well have requested that only married women or widows respond to his call.[123] He may even have used the word "matron." But there is no indication of any process for verifying that women on the jury possessed "matron" qualifications, whatever such qualifications might have been thought to be.

In the 1809 murder trial of Mary Bateman, at York, the defendant was a person of local notoriety, commonly referred to as "the Yorkshire witch." After being sentenced to death, she pleaded that she was twenty-two weeks pregnant, and the judge ordered the sheriff to impanel a jury of matrons. According to the report of the case, this order

> created a general consternation among the ladies, who hastened to quit the court, to prevent the execution of so painful an office being imposed upon them. His Lordship, in consequence, ordered the doors to be closed, and in about half-an-hour 12 married women being impaneled, they were sworn in court, and charged to inquire "whether the prisoner was with quick child?"[124]

Similarly, in *Regina v. Wycherley,* decided in 1838, Baron Gurney, after ordering the sheriff to impanel a jury of matrons, added: "Let all the doors be shut, and no one be suffered to leave the Court."[125] To this statement, two reporters, Carrington and Payne, appended the following footnote: "We believe that the reason of the order for closing the doors of the Court (which is always given before a jury of matrons is impaneled), is to prevent the ladies from the leaving the Court, and thus preventing a jury of matrons *de circumstantibus* from being impaneled."[126]

Such direct evidence of the impaneling process does not appear in earlier cases,[127] but indirect suggestions can be found in the Newgate Calendars.[128] For example, in 1714, Captain Alexander Smith asserted that prisoners regularly had "Matrons of [their] own Profession ready at hand, who, right or wrong, bring in their wicked Companions quick with Child."[129]

Since juries of matrons were usually "*de circumstantibus,*" it is interesting to reflect on the nature of the surroundings. Before the mid-eighteenth century, matrons at the Old Bailey could not have been "captured," as in the nineteenth-century cases, by closing the doors to the courtroom, because there were no doors to close. As Gerald Howson pointed out, historians frequently lose sight of the fact that, until 1737, the Old Bailey was an open-air edifice, almost an architectural cutaway, designed to protect the court against infectious disease that might be carried by prisoners or witnesses.[130] Engravings of the court as it then appeared suggest that onlookers at trials stood in the open area, a courtyard called "Sessions House Yard," reached through an alley. Howson states that "seen from Sessions House Yard, a trial at the Old Bailey must have resembled nothing so much as a giant Punch and Judy show."[131] The outdoor setting may have been unappealing to genteel members of society, and in winter months or inclement weather it must have diminished the natural supply of onlookers. If so, this could give weight to jury-packing accusations such as those of Captain Smith mentioned earlier.

A second procedural inquiry is what the matrons were charged to do and whether they in fact carried out their charge. An early OBSP states simply that the three female prisoners who pleaded their bellies were "by a jury of Women found Pregnant,"[132] but officially the jurors' job was more subtle. As has been noted, the jurors' task was to determine whether the prisoner was "quick with child." The notion of quickening was conceptually central to the role of the jury of matrons because, until the late eighteenth century, the belief was widespread that human life had not begun before this event.[133] Such a belief was to be scotched by medical advances, but it was firmly in place throughout most of the centuries of existence of the jury of matrons.[134] As stated by Blackstone, execution was stayed only "if they bring in their verdict *quick with child* (for barely, *with child,* unless it be alive in the womb, is not sufficient)."[135]

How faithful the juries were to their charge cannot be known exactly. Certainly, the question is meaningless if the jury was packed in the prisoner's favor, as was surely true on occasion. But the jury determinations were almost always expressed in terms of "quickening." Sometimes the jury return was written that a prisoner was, or was not, "quick with child";[136] but most were returned "with quick child" or "not with quick child."[137] Clearly, the honest juries of matrons had the notion of "quickening" in mind; the child's movement—movement that they could feel—was the best possible evidence to support their decision. And, as earlier noted, frequently the juries returned verdicts that prisoners were not with quick child. Of the prisoners who pleaded their bellies in the sixty-six years reflected in Appendix 1, 138 out a total of 296 women, or 47 percent, were found not with quick child. Percentages for individual years varied, and some patterns of abuse are evident, but the overall figures indicate that many juries went about their task conscientiously. In one instance, a jury expressly found that a prisoner was "with Child, but not Quick."[138]

The final inquiry in this discussion on how the jury of matrons worked is the question of ultimate importance to the prisoners: Did pleading their bellies improve their chances for survival? Undoubtedly, many prisoners, if genuinely pregnant, would have pleaded their bellies to allow their unborn children to live even if the device had offered no chance to redeem their own lives. Further, most prisoners would naturally attempt to delay their trip to the gallows as long as possible. Even if the chance for a pardon was unclear or apparently nonexistent, there was nothing to lose by the attempt; the prisoners were already under ultimate sanction.

The fact is, however, that gaining time was of considerable value. Fervid efforts were often made to gain reprieves for prisoners, and these sometimes worked, sometimes unexpectedly.[139] A reprieve provided time to evaluate whether a prisoner should be pardoned, either totally or conditionally upon transportation.[140] What is of particular interest is whether a reprieve for pregnancy gave the prisoner a better than ordinary chance of escaping the gallows. James Cockburn states that in the assize records, "an overwhelming majority of those reprieved on the ground of pregnancy were released."[141] Further, writing about trial jury verdicts and pardons in eighteenth-century Surrey, John Beattie states that few women who were reprieved were ultimately executed, because a successful plea of pregnancy "was likely to be tantamount to a pardon."[142] In a study of seventeenth-century sessions in Middlesex, Peter King makes similar, albeit cautious, observations about women granted a pregnancy reprieve: "There is no evidence as to whether the sentences were always carried out after the lapse of time. A number of women received pardons and there was a tendency for justices to be lenient with pregnant women."[143]

The evidence I have examined in the Gaol Delivery Books, the OBSP, and the Newgate Calendars does not permit a conclusion that a successful pregnancy plea was "tantamount to a pardon." Neither the Gaol Delivery Books nor the OBSP regularly reported the ultimate fate of capital offenders who were reprieved. Some such information appeared from time to time that, while not sufficient to support broad generalizations, is nevertheless of interest. The OBSP for December 1684 reported that "Jane Voss, who formerly Pleading her Belly, has a long time continued in Prison, [was] ordered to be Executed upon her former Sentence."[144] Similar entries appear for other prisoners in 1698, 1703, 1711, 1712, and 1716.[145] Furthermore, the Newgate Calendars recite the eventual execution of a number of female prisoners after their respites for pregnancy.[146] But there are also indications of a number of pardons having been given after respites for pregnancy. The OBSP for September 1686 included a formal list of fifty-three prisoners who were granted royal pardons on July 26, 1686. There were two categories: those who were granted a free pardon and those who were granted a pardon conditional on transportation. Included in the first category was Elizabeth Churchill and in the second Rebeckah Rose, both of whom had been respited for pregnancy in April 1686.[147]

In the OBSP for October 1688, another list of free pardons was set out. This time three women were listed who had earlier pleaded their bellies—one who had been found with quick child in April 1688 and two who had been found not with quick child (in April and July 1688).[148]

It was not unusual for female prisoners who pleaded their bellies to stay in limbo in prison for lengthy periods. Sometimes the continuation in prison was regularly logged by the recordkeepers. For example, the Old Bailey Sessions Books for January 1758 at the Greater London Record Office (London Metropolitan Archives) show two women as respited for pregnancy, and thereafter formal entries for each of them appeared regularly. The following (February 1758) is representative:

> Margaret Larney-Attainted last Session of High Treason in diminishing the gold Coin of this Realm & received judgment to be drawn on a Hurdle to the place of Execution & burned to Death. But being by a jury of

> Matrons found with quick Child Is ordered to remain safe in Gaol until she shall be discharged by due course of Law.[149]

Entries for Margaret Larney ran for a relatively short period of months, but for the other prisoner, Elizabeth Tomkinson, the entries ran until September 1759.[150]

Abuses

A major question not yet squarely faced is the extent to which fraudulent appeals to juries of matrons became a tactical ploy to gain time.[151] Abuse of the jury of matrons could take several forms. I have already referred to Captain Smith's early eighteenth-century jury-packing assertion. Two other forms of abuse were skillful fakery by the prisoner to demonstrate pregnancy and contriving to become pregnant while in prison awaiting trial. I first address the scope and nature of assertions about these abuses and then turn to the OBSP evidence.[152]

In his *Travels Over England,* written in 1698, the Frenchman Misson wrote:

> The Women or Wenches that are condemn'd to Death, never fail to plead they are with Child, (if they are old enough) in order to stop Execution till they are delivered. Upon this they are order'd to be visited by matrons; if the Matrons do not find them Quick, they are sure to swing next Execution-Day; but very often they declare that they are with Child, and often too the poor Criminals are so indeed; for tho' they came never so good Virgins into the Prison, they are a Sett of Wags there that take Care of these Matters. No Doubt they are diligent to inform them the very Moment they come in, that if they are not with Child already, they must go to work immediately to be so; that in case they have the Misfortune to be condemn'd, they may get Time, and so perhaps save their Lives. Who would not hearken to such wholesome Advice?[153]

Misson's colorful description was echoed in popular writings of the early eighteenth century, a period when crime in England, particularly London, was increasing sharply. Public imagination was fired by two notorious criminals—Jonathan Wild and Jack Shepherd;[154] in the words of one of John Gay's biographers, London had "suddenly become Newgate-conscious."[155] Defoe's *Moll Flanders,* first published in 1722, contains several references to "pleading the belly," a phrase that Defoe saw no need to interpret for his readers.[156] At one point, one of Moll's fellow prisoners in Newgate explains why she is not in immediate fear of being hung: "I pleaded by belly, but I am no more quick with child than the judge that tried me."[157] Similarly, in the opening scene of Gay's *Beggar's Opera* (first published in 1728),[158] the following exchange takes place between Mr. Peachum, the thief-taker, and his sleazy assistant, Filch:

> Filch: Sir, Black Moll hath sent word her trial comes on in the afternoon, and she hopes you will order matters so as to bring her off.
>
> Peachum: Why, she may plead her belly at worst; to my knowledge she hath taken care of that security.[159]

And, in the third act, Filch enters in a state of exhaustion and explains his condition to Lucy Lockit thus:

> Lockit: Why, boy, thou lookest as if thou were half starved like a shotten herring.
>
> Filch: One had need have the constitution of a horse to go through the business. Since the favorite child-getter was disabled by a mishap, I have picked up a little money by helping the ladies to a pregnancy against their being called down to sentence. But if a man cannot get an honest livelihood any easier way, I am sure 'tis what I can't undertake for another session.[160]

These cynical references to a humanitarian legal procedure run amok also appear in the Newgate Calendars in narrative descriptions of notorious criminals. "Captain"[161] Alexander Smith, in describing the fate of Mary Carleton (known as "The German Princess"), stated that, after having been found guilty, "She now had but one Shift more, and that was an Old *Newgate*-Trick, to plead her Belly; whereupon a jury of Women was found out, and sworn."[162] Smith also wrote that Nan Harris, after being sentenced to death for a theft of calico,

> pleaded her belly, and used the old Stratagem of drinking new Ale-very plentifully, to make her swell, cramming a Pillow in her Petticoat to make her look big; and having Matrons of her own Profession ready at hand, who, right or wrong, bring their wicked Companions quick with

> Child, to the great Impediment of justice; but though she had the good Luck to impose thus on the Bench, after she had been condemn'd once before, yet at the end of 9 Months (all which while she was not wanting to make herself pregnant, if all the Men in the Jayl could do it, but they work'd in vain). . . .[163]

While it is hard to imagine the use of a pillow to any advantage with an honest jury, the device could give courtroom verisimilitude to a corrupt verdict. It is, of course, interesting to see the similarity between Smith's assertions and those of Misson,[164] as well as the behavior of Gay's character Filch.

Against this background it is time to take up the OBSP data shown in Appendix 1. I have already observed that over the years covered by the OBSP used in this study, women who pleaded pregnancy were found to be with quick child only slightly more than half the time (53 percent). What is arresting, however, is to break down these data to correspond with the accusations of abuse just presented. Between 1698, the year in which Misson wrote, and 1727, the year in which Gay completed *The Beggar's Opera,* 62 percent of all women sentenced to death pleaded pregnancy, and, of these, 61 percent were successful before juries of matrons. For one five-year period, 1714–1719, during which Gay was walking the streets of London and Defoe was writing *Moll Flanders,* ninety-two of the 112 females sentenced to death—an astonishing 82 percent—pleaded their bellies. The peak year was 1716, in which all twenty-four—100 percent—of the women sentenced to death pleaded pregnancy, eighteen of them successfully. Even acknowledging that pregnancy was a common, largely unavoidable condition for many women throughout the period, these statistics are unnaturally high. They lend credence to the assertions of Misson and Captain Smith, and to the depictions of Gay and Defoe.

Gradual Disappearance

Ultimately, the jury of matrons became obsolete. Medical expertise in the second half of the nineteenth century could no longer be ignored. From the early 1700s into the 1900s, the jury of matrons continued to function, but with decreasing regularity.

The job of honest jury matrons of the late seventeenth or early eighteenth century was to determine by inspection whether a female prisoner was "quick with child." There were cases, surely, that were easy, such as advanced states of pregnancy with easily discernible fetal movements or women beyond child-bearing age.[165] But the inquiry was often difficult, even supposing a jury made up of women with personal experience with childbirth. There was simply no scientific way to resolve the question.

Midwifery was, even then, an ancient calling, but a quick glance at seventeenth-century treatises on the subject confirms the primitive nature of the understanding of pregnancy then prevalent. For example, the authors of *The Compleat Midwife's Practice* (1656) observed that "false conception hath many signes, common with the true conception; as the suppression of the flowers, depraved appetite, vomitings, swelling of the belly, and of the breasts; so that it is a hard thing to distinguish the one from the other."[166] They enumerated the signs unique to false conception as follows:

> For in false conception, the face is ordinarily puffed up, the breasts, that at first were swollen, afterwards become everyday more than other softer and lanker and without milk. In fine, the face, the breasts, the arms, the thighs and groynes grow lank and meager: The belly waxes hard, as happens to those who are troubled with the Dropsie, and almost of an equal roundness; with many pricking pains, at the bottom of the belly, which have scarce any intermission; which is the cause that they can hardly sleep, being encombered with a heavy and dead burthen.[167]

The authors then observed that in a true conception, "the Male Infant begins to move at the beginning of the third moneth [*sic*], for the most part, and the female at the beginning of the third or fourth month," compared with false conception, where "there be a kind of motion, which is not enliven'd that proceeds from the expulsive faculty of the mother, and not from the *mole.*" The "true mole" refers to the fetus in its formative stages, but four varieties of "false moles" are also identified.[168] The authors' definition of the "true mole" bears repeating because it relates to the legal principle that human life did not begin before the "quickening":

> The true mole is a fleshie body, filled with many vessels, which have many white, green, or black lines, or membranes; it is without thought, without motion, without bones, without bowels or entrailes; receiving its nourishment through certaine veins; it lives the life of a plant, without any figure or order being engendered in the concavitie of the matrix, adhering to the sides of it, but borrowing nothing of its substance.[169]

By the nineteenth century, medical experts were presenting a different view. In 1797, one medical practitioner, John Jones, characterized as a common error "That when the mother first perceives the child to move, it is the very time when its life commences."[170] Later, in an influential treatise on medical jurisprudence published in 1823, Dr. Theodric Beck rejected the theory that life does not commence before the quickening. He reasoned that "The foetus, previous to the time of quickening, must be either dead or alive" and "that it is not the former, is most evident from neither putrefaction nor decomposition taking place, which would be the inevitable consequences of an extinction of the vital principle."[171] He acknowledged that "Foetuses do actually die in the uterus before quickening," but "then all the signs of death are present." His logical conclusion was that the embryo, before quickening and absent signs of death, "must be in a state different from that of death, and this can be no other than life."[172] Even the definition of the "true mole" presented earlier did not deny the existence of "life" before quickening; it was merely viewed as "the life of a plant."[173] Nevertheless, Beck pointed out that nineteenth-century medical research had demonstrated through early stethoscopic detection of heartbeats and other means that "the foetus enjoys [human] life long before the sensation of quickening is felt by the mother." Indeed, Beck concluded that the embryo possesses "vitality from the very moment of conception."[174]

Quickening nonetheless continued, in the nineteenth century, in criminal cases, to be a required element of the jury finding.[175] Dr. Michael Ryan, in his early nineteenth-century book on medical jurisprudence, observed that this jury task was one "which the whole faculty of physic, in every part of the world, could not determine, in the early months of pregnancy." He added: "It would be as wise to appoint a jury of infants to examine these Questions."[176]

Examples are not wanting of erroneous determinations by juries of matrons. Several such examples were marshaled in an article in the *Med-*

ical Times and Gazette of January 27, 1872, to support the argument that "it is high time that this absurd trial by a jury of matrons were done away with."[177] An Old Bailey case in 1847 was reported in which a jury of matrons examined Mary Ann Hunt and returned a negative verdict; "yet, three months after, she gave birth to a full-grown child." Further: "In Wright's case, at the Norwich Assizes, in 1832, a similar verdict was returned; and in this case, also, the woman would have been executed, had not several Medical men represented to the presiding judge that the method taken by the jury to determine quickening was insufficient."[178] In March 1872, the *Medical Times and Gazette* reported the case of Rachel Busby,

> who was sentenced to death at the last assizes at Oxford for the murder of her child, has just given birth to a stillborn infant at the county gaol. Twelve 'matrons' were impaneled at the trial, but they found there was no ground for a respite, and but for the exertions of some philanthropic gentlemen at Oxford the convict would then have been executed.[179]

How often pregnant women were actually executed after erroneous jury of matrons determinations cannot be known.[180] Hayward reports that after the jury of matrons found Katherine Fitzpatrick and Mrs. Holmes not quick with child, "both to the time of their death averred they were so, and seemed exceedingly uneasy that their children should die violent deaths within them."[181]

Further complicating the task of the honest jury of matrons was the likelihood of dishonesty on the part of the prisoner. Midwives and doctors acknowledged the deceptive potential. Cazeaux, in a widely used French treatise on midwifery, wrote: "Some females, from the desire to simulating pregnancy, have acquired the power of contracting their abdominal muscles in so singular a manner, that many able accoucheurs have been deceived and believing that they felt the foetal movements, have consequently pronounced them pregnant."[182] Likewise, Dr. Taylor noted that "medical practitioners of repute have been deceived for a time by this artifice," but he added that "this occurred before the discovery of chloroform or the stethoscope."[183] In 1872, Dr. Thomas Madden, referring to cases in which qualified medical men declared that women were not pregnant until almost the moment before delivery, observed that such cases "show the absurdity of the law in committing the solution of a question of such gravity to any twelve matrons, however ignorant, who may happen to be present when the plea is raised."[184]

Further, the matrons were confronted with contrivances beyond mere muscular manipulation. I have earlier mentioned Captain Smith's reference to "the Old Strategem of drinking new Ale very plentifully, to make her swell."[185] More sophisticated techniques were no doubt resorted to, as is suggested by the case of Elizabeth Cellier.[186] Referred to as a "celebrated midwife," Mrs. Cellier was acquitted of high treason in King's Bench in the spring of 1680, only to be brought to trial again at the Old Bailey for libel arising out of the account she wrote of her acquittal. She was convicted and was sentenced to stand in the pillory. To avoid that ignominy, Mrs. Cellier feigned pregnancy and pretended that she had suddenly commenced her labor. According to Prance's account of the incident, "after a world of groanings and a thousand bewitching wry faces, an able physician and several discreet women were sent for," after which "They searched her so narrowly that they discovered the whole cheat, and found that the good lady was no more with bearn than the town-bull, but only having over night privately gotten a bladder of blood had used her skill in creating the necessary symptoms, and, preparing certain clots of it, had put them in her body."[187]

The task of the honest jury of matrons, then, was often formidable, with the decision turning on indistinct or "doctored" evidence, and with as many as two lives hanging in the balance.[188] One option was for the jury to say that they did not know the answer. This was done by juries of matrons from time to time, and in these cases there was apparently no insistence that the jury be isolated without food or drink until a decision was reached, as theoretically would have been done with the ordinary trial jury.[189] When the jurors who examined Deborah Churchill in 1708 reported that they were ignorant whether or not she was with child, "the court, willing to allow all reasonable time in a case of this nature, respited judgment for six months; at the end of which time she received sentence of death, as there was no appearance of her being pregnant."[190] Further, in the trial of Patrick Ogilvie and Catherine Nairn in Edinburgh[191] in 1765, counsel for Mrs. Nairn filed a petition suggesting that the prisoner was three months pregnant, but a special committee of five skilled midwives examined her and deposed that "they cannot give a positive opinion, whether [Mrs. Nairn] is pregnant or not."[192] As a result, sentencing was delayed, and regular visits by the midwives to the prisoner were arranged.

During the nineteenth century, a change occurred. When juries found themselves unable to resolve a pregnancy question, the assistance of an accoucheur or doctor was ordered. It is reported that when Ann Hurle, in 1804, "so contrived to baffle the skill of the women appointed to examine her, that they could not come to any satisfactory decision . . . the sheriffs had recourse to the judgment and experience of Doctor Thynne, whose report negatived the plea of the prisoner."[193] On occasion, medical assistance was provided to the jury from the beginning of its deliberations, as in the case of Margaret Crimes, alias Barrington, tried at the Old Bailey in 1809. Her jury of matrons reportedly "retired with the prisoner" and were "assisted by a surgeon of eminence," who was also sworn.[194]

In a third variation, it sometimes happened that the jury, in the midst of its deliberations, sent out a request for medical help. In *Regina v. Wycherley,* a case in the Court of Exchequer in 1838, the jury sent out a request for a surgeon, to which Baron Gurney responded: "I think that I ought not, considering the terms of the bailiff's oath, to allow a surgeon to go to the room in which the jury of matrons is, and that they should come into Court."[195] Accordingly, the jury of matrons returned to court, and a Mr. Greatorex, a surgeon and accoucheur (reportedly also the husband of the forematron of the jury), individually retired with the prisoner to examine her. After Mr. Greatorex gave his opinion that the prisoner was not quick with child, the jury of matrons again retired and returned a like verdict.[196] In reporting *Regina v. Wycherley,* Carrington and Payne described in a footnote an earlier case at Chester in which a surgeon went into the room with the jury of matrons and the prisoner,

> which seems not only to have been in some degree inconsistent with the terms of the bailiff's oath, but was also open to the objection, that the surgeon was thus giving evidence out of the presence of the judge, which evidence might possibly be of a nature to be perfectly inadmissible in point of law, as being hearsay or the like.[197]

Two cases involving a jury of matrons occurred in the 1870s. The first, described in the *Medical Times and Gazette,* was in January 1872 and involved a request by a jury of matrons for help in their examination of Christiana Edmunds. "Half an hour after their retirement a messenger came into Court and an inquiry was made for an accoucheur. One was found—Mr. J. Beresford Ryley, of Woolwich—and he was directed to assist the matrons."[198] The jury eventually decided that the prisoner was not pregnant. The *Medical Times and Gazette* editorialized as follows:

> Wisely, in the Edmunds case, did the jury seek Medical assistance. Mr. Ryley had no difficulty in deciding, by a brief application of the stethoscope, that the woman was not quick with child; and yet such of the matrons—many of whom, he states, were of good social position and unusual intelligence—as had come to any conclusion on the subject under consideration, had arrived thereat on such insufficient grounds as to render their opinion utterly valueless. The continuance of the present law is, then, we think, a scandal and a disgrace to our system of judicature. Juries of matrons, where Medical assistance has not been sought, have fallen into grievous errors; nor have they erred, as a rule, on the side of mercy. The fact that a woman is pregnant, much more the fact that the pulsations of the foetal heart are audible, or the negatives of these, can only be made out by competent Medical examination. Juries of matrons to try these questions ought forthwith to be abolished.[199]

The second case was reported in *The Law Times* in July 1879. Kate Webster pleaded her belly and, "Upon this a scene of uncertainty, if not of confusion, ensued, certainly not altogether in harmony with the solemnity of the occasion." Mr. Justice Denman observed that, "after thirty-two years in the profession, he was never at an inquiry of this sort." Although no one seemed to know what should be done, eventually "the right course was stumbled upon, and the jury of matrons retired with the prisoner to a private apartment, there to ascertain the fact to be inquired of, Mr. Bond, the surgeon, being sworn as a witness and accompanying them."[200] When the jury and Mr. Bond returned, Justice Denman questioned Mr. Bond instead of requesting the jury verdict. Bond was certain the prisoner was not with quick child, but, not being an accoucheur, he could not say whether she was pregnant. Reportedly, Justice Denman urged the jury to accept Mr. Bond's opinion, stating that the question was "not whether the prisoner is in a state of pregnancy, but whether she is or is not quick with child."[201] The president of the

Obstetrical Society of London wrote a letter about this case to the editor of *The Times,* observing in dismay that "here we have a Judge in the 19th century ruling that it is necessary that a criminal should be quick with child before execution was stayed, a rule based on the obsolete medieval assumption that the unborn child is not alive until the so-called 'quickening.'"[202]

After Kate Webster's case in 1879, nothing was heard of the jury of matrons for more than two decades. Astonishingly, however, the procedure resurfaced in the twentieth century, according to two reports in *The Times*. In both cases, however, the description of the jury's role suggests that the jury was to base its verdict on medical evidence presented in court, instead of on a private physical examination of the defendant.

On December 11, 1913, Ada Annie Williams was convicted at the Central Criminal Court of murdering her four-and-one-half-year-old son, after which she claimed she was pregnant. Justice Ridley ordered that all the doors be shut, since "According to the authorities the jury may be empanelled forthwith, *de mulieribus curcumstantibus.*"[203] The report then states that "Dr. Sass, deputy medical officer of Holloway Prison, gave evidence that the prisoner was pregnant, and the jury found a verdict accordingly."[204]

The last known use of a jury of matrons was reported by *The Times* on July 19, 1917. On the previous day, a young woman named Stevens was convicted of infanticide and was sentenced to death, but she claimed pregnancy. Justice Lawrence ordered that a jury of matrons be impaneled, "and after hearing medical evidence they returned a verdict that the prisoner was pregnant."[205] Accordingly, the death sentence was respited.

As a part of the customary law of England that had been called into play rarely since the mid-eighteenth century and hardly at all since the early nineteenth century, it did not become necessary formally to abolish the jury of matrons or to replace it with a more modern procedure. Such a procedure was, however, proposed. The Criminal Code introduced in the House of Commons in 1879 (and again in 1880) contained a provision abolishing the jury of matrons, substituting in its place a requirement that the court "direct one or more registered medical practitioners to be sworn to examine the woman in some private place, either together or successively, and to inquire whether she is with child of a quick child or not."[206] By comparison, the State of New York in its 1881 Code of Criminal Procedure provided in §500 that, "If there is reasonable ground to believe that a female defendant, sentenced to the punishment of death, is pregnant, the sheriff of the county where the conviction took place must impanel a jury of six physicians to inquire into her pregnancy."[207] In England, the jury of matrons died a natural death of obsolescence.[208]

Conclusion

Before medical knowledge about pregnancy acquired some sophistication in the nineteenth century, all that was required for a determination about pregnancy was that a special opportunity for inspection and observation be made available. In the early phases of the jury of matrons, the question of pregnancy was not one regarded as requiring special training. Yet it would have been foolish and indelicate to ask a jury of male freeholders to examine the body of a female litigant or prisoner to ascertain the existence of a condition that male jurors could not possibly have experienced. The jury of matrons was the logical answer, and it had deep historical antecedents. Midwives could have been required, but the tradition in England of trial "by the country"—by a jury of twelve—was venerable, and rounding up twelve midwives every time a prisoner pleaded her belly would have been altogether impracticable.

There have been other examples in English law of the use of "specialty" juries to decide questions that ultimately became the province of medical expertise. One example is the use of the civil commitment jury in insanity cases.[209] Another is illustrated in the OBSP for February 1818, when a defendant, George Spicer, refused to plead, claiming to be totally deaf. A jury was impaneled "to try whether he stood mute willfully, maliciously, and obstinately, or by the visitation of God."[210]

Long before the jury of matrons was replaced by the doctors, however, a chapter of corruption in its history was written at the Old Bailey. Seized upon as a desperation lifeline by women facing execution, the jury of matrons flourished in the late 1600s and early 1700s. As shown by the data in Appendix 1, a high proportion of the females sentenced to death pleaded their bellies in many of the years in the last two decades of the seventeenth century and the first two decades of the eighteenth. Assertions that often the juries were packed and that often the pregnancies were contrived while the prisoner was in gaol were likely true. But recourse to the jury of matrons decreased sharply during the 1720s, and by the 1760s the appearance of the jury was quite sporadic. According to the OBSP, no more than one prisoner pleaded her belly at any sessions after 1762, regardless of the number of females who were sentenced to death.[211] This change is striking, and the reasons for it are unclear. Official efforts to curb the abuse of 1715–1720 might have occurred, although I have discovered no such evidence.[212] Perhaps more care was taken by the sheriffs and judges in the impaneling process; this might have been true especially after 1737, when the Old Bailey courtroom became fully enclosed and thus more hospitable to curiosity-seeking matrons among the middling gentry. No doubt, also, the increasing use of the expedient of transportation and a generalized leniency in the treatment of female prisoners played a part.

To the extent that the early-eighteenth-century abuses were due to packed juries of matrons, they were a corruption of legal process. But it is not likely that all twelve matrons on a given jury were cronies of the prisoner, and another interpretation is possible. It was widely recognized, as many historians have noted,[213] that eighteenth- and nineteenth-century trial juries often mitigated the rigors of the penal laws by what has been termed "jury nullification," or "pious perjury"—most commonly by finding that the value of stolen goods was just under the amount required to make the theft a felony, even though the goods were manifestly worth more. Perhaps the behavior of juries of matrons was a variation on this theme. If the prisoner's claim of being with quick child had any plausibility, what was the harm in allowing a respite? There was no risk to the jurors of being attainted or even penalized for a false verdict. The prisoner would eventually be hung or transported, and there was some chance of saving the life of an innocent unborn child. Such, at least, could have been the reasoning of those members of the jury who did not have their minds made up in advance.[214]

Even so, as the "Newgate-consciousness" of the early eighteenth century faded, and as law enforcement in London began to be strengthened,[215] the frequency with which the jury of matrons was impaneled diminished. Likewise, the percentage of women who successfully pleaded pregnancy dropped.[216] By the late nineteenth century, the obstetrician-gynecologist had come into existence as the recognized expert on the subject of pregnancy. With these developments, the jury of matrons became superfluous. By century's end, it had virtually vanished. The jury of matrons' surprising history is an example of a legal principle founded on humanitarian values that was abused in order to palliate the harshness of the penal laws and that ultimately perished not by continued abuse but by the growth of science.

6 The Self-Informing Jury

The expression "self-informing jury" customarily refers to juries formed in England from the twelfth to the sixteenth centuries under circumstances in which the jurors themselves would be the experts. They were expected to know or to find out the facts of the event or events in dispute and ordinarily would decide without the help of any documentary or testimonial evidence given in court. How pure this process was, even in the early centuries, is a matter of ongoing scholarly debate, but there is general agreement that the transformation to the modern understanding of the jury's role (to decide based solely on evidence presented in court) was well under way by the 1500s.

The ongoing historical assessment of the self-informing jury has centered on the question of how the jurors came to possess the facts of the event or events in dispute. In this chapter, I re-examine the classic model through two sets of source materials—first, the Selden Society's published annual volumes and second, David Seipp's expanding database of Year Book cases.[1] There is some overlap, since the Seipp database includes some of the Selden Society Year Book volumes, but also included are volumes published by the Ames Society, the Rolls Society, and abridgments, as well as old printed but untranslated Year Book editions.

Citing Pollock and Maitland's *History of English Law Before the Time Of Edward I*, John Dawson in his *History of Lay Judges* observed that "It was certainly never supposed that all the members of every jury would have been eyewitnesses of the events about which they spoke."[2] Pollock and Maitland acknowledged that it had become a commonplace to say "that in old times 'the jurors were the witnesses,'" but, they added, the expression "does not quite hit the truth." They gave as the explanation for the juries of old the fact that in the early days juries had arbitral, communal, and quasi-judicial elements.[3] As to "the manner in which the jurors came to their verdict," they noted that the jurors would have had advance notice of the trial, and "We know of no rule of law which prevented them from listening during this interval to the tale of the litigants; indeed it was their duty to discover the truth."[4] Further, "We know of no rule of law which would have prohibited the jurors from listening in court to persons whom the litigants produced and who were capable of giving information, though we do not think that as of yet such persons were sworn."[5]

In a recent work entitled *Judicial Tribunals in England and Europe, 1200–1700: The Trial in History,*[6] Daniel Klerman posed the following question as the title of his chapter: "Was the Jury Ever Self-informing?"[7] Using a variety of printed and manuscript sources, Klerman responds to recent scholarship suggesting "that some fourteenth century juries may not have been self-informing" and "that fifteenth century jurors heard evidence in court."[8] After a review of selected trial accounts, plea rolls,[9] and Year Book reports, Klerman concludes that the thirteenth-century jury, at least, was indeed self-informing, despite the fact that it sometimes heard witnesses at trial.[10] Klerman's conclusions reinforce similar views already expressed by Thomas Green in his concluding retrospective chapter in *Twelve Good Men and True.* Green pointed out that the evidence contributed by McLane, Post, and Powell,[11] while not "inconsistent with the possibility of in-court prosecution testimony alongside self-informing," nevertheless made it appear "that self-informing was at the very least one inevitable significant aspect of the medieval trial."[12]

Against this background we can examine the evidence produced by the Selden Society volumes and by David Seipp's database. Seipp has given a preview in a summary article, in which he points out that, in addition to testimony, medieval jurors at times were presented by the parties in open court with writings that the jurors took with them during their deliberations.[13] His examination of the Year Books also confirms "that a large part of the process of informing juries about matters in dispute in the fourteenth and fifteenth centuries took place informally, outside of court, and before the date of trial."[14]

The cases that follow are largely corroborative of the views of the self-informing jury that have been given by Pollock and Maitland, Green, Seipp, and Klerman. The cases demonstrate the richness of the source material that the Selden Society has been faithfully and laboriously producing for nearly 120 years and that is being substantially augmented by the Seipp entries.[15]

Juries That Seemingly Knew the Facts Without Recourse to Extraneous Evidence

Preliminarily, it should be stated that although early juries were expected to know the facts, there were times when they either did not know or were jurisdictionally restricted. Thus, in a case in Common Pleas in 1327, a judgment was reversed because it had been rendered on a matter that had happened in another county, and "jurors do not become knowledgeable about matters that happened in another county."[16] In 1335, when an inquest was asked whether an infant was married or unmarried, "They said that they could not know that because the infant was living in another county"; thus, "it could not fall in their knowledge."[17]

Another preliminary matter that is reflected in the records is that in order for the court to depend upon jurors to produce the knowledge necessary to resolve the dispute, the jurors had to be seen as responsible and trustworthy. Therefore, in some cases, jurors were dismissed because they were "paupers and unworthy."[18]

Other limitations occasionally played a part besides poverty. In a case in 1276, the issue was whether one John was the son of the lately deceased Marjorie. The male jurors who were called found that the child had been born and named "John" by the women present at the birth, "but they definitely say that he was never heard to cry out within four walls."[19] This finding was later reviewed by the king and council, and since it was "not permissible that males should be present at such intimate affairs [as the birthing]," and "because a woman is not admitted to make inquisition in the king's court," it could not be clear to the court whether the boy was born alive.

Limitations aside, the obligations on jurors in the early days of the Eyre were considered by Maitland and others to be weighty. In their introduction to Selden Society volume 24, *Year Book of the Eyre of Kent, 6 & 7 Edward II (1313–1314)* (1909), Maitland and his fellow editors L. W. V. Harcourt and W. C. Bolland described the articles of the Eyre for the presenting jurors at the Kent Eyre of 1313 as demanding "a complete knowledge of every breach of the law, both criminal and civil, within their several hundreds since the last Eyre, that is since 1294."[20] The editors emphasized that the jurors were required to "cudgel their brains and ransack their memories lest haply they forget one single crime or tort," for "they will amerced [fined] for any omission when the Justices detect it, and detect it they almost certainly will." The jurors "must also be quite sure that every tittle of what they present is the truth, for amercements and fines again await any variation from the strict, provable historical fact."[21] The editors later speculate about how the jurors could possibly inform themselves of all the facts they were expected to know, especially since they did not keep diaries and had no access to court rolls or coroners' rolls. Nevertheless, according to the procedure at the Eyre, "there are the four men and the reeve from every town," and they "may be expected to know something of their own local affairs, and they are there for the special purpose of putting their local knowledge at the service of the jurors."[22] And then "there are the jurors themselves."[23]

As to the jurors themselves, the knowledge standard that the jurors were held to varied in different types of cases. Presenting jurors were more likely to be self-informing than trial jurors. Also, in describing the procedures for the Grand Assize in his introduction to Selden Society volume 77, *Royal Writs in England from the Conquest to Glanvill* (1958–59), R. C. Van Caenegem relies on Glanvill for the proposition that "if the jurors were ignorant, new must be appointed until knowledgeable ones were found."[24] Further, "To be knowledgeable they had to have knowledge of the matters by their own seeing or hearing, or by the word of their fathers or by such indications that deserve the same confidence as their own observations."[25]

In ordinary cases, this strict standard was not applied. C. T. Flower in his *Introduction to the Curia Regis Rolls, 1199–1230,*[26] generalized as follows: "Since the jurors merely told the tale as it occurred to them to tell it, it is possible to say that in some cases they gave evidence, in others they went so far as to state the law, in others they emphasised the fact that they were speaking either of their own knowledge or of hearsay, as the case might be, or even confessed total or partial ignorance of the facts."[27] When the jury confessed ignorance, "Generally the Court made the best it could of such verdicts," usually accepting them if the ignorance was only partial or related to a legal question.[28]

Although it was not necessary for the jurors to be eyewitnesses, there were some such occasions, and these are the clearest self-informing cases. In a King's Bench case, in 1283, the trial jurors spoke of the danger to men who had been wounded in a fierce mêlée over the collection of tithes, and when they were asked how they knew about the danger, they said it was "by this, the coroner who was there with the jury caused the arrow to be drawn from the wound in the presence of some of [the trial jurors]."[29] Similarily, G. O. Sayles, in his introduction to *Select Cases in the*

Court of King's Bench Under Edward I (Vol. III),[30] describes a 1332 contempt case involving an assault upon a man who was coming up the stairs outside the door of the hall of pleas and states that this was "tried by a jury of twenty-four from among those who were present at the time outside and inside the hall."[31] In a 1336 case involving the origin of a letter said to have been delivered at the Castle of York when the county court was there, a jury of twenty-four was impaneled, "as well knights as others etc. from among those who were in the castle on that day."[32]

Apart from eyewitnesses, many examples could be given of cases in which the level of factual detail supplied by the jurors yields a fair inference that at least some of the jurors were well acquainted with the events in dispute.[33] A representative example is a land dispute decided in 1276 by the Court of King's Bench. An assize of novel disseisin had been held at East Grinstead between Matilda of Kingsfold, demandant, and Adam Pinchunne; his wife, Agnes; and two others. Matilda had been forced off her brother Simon's land after his death by Adam and the others on behalf of Adam's wife, Agnes, who was the late Simon's daughter. Simon had maintained Agnes's mother as his wife, and apparently Agnes had been declared by the recognitors to be entitled to inherit Simon's land. The recognitors, Adam, Agnes, and the others were summoned to the King's Bench, where Matilda claimed that the jury "were not examined whether the country considered her [Agnes's mother] his [Simon's] wife or whether he married her in the face of the church or not, wherefore she asks for the jury to be more fully examined upon these articles."[34] Accordingly, the court questioned the jury further, and the jury said that Simon and Agnes's mother had never married—that they had been caught "in fornication" and that, afterwards, Simon promised to marry Agnes's mother but never did so in the face of the church. Thus, Matilda of Kingsfield was declared the heiress.

Community Consensus

As Thomas A. Green observes, some of the early court proceedings "generated a communal sorting-out process that began as soon as the order for the sessions was announced."[35] This is evident in the very first case in the very first Selden Society volume, Maitland's *Select Pleas of the Crown (A.D. 1200–1225)* (1887). Denise, the wife of Anthony, accused Nicholas Kam of killing her husband, and although Denise did not see the killing, "the jurors being asked, say they suspect him of it; the whole county likewise suspects him."[36] In another of Maitland's cases, Christiana claimed that two men killed her husband, one of whom (Ralph) was taken and put in gaol, and that there, according to the sheriff, he died. But "the jurors say that after he was put in gaol, they saw him going about the country"—in fact, "the whole county" said that Christiana withdrew her suit and released Ralph.[37] Interestingly, the jury was apparently not fully informed, because the court required that plaintiff and defendant "be under good pledges" until the court could talk to the person before whom Christiana supposedly withdrew her plea.[38] Most of the cases of this type would have been associated with the Eyre before that process was eliminated in the late thirteenth century.[39] This was not invariably so, as is shown by a 1322 King's Bench case in which the jury was asked whether the plaintiff was guilty of arson, and "the inquest said that it was common knowledge at the time of the taking and therefore said yes."[40]

One of Maitland's cases decided by the King's Bench in 1220 shows both detailed factual assessments and community consensus. One Hamo Moor claimed that Philip King stole a mare from him, but Philip thought the man he had gotten the mare from, Edward, must have stolen it. Edward produced Elis Biggun, who warranted that he sold the mare to Edward. Hamo then accused Elias of having stolen the mare. The jury was formed of eight men of the vill of Cheshunt, eight of the vill of Waltham, eight of Wormley, and eight of Enfield. The eight men of Waltham swore under oath that they believed the mare was foaled to Hamo, for "all the countryside says so."[41] The men of Cheshunt said they did not know if the mare was foaled to Hamo, though they rather thought not, but "they know well that Edward gave her to Philip as a marriage gift," and "they know well that in the presence of the whole parish of Cheshunt, Elias said that he [took up the warranty] for God's sake . . . and not for lucre." But, "As to the marriage portion of Edward's daughter they have heard nothing." The men of Wormley said they knew not whether the mare was foaled to Hamo, but "they know well that Edward gave her as a marriage gift . . . to Philip." And, finally, the eight men of Enfield swore that "they well believe the mare was Hamo's and foaled to him, for all men say so," and "they know well that Elias never sold her to Edward" and that Elias took up the warranty "for money, to wit, for ten marks."

Finally, some cases involved issues that undoubtedly would have been the subject of community gossip, and, although these do not explicitly reflect jurors stating a community consensus, the cases have something of that flavor. In one of Maitland's early cases, a young woman accused two men of robbing her and taking her cloak, but the jury was not persuaded, "And it is testified by the jurors that they [the accused men] did not rob her, and that she is a hireling, and that a man lay with her in a garden, and the boys hooted her, so that she left the cloak and the boys took it and pawned it for two gallons of wine."[42] In a King's Bench case from 1306, the rector of Springthorpe was accused of conspiracy with the vicar of Blyton, but the rector argued that he had merely been trying to clear up the impression that the prior had demanded a larger contribution from his church than was proper.[43] As the editor, G. O. Sayles, accurately summarized, "the jury disposed of this plausible explanation by informing the judges that these two parsons had sent word round to several rectors of churches asking for their co-operation in conspiring against the prior in retaliation for the destruction he had brought upon them."[44]

Partially Informed Juries

I have already referred to situations in which juries might be only partially familiar with the facts of the dispute.[45] More common were cases in which the facts in dispute were known to but a few of the jurors, who then informed the rest. Andrew Horne, in his *Mirror of Justices,* addressed this question when he took up the subject of attaint. Whether Horne's work can be taken seriously is a continuing question,[46] but it is interesting nonetheless to note Horne's claim that, as had been ordained by an ancient assize, if two of the twelve jurors "are by the full verdict of themselves and the other jurors, or (in case all the jurors are not of one opinion) then by good examination of all the jurors, found to be fit witnesses, this is sufficient."[47]

The pattern of two of twelve described by Horne is not evident in any of the Selden Society sources or in Seipp's database, but we do see instances in which only some of the jurors were knowledgeable. Thus, in the general Eyre, as Maitland and his co-editors remind us, the four jurors and the reeve from every town were expected to know something of their own local affairs and were "there for the special purposes of putting their local knowledge at the service of the jurors."[48] Also, in the days of the general Eyre, trial juries were made up at least partially by the presenting jurors, and the presenting jurors came from the hundreds in which the crimes were committed.[49]

In a 1292 King's Bench action alleging false and malicious testimony at a Nottingham gaol, the court ordered a jury of "twelve of the more lawful and discreet men of the whole county of Nottingham, six of whom should be knights girt with the sword, and also twelve of the more lawful and discreet knights of the body of the county, who were present at the gaol delivery."[50] Obviously, the twelve who were at the gaol delivery would inform the other twelve about what happened.

Jury Composition, Geography, and Local Knowledge

In *Gyse v. Baudewyne,*[51] the plaintiff accused the defendant of forcibly abducting (ravishing) his wife, but the defendant claimed that the woman was his own wife, not the plaintiff's. Defendant's attorney prayed that the case be inquired by a jury of "the place where the espousals were made," but the Chief Justice said that "It is not for this court to inquire as to where the espousals were made, nor will we direct the bishop to inquire whether she was your wife." The issue was joined and the case was sent to the jury, but the report of the case ends by stating: "And note that the jury was not to come from the neighborhood where the espousals [with the defendant] were said to have taken place. And this is hard [upon him]."[52]

As the *Gyse* case shows, securing a jury from the neighborhood where the facts would most readily be known was thought to be an important protection for an accused party. This concern is prominently displayed in cases where the factual events straddled two locations. Frequently, this resulted in the formation of mixed juries from both locations, examples of which can be found well into the fifteenth century.

In a 1442 Common Pleas case, for example, plaintiff claimed that defendant assaulted him at one place; defendant responded that plaintiff assaulted him at another place; and the *venire facias* was awarded to bring jurors from both venues, both of which were in the same county.[53] In another assault case, the incident began in one county, and the defendant ran away into another county, where the plaintiff followed and resumed the fight. The writ was filed in the second county, and, after debate, by order of Chief Justice Prysot, the *venire facias* was awarded to be tried by both counties.[54]

More difficult than the assault cases were disputes about entitlement to land, which in turn raised questions of bastardy or the age of a party at the time of a claimed marriage. In these cases, the land would be at one place and the birthplace or marriage place at another. The usual method in such situations was to impanel a jury constituted of jurors from both places.[55] This was not the invariable outcome, as there were differences of views among the justices.[56] Yet, within practical limits, the notion that the jury should be formed from the location likely to produce the best local knowledge persisted well into the late fifteenth century.[57]

Early Cases Containing Evidence Beyond Juror Knowledge[58]

In volume 34 of the Selden Society series, the editors, Paul Vinogradoff and Ludwik Ehrlich, mention two cases as "interesting for the history of trial by jury: they show that by 1312–1313 evidence of witnesses and of documents used to be produced by the parties before the assize and that counsel addressed the latter in interpretation of evidence."[59] This may be too sweeping a generalization, judging at least by the cases cited in support. The report of the first case, *Atte Gracechurch v. Selmerie,* merely indicates that counsel made statements "in evidence to the assize" but says nothing about witnesses.[60] In the other case, the report states that "the party put forward a fine in evidence to the inquisition," but the fine was refused because "it would have been a bar if it had been put forward (before so that) the inquisition would not have been joined."[61]

Another early-fourteenth-century case, however—this one in Morris Arnold's first volume of *Select Cases of Trespass from the King's Courts 1307–1399*[62]—is unusually explicit. In *Reynham v. Hatton,*[63] the defendants' attorney produced a written deed by the plaintiff releasing defendants from all actions and demands plaintiff had against them. The release was witnessed by five men from Surrey. At trial, after jurors were chosen by consent of the parties, four of the five witnesses to the release "come along with the aforesaid jurors and are likewise sworn."[64] The jurors later reported that they examined each of the four witnesses "by himself and separately," and, because the witnesses "disagree in their statements in all respects," the purported deed of release was rejected. Then, "in order that the truth of this deed be known more openly and evidently," the justices called the four witnesses before them, examined each one separately, and agreed wholeheartedly with the jury, ordering that "the statements of the aforesaid witnesses be regarded as frivolous and held for naught."[65]

In his contribution to the British legal history conference in Edinburgh, in 1999,[66] David Seipp summarizes what the Year Books tell us about evidence that juries of the fourteenth and fifteenth centuries might legitimately consider other than their own knowledge. He gives numerous Year Book examples in which writings such as deeds and charters were presented by the parties in open court, and the jurors took the writings with them during their deliberations.[67] If a deed or a charter was disputed and the document had attesting witnesses, those witnesses would be summoned to court and sworn, and, as in the *Reynham* case, they also went with the jurors during their deliberations.[68] Nevertheless, as Seipp cautions, there were rules about what the parties and their counsel could and could not do.[69]

In a 1315 King's Bench action,[70] for example, the report states that one of the jurors of the inquisition, Roger de la Leye, had received outside of court and before being placed on oath, but for the information of his fellow jurors, a charter of King Henry, which Roger got from one Robert Moysent. Roger and Robert acknowledged this in court, and both were committed to the marshal, after which they "made fine with the King."[71] Later in the century, an attaint was heard by the King's Bench pertaining to the Sussex assizes of June 18, 1389.[72] The issue at the trial was whether John Wantley had been unlawfully disseised by the five defendants of Wantley's free tenements in Horsham, and recognitors were summoned. When they came to give their verdict, "the justices were given to understand that, after the recognitors had departed from the court to discuss among themselves their aforesaid verdict, they received various pieces of evidence outside the court from the aforesaid John Wantley."[73] The recognitors were examined under oath, and they admitted that, after they had left court to discuss their verdict among themselves, "they sent a certain Henry atte More to the aforesaid John Wantley to get certain court rolls so that they could have information therefrom for the purpose of declaring their verdict."[74] Wantley complied with the jurors' request, sending the court rolls by his serjeant, one "Richard atte Lawe." Henry atte More and Richard atte Lawe were present in court and admitted these things under oath, after which the recognitors were "completely discharged from declaring their verdict," and "the twelve recognitors . . . as well as Richard atte More and Richard atte Lawe, [were] committed to prison." Each of the jurors paid a fine of 3s. 4d. before being released. Richard atte More and Richard atte Lawe paid fines of twice this amount.

John Wantley at first asked for a jury trial, but eventually settled by paying a fine of 20s.[75]

An alternative to bringing outside evidence or witnesses into court was to adjourn the trial and instruct the jurors to investigate the matter in dispute further. According to the indictment in a murder case, in 1380, the coroner and the sheriffs of London summoned a jury from Langbourne ward and its three adjacent wards and, after having them view the body of the victim, inquired of the jurors "how and in what way he came to his death."[76] The jurors said that they were "at the moment completely ignorant" of who the malefactors were or how the slayings had been committed.[77] The case was put over to the following week to give the jurors time to inquire more fully, but by the following Monday the jurors had discovered nothing more, so they were ordered to come again approximately a month later. When they returned as ordered, they recounted the details of a quarrel and identified and indicted the accused murderers.

A last case with regard to educating the jury beyond its own knowledge is too colorful to omit. In 1390, before the Court of King's Bench, a dispute concerning the right to certain tenements had been tried at the Norwich assizes before John Cassy, Chief Baron of the Court of Exchequer.[78] After the case had been heard and the jurors had retired to deliberate, Baron Cassy learned that there was a stranger in the room with the jurors. Cassy summoned the jurors, who explained that, since they did not know how to read or understand deeds that had been delivered to them in evidence, one of the jurors found the stranger (whose name they did not know) and brought him in to read the deeds and to explain them to the jurors "in the mother tongue." The juror who had procured the stranger was committed to the marshal and paid a fine, but the Court of King's Bench decided that the other jurors were innocent and could proceed with the trial.[79]

Community Custom

Early juries often articulated and applied community customs. This role is close cousin to the primary purpose of juries of merchants, both those from the medieval trade fairs and staple towns and early modern merchant juries in London. Several of the Selden Society volumes are devoted to cases in which juries declared and applied local customs, such as Mary

Bateson's two volumes on thirteenth- and fourteenth-century Borough Customs[80] and Maitland's *Select Pleas in Manorial Courts.*[81] A smattering of community-custom determinations by juries also runs through other volumes in the Society's series. In a 1283 King's Bench case, for example, an abbot alleged extortion against a countess, and a jury was impaneled to ascertain the prevailing customs, which they declared in detail. They were even asked to state what was meant in those parts by "court" and by "hundred." They responded that a court is a place where knights and freemen come together and do suit every three weeks for their tenements and discuss the pleas that belong to the court baron and likewise the pleas that belong to the sheriff by the returns of writs.[82] Further, "They call a hundred the meeting of males over twelve years of age, with the exception of ecclesiastics, twice a year to maintain the peace of the Lord King, where there is no pleading but presentments only are made of the articles of the Crown."[83]

Declaring local customs is not quite the same as coming to court with factual knowledge, but it is analogous. Indeed, the odds seem higher that local jurors would be equipped to declare local custom than that they would have in hand the facts of a specific dispute.

Conclusion

Reports of presentments and trials from the thirteenth through the fifteenth centuries confirm the validity of the expression "self-informing jury." The sense of the cases is that practical methods were used to determine what happened. Sometime the jurors came to court sufficiently informed to reach a judgment without help. Sometimes the cases were adjourned so that the jurors or the court, or both, could investigate. And, at other times, the jurors, while in court, were given relevant documents and questioned the parties. Underlying the process was a consensus that the first and best step was to find jurors—some, at least—who had personal knowledge of the facts. To that extent, the self-informing jury can be thought of as a primitive version of the jury of experts.

7

The English Origins of the Special Jury

Special juries do not exist, as many people seem to suppose, by the authority of a modern statute; on the contrary, they are as ancient as the law itself, and were always struck, as they are at this day, by direction of the Court, when trials were had at the bar and not at *nisi prius*. —Thomas Erskine, Esq., November 15, 1793[1]

During the eighteenth and nineteenth centuries, the special jury emerged in English common and statutory law as a familiar feature of the civil trial.[2] Ordinarily, the term "special jury" appeared in case reports and statutes without explanation or definition, suggesting that the concept was widely understood.[3] As the Erskine quotation indicates, however, the origins of the special jury were not well understood as of the late eighteenth century, never having been subjected to careful historical study.[4]

Close examination of the usage of the term "special jury" since its appearance in cases and legal literature during the second half of the seventeenth century reveals two fundamental points. First, a special jury might satisfy any or all of the following definitions: a jury of individuals of higher social class than usual; a jury of experts; and a "struck jury," that is, one formed by a special procedure that allowed the parties to strike names from an unusually large panel of prospective jurors.[5] Second, various juries were formed before and after the seventeenth century that met the first two of these definitions, even though these juries were never expressly denominated "special." For example, in cases of national importance, grand juries have often been made up of leading citizens.[6] The same was true of petit juries in cases that involved such issues as high treason or seditious libel.[7] Juries of experts ranged from panels of cooks and fishmongers[8] to the all-female jury impaneled to ascertain whether a female defendant was pregnant.[9] Only the third definition, the struck jury, came to be consistently identified as the special jury.

This chapter traces the history of all three useages of "special jury" from the earliest era for which meaningful records were accessible to 1730, the year of Parliament's first significant enactment concerning the special jury.[10] Part I deals with the first two kinds of special juries identified: juries of higher-than-ordinary social standing and juries of persons with special knowledge or expertise. Part II examines the characteristics of the struck jury, culminating in its statutory recognition in 1730. The continuing history of the special jury in England until its disappearance in the late twentieth century follows, in chapter 8.

I. Qualifications of Jurors

Several identifiable objectives recur in the statutes and rules of court that establish qualifications for jurors. First, the statutes and rules sought to ensure that persons of understanding and intelligence served on juries, even though the level of concern varied according to the nature and importance of the litigation. Second, they sought to ensure that jurors had sufficient wealth to be presumptively immune from bribery. Third, they sought to curtail the avoidance of jury service by "men of quality." These measures were also meant to prevent impaneling officers—usually sheriffs and coroners—from manipulating jury panels or from accepting payoffs from persons who wished to avoid jury service.

A. The Problem of Filling Juries with Capable Individuals

Encomiums heaped upon the English jury by law writers over the centuries presuppose the availability of able, intelligent men to serve as jurors.[11] This unrealistic presumption is well illustrated in Sir John Hawles's seventeenth-century tract, *The Englishman's Right: A Dialogue Between a Barrister at Law and a Juryman.*[12] Among the qualifications Hawles gave for the common juror was "to read, and understand, the fundamental laws of the country," such as the Magna Carta, the Petition of Right, and the "late, excellent act for Habeas Corpus's."[13] Hawles recommended also, as "books frequent to be had, and of excellent use to inform any reader of competent apprehension," Horne's *Mirror of Justices*, Coke's *Institutes*, and *Vaughan's Reports*.[14]

Other sources, however, portray common jurors as a dismal rabble. A 1607 Proclamation for Jurors issued by James I declared that jury service "oftentimes resteth upon such as are either simple and ignorant, and almost at a gaze in any cause of difficulty," or else upon those who "are so accustomed and inured to pass and serve upon Juries, and they have almost lost that tenderness of Conscience, which in such cases is to be wished, and make the service, as it were an occupation and practice."[15] Later seventeenth-century voices were heard to the same effect. Thus, John March, after discussing the characteristics enumerated by Coke as desirable in jurors, observed: "Yet for all this, when I again consider what weak and ignorant Juries are for the most part returned, I cannot sufficiently wonder and lament, that men's lives and fortunes should depend upon such men's verdicts."[16]

This problem often was attributed to corrupt sheriffs, who excused all who could afford to pay, leaving only the poor and the ignorant to serve on juries.[17] Several of the jury statutes identified in Appendix 4 reflect this theme. For example, in "An Act against Sheriffs for abuses,"[18] Parliament referred to "great extortions and oppressions" caused by "subtle and untrue demeanor of Sheriffs and their ministers" and as a remedy provided that justices of the peace at criminal quarter sessions might reform jury panels to ensure panels that were "good and lawful."[19]

Parliament did not solve the problem. As James Cockburn observed in his invaluable history of English assizes, sheriffs and undersheriffs in the mid-seventeenth century "were repeatedly censured . . . for returning insufficient freeholders for jury service, and ordered to compile new books of freeholders."[20] More particularly, "seventeenth-century undersheriffs commonly oscillated between two equally unacceptable courses: they either warned indiscriminately all the county's freeholders to attend for jury service, or failed to summon any at all. In consequence bailiffs customarily took up 'men of all sorts' at assize time to form the tales de circumstantibus[21] by which deficient juries might be made up."[22]

The evidence is not entirely one-sided and is subject to demographic variations. In his study of seventeenth-century grand-jury practice in Cheshire, John Morrill concluded that grand jurymen "came from a coherent social group, the middling freeholders . . . [who] were separated from the humbler freeholders less by wealth than by official recognition of their capacity to perform disinterested tasks for the good of the local community."[23] In Cheshire, moreover, "trial juries were drawn from exactly the same group as grand juries. The point is worth making because it has been commonly assumed that trial juries comprised men of lower status."[24] But if not one-sided, the evidence is surely lopsided in suggesting a more than occasional problem throughout the seventeenth century and earlier in obtaining honest and intelligent jurymen.

B. Juror Qualifications: Property-Holding and Quality

1. Specific Property Requirements

As stated by the authors of a mid-seventeenth-century text on jury trial, "It is the general course of the World, to esteem men according to their Estate"; thus the law requiring jurors to be property holders[25] was justified, "for if men of less Estates should serve in Juries," they would be only those who "had more need to be relieved by the 8d.[26] than discretion to sift out the truth."[27]

During and after the reign of Elizabeth I, Parliament sought to ensure that jurors were men of property. As John Baker has explained, "According to medieval thinking, the likelihood of corruption varied in inverse proportion to wealth, and so the root cause of perjury in jurors was considered to be the impanelling of men of insufficient substance. . . . A typical fifteenth century reaction to the prevalence of corruption was to make the qualification even more exclusive."[28]

In Appendix 4, I tabulate all attempts by Parliament from Magna Carta until 1730 to produce responsible and effective jurors. As the table indicates, Parliament experimented with a variety of formulae in different courts and in different types of cases, but a forty-shilling requirement was the general rule in the central courts for more than three centuries. The statute of 27 Eliz. 1, c.6 (1584–85),[29] doubled the standard to four pounds, and the new figure was retained for almost eighty years. Then, in 1664, Parliament raised the requirement to twenty pounds "for reformation of abuses in Sheriffs and other Ministers, who for reward do oftentimes spare the ablest and sufficientist, and return the poorer and simpler Freeholders less able to discern the Causes in question, and to bear the charges of appearance and attendance thereon."[30] By its own terms, the new requirement expired thirteen years later,[31] after which, presumably, the four-pound requirement of the statute of 27 Eliz. 1, c.6, revived. But, in 1692, expressly as a replacement for the expired twenty-pound rule of the statute of 16 & 17 Car. 2, c.3, § 1 (1664–65), Parliament required a ten-pound freehold for jurors in all central courts (at Westminster, on assize, and at *nisi prius*), as well as in quarter sessions, oyer and terminer, and gaol delivery,[32] cities and towns excepted.[33] This standard remained in effect until 1972,[34] though intermittently Parliament determined that certain leasehold or personal property holdings were the equivalents of the ten-pound freehold for purposes of jury qualification.[35]

Overall, the freehold requirements[36] were, if not a complete failure as a method to ensure honest and intelligent jurymen, of very limited value. The statutes suffered from two familiar problems—ineffective enforcement and obsolescence. John Baker contends that increasingly higher property qualifications helped to foster underenforcement; the higher qualifications "made it difficult for sheriffs in some parts of the country to find enough men to return, a difficulty which was exacerbated by the habit of selling exemptions,"[37] leading in turn to a reduction in the property qualification.[38] The property requirement for nonurban areas, however, was not decreased; it was doubled during Elizabeth I's reign.[39] Moreover, the sheriff's exemption of the richer freeholders occasionally overloaded the jury panels with poorer freeholders who then faced the choice of buying their way off the panel or, "by delays and by adjournments, being kept for a week or a fortnight, so that they lose their work and are wholly impoverished."[40]

In contrast, the jurors who were required to travel from outlying counties to Westminster cannot have been poor, given the time and expense involved in the journey, for which they were not reimbursed.[41] Most country jurymen preferred to risk a fine for nonappearance rather than undertake the journey, since the fine, if assessed, probably would be less than the expense of the trip.[42] As George Sayles observed, "The declaration that no jury came is one of the most monotonous commonplaces of the records [of the Westminster courts]."[43]

Instead of locating and fining nonappearing jurors, another way to enforce the property qualification was to amerce (fine) the sheriff for returning panels of unqualified jurors. Few cases that followed this approach are reported.[44] Perhaps one reason why there are not more reported cases is the availability of a simpler enforcement mechanism. It was universally accepted that parties could challenge prospective jurors for failure to meet the freehold requirement, thereby ensuring that only qualified men served. How frequently the right was exercised is uncertain.[45]

Even if challenges of prospective jurors had effectively enforced the property qualification, the problem of obsolescence remained. A fixed property qualification was of limited utility in the face of the constantly changing value of money. Writing in the 1560s,[46] Sir Thomas Smith described "yeomen" as those "next unto the nobility, knights and squires . . . [who] are more travailed to serve in [the commonwealth] than all the rest."[47] He then added, "I call him a yeoman whom our laws do call Legalem hominem, a word familiar in writs and enquests, which is a freeman born English, and may dispend of his own free land in yearly revenue to sum of xl. s. sterling: This maketh (if the just value were taken now to the proportion of monies) vi. l. [£] of our current money at this present."[48]

Using Smith's rate of inflation, the forty-shilling requirement of the statute of 2 Hen. 5, Stat. 2, c.3 (1414), had been devalued threefold by, for example, 1560.[49] Yet, it was not until twenty-five years later that Parliament nominally increased the property requirement to four pounds.[50]

In his seventeenth-century treatise, *The Office and Authority of Sheriffs,* Michael Dalton incorporated Smith's devaluation rate, noting that the old forty-shilling requirement "doth make at this present, at the least six pounds of our money."[51] Dalton did not speculate on the comparative value of seventeenth-century money, but Edward Waterhous did in his commentary on Fortescue, published in 1663.[52] Observing that, in Fortescue's time (around 1470), forty shillings may have served as a measure of property "somewhat considerable, as a convenient support to life, and a delivery of the Possessor from temptation to perjury," Waterhous argued that the value of a juryman's fortune should be enhanced "according to the value of Rents, and Prizes now; (40 l. a year being as little for a Free-holder now to have in Estate, as 40 s. then)."[53] If Waterhous's parenthetical comparison was accurate,[54] the four-pound requirement of 1584[55] had become a trifle, and even the increase to ten pounds in 1692[56] would have been quite small. Working the comparison backward, the four- and ten-pound requirements would, in fifteenth-century money, be worth two and ten shillings, respectively. Whatever the exact comparisons, it seems fair to conclude that the property qualification declined in real value from the sixteenth century on. Parliament allowed the 1664 increase to twenty pounds to expire, and proposals for a major increase in the property qualification never succeeded.[57]

2. General Quality Requirements

Edward Waterhous admonished the sheriffs to take notice "that the King's Courts of Justice are never . . . better pleased, than when they see Panels and returns of Knights, Esquires and Gentlemen, of rank and quality before them."[58] If statutory property qualifications did not produce able jurymen, other methods were available. There is a long history of attempted control over jury quality by the king, the court, and the parties.

a. Juries of Knights Coke observed that, in ancient times, juries consisted entirely of knights.[59] Jury service by knights on the grand assize was standard medieval procedure,[60] but, as C. T. Flower noted, knights "also formed the backbone of juries in possessory assizes."[61] On occasion they were put on a jury by royal order[62] and on occasion by judicial order.[63] Before the invention of techniques to force a recalcitrant prisoner to plead how he would be tried,[64] courts on a number of occasions ordered strong juries when a defendant either stood mute or expressly refused to put himself upon the country.[65] These "strong juries" ordinarily consisted of twenty-four knights,[66] but on at least one occasion "a specially strong jury of thirty-six" was impaneled.[67]

b. State Trials The medieval concern about the service of knights on juries occurred in unexceptional cases. Later, in cases of importance to the government, it became common to impanel "special" trial juries of "men of quality and substance." A brief survey of the decisions reported in *State Trials* illustrates this pattern. In scores of such cases, including some of the most notorious trials in English history, juries consisted of knights, esquires, or gentlemen.[68]

Occasionally, the court took part overtly in jury selection. The report of Lady Alice Lisle's trial, in 1685, for high treason notes that "it being a cause of great expectation and moment, the lord chief justice[69] ordered the sheriff to take care, that a very substantial jury should be returned, of the best quality in the county."[70]

When defendants requested substantial juries, they had mixed success. In his felony trial at the Croydon assizes, in 1590, the Puritan minister John Udall stated, "I do desire to be tried by an inquest of learned men; but seeing I shall not, I am contented to be tried by the ordinary course, as these men before me are, that is, as you use to say, by God and the country."[71] But, in the proceedings against William Acton for murder in

1729,[72] the crown solicitor unsuccessfully sought to avoid drawing a second jury from the same panel that had produced a jury that acquitted Acton in his first trial.[73] Defense counsel's response to the crown solicitor's attempt was that "The other panel[74] cannot write; these are men of ability and experience."[75]

Further, in the trial of the elderly Sir Thomas Gascoigne, baronet, for high treason, Gascoigne requested "a jury of gentlemen, of persons of my own quality, and of my own country, that may be able to know something how I have lived hitherto,"[76] to which Lord Chief Justice Scroggs replied: "Tell him he shall have a good jury of gentlemen of his own country."[77] The jury sworn consisted of one knight and eleven esquires,[78] despite the remark by the Attorney General, "I perceive the best gentlemen stay at home," and the response by Serjeant Maynard, "Yes, it is so small a business."[79]

The cases in *State Trials* demonstrate that, in lawsuits of national importance, jury panels of well-bred men were returned almost as a matter of course. Although the precise dynamics remain obscure except in those few instances of overt directions from the crown or the court, it is clear that the sheriff was the key to the impaneling process. Customarily, he decided how large a panel should be returned in crown cases[80] and who should be on the panel. Jury composition could be influenced in this manner much more effectively than by statutory property qualifications. The practice did not necessarily produce juries predisposed toward guilty verdicts, but it may have tended in that direction. The commoner was not convinced that a jury of men of quality "chosen" by the impaneling officer secured a fair trial, despite the availability of challenges; he was more apt to suspect that such jurymen were partial to the crown.[81] This was true of both petit[82] and grand juries,[83] in trials at Westminster Hall[84] and on assize.[85] Indeed, accusations of jury-packing invariably accompanied trial by jury, of whatever kind.[86]

3. Specific Traditions Requiring Jurors of High Social Standing

Parliamentary legislation and efforts by the court, the crown, and the parties show a long history of concern for ensuring able jurors. In addition, it was well established that specific types of cases or inquests required juries made up wholly or partially of "men of quality."[87]

a. The Grand Assize A defendant in possession of disputed land could invoke the grand assize[88] as an alternative to trial by battle.[89] The grand assize was distinguished by its special composition and method of selection. As stated by C. T. Flower, "The mere fact that the jurors had to be knights gave the grand assise a pre-eminence, since freedom was a sufficient qualification for jurors under the possessory assises."[90] Pollock and Maitland make clear that the jury in the grand assize was, originally at least, only the twelve knights impaneled; the four knights who selected them did not participate in the verdict.[91]

Assembling four knights as selectors and twelve knights as jurymen was no simple task, but the requirements were flexible. Even in the formative years of the grand assize, it is noted in Glanvill that, with the consent of the parties, the court might award that, although all four knights had not come, one of them might elect the twelve by joining with two or three other knights of the same county if any such could be found in court, even if they were not summoned for that purpose.[92]

Much later, in his *Commentaries upon Original Writs,* William Hughes described a case in which the sheriff returned two knights and two serjeants as selectors, because "there were not more Knights within the County who were not of affinity to the one [party] or to the other."[93] Acknowledged to be an insufficient return, the court allowed it to stand *ex assensu partium,*[94] with Hughes adding, "and yet it was conceived, that if the Sheriff had returned Gentlemen, and called them Knights, it was sufficient, and not traversable whether they were Knights or not."[95]

Over time, the grand assize atrophied, but it was not formally abolished until the nineteenth century.[96] Both in terms of the unusual quality of the jurors and the special selection procedure, the grand assize can be viewed as an antecedent to the later development of the special jury.

b. Attaint From the thirteenth to the sixteenth centuries, the writ of attaint hovered over common jurors in civil actions, admonishing them to behave honestly. The attaint "consisted in summoning a jury of twenty-four, and the proceedings were not merely a reconsideration of the facts in dispute, but also a criminal trial of the first jury for perjury."[97] If found guilty, the original jury faced severe punishment: "They were imprisoned for a year, forfeited their goods, became infamous, their wives and children were turned out, and their lands laid waste."[98]

The relevance of the attaint to this study lies again in the special quality of the attaint jurors.[99] Fortescue observed that the jurors of attaint were to be persons "having much greater patrimony than the first jurors,"[100] and the statutory property qualifications support his statement. In 1436, Parliament passed a requirement that attaint jurors each possess a twenty-pound freehold in cases involving pleas of land worth more than fifteen shillings or pleas of personalty worth more than forty pounds.[101] City and borough courts were excepted,[102] but, near the end of the fifteenth century, Parliament required attaint jurors in London to have one hundred pounds in real or personal property.[103] During the first half of the sixteenth century, the various property-holding requirements for attaint jurors were reduced somewhat, but they remained substantially higher than the requirements for common jurors.[104]

c. The Grand Jury The accepted wisdom of the law writers of the seventeenth century held that members of the grand jury were generally men of "Great Worth,"[105] who were "ingenious and learned."[106] Zachary Babington observed that grand jurors might be "called Grand in respect of the quality of their Persons, and greatness of their Estates, ability of their Judgments (being of good Education)."[107]

Doubtless, these characteristics were present on occasion, such as in cases reported in *State Trials*. For example, in *Rex v. Messenger*,[108] the defendants were indicted after "having been several times examined, upon confession of some, and pregnant proof against others, by a special jury of several knights, esquires and gentlemen, of very great worth and esteem, of the county of Middlesex."[109] Similarly, Bishop Burnet describes the grand jury that shocked the court by returning an ignoramus bill[110] against Lord Shaftesbury[111] as having been "composed of many of the chief citizens of London."[112]

Nevertheless, after extensive research on sixteenth- to early-eighteenth-century assize calendars, Cockburn concludes that William Blackstone's contention that grand juries in his day usually consisted of "gentlemen of the best figure in the county" is not true of earlier centuries. Respected local freeholders—those "sufficient inhabitants" on whom community service as tithingmen, constables, and coroners rested so heavily—with a leavening of junior magistrates and lesser gentlemen would perhaps describe more adequately the composition of sixteenth- and seventeenth-century grand juries.[113] Other recent work on the grand jury confirms Cockburn's conclusion.[114]

C. Juror Qualifications: Special Knowledge or Expertise

Jurors with qualifications other than minimum property holdings traditionally were impaneled in certain types of cases. One such type (matrons) has been fully discussed in chapter 5. Jurors in these cases have been "special," even if not so called, because they were selected for their particular knowledge or expertise. Another example from the late eighteenth and early nineteenth centuries is addressed in chapter 8—juries of merchants who were well versed in mercantile customs and who helped articulate and organize principles of commercial law.[115] These uses of the jury as a resource of particular knowledge were not new. As Thayer stated, "[w]hat we call the 'special jury' seems always to have been used. It was a natural result of the principle that those were to be summoned who could best tell the fact, the *veritatem rei.*"[116] These juries included not only jurors supposedly knowledgeable of the facts in dispute but also jurors who had special expertise or understanding.

1. Hundredors

As is discussed in chapter 6, originally jurors were presumed to know the facts in dispute because they were residents of the vicinity where the dispute arose. The early statutes called for jurors who were "next Neighbours,"[117] those who "have best Knowledge of the Truth, and be nearest."[118] In time, the concept that all jurors be "next Neighbours" proved unworkable. The diluted variation that arose required that each common jury contain a certain number of "hundredors."[119] The term "hundred" escapes uniform definition, but historically it refers to a subdivision of a county, measured either by a number of villages or by population.[120] According to Dalton, "hundredors be men impanelled, or fit to be impanelled upon a Jury for any Controversy, and dwelling within the Hundred where the Land lieth, which is in question, &c. whereby they (by intendment of Law) may have Notice *de rei veritate,* or better knowledge of the Cause."[121]

Coke reported that common law required four hundredors to be on a jury "in a plea real, mixt, and personal."[122] The statute of 35 Hen. 8, c.6 (1543–44)[123] altered this rule by requiring that six hundredors be returned on *nisi prius* panels, if available "within the said hundred where the Venue lieth."[124] During Elizabeth I's reign, Parliament decreed that the appearance of two hundredors would suffice in trials of personal actions.[125] In 1705, Parliament eliminated altogether the requirement of hundredors for civil cases.[126]

Of special interest to this study are the cases in which one party challenged the jury for want of hundredors after both parties had formed the jury through the struck-jury procedure. Some judges were naturally irked to receive such a challenge when hundredors on the panel had been struck off the panel by one of the parties. During the seventeenth century, the King's Bench allowed two such challenges,[127] but the Court of Exchequer ruled otherwise. Chief Baron Hale stated that "It is against the common course to take a challenge for want of hundredors . . . where there are but twenty-four left by the parties themselves."[128] Later, in the 1724 decision of *Rex v. Burridge*,[129] the King's Bench held that when the parties consented to the rule for a special jury, they impliedly waived their rights to challenge for want of hundredors.[130]

By the mid-sixteenth century, it was fanciful to view the hundredor requirement as likely to produce jurymen who were "experts" in the sense of being especially knowledgeable about the facts in dispute. Arguably, the requirement never had this effect but was merely a transitional device that preserved the appearance of the old jury of witnesses while the jury assumed its new role of deciding the facts based on evidence presented in court.

2. Jurors in Trials of Aliens, Clerics, and Others

Another specially constituted jury long present in the law pertained to trials of aliens or foreigners. An alien had the right in most cases to request a trial *de medietate linguae*.[131] Thayer observed that "The jury of the 'half-tongue,' *de medietate linguae*, was founded on considerations of policy and fair dealing, rather than a wish to provide a well-informed jury."[132] Undoubtedly, the concept was akin to the sentiment expressed by Sir Thomas Gascoigne in his request for "a jury . . . of my own country, that may be able to know something how I have lived hitherto."[133]

The tradition was old and varied and was not limited to the central courts. Parliament provided an early articulation of the principle in the following 1354 enactment:

> And that in all Manner of Inquests and Proofs which be to be taken or made amongst Aliens and Denizens, be they Merchants or other, as well before the Mayor of the Staple as before any other Justices or Ministers, although the King be Party, the one half of the Inquest or Proof shall be

> Denizens, and the other half of Aliens, if so many Aliens [and Foreigners] be in the Town or Place where such Inquest or Proof is to be taken.[134]

The statutory reference to the Mayor of the Staple reveals antecedents from the law merchant.[135] An inquest before the staple courts "was to consist wholly of aliens when both parties to the suit were aliens; wholly of denizens when both parties were denizens; and half of aliens and half of denizens when one party was an alien and the other a denizen."[136] And, as Hubert Hall observed, "These juries of 'the half tongue' were no new expedient, for even Jews had long ago received this right."[137] The right to which Hall referred is documented by J. M. Rigg in his study of the thirteenth-century rolls of the Exchequer of the Jews.[138] The Exchequer of the Jews was essentially a branch of the central Court of Exchequer, with similar procedures, the most important modification being "the right of a Jew to trial by a panel 'de medietate' when impleaded by a Christian upon a cause of action arising within the Jewry."[139]

There were other variants. Mary Bateson identified fourteenth-century borough customs that called for a jury of which half the members were burgesses in the trial of any burgess outside the borough.[140] In general, the "half-tongue" principle applied to Welsh defendants, though not to Scots.[141] Further applications occurred in the university and ecclesiastical courts. Blackstone observed that when a university scholar was indicted at the assizes or elsewhere for treason, felony, or mayhem, the vice-chancellor of the university could claim jurisdiction, and the resulting trial was before the high steward and a jury formed "*de medietate*"—half from a panel of eighteen freeholders returned by the sheriff and half from a panel of eighteen matriculated laymen returned by the beadles of the university.[142] And, under a writ of *jure patronatus* concerning church patronage, the dispute could be tried by the bishop or by a specially appointed commission, before "a Jury of six Clergymen and six Laymen of the Neighbourhood, or of as many more as the Bishop pleases; the Proportion being observed of Clergy and Laity, that there be as many of one Sort, as the other."[143]

It is clear that the *de medietate* concept, known also in the literature as a "party jury,"[144] had wide application. Although there are other interpretations,[145] Thayer was surely correct in suggesting that the concept grew out of notions of fair dealing,[146] spurred primarily by the idea that some members of the jury should speak the defendant's language.[147] The practice books give examples of *venires* calling for the aliens to be natives of the defendant's country, sometimes even of the defendant's city of residence.[148] Yet, this practice did not persist. Pulton observed that the trial *per medietatem linguae*[149] was available at the king's grant even before the statutes of 27 Edw. 3, Stat. 2 (1353)[150] and 28 Edw. 3, c.13 (1354), but, because the statute of 27 Edw. 3, Stat. 2, applied only to civil actions in staple towns,[151] it "did not remedy the mischief, where the king was party."[152] Thus, "the before rehearsed statute of 28 E. 3. was provided, which maketh mention generally of aliens: therefore it is not material of what nation those aliens are."[153] Eventually, it would suffice for each of the six alien jurors to be from a different nation.[154] This ludicrous image of a polyglot jury is hardly consistent with the original justification for this type of trial.

There was additional erosion of the concept. By statute, trial *de medietate* was unavailable to "Egyptians," that is, to rogues and vagabonds commonly known as gypsies.[155] Likewise, this privilege was unavailable in treason trials,[156] in actions or suits that concerned statutes that regulated imports and exports,[157] and in inquests to assess damages by a writ of inquiry upon a default judgment taken against an alien.[158] The privilege was also inapplicable to grand juries,[159] and, if a defendant in a criminal action pleaded not guilty and allowed a common jury to be returned, he waived his right to a party jury.[160]

By the late eighteenth century, therefore, the party jury had become more form than substance, even though it was still available. Perhaps never viewed as a jury of experts, the party jury emerged to ensure a jury able to understand the point of view of the alien party. In this sense, its animating spirit was similar to that of the special jury of the eighteenth century.

3. Other Experts

In chapter 8, the instrumental use of merchant juries in the late eighteenth century by Lord Mansfield in the Court of King's Bench, continuing in the nineteenth century under Lord Ellenborough and other judges, is explained. Merchant juries, however, existed long before Lord Mansfield. In some instances, merchant status ensured quality rather than expertise,[161] but usually it was otherwise. The distant heritage, of course, was the law merchant. Thus, "In a Court of Piepowders the trial is by the Merchants."[162] And the Carta Mercatoria of Edward I (1303) provided that a foreign merchant might have six foreign merchants on the jury.[163] Many examples of juries of merchants, or "merchants and next neighbors," can be found in the thirteenth-century records of the Fair Court of St. Ives.[164]

Given this background, the regular use of merchant juries would be expected in the central courts during the sixteenth and seventeenth centuries, a period when legal questions of mercantile importance appeared with increasing frequency. Writing in the mid-seventeenth century, Matthew Hale observed that, when a question of *lex mercatoria* arose in the common-law courts, "if it be a question touching the custom of merchants, merchants are usually jurors at the request of either party."[165]

Nevertheless, few reports of such cases exist.[166] In his *Regestrum Practicale,*[167] William Style mentions a 1646 King's Bench decision in which the court granted a motion for "a Jury of Merchants . . . to try an issue between two Merchants, touching Merchants affairs," because "they might have better knowledge of matters in difference which was to be tryed, than others could who were not of that profession."[168] In the 1649 case of *Pickering v. Barkley,*[169] the court held that a contract was to be interpreted according to the custom of merchants and summoned merchants to decide the issue.[170]

Assorted cases can be identified that indicate the courts' readiness to impanel other juries of experts on an ad hoc basis. Thayer stated that jurors were occasionally "men of particular trades," citing a 1394 jury of "cooks and fishmongers, where one was accused of selling bad food."[171] A further example arose in the 1663 libel trial of John Twyn.[172] One of the defendants stated: "We desire we may have a jury of booksellers and printers, they being the men that only understand our business."[173] Lord Chief Justice Hyde replied: "There are those already that understand it as well as booksellers or printers; besides, half the jury are such, and they are able to make the rest understand it."[174]

Later, in 1700, Holt reported an anonymous case involving a dispute between an earl and one of his farmers over the value of improvements on the land.[175] Holt indicated that the first jury of farmers gave £200 damages, which the court considered excessive. But on the second trial, "a Jury of Gentlemen [was] order'd, who only gave 40 *l*."[176] The court considered this insufficient and granted the farmer's motion for a third trial.[177]

G. O. Sayles reported early King's Bench cases in which juries of clerks and attorneys were impaneled to deal with alleged falsification of writs by attorneys,[178] extortion by court officials,[179] and similar behavior.[180] The problem of corrupt behavior by officers of the court persisted over the centuries, and expert juries of inquiry became a regular part of the administration of the Court of Common Pleas in the fifteenth, sixteenth, and seventeenth centuries. From an examination of fifteenth-century plea rolls, John Baker has ascertained that official inquiries into alleged misconduct by an attorney or officer occurred "very occasionally."[181] In 1566, Lord Chief Justice Dyer ordered a sixteen-member jury of attorneys,[182] and, in 1654, Common Pleas issued a rule calling for a jury of clerks and attorneys to be impaneled once every three years "to enquire of Abuses, Extortions, &c. of Attornies."[183] Undoubtedly, these juries of inquiry functioned as investigative committees or special commissions more than as traditional juries addressing specific factual disputes. Yet, in their role of applying expertise to the identification and evaluation of behavior differing from the norm, they resemble the later merchant juries that applied expertise on mercantile customs to the commercial behavior of the litigants.

II. Emergence of the Struck Jury

The headnote to Section 15 of the 1730 "Act for the Better Regulation of Juries" declares that, "In Trials of Issues at Westminster, on Motion of the Parties, Judges may order a special jury."[184] The full text of Section 15 is as follows:

> And whereas some Doubt hath been conceived touching the Power of his Majesty's Courts of Law at Westminster, to appoint Juries to be struck before the Clerk of the Crown, Master of the Office, Prothonotaries, or other proper Officer of such respective Courts, for the Trial of Issues depending in the said Courts, without the Consent of the Prosecutor or Parties concerned in the Prosecution or Suit then depending, unless such issues are to be tried at the Bar of the same Courts; Be it declared and enacted by the Authority aforesaid, That it shall and may be lawful to and for his Majesty's Courts of King's Bench, Common Pleas and Exchequer at Westminster respectively, upon Motion made on Behalf of his Majesty, his Heirs or Successors, or on the Motion of any Prosecutor or Defendant in any Indictment or Information for any Misdemeanor, or Information in the Nature of a Quo Warranto, depending or to be brought or prosecuted in the said Court of King's Bench, or in any Information depending or to be brought or prosecuted in the said

> Court of the Exchequer, or on the Motion of any Plaintiff or Plaintiffs, Defendant or Defendants in any Action, Cause or Suit whatsoever, depending or to be brought and carried on in the said Courts of King's Bench, Common Pleas and Exchequer, or in any of them, and the said Courts are hereby respectively authorized and required, upon Motion as aforesaid, in any of the Causes before-mentioned, to order and appoint a Jury to be struck before the proper Officer of each respective Court for the Trial of any Issue joined in any of the said Causes, and triable by a Jury of twelve Men, in such Manner as special Juries have been, and are usually struck in such Courts respectively, upon Trials at Bar had in the said Courts, which said Jury so struck as aforesaid, shall be the Jury returned for the Trial of the said issue.

William Blackstone, in his *Commentaries,* wrote that "Special juries were originally introduced in trials at bar, when the causes were of too great nicety for the discussion of ordinary freeholders," or, alternatively, "where the sheriff was suspected of partiality, though not upon such apparent cause, as to warrant an exception to him."[185] Blackstone stated that if the court granted the motion for a special jury in either situation, the sheriff was then "to attend the prothonotary or other proper officer with his freeholder's book; and the officer is to take indifferently forty-eight of the principal freeholders in the presence of the attorneys on both sides; who are each of them to strike off twelve, and the remaining twenty-four are returned upon the panel."[186]

It is not evident why Blackstone attached the struck jury procedure to the case of the "unindifferent sheriff" (which was the customary expression used for the partial or biased sheriff). That situation presented a potential problem wholly unrelated to the procedure for striking a jury in a trial of great consequence. In the latter instance, parties sought a highly capable jury of qualified individuals who would apprehend the importance of the case and would behave responsibly. This goal was accomplished by requiring the large panel of exceptional individuals. The panel could have been reduced from forty-eight to twenty-four by an appropriate court officer, but, perhaps to avoid overt appearances of jury packing, the parties were given that task. In the unindifferent-sheriff situation, there was neither a need for a larger panel than usual nor a need for jurors of exceptional ability; the problem was simply to avoid the alleged bias. This had been a recognized problem for centuries. The standard illustration in the legal literature from the fifteenth to the eighteenth centuries was a sheriff who was a "cozen" (cousin), or kindred, to one of the parties, in which case it was uniformly stated that the plaintiff could have the *venire* directed to the coroner, not the secondary.[187]

In my full study of the origins of the special jury (from which this chapter is adapted), I work through a possible explanation for Blackstone's reference to sheriff partiality—an explanation based on successive editions of seventeenth- and early-eighteenth-century practice books that were in all likelihood among Blackstone's sources.[188] There is no need to repeat that speculation here, except to recognize the basic point that the "unindifferent-sheriff" situation can be put aside, having had no significant part in the emergence of the struck jury.

Blackstone's other category—cases "of too great nicety for the discussion of ordinary freeholders"—had, however, long been linked to the struck-jury procedure. For example, Duncombe, in his 1665 treatise on trial by jury, observed that "in matters of great consequence," the court could summon jurors who owned property above the four-pound-per-annum minimum. "But in such Cases (every one knows) the Court most commonly orders the Prothonotary to choose 48 out of the Sheriff's Book of Freeholders, of the most substantial men in the County, and the Parties strike out 12 apiece, then the Sheriff returns the rest."[189]

Earlier, William Style, in his 1657 *Regestrum Practicale,* wrote that, "Upon a motion and an Affidavit made in Court that the Cause to be tried at the bar, is a Cause of very great consequence, the Court will make a Rule for the Sheriff to return 48 Jurors upon the Jury."[190] A trial at bar was conducted by the full common-law court in London, rather than by a single judge (at *nisi prius,* at it was called), and, as is explained more fully later, trials at bar were characteristically trials "of great consequence." Style merely said that, for such a case, a double-sized panel (forty-eight instead of twenty-four) could be returned. But, in the 1694 edition of Style's *Regestrum Practicale* (published long after Style's death, in 1679), the editor John Lilly added that "each party to strike out 12 by one at a time, the Plaintiff or his Attorney to begin first, and the remaining 24 shall be the Jury to be returned for the Trial of the Cause."[191]

Since these early practice books tied the special jury procedure to trials at bar, they may have caused the uncertainty (resolved by the 1730 statute) about whether the struck jury could be granted by the common-law courts on the motion of only one party in cases *not* to be tried at bar. That there was uncertainty is clearly shown by the well-known *Trial of the Seven Bishops*[192] in King's Bench in 1688. The report contains extended colloquies between Chief Justice Wright and Sir Samuel Astry, Master of the Crown Office, on a variety of procedural points. Astry had been the chief clerk on the crown side for a dozen years and had been a civil practitioner for the twenty years previous.[193] By the tone of the exchanges, it is clear that Chief Justice Wright deferred to Astry's experience on court procedures, despite the dour comment from defendants' counsel that "Sir Samuel Astry has not been here so very long, as to make the practice of his time the course of the court."[194] One of the procedural points that arose concerned a request by defendant's counsel "that in the return of the jury there may be forty-eight returned."[195] The Attorney General[196] responded: "I tell you what we will do; sir Samuel Astry shall have the Freeholders Book, if you please, and shall return twenty-four."[197] Counsel for the defendant rejoined that "Eight and forty has been always the course, when the jury is returned by sir Samuel Astry."[198] Counsel then agreed to follow whatever the usual practice was, and Chief Justice Wright asked: "What is the usual course, sir Samuel Astry? Do you use to return twenty-four, or forty-eight, and then strike out twelve apiece, which I perceive they desire for the defendants?"[199] Astry responded: "My lord, the course is both ways, and then it may be as your lordship and the court will please to order it."[200] Chief Justice Wright ordered forty-eight because "that is the fairest,"[201] with which counsel for both sides were content.[202]

By 1700, the struck-jury procedure had become a recognized feature of court practice. The first express statutory reference to the special jury had occurred in 1696,[203] and, in that same year, two King's Bench rules dealt specifically with procedural aspects of striking the jury.[204] During the first three decades of the eighteenth century, the struck jury crept by degrees into a number of the practice books.[205] By the 1730 enactment, the procedure was fully established.

B. Relation to Trials at Bar

Blackstone's view that special juries were "originally introduced in trials at bar, when the causes were of too great nicety for the discussion of ordinary freeholders"[206] was probably correct, but Robert Richardson's flat statement, in 1739, in his widely used King's Bench practice book, that "All Issues to be tried at the Bar are to be tried by a Special Jury struck by the Secondary"[207] was surely incorrect. Older authorities partially illuminate the relation of the special jury to the trial at bar.[208] Although there clearly was an historical connection between the two, its exact nature was never well defined. Style again provides a suitable starting point.

According to Style, trials at bar were granted in two situations—where the trial presented difficult questions or involved great value.[209] In either case, "it is fit the Trial should be at the Bar, where Trials are more solemn, and where more time may be spent in the Trial than can be at the Assizes."[210] Citing a 1648 rule of King's Bench, Style noted that "the old use of practice" allowed only ten such trials per year because "Trials at the Bar are a great hindrance to other businesses which are more proper for the Court."[211] Nevertheless, on May 1, 1650, the King's Bench increased the maximum number of trials at bar to twenty per year, all to be conducted, as had been true earlier, during Easter term.[212] At some point after 1670, the year of Style's second edition, the limitations on the number of trials at bar and their confinement to Easter term disappeared; Lilly's revision of Style in 1694 noted that trials at bar "are now more desired than anciently they were" and that "the Court doth not think fit to limit them to any number."[213]

In *Lord Sandwich's Case,*[214] the King's Bench, in 1699, acknowledged that "Where there is value or difficulty, we are bound of common right to grant trials at the bar," but the court denied a motion for a new trial at bar.[215] The court reasoned that, even though the value of the property in question was large, only the execution of a conveyance remained in dispute.[216] An unreported case supports the intimation in *Lord Sandwich's Case* that Chief Justice Holt was not pleased by the proliferation of trials at bar. In *Drake v. Nicholle,*[217] Raymond moved for such a trial, alleging that a large sum (£150) was in dispute; Chief Justice Holt denied the motion, stating "the value is not all but the difficulty must be regarded."[218]

In *Fuller v. Mountjoy,*[219] Chief Justice Parker observed that "the real purchase money as 2000£ may be said to buy an 100£ annuity"; thus, a general rule of £100 income per annum real estate or £2000 personalty was established.[220] Despite Chief Justice Holt's reservations, the "value or difficulty" formula persevered[221] until a swing of the pendulum back to a more sparing allowance of trials at bar can be observed, beginning in the late 1720s and becoming established in the 1730s. In 1725, the court had, on the strength of precedent, granted a trial at bar where the disputed matter was of trifling value but required lengthy testimony,[222] but, in 1728, the new attitude of King's Bench was expressed in *Goodright v. Wood*[223] There, "the Court laid down two Rules, that they never grant these Trials [at bar] merely for the Consequence of the Cause, though it be of ever so great a Value; nor ever for the Length of Examination, where 'tis of a very small Value; and in Ejectments the Rule has been not to allow them but where the Yearly Value of the Land in Question is 100 *l.*" The court added that "a general Swearing of the Length of a Cause, though there is Value too, will not be sufficient, unless there is a probable Foundation laid for them to believe it."[224]

Further, in the 1741 Common Pleas case of *Frost v. Whadcock,*[225] plaintiff supported his motion for a trial at bar by citing the need for a close examination of title, involving many witnesses, to which the court responded: "As to strict Examination, it is necessary in all Cases, and is nothing with Respect to a Trial at Bar."[226] There being "no Nicety in this Point, or Difficulty, so as to require the Attention of the whole Court," the court denied the request in favor of "a Day extraordinary at the Assizes, where an examination of a great Number of Witnesses is most proper, and least expensive."[227]

A further limitation on the trial at bar was its unavailability in the City of London. By the city's charter, London jurors could not be required to journey outside city limits.[228] Moreover, "It was said by Rolle Chief Justice, that the City of Bristol will not bring a matter to be tryed here at the Bar, no more then the City of London will."[229] The same rule existed generally regarding the counties palatine, as Coke's report of a 1568 Common Pleas case indicates.[230]

With these general rules on the availability of a trial at bar as background, some features of the connections between the special jury and the trial at bar can be identified. First, not every trial at bar used a special jury. *Mr. Farington's Case,*[231] a 1682 murder trial, clearly illustrates this fact. There, the court ordered a trial at bar upon good cause shown, after which a request was made that a special jury be struck "as is usual by the Secondary in Civil Causes upon Trials at Bar."[232] The court denied the request as "contrary to the Course of the Court in capital Causes."[233] Otherwise, the defendant would be deprived of his right of thirty-five peremptory challenges.[234]

Conversely, not every special jury case was a trial at bar during the formative years under discussion. A majority of the reports of seventeenth-century special-jury cases state that the trial was at bar, but many of them are silent on the subject, and the trials may not have been at bar.[235] Moreover, by the second half of the century, courts on assize could order special juries. Lilly reports a ruling by Chief Justice Glynne that states that a struck jury could be awarded at *nisi prius,*[236] and, in the 1724 decision of

Rex v. Burridge,[237] Chief Justice Charles Pratt observed that "above thirty years ago there were several [such] precedents" in which struck juries were ordered, even without the consent of the parties.[238]

Although the special jury may have deep roots, it was not well recognized until the second half of the seventeenth century. Even then, judges and leading practitioners were uncertain about the procedure. Trials at bar, in contrast, were both familiar and common. It is unreasonable, therefore, to assume that struck juries invariably accompanied trials at bar for important or difficult cases. The sheriff may well have produced a "special," nonstruck jury as a matter of course for trials of sufficient moment to command the full court's attention; in this sense, the special jury and the trial at bar seem to have been linked at least through the 1600s. During the late 1600s, however, the number of trials at bar increased significantly, reaching cases of trifling consequence that promised complicated or extended testimony. When this happened, even the special, nonstruck jury probably was not returned on a consistent basis. Additionally, the increasing use of the special jury at *nisi prius* by the end of the century and the unavailability of the special jury in capital cases further distanced the two concepts. By the time of the statute of 3 Geo. 2, c.25 (1730), the special jury had become synonymous with the struck jury and had acquired a life of its own.

C. Procedural Questions

Some procedural features of the special jury were settled before the statute of 3 Geo. 2, c.25 (1730). In 1696, the King's Bench ruled that if attorneys for both parties received proper notice and only one side appeared, "he that appears shall, according to the ancient course, strike out twelve; and the Master shall strike out the other twelve for him that is absent."[239] Also, by a separate rule in the same year, the court ordered that the rule for a struck jury must specify that the Master is to "strike forty-eight, and each of the parties shall strike out twelve," or else "the Master is to strike twenty-four, and the parties have no liberty to strike out any."[240]

Whether before the 1730 statute the consent of both parties was always required for a special jury is unclear.[241] The early-eighteenth-century practice seems to have been as follows: When a party requested a special jury, the opposing party was given notice and time to respond.[242] A special jury would be ordered where good cause existed, even over the objection of one or both parties.[243] The court might find good cause in the innate importance of the case, and the court could order a special jury on its own motion or on the motion of one of the parties. A unique and interesting variation on this pattern is an unreported anonymous case in 1710 in which the King's Bench accepted the prospect of jury-packing as good cause not to allow a special jury. The court granted the defendant's motion to discharge a rule for a special jury after he argued: "The suit is between the Lord of a Manor and his Tenants. They will get all Lords of Manors returned. I pray it may be tryed by a Common Jury."[244]

The 1730 statute, titled "An Act for the Better Regulation of Juries,"[245] made clear that consent of both parties was not required. In a 1737 decision, the Court of King's Bench summarized the pre-1730 practice by stating that, "though it was not unusual, before the said act, to grant special juries without consent, yet in some instances, and for special causes, it was and might be done."[246]

With regard to the expense of a special jury, the 1730 statute required the applying party to pay the costs of striking the jury.[247] Previously, perhaps because courts customarily impaneled special juries with the consent of both parties, the practice had been for the parties to share equally the costs of striking the jury.[248] The amounts of the fees were not fixed by rule of court or by statute. In a 1694 table of customary fees, the fees due Mr. Richard Aston, Secondary of the Court of King's Bench, included: "For Returning Juries to Try Causes at the Bar, each Party give what he pleases."[249] According to Richardson, "The Secondary and Under-Sheriff had formerly each a Guinea a Side from Plaintiff and Defendant."[250] And, in 1730, a tabulation of the fees of Mr. Samuel Clarke, Secondary of King's Bench, showed one pound, one shilling due from each party "For the nominating and striking all special Juries for Trials at the Bar and otherwise."[251]

In addition to the costs of striking, fees were paid to special jurymen. Chief Justice Lee observed in 1737 that "there has not been any Rule settled about the Sum that it is reasonable to give the Jury upon a Trial at Bar,"[252] but the Master of the King's Bench Office certified that "he never allowed less than a guinea to each special juror in London."[253] One case of a trial at bar was cited in which each juryman received five guineas,[254] and one justice questioned why a special juror should receive more than a common juror, because the former was better able to bear the cost of jury service than the latter.[255]

A final point of procedure pertains to the use of talesmen. Originally, talesmen were summoned by a specific rule for a fixed number of additional prospective jurors when the initial panel did not yield a full jury.[256] As Appendix 4 shows, statutory property qualifications were set for talesmen in 1692 at a level half that required for the initial panel of jurors, certain courts and types of cases excepted.[257] The old requirement of an order for a fixed number of talesmen generated delay, especially when there was no assurance that the order would produce a full jury.[258] Thus, Parliament authorized the tales *de circumstantibus* in the mid-1500s,[259] permitting deficiencies in jury numbers to be filled from among the bystanders in court upon the prayer of the plaintiff or defendant. The tales *de circumstantibus* was not allowed for trials at bar,[260] but it was available for special juries called at *nisi prius* or on assize, despite the possible dilution of the quality or expertise represented by the special jury.[261]

D. Relation to "Good" Juries

More elusive than the connection between the special jury and the trial at bar is the relationship of the special jury to the "good jury." The expression "good jury" became a term of art, at least by the early eighteenth century. For example, in the 1727 case of *Rex v. Chipping-Norton,*[262] King's Bench granted the defendant's motion "that he might have a good Jury" but denied him a special jury since the Attorney General would not consent to the latter.[263]

Loosely described by Tidd as "a better sort of common jury,"[264] a good jury typically was returned by the sheriff pursuant to a writ of inquiry[265] to ascertain the amount of damages owed to a successful plaintiff. The good jury was not automatic in such cases; it was impaneled at the plaintiff's request, often after the recovery of a default judgment.[266] The term "good jury" may have originated in the form of the writ of inquiry, which directed that the inquest be conducted by "duodecim proborum et legalium hominum,"[267] or twelve good and lawful men. By comparison, the writ for a common jury called for twelve "free and lawful men of the neighbourhood," or "free and lawful men of the body of your county."[268]

The seventeenth- and early-eighteenth-century practice books do not mention the good jury. Possibly this omission reflects the local nature of the inquiry before the sheriff in the venue where the dispute arose, yet even the late-eighteenth-century practice books that deal with sheriffs and undersheriffs are silent on the subject.[269] Nevertheless, in 1720, the Court of King's Bench was able to refer to "the common rule for a good jury,"[270] and Common Pleas later observed that "The practice of ordering a good jury existed long before the passing of the Acts which regulate special juries."[271] Tidd expands the latter point by noting that the use of good juries at *nisi prius* preceded the introduction of special juries.[272]

Several good-jury cases not initiated by the writ of inquiry occurred before the statutory endorsement of the special jury in 1730.[273] In 1665, King's Bench refused a request for a special jury in a new trial granted because of an initial verdict that was contrary to the evidence.[274] The court did not want to set an "ill example" by impaneling a special jury whenever a common jury went wrong but instead compromised and ordered a good jury.[275] In 1724, the court also awarded a good jury in the retrial of a complex property dispute.[276]

Initially, the consent of the parties was required for a good jury. In *Bishop of Sarum v. Ashe,* decided in 1710, Justice Powell responded to a motion for a good jury in an action of *scandalum magnatum* by stating: "We can't do it; all Rules for good Juries are by consent."[277] Some years later, however, King's Bench pointed out, in *Rex v. Burridge,* that, "If an affidavit be laid before the Court of suspicion that there will not be a fair jury, and the adverse party will not consent to a good jury, we will rule one without consent."[278] The problem of suspected bias in jurymen could have been corrected by challenges, but perhaps the alternative of the good jury arose in cases where the suspicions of bias were not specific enough to sustain particular challenges. This possibility may be reflected in the 1714 case of *Dux Leeds v. Hill Morton,*[279] in which the court granted the rule for a good jury "because there was a complaint made against the common panel."[280]

Very little is known about the identity and social standing of good jurors returned during the seventeenth and early eighteenth centuries.[281] Absent special cause, motions for good juries were occasionally denied in London and Middlesex because "all are presumed to be good there."[282] As with special juries, the sheriff undoubtedly used his discretion in tailoring the quality of the jury to the importance of the case. In one case, in 1720, the Court of King's Bench observed that a good jury "is often made up of gentlemen who are in the commission, that is, of justices of the peace."[283]

Conclusion

As is shown in the next chapter, the special jury of the late eighteenth and early nineteenth centuries was typically drawn from a special class of men of above-average wealth or standing in the community, often the merchants. This practice began as a custom without statutory mandate. The statute of 1730 was procedural only, with no qualitative requirement for special jurors. In the early eighteenth century, the special jury was equivalent to the struck jury, and, although it was the customary procedure in trials at bar, one judge asserted, in 1710, that, "in a Tryal at Bar, the Jury is returned by the Master. The Jury is special only because it is returned in a special manner, it is no Objection that a man is a Common Juror."[284] In the late eighteenth century, Lord Mansfield frequently used special juries of experts (merchants). Under Mansfield's successor, Lloyd Kenyon, the special jury was still used frequently, and this pattern continued under Kenyon's successor, the able but domineering Lord Ellenborough. Accusations of the packing of special juries,[285] however, brought the special jury under the scrutiny of reform-minded Parliaments in the nineteenth century, resulting in additional legislative requirements.

8

Special Juries in England

Nineteenth-Century Usage and Reform

Special juries were used in the late eighteenth and nineteenth centuries in a surprisingly diverse array of courts and locations. Apart from the mainstream experience in the central courts in England, Scotland, and Ireland, the special jury appeared in other courts in England, in the farthest reaches of the British Empire, and in a number of American jurisdictions. Here is a sampler: the Court of the Sheriff of Middlesex;[1] Inquisition of Damages conducted by the Deputy Sheriff of Middlesex at the King's Arm Tavern;[2] Her Majesty's Court of Probate;[3] the Liverpool Court of Passage;[4] the Circuit Court at St. John, New Brunswick;[5] the Supreme Court of Prince Edward Island;[6] the Court of the Recorder of Bombay;[7] and the U.S. Supreme Court.[8]

This chapter examines special-jury usage and reform in England in the late eighteenth and nineteenth centuries. During its robust life in England in the late eighteenth century, the special jury was used frequently and instrumentally by Lord Chief Justice Mansfield in the shaping of a coherent body of commercial law. Widely regarded as the founder of English commercial law, Lord Mansfield was well known for his repeated use of merchant juries in the Court of King's Bench, particularly in the 1770s and 1780s. Indeed, by the century's end, Mansfield's special jurors appear to have attained something of celebrity status. As Lord Campbell observed, in his *Lives of the Chief Justices:* "Several of these gentlemen survived when I began to attend Guildhall as a student, and were designated and honoured as 'Lord Mansfield's Jurymen.' One, in particular, I remember, Mr. Edward Vaux, who always wore a cocked hat, and had almost as much authority as the Lord Chief Justice himself."[9]

Juries of Merchants

Particularly in insurance cases, or cases involving bankers' customs with regard to bills of exchange or promissory notes, the merchant jury was often a helpful source of expertise for the court and the parties. Lord Mansfield stated in *Lewis v. Rucker* (an insurance case):

> The special Jury, (amongst whom there are many knowing and considerable Merchants,) . . . understood the Question very well, and knew more of the Subject of it than any Body else present; and formed their Judgment from their own Notions and Experience without much Assistance from anything that passed.[10]

It is unclear whether Lord Mansfield was able to influence special-jury selection so that only trusted merchants were returned in commercial cases. Some evidence suggests that this may have been possible, through the combined effect of a loyal court official who selected the names for the jury panel and the practice of filling up a jury with talesmen when fewer than twelve members of the special-jury panel appeared.

Through a study of Lord Mansfield's trial notes (about half of the notebooks filled by Lord Mansfield during his thirty-two years on the bench are known to survive), I have identified approximately six hundred special-jury cases in trials he conducted.[11] Of these, 27 percent were involved with the purely commercial subjects of insurance, bills of exchange and promissory notes and another 34 percent dealt with general "business"-type subjects, such as debt, special contract or covenant, patent, goods sold and delivered, work and labor performed, and money had and received. Eight percent of the cases were devoted to bankruptcy questions. The remaining 31 percent involved noncommercial subjects, such as negligence, trespass, trover, assault, criminal conversation, nuisance, ejectment, libel, and perjury.

Yet, it is clear that the merchants became the backbone of the special juries impaneled in London and Middlesex in the late eighteenth century. It is generally assumed that, thereafter, merchants continued to populate London special juries, as is reflected in the 1817 libel case of *Rex v. Wooler,* where Lord Ellenborough stated: "The law does not absolutely require that the jurors be merchants, but the practice certainly has been within the City of London to take such only as came within that description."[12] A jury list in the Corporation Records Office in London tends to confirm Lord Ellenborough's statement. Four hundred and ninety-nine jurors are named from twenty-eight London wards. Of these, 477 are shown as merchants, the remaining twenty-two falling into a variety of occupations ranging from banker to slop seller.[13]

In sharp contrast to this evidence, however, is the 1817 report of a special committee appointed by the Mayor and Aldermen of London to examine and evaluate jury lists for the central courts sitting in Guildhall. The committee observed that, "Although it is obvious, that, within the City of London there must be an immense number of Persons who are eligible to serve on Special Juries," the Special Jury book contained only 485 names, and almost half of these were found not to be London householders and were thus unqualified. Of the remaining 257 special jurors, the committee found that only eighty-eight fell within "the modern acceptation of the term Merchants," while the rest were "of those usually styled Tradesmen, and not Merchants." The committee explained that these data were developed "to shew that the practice of a Special Jury being composed exclusively of Merchants, which has been the alleged plea for the past practice, is as unfounded in fact as it is utterly unsupported by any principle of Law."[14]

Whatever their composition, special juries were frequently impaneled in the nineteenth century. Lord Mansfield's endorsement of merchant juries encouraged the use of special juries in commercial cases, and it had already been made clear in eighteenth-century legislation that a special jury would be available to any party ready to pay for it.[15] By the turn of the nineteenth century, arranging for a special jury involved nothing more than a bit of paperwork.[16]

After Lord Mansfield, special juries of merchants continued to be influential, especially during the first half of the nineteenth century, under Lords Ellenborough and Campbell. Acknowledging the frequent use of merchant juries, however, is one thing; understanding the workings of the process is another. How often were "juries of merchants" formed, and how did this happen? And what part did the merchant jurors' expertise actually play in the decisions and in the formulation of common-law doctrine in commercial cases?

There was no entitlement to a jury of merchants. As was explained in chapter 7, the 1730 statute on special juries endorsed them without definition other than by reference to the practice of impaneling special juries already established in the courts and by describing the procedure—producing a panel of forty-eight names, which was then reduced to twenty-four by the parties' taking turns striking out names. In my Mansfield work, I describe a 1773 case involving the Goldsmiths' Company in which the Recorder of London had summoned a jury of merchants.[17] The barrister John Dunning challenged this, remarking, "With the same propriety that the order specifies a Jury of Merchants, it might have specified a Jury of Goldsmiths to be summoned."[18] Opposing counsel, Serjeant Burland, observed that orders for juries of merchants had frequently been made; Dunning said perhaps this was so, but only with consent. In the case being argued, "it was agreed to have a Special Jury not confined to Merchants only."

Reported cases confirm Serjeant Burland's remark that juries of merchants were frequently impaneled. Sometimes special juries or juries of merchants were ordered by the Court of Chancery in referring a question to the law courts for jury-trial resolution. In an anonymous case in 1722 in which Chancery referred a question to law, the Court remarked that "it is proper to move the Court of Chancery for a special jury, if the circumstances of the case require it; and the court will grant the same, as they did in the case of *Attorney General* and *Snow.*"[19] At common law, special juries were impaneled at the request of one of the parties, but since questions referred by Chancery to the law courts were designed, according to the common expression, "to inform the conscience of the Court of Chancery," orders from Chancery calling for special juries or juries of merchants were ordinarily complied with.[20]

But what, exactly, did juries of merchants do? We can imagine models at two extremes, one passive and one active. The first would be a jury of impassive experts upon whom the court would rely to do the right thing. The second would be a jury of experts who were permitted, perhaps encouraged, to participate in the trial and to articulate, where relevant, mercantile practices. Both models find support in the cases, but, as I will show, the active model came to dominate as the eighteenth century ended and continued well into the nineteenth century.

The question of how active the jurors were is of interest in considering how common-law principles and doctrine came to be articulated and agreed upon in a system with jury trial as its mainspring. The problem of the inarticulateness of the general verdict has often been recognized as an impediment to the growth of the common law. As Lord Mansfield remarked in *Vallejo v. Wheeler,*[21] "it is not easy to collect with certainty from a general verdict, or from notes taken at *nisi prius,* what was the true ground of decision," and for this reason Mansfield, in *Vallejo* "as in all doubtful cases, . . . wished a case to be made for the opinion of the Court."[22] As to merchant jurors, perhaps Mansfield's best-known observation is that quoted earlier from *Lewis v. Rucker,* where he stated that the jurors "formed their judgment from their own notions and experience, without much assistance from any thing that passed."[23] This, of course, suggests more the passive model of the jury of merchants than the active.

Another example on the passive side is a 1744 decision, *Banbury v. Lisset,*[24] which presented the question of whether a document drafted by the parties constituted a bill of exchange. Chief Justice Lee observed that "it was not within the power of the parties to make what form they please pass for such a bill, but it ought to be agreeable to the lex mercatoria: the privilege arises from the convenience to trade, which is not consulted in this case . . . : however, being a mercantile transaction, he left it to the special jury of merchants: who found it to be no bill of exchange."[25]

In the post-Mansfield era, a more active role for juries of merchants emerged, especially after the chief justiceship of King's Bench passed from Lloyd Kenyon to Ellenborough. Looking back on this time in an 1831 case that involved the sharing of profits between partners, Lord Chancellor Brougham remarked that the question had come "with peculiar advantage under the cognizance of a learned judge like Lord Ellenborough, and a special jury of merchants in the city of London, who declare what is the result of the facts: no judge ever had greater experience in mercantile law, and no men are better able than those juries to decide by their good sense and mercantile habits."[26]

Clearly, Ellenborough believed in the active model of the jury of merchants. In *DeTastet v. Baring,*[27] a dishonored bill of exchange had been drawn from London to Lisbon while Lisbon was blockaded by a British squadron, and the question was whether any exchange or re-exchange of the bill could be allowed, given the state of war between the two nations. Ellenborough was the trial judge, and, in presenting the case to the Court of King's Bench for argument, he

> stated the manner in which he had left the case to the jury: which he observed was a special jury consisting of many eminent merchants conversant with the subject, and therefore he had encouraged them to take an active part in the examination of the witnesses; which they had done: and they had drawn their conclusion from the whole evidence, in favour of the defendants against the claim of re-exchange.[28]

It is unclear how often merchant jurors were encouraged to participate in the examination of witnesses, though undoubtedly the *DeTastet* case was not a singular instance. Repeatedly in cases that were heard over more than half of the nineteenth century, the judges showed deference to the merchant jurors, as shown in the case reports. For example, in *Prescott v. Flinn*,[29] the Court of Common Pleas declined to order a new trial on a question of a clerk's authority to endorse checks because at the first trial, "the evidence on this subject was left to a special jury of merchants, who have the right to bring their own knowledge of the general course of business in aid of their judgment on the particular occasion, and they have declared themselves satisfied that the Defendants have, by their conduct, shewn that this clerk had authority to indorse." And, in *Foster v. The Mentor Life Assurance Company*,[30] which required an interpretation of a life insurance policy, Lord Campbell stated: "Upon the whole, I am of opinion that a special Jury of the city of London, gentlemen more familiarly acquainted with such transactions than we are, have arrived at a right Conclusion, and that their verdict ought not to be disturbed."[31]

There are many other instances in the reports of deference by the judges to juries of merchants in the late eighteenth and through much of the nineteenth centuries. Illustrative are the following:

Justice Grose (King's Bench): "Now it must be remembered, that this cause was tried by a special jury of merchants of London, persons peculiarly conversant in commercial transactions, and who perfectly well knew the ordinary risk of such a voyage, and what would vary that risk; and they were of the opinion that the underwriter was not liable."[32]

Chief Justice Eyre (Common Pleas): "If I had continued to doubt I should be unwilling to interfere with a verdict of a special jury of merchants on a subject of this kind, unless I clearly saw that some principle of law had been mistaken; or unless I was bound by authorities to pronounce that verdict wrong."[33]

Justice Chambre (Common Pleas): "Whether that explanation would have been satisfactory to any of us, sitting as jurymen, I do not know; it has been submitted to a special jury of merchants, who are very competent judges, and they have found on it, and . . . I think they have judged rightly."[34]

Chief Baron Abinger (Exchequer): "There was no misdirection upon the letter, the meaning of which, as part of a mercantile correspondence, was left to the judgment of a jury of merchants."

Chief Justice Tindal (Common Pleas): "The whole case as to the debt due to the factors was summed up, and left to the consideration of the jury, as mercantile men, to draw their own conclusion whether there was a debt or not"; "plaintiffs objected altogether to the principle on which the account was made up by the factors. But, without entering into a discussion on the point, we think this matter was a question peculiarly for the consideration of a jury of merchants; and we cannot see that they have come to a wrong conclusion."[35]

Lord Chancellor Cottenham: "It does appear to me to be, of all others, a case which ought to be decided by a Court of law with the assistance of a jury of merchants, who are familiar with the subject-matter, and much better competent than any Judge can be to put a construction upon mercantile terms, and to take a right view of the transactions as between merchants who are in the habit of dealing with questions of this sort."[36]

Justice Crowder (Common Pleas) (in chambers, ordering a change of venue from Middlesex to London in a contract dispute over the sale in London of indigo): "I certainly thought that the action would, from its nature, be more satisfactorily tried by a jury of merchants."[37]

Justice Crowder (Common Pleas): "The question as to the amount and mode of estimating the damages was very fully gone into. The evidence upon the subject was that of mercantile men, peculiarly conversant with the matter: and the jury was a special jury of Liverpool merchants, than whom none could be more fit to decide such a question. And I must say that I do not consider the amount excessive."[38]

Justice Keating (Common Pleas): "Whether or not there had been a breach of contract was for the consideration of the jury. . . . Now, here was a special jury of London merchants, who must be taken to be perfectly well aware of the rule of law that a man must at all events perform his contract: and they came to the conclusion that this defendant did not absolutely refuse to proceed to Copenhagen."[39]

Further manifestations of the active model of the jury of merchants are found in case reports that contain volunteered observations by jurors about mercantile practices, often strongly influencing the outcome, and in a case that caused insurance companies to change their practices in response to the verdict. The latter case, *Cantilton v. The London Assurance Company,*[40] was before Chief Justice Dudley Ryder in King's Bench in 1754; the jury of merchants was of the opinion that a term of a policy ("unless the ship be stranded") constituted a condition. This evidently caused "the great assurance companies of London" to drop the words from their policies.

In *Hoare v. Dickson,*[41] a case that came before Baron Parke at the Surrey assizes in 1849, "the jury (a special jury) expressed so strong an opinion—in which the learned judge coincided—that there was no ground for the action, that the plaintiff's counsel consented to be nonsuited."[42] And, in *Rucker v. Lunt,*[43] at the London sittings of the Court of Exchequer at Guildhall, in 1863, insurance brokers sued to recover a commission of 10 percent, and, "One of the jurymen said that he himself and one or two of his colleagues had experience in like matters, and were convinced that such was the understanding in London." Baron Martin recollected that such a custom had been "found by a special jury at Guildhall about thirty years ago." Defendant's counsel threatened to call witnesses to express the contrary view, but after plaintiffs called two witnesses who endorsed the custom, defendant's counsel said that he could not hope for a verdict, and the jury found for the plaintiffs.[44]

A good example of the volunteered comment by a merchant juror is found in *Brough v. Whitmore,*[45] an action on an insurance policy for coverage of the loss of a ship's stores and provisions, which had accidentally burned while in a warehouse during ship repairs. At the trial before Lord Kenyon, defendant claimed that the provisions were not protected by the policy, "but one of the [special] jury said that it had been determined in Lord Mansfield's time that they were included under the word 'furniture,' under which decisions the merchants in the city had since acquiesced; on which the plaintiffs obtained a verdict."

Other instances are supplied in cases tried before Lord Ellenborough in the King's Bench. In *Wright v. Shiffner,*[46] Lord Ellenborough stated his understanding of the application of the terms of an insurance policy written on a voyage from Surinam in the West Indies to London, after which "Mr. Taylor, a special juryman, said, that this was the construction universally put upon these policies in the city of London." This gave plaintiff the verdict. In *Gantt v. Mackenzie,*[47] the question concerned damages payable by the drawer of a dishonored foreign bill of exchange, and "Lord Ellenborough left this upon the custom of merchants, to the gentlemen of the special jury: who said, the holder of the bill was entitled to £10 per cent damages, and that interest was to be allowed only from the time when the bill was presented for payment." In another case, the jurors explained a practice in legal terms. Plaintiff in *Spear v. Travers*[48] sued successfully for undelivered goods that had been paid for, and in giving the verdict, "The gentlemen of the special jury observed, that in practice the indorsed dock warrants and certificates are handed from seller to buyer as a complete transfer of the goods." Numerous comparable examples of influential merchant juror opinions appear in the reports.[49]

One case in the Court of Common Pleas in 1832 shows how blurred the line was between merchant juror and witness. In *Elton v. Larkins,*[50] the question was whether a person buying a policy of insurance was obliged to state to the underwriter facts that were contained in Lloyd's List, which the underwriter could inspect. The court ruled that disclosure was required and, in reaching the decision, heard the testimony of a witness named Willis. At the time, Willis was serving as foreman of the special jury in a cause being heard by the Court of King's Bench, but Chief Justice Tenterden permitted Willis to leave the jury box to come into the Common Pleas to be examined, where Willis stated, among other things: "It is my practice, in an extensive connection as a broker, to communicate all information as to the time of sailing."[51]

A final question about the jury of merchants cases, perhaps the critical question, is how the legal community viewed the merchant jury pronouncements. Were they law? If so, how so? In *Brough v. Whitmore,*[52] where a special juryman explained that a ship's stores and provisions came within the term "furniture" in an insurance policy, Lord Kenyon was a bit forlorn in his opening remarks, declaring: "On the trial of this cause I had nothing to guide my judgment on the construction of this instrument but the words of the policy; and when it was stated that 'provisions' were included in the word 'furniture,' I confess I was somewhat at a loss to know to what extent the underwriters were liable on words so indefinite as these which are used." He then wondered aloud about whose job it was to say what the words meant, observing that he thought "the rule of law is to be given (not by merchants) but by the Court," yet, "when a question arises on the construction of the words of an instrument which are in themselves ambiguous, it is a matter fairly within the province of those who alone act upon such instruments to declare the meaning of them."[53] He added that only help from Lombard Street on the uniform practice of merchants and underwriters rendered insurance policies intelligible.

Years later, in *Lucas v. Dorrien,*[54] the question before the Court of King's Bench was whether an endorsement of the delivery checks or warrants of the West India Docks would pass the property in the goods covered by the warrants, and both sides naturally referred to *Spear v. Travers,*[55] where the special jurors had said that endorsed dock warrants effected a complete transfer of goods. In *Lucas,* Serjeant Best tried to shake off the earlier case by observing: "The special jury [in *Spear*] certainly mentioned the practice. The usage of merchants is undoubtedly part of the law of the land; but these ephemeral practices are not."[56] The court, however, was not persuaded, and, in his opinion, Justice Dallas observed that he had been "several times stopped by a special jury, they being satisfied that the goods pass from hand to hand by indorsement of these instruments," and that "All special juries cry out with one voice, that the practice is, that the produce lodged in the docks is transferred by indorsing over the certificates and dock warrants."[57]

Clearly, therefore, merchant jurors played an important role in articulating mercantile practices that had legal implications. It is too much, however, to say that undisputed merchant practices that were brought out in litigation automatically became part of the common law. Practices might do so, as in *Spear* and *Lucas,* where they made sense to the court and offended no established legal principle, but not otherwise. In a case before Lord Kenyon, for example, a special juror stated that the practice among underwriters was to subscribe a slip or short memorandum of proposed insurance that was considered binding in the ordinary course of business, but Lord Kenyon said that, "whatever obligation of this kind there might be in point of honour and good faith, the underwriter certainly would not be bound in law, for the assured in order to support his claim in a Court of justice must produce a stamped policy."[58] And, in *Rickford v. Ridge,*[59] Lord Ellenborough simply rejected as nonsense a banking practice that everyone agreed was uniformly followed. Bankers from Fleet Street testified that they often waited overnight to present for payment checks that came in the post after the banks' daily shipments of checks for payment had gone out, but a special juror "observed (and it was on both sides allowed to be so), that the practice is different with all London bankers east of St. Paul's, who present for payment all checques and bills the very same day they receive them by the post." Ellenborough said: "I cannot hear of any arbitrary distinction between one part of the city and another. It is not competent to bankers to lay down one rule for the eastward of St. Paul's, and another for the westward."[60]

In the *Rickford* case, the result reached by the special jury—that it was reasonable to wait until the next day to present the late-arriving checks for payment—was agreeable to the court. As was discussed in chapter 3, however, precisely the same issue had come before King's Bench some years earlier in a series of cases in which special juries stubbornly insisted on what can be called, for short, "same-day deposit."[61] These cases reveal a struggle within the Court of King's Bench about whether the court had the power to declare as a matter of law what a reasonable time should be for making the deposits, thereby sweeping away jury verdicts. Justice Francis Buller argued strongly that the court should declare the matter one of law, characterizing the cases as reflecting "great discredit on the courts of *Westminster.*"[62] Lord Mansfield ultimately agreed with Justice Buller but, perhaps in deference to special jurors with whom he had worked for so long, was very hesitant to take the step. Yet, it was a step that had to be taken; otherwise, juries, special or not, would be empowered to insist upon verdicts that in the eyes of the judges were senseless. A good example of the difficulty is *Scrimshire v. Alderton,* decided by the Court of King's Bench in 1743.[63] There, the question was whether a farmer who had consigned goods to a factor had an action against a buyer who had arranged purchase of the goods from the factor, after which the factor had failed before being paid by the buyer. Chief Justice Lee thought the action was valid and directed the jury to find for the plaintiff farmer, but the jury "went out and found for the defendant; were sent out a second, and a third time to re-consider it, and still adhered to their verdict; and being asked man by man, they separately declared they found for the defendant." Justice Lee granted a new trial, and the case came on again, this time before a special jury. Justice Lee "declared, that a factor's sale does by the general rule of law create a contract between the owner and buyer."[64] Nevertheless, the jury found for the defendant, telling the court that, under the circumstances proved, they thought the buyer answerable to the factor only. There the case ended, however unsatisfactorily to the court.

Nineteenth-Century Class Consciousness and Reform

Alongside the continuing use of juries of merchants as the nineteenth century progressed, the special jury came to be requested by parties not to gain specific expertise but primarily to ensure a higher class of jurymen than would otherwise appear. This fact was noted with distaste by Sir William Erle after his retirement as Chief Justice of the Court of Common Pleas. In testimony in May 1868 before the Select Committee on Special and Common Juries of the House of Commons, Sir William stated:

> I believe the intention of the Legislature has been departed from, and to my mind a very pernicious custom has been introduced, whereby the right to resort to a special jury has been so given as to foster the notion of there being class prejudices pervading the jury box, and that a party wanting to rely upon a certain class of prejudice, would take one jury, or the other accordingly.[65]

That special juries were used regularly during the eighteenth and nineteenth centuries in noncommercial settings is clear, as has already been noted.[66] Special juries were traditionally impaneled, for example, in libel cases.[67] Special juries were also used occasionally in marital cases involving alleged infidelity—criminal conversation.[68] These noncommercial cases undoubtedly contributed to the increasing popularity of the special jury.

I earlier indicated that approximately six hundred cases are shown in Lord Mansfield's surviving trial notes as having used special juries. The surviving notes cover a thirty-year period, but they represent only about half of Lord Mansfield's trial sittings. Taking into account the other half—and the fact that Mansfield did not always record the presence of a special jury—a fair extrapolation might suggest a special-jury volume of at least fifteen hundred cases, or an average of fifty per year. This figure is probably conservative, and it speaks only to one judge on one of the central courts sitting at *nisi prius* at Guildhall and Westminster. For comparison, a parliamentary study in 1854 showed that 162 special juries were summoned during the calendar year 1853 to the several courts sitting at *nisi prius* at Guildhall, broken down as follows: Queen's Bench, seventy-five; Common Pleas, thirty-seven; Exchequer, fifty.[69] Estimating a volume at Westminster of two-thirds that at Guildhall, this would yield 125 special-jury cases for the year in Queen's Bench at both locations, which would be a much higher volume than I have hypothesized for Lord Mansfield. A further comparison of interest is between the 1854 figures and figures taken from the 1817 special committee report for the City of London. In 1854, the number of special-jury cases at Guildhall for Queen's Bench and Common Pleas combined was 112. In 1817, these two courts at Guildhall heard 114 such cases in three terms,[70] indicating a higher volume for the whole year. If cases were relatively evenly distributed throughout the terms, the 1817 total was just above 150 cases, significantly higher than the comparable figure for 1854.

The burgeoning popularity of the special jury during the middle of the nineteenth century can be illustrated by the testimony in 1867 of William Erle before the Select Committee on Special and Common Juries:

> I may mention that after term there are always sittings to try special jury cases. Three courts of the three superior common law courts for the trial of special jury causes, and very often more than that. At this moment there are two Courts of Common Pleas sitting to try special jury cases. Special jurors are also wanted in Chancery in the Divorce Court, and a great many Sheriffs' Courts that are held for compensation cases; and also in cases where there is no plea, they may settle damages to any amount in the Sheriff's Court.[71]

Despite its extensive use, the special jury did not escape the spreading reform sentiment of the nineteenth century. As earlier noted, Chief Justice William Erle decried the transformation of the special jury into an adjunct of the class system,[72] while the special investigatory committee in London earlier uncovered a downgrading in many special jurors from merchant to tradesman.[73] These were but two of a number of nineteenth-century sources that direct accusations of corruption and abuse at the special jury, especially concerning alleged jury-packing.

As explained in chapter 7, the special jury was first mentioned in an act of Parliament in 1696,[74] but it was not until 1730 that Parliament squarely endorsed the practice.[75] In 1751, Parliament enacted provisions concerning who was to be responsible for the cost of a special jury and directing that fees extended to special jurymen should not exceed one guinea apiece.[76] Yet, other than requiring the sheriff to attend the secondary or prothonotary with his freeholders book, the eighteenth-century legislation on special juries did not regulate how the list of prospective special jurors would be formed, or how the forty-eight names would be selected from the list.

It was not surprising that allegations emerged that the sheriff or the secondary, or both, were manipulating the book to ensure that only chosen men formed the jury panels. This was particularly true in libel cases, about which the public was easily inflamed. Accusations of jury packing were not new in the late eighteenth and early nineteenth centuries,[77] but they grew in quantity and vehemence in the context of the special jury. Even in Lord Mansfield's time, John Horne asserted, in his well-known self-defense to libel charges brought against him, that "The special jurors in the counties, especially in Middlesex, great numbers of them, are qualified by the crown; they are esquired by the crown; and these crown esquires always attend upon the special juries."[78] Indeed, in November 1771, an editorial in *The Craftsman* observed that despite the popular recognition of juries—in particular, special juries—as "the Palladium of our Constitution," yet "we are assured, that such certain means is always taken in the fixing of Special Juries, that an eminent Tradesman of Westminster (who has long engaged his Attention on the Subject) has offered a very considerable Wager that he Names, on any Occasion beforehand, seven or eight of any Special Jury, at Westminster Hall."[79]

These were but polite preliminaries to Jeremy Bentham's tract *The Elements of the Art of Packing, as Applied to Special Juries.*[80] Written in 1808 but withheld from publication until 1821 because of its incendiary nature,[81] Bentham's tract alleged that a "regular corps" of special jurors had been developed, with "the members nominated in all cases by the dependent of the judge, that is in effect by the judge himself."[82] Elaborately supported by a few facts and plentiful argument and expanded into a broadside against government repression of freedom of the press, Bentham characterized the secondary (who, among court officers, was also called "the Master") as the Master Packer—a lackey who freely manipulated those loyal jurymen who constituted the "Guinea trade."[83] The latter expression came from the fact that each special juryman was paid one guinea per case while sitting.[84]

Bentham was not alone in his invective. Reference was earlier made to *Rex v. Wooler,*[85] in which Wooler, the editor of a publication known as *The Black Dwarf,* was convicted of libel. Wooler published his own story, asserting that the special jury that convicted him had been rigged by representatives of the crown.[86] On this point, Wooler was partly right. The crown *attempted* to fix his jury. The full report, in manuscript, of the

1817 special committee in London contains a deathbed affidavit from a Mr. David Walker, who had been for many years a clerk in the Office of the Secondary of London. The Secondary, Mr. Collingridge, had previously appeared before the committee and had denied any intervention by the Solicitor of the Treasury or his representative in the *Wooler* case. Walker, however, affirmed that a representative of the Solicitor of the Treasury came seeking Mr. Collingridge when Collingridge was out. The messenger grew tired of waiting, and Walker said:

> He then shewed me a letter from the Solicitor of the Treasury to Mr. Collingridge requesting to know whether certain persons the names of whom were enclosed in a list "were good men." The Gentleman then asked me the question as to their political Opinion and which were good men, & I said yes, they are all good men and he replied but mark some of the names of the best.

Collingridge was recalled before the committee, and, although he acknowledged that the event had taken place, the best part of the story was never known, not even to Wooler. Walker affirmed that, after he was importuned by the messenger to "mark some of the names of the best," he "considered it very improper & refused for a long time." When the messenger continued to insist, Walker complied, but, in his own words, "thinking it would be highly improper for a Clerk in the Office to further the Views of Ministers in reference to the Juries, I marked two or three of the names as good men whose political Opinions I knew to be in favor of liberty," and "these persons were left on the list at striking which I believed they would not otherwise have been."[87]

Sufficient agitation about jury packing took place to provoke a new legislative formula. In the County Juries Act of 1825, Parliament discarded the procedure calling for the sheriff and the secondary to prepare a panel of forty-eight names for each special jury. Instead, a system for anonymous balloting was established that required random selection from forty-eight numbered cards placed in the ballot box, with numbers corresponding to eligible special jurors.[88]

To deal with the quality of special jurors, Parliament provided, for the first time, that only individuals who fell in the categories of merchant, banker, or esquire (or person of higher degree) could serve.[89] Sheriffs were directed to extract from the jury books the names of all men who fell within these classifications and to arrange them in a separate, numbered "special jurors list," thus providing the numbers to be used in the balloting.

Jeremy Bentham was dismayed by the 1825 enactment. On 7 April 1827, he wrote to Sir Robert Peel as follows:

> Sir,
>
> *Jury packing* is now my theme. In the framing of the Jury Act, on which your name is stampt, which of two objects—*abolition* or *establishment*—was the one really aimed at, I declare myself with all sincerity, utterly unable to determine. . . . An entire work of mine has been directed to this subject. I can not quit it in the state in which, led to it of late by accident, I was no less surprised than mortified at beholding it.[90]

Bentham proposed amending the Jury Act and questioned Peel on his willingness to endorse such an action, but on April 9, 1827, Peel wrote to Bentham the following terse response: "Sir, I beg leave to acknowledge the receipt of your Letter of the 7th. April—and to inform you in reply to your question that I am not prepared to bring in a Bill for the alteration of the Jury Act in the mode you suggest."[91]

The 1825 Act, nevertheless, was an attempt by Parliament to elevate and unify the qualifications of special jurors. According to Chief Justice William Erle, "'Merchants' may have been designated as being supposed to be men conversant with commerce, and as being competent to deal with matters compared in our law merchant; 'bankers' were supposed to be conversant with the questions relating to money; and 'esquires' may have been specified as being persons conversant with rural interests."[92] Such an explicit intent is not evident in the committee work that led to the 1825 enactment, but, in any event, the scheme was a failure. No definitions of the terms "merchant," "banker," or "esquire" were given, leaving officials with abundant local discretion to construe the terms as convenience or cupidity dictated. Testimony before later parliamentary committees revealed a galaxy of interpretations and abuses. A merchant was described as a businessman with two or three clerks[93] or as one who exports or imports,[94] but the category excluded tradesmen, such as wine merchants,[95] drapers,[96] or beer sellers.[97] On the other hand, many individuals were said to be classed as merchants who in fact were not, either because the enrolling clerks were not capable of making the fine distinctions necessary[98] or because "merchant" was the description given by the resident to the enrolling officer (usually the ward overseer or vestry clerk), who had no information to the contrary.[99] Even before the County Juries Act of 1825, the looseness of the term "merchant" had been noted in connection with London juries. An article in *The Newgate Monthly Magazine* in 1825 quoted from a pamphlet entitled "The Law of Libel," as follows:

> In the City of London special jurors are *to be taken from merchants only.* The law gives no such direction, but the practice, the court says, is a good one, no matter how it began, or how opposite it may be to the law. But then in respect to the practice, who is a merchant?—in former times every man who dealt by wholesale; in a more restricted sense, a man who deals with foreign countries only. In which of these senses, then, it may be asked, is the word understood by the City of London jury selecter or packer? The answer is in no one of them. The Master of the Crown said, a *rag* merchant was not a merchant, and a *wine* merchant was a merchant, so he rejected the *rag* merchant and took the *wine* merchant. A *banker* was not a *merchant* so he rejected a *banker,* any one was a *merchant* whom he pleased to call one, no one was a merchant whom he chused to say was not a merchant.[100]

Beyond the term "merchant," there were other uncertainties. On occasion, the description of a resident's occupation was given by his servant.[101] In some jurisdictions, "esquires" were only those few individuals who fell within the legal definition,[102] in which case country gentlemen, no matter how wealthy, would not qualify.[103] More often, the term "esquire" was expanded according to the individual discretion of the sheriff, undersheriff, or enrolling clerk.[104] Indeed, one witness indicated that some jurymen were on two lists, qualifying as esquires in the wards where they lived and as merchants in the wards where they worked.[105]

These practices left no hope of a uniform application of the statutory terminology. Sometimes the actions of the overseers or vestry clerks were honest attempts to comply with the statutory scheme, and usually this meant downgrading the residents' own exalted descriptions of themselves.[106] At one time in Kent and Sussex, however, common jurymen were so plentiful and service on common juries so infrequent that special jurors maneuvered to downgrade themselves off the special-jury lists.[107] Usually this was accomplished by well-placed words with the vestry clerks or with the secondary; suggestions of bribery were common, even if not supported by hard proof.[108]

Two additional abuses of the special-jury system were the subject of protest during the nineteenth century. Already mentioned was the fact that each special juryman received one guinea for his service, which was vastly more than the shilling or eightpence paid to common jurors. With a good run of cases, the special juror could achieve an acceptable living,[109] and this was what Bentham called "the Guinea trade."[110] The popular vernacular was cruder, referring to these special jurors as "guinea pigs."[111] John Horne accused the government of creating such a class of jurors by "esquiring" them.[112] Another theory, offered in testimony before House of Commons investigative committees, was that this corps of jurors grew up as talesmen—that is, individuals who lay in wait in the environs of the courthouse to be available to fill up special juries when, as often happened, too few of the regular jury panel of twenty-four appeared to produce twelve jurors.[113]

The existence of a corps of "professional" special jurors receives statistical support from the investigative reports of the Select Committees of the House of Commons and the City of London. The 1817 London report reveals that many of the special jurors were "regulars." A few served in almost half of the 114 cases studied, and nine others (out of the total number of special jurors of 274) served in one-third or more of the cases.[114] Even more dramatic are the figures contained in returns of jurors supplied by sheriffs and other local officers to the House of Commons in 1823.[115] These data describe persons in the jury list who were named to serve in special-jury cases and thus do not include talesmen. For the crown side of the Court of Exchequer, reports for the years 1820, 1821, and 1822 reveal among the special jurors a hardy crop of perennials. As an arbitrary definition, the jurors who were named at least twenty times in one of the three years and a significant number of times in at least one of the other years were identified. There were fifty-five such jurors.[116] Taking a slightly different slice of the special jurors reported for the crown side of the Court of King's Bench, the fifty-three persons who were named fifteen or more times to special juries (constituting 3 percent of the total list) represented 62 percent of the total special-jury service. Significantly fewer special-jury nominations occurred in the Court of Common Pleas during these years, but many of the names that appeared most frequently also appeared in the groups of regulars in the King's Bench and Exchequer. No reports were given from the civil sides of King's Bench or Exchequer.

Mr. E. H. Lushington, Chief Clerk in the Crown Office of the Court of King's Bench, appended an explanatory comment to the data he returned, stating:

> Upon prosecutions of a private nature, the parties or their attorneys frequently examine the old lists, and fixing upon one, which appears to them to contain the names of persons whom they know to be in habit of attending upon the trial of Special Jury causes, they, of their own accord, and by consent, adopt such as the established list, instead of having a nomination made indiscriminately from the Sheriff's clerk. This occasions the frequent recurrence of the names upon the nomination.[117]

A similar point was independently made by the Clerk to the Prothonotaries of the Court of Common Pleas.[118] Mr. Lushington, of the Court of King's Bench, added that this process of taking special jurors by consent was never followed in prosecutions of offenses of a political nature or in indictments or informations for sedition or blasphemy, but that only thirteen such cases had occurred in the three years covered by his report.[119]

It is difficult to know how much weight to give to this general explanation of the repetition of special jurors. Tending to diminish the suggestion's validity is the fact that the professional jurors actually served in fewer than half of the cases for which they were summoned. This fact also suggests that these professional jurors were not in it for the money and that the "guinea pig" designation more properly described the talesmen. In any event, the fact that professional jurors existed, augmented by regular talesmen, came to be regarded in the nineteenth century as an odious feature of the special jury, even if it was not viewed so in the earlier era of Lord Mansfield and his merchant juries.

A final problem with special juries that boiled over during the nineteenth century was described in the following terms by commissioners of inquiry in 1851: "It is well known to be a frequent practice for defendants who wish for delay, to obtain a rule for a special jury, which practically, in London and Middlesex, has the effect of postponing the trial."[120] Chief Justice William Erle of the Court of Common Pleas put the point more bluntly:

> Frequently, the vexatious exercise of the right to a special jury is on the part of the defendant; defendants who have not money, cast about for

time, and a special jury is one of the common resources they avail themselves of.[121]

In the Juries Act of 1870, Parliament returned again to the nagging problems of special juries. New procedures were established for the preparation of special-juror lists, jurors were not to serve more than once per year, and the practice of nominating and reducing special juries, long prevalent in London and Middlesex,[122] was abolished.[123] Most significant, the qualifications for special jurors were altered. Definitions of the terms "merchant," "banker," and "esquire" were not fashioned, but the following additional persons were added to the ranks of potential special jurors: any person occupying a dwelling house rated at one hundred pounds or more in large towns and cities, or fifty pounds elsewhere; any person occupying a farm rated at three hundred pounds or more; or any person occupying nonfarm premises rated at one hundred pounds or more.[124]

Three years after the passage of the Juries Act of 1870, a member of Parliament connected with a manufacturing establishment testified before the Judicature Commissioners (who were assessing the desirability of establishing Tribunals of Commerce to be presided over by two experienced merchants) as follows: "My opinion is decidedly that two men of mature judgment and long experience are a more secure jury to appeal to than an uncertain special jury which I often see collected together, who have no knowledge whatever of the circumstances which they are going to inquire into."[125] Another MP who was a shipowner engaged in commerce testified that the quality of special jurors at Guildhall had deteriorated. Responding to a reference to the former system of juries at Guildhall under which special jurors were required to be merchants, bankers, or esquires, the MP stated: "You get a very different class of men now."[126]

Conclusion

The special jury lingered on the statute books until the mid-twentieth century. In 1949, the provisions for special juries were abolished except for the City of London Special Jury, and that reservation was eliminated in 1971.[127] In the mid-1980s, the Fraud Trials Committee considered reviving the special jury (in the form of a jury of experts), but the proposal was rejected because, in the Committee's view, "we do not believe that special jurors would have the degree of special knowledge or expertise which would be required in order properly to grasp the points of concern in a complex case."[128]

As with most features of the English jury, the special jury traveled to the United States, took root, and prospered until late in the twentieth century. Somewhat surprisingly, remnants of the special jury yet survive in a few states. The full story is told in chapter 9.

9

Special Juries in the United States and Modern Jury Formation Procedures

In this final chapter, I explore the history of the special jury in the United States and relate it to two fundamental features of the institution of trial by jury. The first is what every schoolchild learns: No one who claims to be innocent can be sentenced to jail unless found guilty of wrongdoing by a jury of his or her peers. The second is the requirement that the pool of potential jurors used by the courts must comprise, as nearly as possible, a reasonable cross-section of the community.[1] A requirement that a defendant's trial jury should contain a representative number of his or her peers (taken from a class that would represent a distinct constituent group in the community), instead of the peers merely present in the jury pool, could link these two concepts. This additional step, although taken in the past and recently advocated by a few reformers, has no support in contemporary jury practices.

The "jury of peers" notion has an ancient lineage that still reverberates as a supposedly important part of every American's heritage. An opinion in 1996 of the U.S. District Court for the Eastern District of Pennsylvania, disposing of a show-cause order against a woman who failed to appear for jury service, illustrates the modern, nostalgic perception of this heritage. Judge Hutton wrote that "The right to a trial by a jury of one's peers is one of the cornerstones of the American judicial system. It is a birthright cherished by generations of American citizens."[2] A 1968 Supreme Court discussion of the objectives of the framers of the federal and state constitutions similarly concluded that "Providing an accused with the right to be tried by a jury of his peers gave him an inestimable safeguard against the corrupt, or overzealous prosecutor and against the compliant, biased, or eccentric judge."[3] Consider also the 1995 convic-

First woman jury, Los Angeles, November 3, 1911, from the George Grantham Bain Collection. The California constitution was amended in October 1911 to give women the vote, and on November 3, 1911, this all-woman jury acquitted A. A. King, editor of the *Watts News,* who stood accused of publishing obscenity, having quoted in the newspaper language used by a city councilman. Courtesy of the Library of Congress.

tion of former congressman Walter R. Tucker III for extorting bribes while serving as mayor of Compton, California.[4] According to news reports, Tucker wrote to California governor Pete Wilson and to House Speaker Newt Gingrich, stating in his letter that he "was not judged by a jury of [his] peers and . . . did not receive a just verdict."[5]

What did former congressman Tucker mean? Who were the "peers" of whom he claimed to be deprived?[6] According to Henry Toulmin, U.S. Judge for the Mississippi Territory and author of an 1807 book called *The Magistrate's Assistant,* "The fundamental principle of this institution [trial by jury] is, that a man should be tried by his peers or equals, a commoner by commoners and a nobleman by nobles."[7] This proposition, however, is, and for the most part always has been, a fairy tale. Historically, we boasted about juries of our peers while excluding half the pop-

Photograph of three women registering for jury duty at the Hall of Records, New York City, 1937. A *World-Telegram* staff photo, labeled: "They augur no good for love slayers." The three women are identified, left to right, as Mrs. Silvia Haskell, Mrs. Rita Litman, and Mrs. Celia Winer. From the *New York World-Telegram and Sun* Newspaper Photograph Collection. Courtesy of the Library of Congress.

ulation—women—from jury service.[8] We also followed practices that kept racial and other minorities off juries or that left them drastically under-represented. In the not-so-distant past, the United States also maintained requirements of property ownership that excluded the poorest segments of the economic spectrum of society.[9]

Both the jury-of-peers concept and the reasonable-cross-section requirement relate to jury composition procedures. They do so, however, with sharply different objectives. As Judge Toulmin suggested, the jury-of-peers notion is aimed at giving the defendant a fair trial by placing on his jury at least a representative number of people who share the defendant's cultural, linguistic, ethnic, or, possibly, socioeconomic circumstances.[10] Historically, this idea gave rise to the "mixed," or "half-and-half," jury, the jury *de medietate linguae* (literally, "of the half-tongue") discussed in chapter 7,[11] to which foreign defendants would have been entitled. Half of the jury would be citizens of the state where the case was tried, while the other half would be foreigners.[12] The notion was not merely to facilitate communication but also, as expressed by a defendant in a seventeenth-century English case, to secure jurors "of my own country, that may be able to know something how I have lived hitherto."[13] Occasional recent voices have reprised this idea by calling for racial or ethnic quotas for certain types of juries.[14]

The reasonable-cross-section requirement, by contrast, is designed to ensure that members of all significant, or "cognizable," segments of the community have the opportunity to be jurors.[15] This egalitarian requirement pulls strongly against any procedure or tradition that would permit the formation of juries from lists of persons with special qualifications. In U.S. history, one well-known example of such a jury with special qualifications is the so-called blue-ribbon jury, that is, the "high-class" jury.[16] Another historical example is the jury of experts, most notably the merchant juries that were instrumental in absorbing commercial practices into common law.[17] Both of these examples fall within the meaning of the "special jury" used and understood in England for several centuries, as has been elaborated in chapters 7 and 8.

The idea of drawing exclusive special juries from specialized lists seems to be anachronistic today. Elite special juries surely are antithetical to the hard-fought, long-delayed goal of opening up jury service to everyone. Having eliminated the unsavory exclusions of the past, how can there remain a place in modern American society for an exclusive special jury?

I argue that there is still such a place—that our history justifies continued experimentation with jury composition, including the special jury. However desirable the reasonable-cross-section requirement is as a means of keeping members of an increasingly stratified society personally involved in the business of democracy, the requirement contributes little or nothing to other goals, such as coping effectively with jury trial of complex cases or striving for fairness to the litigating parties. Yet the latter goal—picking juries that will be fair to the parties—has long been central to the jury-selection process, especially as embodied in peremptory challenge and *voir-dire* practices. The Supreme Court has outlawed the use of peremptory challenges to eliminate potential jurors on the basis of race or gender as improperly discriminatory and as inconsistent with the reasonable-cross-section requirement;[18] however, *voir-dire* screening, including the use of nondiscriminatory peremptories, continues to be the principal method of ferreting out undesirable jurors.

The *voir-dire* process brings into view another prominent feature of the special jury. Historically, the term "special jury" has had two main connotations—the jury composed of jurors with special qualifications, as discussed earlier, and the jury formed by a special procedure that involves the presentation of a large panel of potential jurors to the parties, who then reduce the panel to a specified smaller number by taking turns striking names off the list. When this procedure is used, the resulting jury usually is referred to as a "struck jury."

As we saw in chapter 8, the special jury is now extinct in England. In the United States, it survives in about a dozen states, though in most of these states it persists solely as a struck-jury formation procedure.[19] For reasons later explained, this procedure often is viewed as being fairer to criminal defendants than is the peremptory challenge, the more customary device designed to protect criminal defendants in jury selection.

The other goal mentioned—coping effectively with jury trial of complex cases—encourages the use of a jury of experts, assuming the jury is constitutionally indispensable in such cases (see chapter 2). Here, too, recent voices have called for the revival or extension of this type of special jury.[20] In actual practice, Delaware is the only state where this occurs, as I later explain.[21]

Part I of this chapter discusses the history and current validity of the struck jury in both civil and criminal cases and deals with the relation between struck-jury procedures and peremptory challenges. Part II explores the history and current validity of special juries in which jurors have special qualifications. Part III discusses the relation between the special jury and the reasonable-cross-section requirement, especially as reflected in Supreme Court cases and other federal cases that deal with peremptory challenges based solely on "protected-group" characteristics such as race and sex.

I. The Struck Jury

It is helpful at the outset to understand the relationship between struck-jury procedures and the jury composed of jurors with special qualifications. Usually there is no official or formal connection. Eighteenth-century American statutes authorizing the special jury typically approved and set out a struck-jury procedure but said nothing about impaneling jurors of special qualities or characteristics. Most of the American statutes followed the 1730 English statute.[22]

Because special juries of "gentlemen of the better rank" had become customary in trials at bar in England, the special jury came to be thought of as regularly composed of such persons, even when the trial was not at bar.[23] This fact is important in understanding the adoptions of the special jury in America. In 1741, for example, New York enacted a statute that copied Parliament's 1730 statute and declared that "his Majesty's Supreme Court of this Colony" could, upon motion,

> order and appoint a jury, to be struck, before one of the Judges of the said Court, for trial of any issue joined in any of the said cases, and triable by a jury of twelve men, in such manner as special juries have by law heretofore been struck, for trials at bar; which jury, so struck, as aforesaid, shall be the jury returned for the trial of the said issue.[24]

As we shall see, New York's statutory treatment of the special jury changed after statehood, but the notion that special jurors were jurors "of the better rank" persisted.

The heritage thus was one of a statutorily endorsed struck-jury procedure that said nothing about who the special jurors should be, yet was undergirded by a custom of filling the special jury with upper-class gentlemen. By the time of American independence, the custom had expanded so that, in commercial cases, special juries of merchants were commonplace.[25]

Against this background, I turn to the struck jury as it took root and prospered in the United States. The formulas in the several states, even in the eighteenth century, were by no means uniform. Clusters of states, however, followed similar patterns, especially as the statutory adoptions spread westward in the nineteenth century

A. States in Which the Special Jury Remains Valid

There are about a dozen states in which the special, or struck, jury remains on the statute books.[26] In several of these, the struck-jury procedure is used in criminal cases because it is viewed as allowing a voir-dire superior to the "jury-box" method.[27] Indeed, as I will explain, this perceived superiority led trial judges in Hawaii to use the struck-jury method in the face of a contrary statutory mandate.

In three states—Delaware, Virginia, and Alabama—the special or struck jury continues to be regarded as a significant part of the jury-trial heritage. The approaches in the three states, however, are very different, and each requires elaboration.

Delaware is a special-jury laboratory. Constitutional challenges to the special jury have been unsuccessful in Delaware, and the current statute is the only one in the nation that overtly authorizes the use of the special jury for complex civil litigation. This authorization is a recent development; the early history began in 1793 when the Delaware legislature passed "An Act for more certainly obtaining returns of impartial juries, and their better regulation."[28] That statute gave the sheriff directions about what to do with the return of the *venire facias,* "unless in cases where a special jury shall be struck by rule of court."[29] A "rule of court" was a court order, and thus it is clear that informal special-jury usage was in place in Delaware during the eighteenth century.

The first detailed statutory recognition of this usage in Delaware came in an 1810 act that provided that a struck jury was required on application of either party "in any action, cause or suit whatsoever" in the Supreme Court or the Court of Common Pleas.[30] According to the Delaware Supreme Court in a 1960 decision, *Nance v. Rees,*[31] the 1810 act could be traced to the English statute of 1730, and "the Act of 1810 did no more than codify into statutory law a practice long followed in Delaware courts as a part of the legal heritage from England.[32] Open to question, however, was whether the procedure applied to criminal as well as to civil cases. In *Rush v. State,*[33] a defendant in a murder case claimed that his request at trial for a special jury should have been granted, but the Supreme Court of Delaware concluded that "The legislative history of the Delaware special jury statute, from its inception in 1810, indicates that special juries were to be confined to courts of civil jurisdiction."[34]

The formula specified in the 1810 statute was one that is now familiar—forty-eight freeholders "most indifferent" and "best qualified" were to be reduced to twenty-four by alternating strikes by the parties.[35] With comparatively minor adjustments, this formula persisted in Delaware for 177 years. In 1987, however, Delaware repealed the statute and replaced it with a single paragraph, which opens with the following sentence: "The court may order a special jury upon the application of any party in a complex civil case."[36] The methodology for impaneling special juries under this law is left, apparently, to court rules or to the ad hoc invention of trial judges.[37] Substantively, the two major changes were the conversion from special juries as a matter of right (as they had been under the 1810 statute) to one of court discretion and the limitation of special juries to complex civil cases. As is discussed later, both the traditional struck-jury statute and the succinct 1987 version survived constitutional challenge in Delaware during the 1980s.[38]

In Virginia, the first statutory appearance of the struck jury appears to have been in 1788 for impeachment trials. The statute provided for the sheriff to return a panel of twenty-four jurors from the senatorial district where the accused resided; then, "The prosecutor for the commonwealth, and the person accused, shall, in open Court, alternately strike one, until the number shall be reduced to twelve."[39] The general availability of the struck jury entered the statute books much later. The Virginia Code of 1849 provided that a trial jury would be formed by reducing a panel of twenty-four to eighteen by lot, after which the eighteen would be reduced to twelve by alternate strikes by the parties.[40] In 1887, however, the Virginia Code was changed to provide: "Any court, in a case where a jury is required, may allow a special jury."[41] The procedure was to summon a panel of twenty qualified jurors, to choose sixteen of them by lot, and to reduce the sixteen to twelve by alternate strikes by the parties. This formula remained until 1950, when Virginia moved to smaller juries for most cases and adopted the struck jury across the board.[42] The 1950 Code specified that juries in minor civil cases (up to one thousand dollars in controversy) should be five jurors out of a panel of eleven; in other civil cases, the jury was to be seven out of a panel of thirteen, "except that when a special jury is allowed, twelve persons from a panel of twenty shall constitute the jury."[43] In all cases, alternate strikes by the parties were to reduce the panel to the number of jurors for the applicable jury.

The jury provisions of the Virginia Code of 1950 remain in place today, except for an increase in the jurisdictional limit for the five-person civil jury from one thousand to fifteen thousand dollars.[44] The only difference between ordinary civil juries and special juries in civil cases is the size of the jury panel and the jury itself. Nothing in the statutory language or case law indicates that special jurors are to be persons of special qualifications.[45] Another provision of the Code of 1950 (still in effect), however, permits the parties to create a jury of three members by consent. The plaintiff selects one juror, the defendant selects a second, and the two jurors in turn select a third, and "any two concurring shall render a verdict in like manner and with like effect as a jury of seven."[46] Although not a struck jury, this jury-by-consent is a special jury in the sense that it is formed by a special procedure. What the jury-by-consent most resembles is arbitration.[47]

Alabama uses the struck jury in both criminal and civil cases. The original 1841 statutory authorization in Alabama for struck juries applied to civil cases "sounding in damages merely" or involving more than one hundred dollars.[48] Alternate strikes were to reduce panels of twenty-four persons to twelve.[49] Alabama later expanded this authorization to "all civil actions triable by jury,"[50] an expansion that is still in operation.[51] The Alabama Rules of Civil Procedure, which control all Alabama courts except district courts, codify the same procedure.[52] The struck-jury method of Rule 47(b) superseded the older method of peremptory challenges that was available in civil cases for which no special jury was selected.[53]

Meanwhile, early in the twentieth century, the struck-jury procedure was made applicable to Alabama criminal cases.[54] A sliding scale was fashioned so that a panel of at least thirty-six is required for capital offenses, twenty-four for noncapital felonies, and eighteen for misdemeanors. This scheme supplanted peremptory challenges in criminal trials.[55] Constitutional attacks on the statutes that apply the struck jury to criminal cases failed.[56]

Other states in which the struck jury remains valid by statute include South Carolina, Indiana, Arkansas, Maryland, and West Virginia.[57] Use of the method of striking jurors in lieu of peremptories, without calling the result a struck jury, is codified in Arizona and Texas.[58] In addition, there is evidence that the method is used pursuant to court rules in Massachusetts and that it has been employed by trial judges as a matter of personal preference in Alaska, Hawaii, and California.[59]

The South Carolina experience with the special jury was unique in its explicit use of merchant juries in the eighteenth century.[60] A 1769 statute authorized special juries in the Charleston Court of Common Pleas, if consented to by both parties in cases involving trade or considerable money or in disputes between merchants.[61] Although the statute referred to ordering "a special jury to be struck," the method of juror selection was by balloting—either from lists of potential jurors that the parties supplied (for trials at bar of causes "of weight and importance") or from regular jury lists.[62] The legislature later observed that the 1769 plan sometimes resulted in special juries "drawn entirely out of the number of those whose names were given in or delivered to the court by one of the parties in controversy," and the law was changed in 1791 to a complicated formula, applicable on consent of both parties, on request of either party, or at the court's discretion in big-money cases.[63] The gist of the formula was that each party was to supply eighteen names of qualified grand jurors; then each party was to strike ten names from the other party's list and identify two names from the twenty rejects to serve as "talesmen" (backup jurors), if needed. This resulted in a panel of twenty names to be summoned for trial.[64] Five years later, this act was repealed, and the next year, the right to a special jury was abolished "except by consent of both parties" because the device had been found to have been "abused to the purposes of delay and chicanery."[65] When both parties consented, however, the 1791 procedure still could be used.

There were other legislative adjustments over time in South Carolina, and, during the twentieth century, the legislature adopted a straightforward struck-jury approach that remains in effect. The current version calls for the clerk in the Court of Common Pleas to supply a list of twenty jurors from "the whole number of jurors who are in attendance," and then alternate strikes reduce this list to the trial jury of twelve persons.[66]

In Indiana, the nineteenth-century statutory authorization of special juries began with the simple declaration that "The Court shall have the power, when the business thereof requires it, to order the impaneling of a special jury for the trial of any cause."[67] This was accompanied by a provision captioned "Jury by agreement," which allowed the parties to "agree upon the jurors to compose a special jury, and notify the Court thereof."[68] Alternatively, the parties were allowed to have a "struck jury, by consent," formed by a return by the sheriff of eighteen competent jurors, reduced to a jury of six via six strikes by each party or by any other number of strikes the parties might choose.[69] When the struck jury was ordered by the court instead of the parties, the Indiana formula was for a panel of the forty "most indifferent" and "best qualified" men to be returned, and each party was to strike twelve, reducing the panel to sixteen.[70] Amendments in 1913 deleted the language that called for the clerk to select forty men "most indifferent" and "best qualified," substituting instructions for the clerk to take forty names from a well-shaken box containing the names of qualified ordinary jurors.[71] In 1988, Indiana repealed the provisions that allowed the court to order struck juries, but the sections that allowed a special jury by agreement or a struck jury by consent remain intact.[72]

The remnant of the struck jury in Arkansas is evident in statutes that grant each party three peremptory challenges. On the criminal side, each party in a misdemeanor case has three peremptories that can be exercised orally, after which the names of twenty-four jurors are put in a box, eighteen names are drawn and entered on a list, each party strikes up to three names, and the first twelve names remaining constitute the jury.[73] In civil cases, the formula is similar, but the process of striking from a list of eighteen names drawn from twenty-four is optional.[74] Previously the state utilized a more typical struck-jury method; on the request of either party, the circuit court had discretion to order that a panel of forty-two names be returned, and this list, after each party's twelve strikes, would be reduced to eighteen names.[75]

Maryland used the struck-jury method for nearly two centuries in jury formation for all trials. Under a 1797 statute, for each civil case the clerks drew a panel of twenty jurors by ballot; then the list was delivered to the parties, each of whom struck out four names.[76] Maryland extended this procedure to criminal cases in 1802, except for capital felonies or treasons, for which peremptory challenges were allowed.[77]

Under current law in Maryland, the procedural rules contain the method for striking names that is used to effectuate peremptory challenges. In civil cases in the circuit court, each side has four peremptories (and possibly more, if alternate jurors are impaneled), which are exercised by striking names off a list "sufficient to provide the number of jurors and alternates to be sworn after allowing for the exercise of peremptory challenges."[78] Larger numbers of peremptories are allowed in criminal cases,[79] and striking names off a jury list occurs only if no party requests alternating challenges.[80]

Until 1985, West Virginia law provided that "any court may allow a special jury in any civil case," and such juries were formed in a typical manner—twenty names to be drawn, reduced to sixteen by lot, and then reduced to twelve by two strikes by each party.[81] By 1985 amendments, the numbers were changed to ten, reduced to eight by lot, and then ultimately reduced to six by one strike each.[82] The original formula was retained, however, for eminent-domain cases.[83]

The last group of active struck jury states I mention only briefly. In Arizona, the rules of civil procedure state that the clerk shall make a list consisting of as many names drawn from the jury box as the court directs, from which the parties alternate in making peremptory challenges until such challenges are exhausted, and the clerk then calls the first eight persons on the list of remaining names to serve as the jury.[84] In Texas, the law provides that in all criminal cases that do not involve the death penalty, "the party desiring to challenge any juror peremptorily shall strike the name of such juror from the list furnished him by the clerk."[85]

The occasional use of a struck-jury method of choosing jurors in Massachusetts is demonstrated by *Commonwealth v. Johnson.*[86] In *Johnson,* the defendant was convicted of rape, and among his challenges on appeal was a claim that the trial judge had deprived him of his peremptory challenges by imposing the struck-jury method upon him.[87] The claim was rejected after the court explained that the struck method was not a system for exercising peremptory challenges but was, rather, "an alternative method for selecting a jury," in which a *venire* pool of about one hundred members is drawn. After *venire* persons from the pool are excused for cause or hardship, the jurors are struck; the defendant strikes two members of the remaining *venire,* the prosecutor then strikes one member, and the process is repeated until twelve jurors remain, who then serve as jurors for the trial.[88]

Similarly, in the 1992 case of *Van Huff v. Sohio,*[89] the Alaska Supreme Court held that the trial court did not abuse its discretion by using the struck-jury method of jury selection, nor was the method inconsistent with the rule used in Alaska for peremptory challenges. Finally, in Hawaii and California, the use of the struck-jury method by trial judges has been held to be improper because it is inconsistent with the method of jury selection prescribed by statute, but if the defendant fails to object to the struck-jury method at trial, or if the defendant cannot show prejudice, its use will not justify reversal of a conviction.[90]

B. States in Which the Once-Authorized Special Jury Is No Longer Valid

New York and New Jersey have especially rich special-jury histories, including, for New York, two U.S. Supreme Court cases. The special jury survived in New York until 1965,[91] but in a surprising, inverted way. Although the special jury remained theoretically available in both civil and criminal cases until its repeal, it was used rarely in civil trials; instead, its most interesting twentieth-century history was in capital criminal cases. Most states with early struck-jury histories followed England's lead and withheld the device from capital cases so as not to reduce the number of the defendant's peremptory challenges. New York, however, fashioned a unique statute in 1896 that provided for special juries only in criminal cases and only in two counties—those having a population of more than 500,000.[92] Special juries were allowable if necessary for a fair and impartial trial or because of the "importance or intricacy" of the case.[93] Special jurors were to be chosen from a special list to be prepared by jury commissioners after personal interviews.[94] In addition to ordinary trial-juror qualifications, each candidate had to have a clean record in the courts, be able to disregard newspaper publicity, disavow any conscientious objection to the death penalty, and be able to resist any negative presumption if a defendant were to decline to testify.[95]

Shortly after the 1896 New York special jury statute was passed, Benjamin Tucker gave a speech at the Cooper Union under the auspices of several labor unions; his talk constituted a scathing criticism of the elitist and exclusive effects of the new law. The speech was published in 1889 under the title "A Blow at Trial by Jury."[96] In his opening remarks, Tucker stated that, instead of the actual title ("An Act providing for a special jury in criminal cases in each county of the State having a certain population, and for the mode of selecting and procuring such special juries; also, creating a special jury commissioner for each of such counties, and regulating and prescribing his duties"), a more accurate title would have been:

> An act providing for the enforcement of those laws of the State of New York which, having found their way into the statute-books only through the insidious machinations of a clique or a cabal or a boss or an interest or a handful of fanatics, are so unpopular with the citizens of the State of New York that a conviction of the violation of them can seldom, if ever, be secured from a jury fairly and impartially impaneled from the mass of sober-minded people.[97]

Many years passed, but eventually Benjamin Tucker's attitude began to be shared by New York judges. In a 1960 decision, *Schuster v. City of New York*,[98] Supreme Court Judge Henry Martuscello wrote a lengthy opinion denying the defendant's motion for a special jury in an action for damages allegedly caused by police negligence in not preventing an informer's murder. The judge observed that "the historic purpose for which the special jury was introduced to common law [was] to provide more intelligent and competent jurors in exceptional cases," and he concluded that the case before him was not sufficiently important or intricate to justify a special jury.[99] In reaching this conclusion, he expressed his strong distaste for the elitist nature of blue-ribbon juries, noting that five separate New York judicial councils or conferences from 1937 to 1952 had recommended abolition of the special jury.[100] Judge Martuscello stated, incorrectly, that special juries "were not authorized in this state" until the 1896 statute and "were not established in civil actions until the enactment of Chapter 602 of the Laws of 1901."[101]

In fact, the special jury in civil cases went much further back in New York history than 1896. That history is laid out by Morton Horwitz in *The Transformation of American Law 1780–1860.*[102] Horwitz describes "the 'struck' or special jury" as "a favorite institution of colonial merchants" that the 1741 statute initially authorized and that a 1786 enactment re-endorsed after independence.[103] In 1801, however, New York codified a detailed struck-jury procedure that, according to Horwitz, "for the first time placed struck juries within the judges' control, permitting them only where the court 'may deem it necessary, by reason of the importance or intricacy of the case.'"[104]

By the time George Caines published his New York practice book in 1808, the special jury had assumed sufficient importance to occupy a full chapter.[105] Caines quoted the 1801 statute verbatim. Among other things, the statute sets forth the New York version of the English procedure: In the presence of the parties, the clerk or his deputy was to copy out of the jury book forty-eight names, which would then be reduced to twenty-four by alternate strikes by the parties; the panel of twenty-four would be summoned for jury service; and on the day of trial, "the jurors so struck shall be called as they stand upon the panel, and the first twelve of them who shall appear and are not challenged, or shall be found duly qualified and indifferent, shall be the jury, and be sworn to try the said cause."[106] Nothing in the act called for a special list of, as Judge Martuscello put it, "more intelligent and competent jurors,"[107] but the act made the special jury a matter of judicial discretion in "intricate or important" cases.[108]

Horwitz points out that the 1801 statute led to a number of special juries between 1801 and 1807, chiefly in marine insurance cases.[109] Thereafter, however, "we hear no more of merchant juries in New York commercial cases of any sort," even though the statute remained on the books, "and indeed special juries continued to be used in libel cases."[110]

In *Schuster v. City of New York,* Judge Martuscello gave the twentieth-century history of the civil special jury in New York on the basis of a total of six cases—four in the first decade, one in 1922, and one in 1935.[111] Declining to make *Schuster* the seventh case, the judge declared: "Juries were intended to serve as instruments of justice. They cannot fulfill that purpose unless they are truly representative of the community. There can be no true equal representation of a community if jurors are selected because of an alleged economic, social or superior educational status. Responsibility in our democracy should be shared by all and not a few."[112] He admonished that "Juries of character, courage, and independence can only exist in an atmosphere where there is no discrimination in their choice because of social, economic or philosophic reasons."[113]

Judge Martuscello's sentiments anticipated, or were in the vanguard of, the "reasonable-cross-section" movement that has since swept the country.[114] They are, of course, open to challenge. It is not self-evident why juries cannot accomplish "justice" unless they are truly representative of the community. Presumably New York would continue to achieve justice in capital criminal cases while special juries persisted.[115]

New Jersey adopted its version of the English special jury practice in 1797 and retained it until 1991. The original act validated the granting of a special jury in any civil case or in any criminal case that did not involve a right to peremptory challenges.[116] When granted, the sheriff was to select forty-eight men from the jury book—men deemed by the sheriff "most impartial and indifferent" and "best qualified as to talents, knowledge, integrity, firmness and independence of sentiment."[117] The parties then were to strike out twelve each, leaving a jury panel of twenty-four to be summoned for trial.[118] New Jersey made significant changes to this scheme in 1851. The new law made struck juries available in any civil or criminal case, but in civil cases the court had to be satisfied (by an affidavit by the party requesting the struck jury) that the nature and importance of the matter in controversy merited the step.[119] Perhaps New Jersey had encountered the same thing that had happened in the English courts—tactical special-jury requests by lawyers seeking only to delay proceedings.[120]

Another significant change made in New Jersey in 1851 was to give the court, in civil cases, the option of ordering either a panel of forty-eight to be reduced to twenty-four or a panel of thirty-six to be reduced to eighteen.[121] The law then remained stable until the end of the century, when New Jersey revised the formula to require a jury panel of ninety-six names, to be reduced to forty-eight by twenty-four strikes on each side, after which the forty-eight names remaining were to be "placed in the box," and "the jury for trial of the case is drawn in the usual way."[122]

These numbers, however, must have become cumbersome, because New Jersey changed the law again and readopted the 1851 standard—discretion in the trial court to grant a struck jury in any civil or criminal case after the nature and importance of the case were established by affidavit.[123] When granted, the order was to "direct the jury commissioners of the county in which the cause is to be tried to prepare a list of 36 or 48 persons or, in special causes or in a criminal cause, a larger number of persons"; the parties or their attorneys were then to strike names until half of the names on the list remained, and the trial jury was to be selected from the remaining names "in as nearly as possible the same manner as a jury from the general panel is required to be selected."[124]

Over the years, New Jersey's struck-jury statutes were tested often in the courts. In *Fowler v. State,*[125] for example, the New Jersey Supreme Court held that the struck-jury statute was valid under the New Jersey Constitution of 1844 and its guarantee of trial by jury. The court observed that the struck jury was derived from English law and had been confirmed by New Jersey legislation in existence when the constitution was passed.[126] Another attack, this time after the 1898 amendments, failed in *Brown v. State.*[127] There, the struck-jury system was claimed to be inconsistent with the defendant's right to challenge potential jurors;[128] however, the New Jersey Court of Appeals disagreed, noting that the struck list of forty-eight names had to be given to the defendant at least twelve days before impaneling, providing ample time to ascertain grounds of objection to individual jurors.[129] Moreover, the defendant was entitled to five peremptory challenges as the names of the trial jurors were drawn from the box of forty-eight names.[130]

After a period of relative calm, several cases decided in the late 1980s contested anew the New Jersey struck-jury system. Because these cases dealt with voir-dire issues, I defer them until the following section on peremptory challenges.[131] Still other cases, scattered across most of the twentieth century, questioned the struck-jury system in terms of its "excluding" effect—its effect of leaving protected groups underrepresented or unrepresented in the jury pool.[132] Finally, in 1991, New Jersey repealed the struck-jury procedure.[133] Two special applications of the struck jury remain on the books, but their retention after the 1991 repeal may have been oversight.[134]

Because a wide variety of historical patterns has been traced, only a brief description follows of comparable struck-jury experience in other states in which the procedure has been repealed. Although this may not be an exhaustive list, the following states, by region, once had struck juries: in the Northeast and mid-Atlantic region: Pennsylvania and Vermont; in the South: Georgia; in the Midwest: Iowa, Michigan, Minnesota, Missouri, Ohio, and Wisconsin; and in the West and Southwest: Nevada and Oklahoma. Some of these states followed the standard English model or a close variant.[135] Often the size of the prestrike panel was smaller than forty-eight.[136] Surprisingly, however, in Nevada, the prestrike panel was to number one hundred, to be reduced to fifty by alternate strikes.[137] At the other end of the spectrum, Iowa, in 1851, legislated a six-man struck jury, reduced from a panel of eighteen,[138] and in 1873, the parties in a struck-jury case were given statutory authority to choose that the verdict should be by majority vote.[139] Iowa repealed these procedures in 1927.[140]

In 1890, the legislature of the Oklahoma Territory passed a statute authorizing a special jury whenever the court's business required it.[141] If ordered, the statute provided that "The parties may agree upon the jurors to compose a special jury."[142] Alternatively, the parties could have the sheriff return a panel of eighteen, to be reduced to six by alternate strikes; otherwise, the "forty to sixteen to twelve" formula used in other states was to be followed.[143]

In Pennsylvania, the struck jury had a long history, starting in the eighteenth century. Initially authorized by statute in 1785, the special jury survived until 1937.[144] By the end of the nineteenth century, however, the status of the statutory authorization was uncertain, as is shown by the following annotation to the special-jury provision in the 1894 Code: "This subject is in a very confused state; but as the right is a common-law one, and the act of 1785 has never been expressly repealed, it seems safer to insert it. There is certainly nothing corresponding to the clear irreconcilability that is necessary to constitute a repeal by implication."[145]

C. The Relationship Between the Struck Jury and Peremptory Challenges

The right to strike a specified number of jurors without giving any reason closely resembles the right to a specified number of peremptory challenges. In practice, however, the two concepts differ in important ways.

The reason the struck jury was inapplicable to trials of capital offenses in England in the eighteenth century was pragmatic. The struck-jury tradition that had crept into practice the century before had settled on a jury panel of forty-eight, with twelve strikes on each side, and this did not accommodate a defendant's right to thirty-five peremptory challenges. There is no evidence that anyone seriously argued for extending the struck-jury procedure to capital offenses by increasing the size of the jury panel from which names would be struck. Had there been any such attempt, another problem immediately would have come into view.

The struck-jury procedure was a preliminary process implemented in the clerk's office before any jurors whatever had been summoned to the courthouse. The struck-jury tradition was that of striking names off a list, whereas the tradition of peremptory challenges was one of eliminating persons who had appeared for jury duty and who stood ready to serve. As Justice Harlan observed in 1884 in *Pointer v. United States,*[146] "The right to challenge a given number of jurors without showing cause is one of the most important of the rights secured to the accused"; therefore, "Any system for the empaneling of a jury that prevents or embarrasses the full, unrestricted exercise by the accused of that right, must be condemned," and the defendant "cannot be compelled to make a peremptory challenge until he has been brought face to face, in the presence of the court, with each proposed juror, and an opportunity given for such inspection and examination of him as is required for the due administration of justice."[147]

Thus, it is obvious that the traditional struck-jury system fell far short of the protection intended by peremptory challenges. Changes in court practice, however, eliminated the problem. In 1986, in the case of *United States v. Ricks,*[148] convicted drug dealers challenged the use of the struck-jury system at their trial by the U.S. District Court for the District of Maryland. In the Fourth Circuit opinion giving qualified approval to the use of the struck jury, Judge Winter noted that, at common law, twenty-four veniremen were returned by the sheriff after the parties had "exercised their strikes against the list" because "Experience demonstrated that twenty-four veniremen were usually necessary to ensure that at least twelve persons appeared."[149] As Judge Winter explained, "The rationale for summoning more than the minimum number required to draw a jury does not exist today where the veniremen are summoned and are present in the courtroom before any exercise of peremptory challenges."[150]

Under modern practice, therefore, the struck-jury method can satisfy statutory rights to peremptory challenges. Indeed, the method is widely viewed from the criminal defendant's vantage point as superior to the traditional "jury-box" method. As the Second Circuit explained in *United States v. Blouin:*[151]

> Within the Second Circuit, both the "jury box" and the "struck jury" methods are used. The goal of the "jury box" system is to fill the box with twelve acceptable jurors, and the system is indifferent whether the parties use all their challenges before acquiescing in a panel, or waive all challenges and accept the first twelve called. The goal of the "struck jury" is to whittle down an initially selected group of normally twenty-eight candidates (twelve jurors plus sixteen challenges) to twelve survivors, and it therefore builds in a preference for the parties' exercising all their allotted challenges. This difference in procedure highlights the different outlooks of the two systems. The "jury box" system tends to focus the parties' attention on one member of the *venire* at a time, as he or she is seated in the box, and prompts the parties to ask, "Is this juror acceptable?" The "struck jury" system, by contrast, emphasizes the overall complexion of the panel and suggests the very different question, "Which twelve of these twenty-eight will be most favorable to my side?"
>
> By permitting full comparative choice among a panel of twenty-eight prospective jurors, the "struck jury" system lets the parties make the most effective use of their challenges, in the sense that through their choices they are able to determine from the initial panel not only who will not serve but also who will serve as the petit jury. The "jury box" system does not afford the opportunity . . . of full comparative choice, for the parties do not know ahead of time who the replacement for a challenged juror will be.[152]

With this explanation in mind, it will not be surprising to learn that convicted criminal defendants have raised on appeal (unsuccessfully) the claim that they have been deprived of the full and effective use of their peremptories when the struck-jury method of impaneling the jury was *not* used at trial.[153] In the *Blouin* case, for example, the court, although admitting that the struck-jury method "affords a more 'effective' opportunity for the use of peremptories than the 'jury box' system," held that both systems fell within trial-court discretion and that neither was mandatory.[154]

The courts, however, continue to face new issues about the struck-jury system. In the Fourth Circuit decision in *United States v. Ricks,*[155] a divided court observed that, "from the historic operation of the struck-jury system and from the careful recitation of facts showing that in each case upholding its validity, the number of veniremen supplied to counsel did not exceed the number of jurors actually required plus the authorized number of peremptory challenges" and held that such a limitation on the size of the panel "is an essential requirement of a valid struck jury system."[156] The dissent called this "a new rule that affects every criminal trial in this circuit"—a rule that prior authority refuted and that worked against the "fair-cross-section of the community" goal.[157]

The history of the struck jury does not support the viewpoint of either the majority or the dissent in *Ricks*. The limitation that the majority articulated cannot be found in "the historic operation of the struck jury."[158] Even though, as the dissent stated, "A large venire . . . enhances the likelihood that the jury will include a fair cross-section of the community,"[159] that goal was never a rationale for the struck jury. The struck jury originated in civil cases, and it gave the parties some degree of control over jury composition that they otherwise would not have had.[160] In doing so, the struck-jury concept was cousin to the jury of peers in that it allowed parties some leeway to pick jurors sympathetic to their lifestyles and circumstances. At least in theory, the same can be said of peremptories.[161] Regardless of whether the number of strikes is limited to the number of peremptories, the struck-jury formula is not complementary to the reasonable-cross-section requirement. The struck-jury formula is a protection for litigants, while the cross-section requirement is a device to protect the citizens' right to serve on juries.[162]

II. The Special Jury Composed of Jurors with Special Qualifications

It is not radical to hope to fill juries with capable people. As already mentioned for Delaware and Indiana,[163] early statutes explicitly called for jurors to be "well-informed,"[164] or "most indifferent" and "best-qualified."[165] The special jury, however, was often thought of as a blue-ribbon, or high-class, jury, somewhat in the tradition of the grand jury.[166] This is but one of at least four types of "special-qualification" juries represented in American jury traditions and practices, each of which is discussed in the sections that follow.

A. The Blue-Ribbon, or High-Class, Jury

In the United States, the practice of impaneling "gentlemen of the better rank" was ordinarily an unwritten custom,[167] although sometimes a statute explicitly required it. In New Jersey, the 1797 statute authorizing the struck jury specified that the sheriff was to select as the struck-jury panel the forty-eight persons from the jury book that he thought were "most impartial and indifferent . . . and best qualified as to talents, knowledge, integrity, firmness and independence of sentiment, to try the said cause."[168] Indeed, the 1929 amendment that dropped these qualifying words was unsuccessfully challenged in court as unconstitutional.[169]

In Georgia, the special jury was expressly linked to the grand jury. From 1796 until 1914, Georgia statutes required special jurors to be taken from the grand-jury list.[170] Grand jurors, in turn, were to be "the persons most able, discreet and qualified."[171]

The struck-jury procedures in New York are those that have been most notoriously associated with jurors "of the better rank." The procedures twice came before the U.S. Supreme Court in the 1940s—in *Fay v. New York*[172] and in *Moore v. New York*.[173] Both times the Court barely upheld the special-jury statutes by a five-to-four vote, over strongly worded dissents by Justice Frank Murphy. In *Fay,* Justice Robert H. Jackson, writing for the majority, explained: "Special jurors are selected from those accepted for the general panel by the county clerk, but only after each has been subpoenaed for personal appearance and has testified under oath as to his qualification and fitness."[174] Justice Jackson reviewed the prior unsuccessful attacks on the New York special jury because of its restrictive composition, after which he turned to the proof presented in the case before the Court. Tabulations and studies of New York jury questionnaires had been presented to show that laborers, operatives, craftsmen, foremen, service employees, and women were systematically excluded from the special-jury panel. The Court was not convinced that the statistics proved "that the jury percentages are the result of discrimination,"[175] stating that "petitioners adduced no evidence whatever that the occupational composition of the general panel is substantially different from that of the special"[176] and adding that women had an absolute exemption from jury service should they wish to exercise it, which apparently they often did.[177] Dissenting Justice Murphy, anticipating later developments, thought that the blue-ribbon jury "denies the defendant his constitutional right to be tried by a jury fairly drawn from a cross-section of the com-

Pen-and-ink drawing by the artist Charles Dana Gibson (1867–1944), published in *Life* magazine, December 22, 1927, captioned "Called for Jury duty." Hardly a reasonable cross-section of the community, most of these prospective jurors can be seen as coming "from the better rank" of society. Courtesy of the Library of Congress.

munity."[178] Justice Murphy admitted that "There is no constitutional right to a jury drawn from a group of uneducated and unintelligent persons" or "chosen solely from those at the lower end of the economic and social scale,"[179] but he observed that the jury "is a democratic institution, representative of all qualified classes of people," so that the jury lists had to include persons "with varying degrees of training and intelligence and with varying economic and social positions."[180] He continued the argument in the *Moore* case, characterizing the New York special-jury panels as "completely at war with the democratic theory of our jury system, a theory formulated out of the experience of generations."[181]

The repeal of the New York blue-ribbon-jury statute in 1965 ended the era in U.S. history when trial juries could be formed from special lists of persons in the upper echelons of society. It is not surprising that this era happened or that it is now closed; nevertheless, the idea of special juries of experts survives. Because experts typically are highly educated, most of them fall in the upper end of the socioeconomic spectrum. It is usually less objectionable, however, to think of selecting special jurors from this segment of society when those jurors are chosen for their expertise, rather than solely because of their social standing.

B. The Jury of Experts

The notion of bringing experts into dispute settlement processes makes good common sense and has an extensive history. Perhaps the best-known example is the use of experts as arbitrators. The idea of expert decision makers is also at the heart of the extensive network of quasi-adjudicatory administrative agencies that has flourished since New Deal days. Another example is the formation of specialty courts, such as a commercial court[182] or the U.S. Court of Patent Appeals.[183] Neither the private arbitrator nor the administrative judge, however, need worry about submitting questions of fact to a jury. Specialty courts must do so, continuing to recognize the preserved right to jury trial embodied in the Seventh Amendment, comparable state constitutional provisions, and statutes.

As has been discussed, the courts have not effectively responded to the robust debate in legal literature about the constitutionality of dispensing with the jury in complex civil litigation.[184] By and large, the argument that a "complexity exception" can be carved out of the Seventh Amendment has not succeeded. One alternative, as earlier noted,[185] would be to revive and expand the use of the special jury and to utilize jurors equipped by education or training to understand the complex issues in dispute. This idea is currently on the statute books in Delaware. Before discussing Delaware's statutory provisions, however, I will lay out the historical use of special juries of experts.

The most common historical example, following the English experience,[186] is the use of the merchant jury for commercial cases. There was such a chapter in New York law, as earlier explained.[187] South Carolina and Louisiana also utilized the merchant jury.

In addition to discussing New York's use of the merchant jury, Morton Horwitz summarized the South Carolina history in *The Transformation of American Law 1780–1860.*[188] According to Horwitz, "Even more than in New York, merchant juries seem to have exerted a powerful influence over the course of development of post-revolutionary South Carolina commercial law."[189] He gives several examples of the power of merchant juries during the 1780s and early 1790s (their heyday in South Carolina), authorized by a colonial statute of 1769[190] and allowed on the court's own motion by an Act of 1791.[191]

The Library of Congress holds a privately printed volume containing South Carolina jury lists from 1778 to 1779.[192] These were copied from original handwritten lists in the South Carolina archives and are broken down by judicial districts, as shown on explanatory maps. Three categories are tracked—grand jurors, petit jurors, and special jurors. Special jurors made up 38 percent of the total number of jurors in Charleston, whereas in other districts the percentages ranged from 2 percent to 8 percent. Clearly, the use of special juries of merchants in the commercial center of South Carolina was well established by the time of American independence, and probably earlier. As Horwitz pointed out, however, parties began to use special juries as a delay tactic, and, in 1797, South Carolina passed a statute that limited special juries to cases in which both parties consented.[193] Thereafter the special jury trail goes cold. Presumably the use gradually died out.[194]

Louisiana is another jurisdiction with a history of actively using merchant juries. In 1807, Louisiana passed a statute that proved to be unique in U.S. history by allowing the trial judge to appoint special jurors who had expertise relevant to the litigated dispute. The statute provided:

> In all cases when the judges shall be of opinion that the matters to be submitted to the decision of a jury, are of such a nature as to require certain information peculiar to certain occupations or professions, then and in that case the judges are empowered, at the request of either party, to direct to be summoned a sufficient number of jurors; being of the occupation, profession or trade, an acquaintance with which is more particularly necessary for the decision of the cause.[195]

The experience in Louisiana with this statute (which was repealed in 1823 and reinstated in 1831) is described by Richard Kilbourne in *Louisiana Commercial Law*.[196] According to Kilbourne, the statute, after its revival in 1831, "remained viable during the antebellum period and even appears in John Ray's Digest of 1870."[197] He attributes this longevity to facts peculiar to New Orleans—its civil-law tradition, the dependence of its economy on international trade, and the concomitant traffic in commercial paper.[198] His own examination of juries summoned during the first three years of the Commercial Court,[199] from 1839 to 1842, showed a large percentage of merchants even when the juries were not special. This abundance of merchants was primarily a result of the fact that often merchants were the only men who met the qualifications for regular jury service.[200]

After the Commercial Court was eliminated in Louisiana, in 1846, the preeminence of merchants on juries, both special and ordinary, undoubtedly dwindled.[201] For several decades, however, the experience with merchant juries in New Orleans represented the closest approximation in the United States to Lord Chief Justice Mansfield's use of merchant juries to incorporate mercantile practices into the common law.[202] Kilbourne names many of the prominent commission merchants, brokers, bankers, directors of insurance companies, and directors of the chamber of commerce who served as jurors.[203] Moreover, he notes that, "Permitting juries of merchants . . . to generate their own laws with a stamp of approval on trade practices had important economic repercussions."[204]

Delaware also has a rich history of special-jury use. As earlier explained, the Delaware statute passed in 1987 allows a special jury to be ordered "upon the application of any party in a complex civil case."[205] The Delaware Superior Court upheld the constitutionality of special juries in *In re Asbestos Litigation*.[206] The court concluded that "qualifications of jurors and the exercise of peremptory challenges, which are the distinguishing characteristics of the special jury procedure, are not constitutionally protected,"[207] and that the statutory change in 1987 that converted the Delaware special jury from a matter of right to a matter of court discretion was legitimate.[208]

In reaching these conclusions, the Delaware court briefly reviewed the English special-jury background, including William Blackstone's reference to "causes of too great nicety for discussion of ordinary freeholders."[209] The court also noted that "The use of special jurors who had particular knowledge or experience in the subject of the trial had been customary in England from early times."[210] At various stages in Delaware, jurors were required to be "the most discreet and judicious freeholders," "sober and judicious persons of fair character," and "qualified to vote at the general election."[211] They were to come from the general jury lists and were to be (initially) the "most indifferent" and "best qualified" or (later) "indifferent and judicious citizens."[212]

Presumably the Delaware legislature, in making the 1987 change in the special-jury law, intended both to make the special jury more exceptional by making it discretionary and to respond to the perceived problem of relying on ordinary juries in complex civil cases. No legislative guidance, however, was given about what constitutes a complex civil case or, for that matter, about how special jurors are to be selected whenever a special jury is ordered in such a case.

The several reported cases that have used special juries or that have responded to motions for special juries under the new law show that the new law may lead more to confusion than clarity. A growing distaste for the special-jury option among superior court judges may be discernible. In four Delaware cases, the court denied motions for special juries, all on the ground that the cases before the court were insufficiently complex. One of these cases, *Amoroso v. Joy Manufacturing Co.*,[213] was a product liability case involving a heavy air compressor, and the court, reasonably enough, saw no complex issues. Less straightforward was a series of asbestos cases in which special jury motions were denied,[214] despite the fact that in a previous trial the jury had been called upon to render its verdict by answering thirty-six pages of interrogatories and that one scheduled case might require jury answers to interrogatories from fifteen or more defendants. The court pointed out that many of the answers to the various defendants' interrogatories would be the same, and prior verdicts in other cases "demonstrated that the issues which are presented in these cases are well within the comprehension and capabilities of jurors who come from the ordinary panels of jurors."[215] The court explained its meticulous habits to assist ordinary juries, pointing out, as well, that "Most areas of science can be described in such a way that they can be understood by people of ordinary intelligence, education and experience," for example, "by avoiding overly technical words and expressions (particularly of Latin origin) and using less erudite verbiage."[216] Responding to defendants' reliance on an article entitled "The Case for Special Juries in Toxic Tort Litigation,"[217] in which the author argues for special juries formed by a system of specific education and experience standards, the court wrote:

> The use of jurors who have expertise which relates to the case also presents problems. One is that many cases involve more than one area of expertise. Another is that in many specialties, experts do not subscribe to a single philosophy or approach, and therefore, the decision could be slanted toward one predetermined philosophy or another and not dependant upon the evidence presented at trial. The use of experts as ju-

> rors could well produce a more prejudiced system of justice than does the traditional jury system.[218]

The court also observed that the proposed scheme would represent a method of selection that is "contrary to fundamental principles of jury trial" and "inconsistent with established principles of justice," requiring "statutory and perhaps constitutional modification."[219]

Yet another motion for a special jury was denied in *Noramco (Delaware), Inc. v. Carew Associates, Inc.*[220] The court was not impressed by the argument that the construction dispute estimated to occupy a two-week trial would involve the proverbial "battle of the experts."[221] The court noted that "The better experts have learned to be able to speak understandably to lay people," adding, "That the expertise may be complex does not necessarily mean that the case is a 'complex civil case.'"[222]

When a special jury is granted, a new question occurs—one that seems obvious in retrospect but that may not have been anticipated. Do the standards for the admissibility of expert testimony require upward adjustment because of the supposed greater capabilities of the special jurors? This question came before the Delaware Superior Court in *Ramada Inns, Inc. v. Dow Jones & Co.*,[223] a libel case that presented an "actual malice" issue. The plaintiff proposed that a Pulitzer Prize–winning journalist, professor, and author testify about journalistic standards.[224] Dow Jones filed a motion in opposition, arguing, among other things, that the testimony should be rejected because "the subject of the testimony is within the comprehension of the average special juror in this case."[225] The Superior Court acknowledged the following test set forth by the Delaware Supreme Court: "Knowledge is specialized only when not possessed by the average trier of fact who lacks the expert's skill, training or education. Consequently, expert testimony impermissibly invades the province of the jury if it embraces matters in which the jury is just as competent as the expert to consider and weigh the evidence and draw the necessary conclusions."[226] Despite case authority from other jurisdictions holding that journalism standards were well within the reach of ordinary jurors, the court was "not persuaded that members of a special jury are sufficiently knowledgeable of the standards and practices of investigative journalism so as to render expert testimony on the subject useless."[227]

The future of the 1987 Delaware special-jury statute remains uncertain.[228] The Delaware Superior Court in *Ramada Inns* published by slip opinion the following method agreed upon with counsel for the selection of the special jury:

1. The parties shall submit to the Court a list of witnesses likely to be called at trial . . . for the Prothonotary's use in furnishing notice to jurors.
2. The Prothonotary shall promptly identify potential special jurors and shall send the appropriate special jury questionnaire to those persons identified.
3. After receiving the responses to the juror questionnaires, the Prothonotary shall select one hundred persons who are qualified as special jurors. . . .
4. . . . The Prothonotary shall provide the Court and counsel with (a) a list of the names of the special jurors selected and (b) a copy of the responses by those individuals to the special jury questionnaire.
5. . . . The parties shall file any written challenges for cause on the ground that individual jurors selected by the Prothonotary do not qualify as special jurors. Any party objecting to such a challenge shall not file a written response but shall reserve his objections until the hearing conducted by the Court or until the prearranged teleconference.
6. The Court shall conduct a hearing in the Court or over the telephone. . . . At that time the Court will consider the written challenges and any oral opposition to those challenges. The Court will rule on each challenge at that hearing.
7. The parties will have the right to exercise peremptory challenges at a date to be determined during the pretrial conference. . . . Each side may exercise up to, and including, six peremptory challenges.
8. After the exercise of the peremptory challenges the Prothonotary shall promptly summon the remaining jurors to appear at the first day of trial. . . .
9. The jury and alternates in this case shall be selected from the remaining array in the same manner as juries are selected in non-special jury cases.[229]

C. Juries for Property Condemnation and Diking District Assessment Disputes

1. Next Neighbors

Thus far in this discussing of special qualifications for jurors, I have considered both the blue-ribbon jury and the jury of experts. I now turn briefly to two features of the larger history of the jury. The first (see chapter 6) is the original notion that jurors were to be "next neighbors" who ought to be in a position to know something about the dispute and the parties, instead of being disinterested strangers requiring proof of facts. One species of jury statute survives in the United Stated that still retains the flavor of this ancient notion. A few state statutes require juries to decide valuation disputes caused by property condemnations effected through eminent domain for public works (usually highways) or resulting from diking district assessments. The West Virginia statute requires the jurors to be "qualified freeholders" in the county where the property in dispute is located.[230] These are the only civil juries in that state that still require twelve members, determined by the parties' alternate strikes of four each from a panel of twenty freeholders.[231] The language of the Washington state statute allows the court to "call a special jury . . . and direct that a jury panel be selected and summoned . . . from the citizens of the county in which the lands . . . sought to be appropriated are situated, as many qualified persons as may be necessary in order to form a jury of twelve persons."[232]

Colorado codified an interesting variation, circling back to the special jury with expertise, for juries in drainage district assessment disputes. To resolve a disputed assessment, the statute provides that the district court shall "cause to be summoned six landowners living outside of the drainage district, who are not interested in any lands or work in said district, or of kin to any of the parties interested," and, "The six landowners shall be men who have some knowledge of the costs and benefits of farm drainage."[233]

2. Juries *De Medietate Linguae*

The second feature of the broader history of the jury previously discussed is the half-and-half jury and its kinship to recent arguments that call for racial quotas for juries in racially charged cases.[234] The half-and-half jury—the jury *de medietate linguae*—was part of the early jurisprudence of several states.[235] This type of jury required that half of the jurors have the special qualification of being foreigners. Judge Henry Toulmin's rationale bears repeating:

> The fundamental principle of this institution [trial by jury] is, that a man should be tried by his peers or equals, a commoner by commoners and a nobleman by nobles; and so liberal was the extension of this principle

> even in the 14th century, that by the 28th of Edward III, ch. 13, it was provided, that in inquests to be taken between aliens and English subjects, one half of the jury should consist of aliens, and the other half of English subjects. We have a similar provision in our own statutes.[236]

The practical difficulty, of course, was finding six foreigners from the defendant's own country. The solution was for the impaneling officer to try his best to find jurors from the defendant's own country but to resort to any foreigners, as necessary. According to an 1803 New York practice book:

> Juries and inquests between aliens and citizens of the United States . . . , the one half shall be citizens of this state, . . . and the other half aliens, if so many there be in the city or county where such jury or inquest is to be taken, and who shall be indifferent between the parties; and if there be not so many aliens or strangers, then as many as shall be found.[237]

In contrast, a South Carolina Justice of the Peace manual published in 1810 stated that the sheriffs in a trial of an alien were to "summon 18 subjects of the nation of such alien, if they may be had, or the subjects of any other nation (except subjects of Great Britain during the war)."[238]

It is doubtful that today's calls for racial quotas for juries in racially charged cases[239]—the modern counterpart of the jury *de medietate*—will be enacted into law. Interestingly, however, the concept was officially recommended in England. The Royal Commission on Criminal Justice issued its Report in July 1993, paragraph 62 of which reads as follows:

> We are reluctant to interfere with the principle of random selection of juries. We are, however, anxious that everything possible should be done to ensure that people from the ethnic minority communities are represented on juries in relation to their numbers in the local community. The pool from which juries are randomly selected would be more representative if all eligible members of ethnic communities were included on the electoral roll. Even if this were to be achieved, however, there would statistically still be instances where there would not be a multi-racial jury in a case where one seemed appropriate. The Court of Appeal in *Ford* held that race should not be taken into account in selecting juries. Although we agree with the court's position in regard to most cases, we believe that there are some exceptional cases where race should be taken into account.[240]

Almost uniformly, case law and secondary literature in England prior to the Royal Commission's Report opposed the idea of racial quotas.[241] In the *Ford* case referred to by the Commission, the Court of Appeal ruled that, "in the absence of evidence of specific bias, ethnic origins could not found a valid ground for challenge to an individual juror" and that a judge does not have discretion to remove a potential juror solely on that ground, not even in the interest of achieving racial balance on the jury.[242] In a 1995 speech to the Leeds Race Issues Advisory Council, the Lord Chief Justice of England stated his opposition to the proposal by the Royal Commission on Criminal Justice, calling it "the thin end of a particularly insidious wedge."[243] He viewed the proposal as a dangerous departure from the time-honored practice of random selection of jurors. In Lord Chief Justice Taylor's opinion, members of the jury should not be regarded "as representing the views of the community, or of discrete parts of it, nor indeed of 'representing' either the complainant or the defendant."[244]

III. The Special Jury, the "Reasonable-Cross-Section" Requirement, and Constitutional Limitations on Peremptory Challenges

In his 1994 book, *We the Jury,* Jeffrey Abramson observes that "The cross-sectional jury is so familiar to us today that we forget how modern is its triumph."[245] He traces the march of the idea from infancy in the 1960s to the Jury Selection and Service Act of 1968, then to the Supreme Court's 1975 decision in *Taylor v. Louisiana,*[246] which raised the concept to constitutional stature under the Sixth Amendment.[247] Abramson gives this summary appraisal: "To say, as the Supreme Court did in its landmark 1975 decision, that only 'representative' juries are 'impartial' juries is to suggest a new way of thinking about how to make jurors capable of impartial justice—a way that stands the classical view of impartiality on its head."[248]

Abramson's appraisal is correct. The fundamental change in opinion that occurred regarding the selection of juries was a shift away from rules that promote fairness to the parties to a lawsuit, especially defendants in criminal cases, and toward rules that are perceived as promoting fairness to society at large and its democratic traditions. The classical model was shaped to produce unbiased jurors who could decide cases unencumbered

A Reconstruction-era mixed jury, illustration published in *Frank Leslie's Illustrated Newspaper,* November 30, 1867, as one of ten sketches by artist James E. Taylor, called collectively "The Operations of the Registration Laws and Negro Suffrage in the South." The practice of impaneling such mixed juries was short-lived and was not revived until the Civil Rights era of the late twentieth century. Courtesy of the Library of Congress.

by any personal agendas. Occasionally—as in the half-and-half jury—this was leavened by a desire to be as fair as possible to a defendant, by having some jurors equipped to understand and empathize with the defendant's cultural and linguistic background. The new model jettisoned this idealism, adopting a brand of realism that frankly acknowledged the existence of sharp ethnic, gender, and racial divisions in society. The best way to account for these divisions in jury composition, the new model posits, is to ensure that all clearly identifiable, "cognizable" groups are fairly represented in the jury pools. This way, in the aggregate, the biased votes by jurors of the various interest groups eventually will cancel each other out.[249]

The next logical development dealt with peremptory challenges. If we insist on a fair cross-section of the community in the jury lists that generate jury panels, surely it is wrong to allow a party to tamper with the chance that various cognizable groups will find representation on particular juries. Thus, it is wrong to allow the exercise of peremptory challenges solely to eliminate blacks, other racial or ethnic groups, or women. A series of Supreme Court decisions established this proposition in the 1980s and 1990s: *Batson v. Kentucky*[250] (disallowing peremptories based solely on race); *Powers v. Ohio*[251] (holding that *Batson* applies regardless of whether jurors eliminated are of the same race as the defendant); *Edmonson v. Leesville Concrete Co.*[252] (holding that *Batson* applies to civil cases as well as to criminal ones); *Georgia v. McCollum*[253] (holding that *Batson* applies to defense counsel as well as to the prosecution); and *J.E.B. v. Alabama*[254] (holding that the *Batson* principle precludes using peremptories to eliminate jurors solely because of their sex). Unsurprisingly, *Batson* led to a call for the elimination of peremptories altogether, on the theory that they are inconsistent with the cross-section idea.[255] A closely divided Supreme Court, however, refused to eliminate peremptories completely in *Holland v. Illinois,*[256] reasoning (in the majority opinion by Justice Antonin Scalia) that the constitutional principle at work seeks jury impartiality, not cross-section representativeness on specific juries. Abramson is nevertheless correct in concluding that "the present position of American law on peremptory challenges is incoherent."[257] He adds that, "Having taken the first step of prohibiting race and sex as grounds for peremptory challenges, the Supreme Court has little logical choice but to take the second and decisive step of banning all uses of peremptory challenges that target specific groups for exclusion from the jury."[258]

Regardless of whether the current position of American law on peremptory challenges is incoherent, we must ask what the implications of the new law are for whatever life may be left to the special jury. If the Supreme Court were to adopt a quota of a specified number of black jurors in a racially charged case, a new special jury would exist because at least some of the jurors would be required to have special qualifications. This is not likely to happen; the idea is out of fashion with the political temper of the times and is incompatible with the cross-section concept.[259]

Short of the racial-quota notion, what are the implications of the new jury rules for the special jury? Clearly, the restrictions that prevent the discriminatory use of peremptories apply to the struck-jury method of jury selection and to the jury-box method.[260] It may be easier, however, to camouflage discrimination with the struck-jury model because the demographics of the entire panel are known from the start, making it easier to pick and choose. A party hoping to eliminate women from a jury may avoid a charge of intentional sex discrimination by merely eliminating most of the women, allowing one or two who seem least objectionable to remain.

Alternatively, the opportunity to discriminate, provided by advance knowledge of the entire panel, could supply real meaning to the jury-of-peers idea. By strategic striking, it often may be possible for a criminal defendant to have some jurors from his own race or socioeconomic circumstances. This possibility falls short of the "affirmative peremptories" argued for by one writer,[261] but it moves in the same direction.

Because the cross-section idea pertains to both civil and criminal cases, as do the rules on peremptory challenges, new questions arise regarding the use of special juries made up of jurors with special qualifications. Despite its extensive history in the United States, this practice survives only in Delaware and in the few states with statutes prescribing special qualifications for jury service in real estate condemnation or drainage district disputes. The number of juries convened for condemnation or drainage district disputes is undoubtedly quite small, and it is unlikely that a serious challenge to those statutes will arise. Were such a challenge to occur, however, the circumstances should be sufficient to justify an exception to the cross-section concept. Sustaining, for example, the Colorado statute calling for six jurors who "have some knowledge of the costs and benefits of farm drainage"[262] would have the effect of excluding large segments of the community from jury service in drainage district disputes, but such an outcome should not be viewed as evil or impermissible. The cross-section requirement and the limitations on peremptories need not blot out entirely the two-plus centuries of American jury tradition. That history was built upon fairness to parties in litigation, a perspective that should not be lost. It would be senseless, of course, to return to the elitist days of blue-ribbon juries and prescriptive disqualifications from jury service. The reasonable-cross-section concept is now rightfully prevalent and strong. It is strong enough not to be shaken by exceptional jury composition procedures when special circumstances justify them.

The Delaware special-jury statute, as implemented in the *Ramada Inns* case, is again illustrative.[263] In *Ramada Inns,* the special jury was assembled through the use of questionnaires designed to produce a panel that could handle a complex civil case. Such a special jury should not be viewed as offending the policy that underlies the limitations created by the Supreme Court on the exercise of peremptories. What is prohibited is intentional discrimination, which a selection process that used neutral criteria shaped by the needs of the case would not demonstrate. This is true even if the criteria could be shown to have a disparate impact on "cognizable classes" entitled to be proportionately represented on the jury rolls. This practice parallels the realm of employment, where specific business needs justify neutral selection criteria in hiring and promotion despite disparate impact on classes protected by the Civil Rights Act of 1964.[264]

The Delaware practice in *Ramada Inns* calls on the parties to stipulate under court supervision to a procedure to produce the special-jury panel and to select the trial jury. The Superior Court does not seem to have responded to the advice that the Delaware Supreme Court offered in *Haas v. United Technologies Corp.*[265] In upholding the pre-1987 special-jury statute, the Delaware Supreme Court called upon its power under the Delaware constitution to supervise the administration of justice and commended to the Superior Court "the delicate and difficult task of drafting a rule of court stating the criteria and guidance for the selection of special juries to ensure 'a cross section of the population suitable in character and intelligence for that civil duty.'"[266] The Delaware Supreme Court admonished the Superior Court to "be mindful of the twin goals of achieving a fair representation of the community on the jury panel while providing for intelligent, educated and competent jurors for the adjudication of complex cases."[267] The Supreme Court concluded:

> We offer as a suggestion, and without fettering the Superior Court's discretion in this matter, that jurors be randomly selected from a special jury pool comprised of individuals meeting specified age, intelligence and educational requirements and, to the extent deemed legally permissible by the superior court, possessing special occupational skills. Perhaps a minimum educational requirement of a bachelor's degree from an accredited college or university might be one of those criteria.[268]

The Superior Court probably chose the wiser course by handling each case ad hoc rather than trying to write a rule of court for all cases. Several factors support this course of action, including the discretionary nature of the special jury in Delaware since 1987, the uncertainty among Superior Court judges about when a case is complex enough to merit such a jury, and the palpable tension between a jury pool composed along the lines suggested by the Delaware Supreme Court in *Haas* and a jury pool that conforms to a cross-section of the community.

Conclusion

The current prevailing philosophy about jury composition, the reasonable-cross-section requirement, is ahistorical. The history of jury composition rules and practices before American independence and in the following centuries, especially those that created or permitted special qualifications for jurors to decide particular types of cases, demonstrates this fact. Such rules and practices define the special jury. Although the term "struck jury" was often used as if synonymous with "special jury," many struck juries were merely juries formed in a specific way, different from the traditional jury-box method, with no statutory or customary second feature calling for jurors to have special qualifications. The typical special jury in both English and American history was a struck jury composed of persons of the better rank, merchants, or others with special capabilities that facilitated understanding the dispute in question.

The rationale behind the typical special jury has always been to improve the decision-making process. In some states, courts have had the power to order a special jury when the nature of a particular dispute calls for it, but ordinarily one or both parties requested a special jury. A party's request for a special jury was a matter of right (although the requesting party might have had to bear any extra cost) or a matter of court discretion. The fundamental point, however, is that the special jury was in aid of the parties or the court.

Occasionally one encounters a claim that the reasonable-cross-section requirement is also in aid of defendants. For example, in *State v. Gilmore,* a New Jersey court wrote: "While defendant in the present case has no right to insist that Blacks serve on his trial jury or that there be proportional representation of Blacks on the jury, . . . he does have the unqualified right to be tried by a fair and impartial jury," and the New Jersey Constitution defines that jury as "a jury drawn from a representative cross section of the community."[269]

This formulation illustrates the air of unreality that so often infects jury discourse. If a black defendant truly were entitled to a jury drawn from a representative cross-section of the community, that jury would include some black members. In fairness, however, the New Jersey court in

State v. Gilmore recognized the following realistic appraisal by the California Supreme Court:[270]

> A party is constitutionally entitled to a petit jury that is as near an approximation of the ideal cross-section of the community as the process of random draw permits. Obviously he cannot avoid the effect of that process: the master list must be reduced to a manageable venire, and that venire must in turn be reduced to a 12-person jury. The best the law can do to accomplish those steps with the least risk to the representative nature of the jury pool is to take them by random means. . . . We recognize that in a predictable percentage of cases the result will be a wholly unbalanced jury, usually composed exclusively of members of the majority group. This is inevitable, the price we must pay for juries of a workable size.[271]

In cases governed by a statutory or constitutional cross-section requirement, the traditional special jury, one drawn from a distinct group of specially qualified jurors, is not permissible. The cross-section requirement protects the rights of the population at large, not those of the parties to a lawsuit or those of the judicial system.[272] Skirmishes will continue over what constitutes a "cognizable group" under the cross-section requirement and what constitutes an impermissible basis for the exercise of peremptory challenges,[273] but judicial support for the cross-section requirement is strong. As the Fifth Circuit baldly stated, "the desire for competency must not be pursued to the extent that a fair cross-section is prevented."[274]

In a 1947 opinion denying a special jury, the Bronx County Court quoted former New York governor Herbert Lehman's address to the legislature: "I recommend that Blue Ribbon Juries be abolished. The use of special or so-called 'Blue Ribbon' juries is not consonant with the preservation of the constitutional right to a trial by jury of peers. It is at war with our basic concepts of a democratic society."[275]

What did Governor Lehman mean? Did he suppose that a democratic society cannot, under any circumstances, allow competence to prevail over representativeness, anticipating the recommendation of the 1960 Federal Judicial Conference?[276] Even if so, special juries in civil cases have been commonplace throughout most of the history of this democratic society. Other juror qualifications that dilute the purity of the trial-by-peers ideal also pervade history. That ideal, moreover, points logically toward a destination that the courts and most commentators reject—the mandatory presence on a trial jury of some persons empathic toward the parties, especially criminal defendants. As a legal commentator wrote, "no constitution or law guarantees a right to trial by a jury of one's racial peers.[277]

Occasional voices still call for a return to something like the half-and-half jury of an earlier era in order to make the jury-of-peers idea realistic in some cases.[278] These voices are likely to remain lonely, as two cases dealing with Spanish-speaking jurors demonstrate. In *Hernandez v. New York*,[279] a jury, from which all Latinos had been eliminated at *voir-dire*, convicted the defendant of attempted murder. The jury composition resulted from the prosecution's use of its peremptories to eliminate all potential jurors who spoke Spanish. The defense challenged this behavior as an improper exclusion of Latinos from the jury pool. Although there was no majority opinion, a majority of the Supreme Court rejected the challenge. According to Justice Sandra Day O'Connor (joined by Justice Scalia), language-based peremptory strikes are not the same as racially based strikes: "That is the distinction between disproportionate effect, which is not sufficient to constitute an equal protection violation, and intentional discrimination, which is."[280] Justice Anthony Kennedy, Chief Justice William Rehnquist, and Justices Byron White and David Souter acknowledged the possibility that, in some circumstances, language ability might properly "be treated as a surrogate for race under an equal protection analysis."[281] They did not find this possibility justified, however, on the specific facts of the case before them.[282]

Following *Hernandez*, the Third Circuit in *Pemberthy v. Beyer*[283] concluded that peremptory challenges based on language ability are not "equivalent for equal protection purposes to the types of challenges prohibited in Batson and related cases."[284] The court, however, cautioned that, "Because language-speaking ability is so closely correlated with ethnicity, a trial court must carefully assess the challenger's actual motivation even where the challenger asserts a rational reason to discriminate based on language skills."[285]

From the standpoint of the history of the special jury, the significance of *Hernandez* and *Pemberthy* is their demonstration of how far the law has moved away from our jury heritage. In the half-and-half jury, the jurors' ability to communicate in the defendant's language was at least one reason supporting the belief that foreign jurors were needed to ensure a foreign defendant a fair trial. Neither *Hernandez* nor *Pemberthy*, however, discussed the relationship between the ability of potential jurors to speak Spanish and the fairness owed the defendants by the jury-trial guarantee. The interest at stake was that of the potential jurors.

Hernandez and *Pemberthy* nevertheless may provide support for the use of higher education as a juror criterion, such as in the selection of Delaware's special juries in complex cases. If attorneys can strike jurors because they speak Spanish, likely eliminating at least three out of four of the Hispanics or Latinos in a jury pool,[286] then attorneys can select educated jurors even if the education criterion has a disproportionate racial or socioeconomic impact. In 1967, Judge Botter of the Superior Court of New Jersey wrote, in response to a complaint about the method for selecting grand jurors:

> I think that legally in the discretion of the jury commissioners a higher education standard can be used for the selection of persons to serve on the grand jury. . . . We may talk about broad economic or social classes. I'm not certain . . . that the grand jurors do not represent a fair cross-section of economic classes. . . . If you accept the proposition that a higher educational standard can properly be used, then you cannot accept the corollary that the use of a higher educational standard must produce intentional discrimination.[287]

This philosophy elevates competence over representativeness and, therefore, may not be permitted whenever the reasonable-cross-section requirement applies.[288] If such a requirement is not preclusive, however, history supports the continuation of experiments with other models, just as Delaware has done. The jury is a remarkably rich and resilient tradition. The richness of that tradition should not be disregarded altogether to achieve the abstract satisfaction of jury lists representative of cross-sections of communities. More often than not, little correlation will exist between the reasonable-cross section and the composition of a particular jury. It is easy to understand the conceptual appeal of the link between the reasonable-cross-section idea and democratic traditions. The reasonable-cross-section idea, however, need not be all-consuming. Other formulas, especially those shaped to achieve fair and intelligent verdicts in specific cases, have achieved historical legitimacy and should be allowed a reasonable coexistence.

Appendix 1

Juries of Matrons Reported in Old Bailey Sessions Papers, 1677–1800

Year[a]	No. of Sessions Covered by Reports Examined	No. of Females Shown to Have Been Sentenced to Death[b]	No. of Females Reported to Have "Pleaded Their Bellies"	No. of Females Found with Quick Child
1677	6	13	0	0
1677–78	7	22	3	3
1678–79	8	23	1	1
1679–80	8	43[c]	3	3
1680–81	8	35	0	0
1681–82	8	21	0	0
1682–83	7	14	0	0
1683–84	8	20	6	3
1684–85	8	28	6	5
1685–86	8	19	13	10
1686–87	8	26	9	4
1687–88	8	13	7	4
1688–89	6	21	8	7
1689–90	8	19	11	9
1690–91	8	51[d]	7	2
1691–92	5[e]	3	2	2
1692–93	7	36	25	20
1693–94	7	24	13	9
1694–95	6	20	11	10
1695–96	5	15	12	12
1696–97	6	18	15	9
1697–98	6	13	10	9
1698–99	2	5	4	1
1699–1700	4	15	11	4
1700–01	0	-	-	-
1701–02	2	2	2	2
1702–03	4[e]	5	5	2
1703–04	4	4	3	3
1704–05	0	-	-	-
1705–06	0	-	-	-
1706–07	4	1	0	0
1707–08	5	4	0	0
1708–09	4	9	1	1
1709–10	3	8	0	0
1710–11	4	5	0	0
1711–12	4[e]	11	4	4
1712–13	4	8	2	2
1713–14	3[e]	9	7	3

Juries of Matrons Reported in Old Bailey Sessions Papers, 1677–1800 (Cont.)

Year[a]	No. of Sessions Covered by Reports Examined	No. of Females Shown to Have Been Sentenced to Death[b]	No. of Females Reported to Have "Pleaded Their Bellies"	No. of Females Found with Quick Child
1714–15	7	18	13	7
1715–16	8	24	24	18
1716–17	8	21	17	11
1717–18	8	22	14	9
1718–19	8	18	17	12
1719–20	8	18	8	2
1720–21	8	18	15	12
1721–22	8	8	5	3
1722–23	8	5	2	1
1723–24	8	7	4	3
1724–25	8	8	1	0
1725–26	8	12	6	1
1726–27	8	10	2	1
1727–28	8	15	0	0
1728–29	8	9	3	2
1729–30	7	4	0	0
1730–31	8	4	2	2
1731–32	8	5	2	0
1732–33	8	6	3	2
1733–34	7	12	6	0
1734–35	8	9	4	1
1735–36	8	3	0	0
1736–37	8	10	2	1
1737–38	8	5	2	2
1738–39	8	6	1	0
1739–40	8	13	3	2
1740–41	8	15	5	1
1741–42	8	8	0	0
1742–43	8	8	1	0
1743–44	8	8	0	0
1744–45	8	9	0	0
1745–46	8	2	0	0
1746–47	8	4	0	0
1747–48	8	4	0	0
1748–49	8	6	5	4
1749–50	8	3	2	2
1750–51	8	5	4	2
1751–52	8	3	1	0
1752–53	8	9	2	0
1753–54	8	4	2	2
1754–55	8	3	1	0
1755–56	8	1	0	0
1756–57	8	4	1	0
1757–58	8	5	4	2
1758–59	8	2	2	0
1759–60	8	2	1	0
1760–61	8	2	1	0
1761–62	8	4	3	0
1762–63	8	6	0	0
1763–64	8	8	0	0
1764–65	8	6	1	0

Juries of Matrons Reported in Old Bailey Sessions Papers, 1677–1800 (Cont.)

Year[a]	No. of Sessions Covered by Reports Examined	No. of Females Shown to Have Been Sentenced to Death[b]	No. of Females Reported to Have "Pleaded Their Bellies"	No. of Females Found with Quick Child
1765–66	8	6	0	0
1766–67	8	2	0	0
1767–68	8	7	1	1
1768–69	8	9	0	0
1769–70	8	8	0	0
1770–71	8	6	0	0
1771–72	8	4	0	0
1772–73	8	4	1	1
1773–74	8	6	0	0
1774–75	8	5	0	0
1775–76	8	2	0	0
1776–77	8	4	0	0
1777–78	8	8	0	0
1778–79	8	10	0	0
1779–80	8	10	0	0
1780–81	8	19	0	0
1781–82	8	15	0	0
1782–83	8	17	1	0
1783–84	8	13	0	0
1784–85	8	12	0	0
1785–86	8	7	0	0
1786–87	8	17	2	0
1787–88	8	11	0	0
1788–89	8	6	0	0
1789–90	8	13	0	0
1790–91	8	9	0	0
1791–92	8	7	1	1
1792–93	8[f]	-	-	-
1793–94	8[f]	-	-	-
1794–95	8[f]	-	-	-
1795–96	8	10	0	0
1796–97	8	5	0	0
1797–98	8	10	0	0
1798–99	8	7	0	0
1799–1800	8	7	0	0

Sources: For the years addressed by this appendix (1677–1800), I initially used the OBSP held by the British Library, the Guildhall Library for the City of London, and the Harvard Law School Library. Subsequently these OBSP sets were supplemented by Old Baily Proceedings Online, compiled by Tim Hitchcock and Robert Shoemaker, at http://www.oldbaileyonline.org.

[a] Of the eight Old Bailey sessions held annually, the first was in December and the last in October. The intervening sessions customarily were held in January, February, April, May, July, and September. Also, the Julian calendar was used in the OBSP through December 1751, in which the calendar year commenced on March 25. All pre-1752 dates were converted to the new-style (Gregorian) calendar for this tabulation.

[b] The characterization of prisoners as male or female is based solely upon the given names stated in the reports. Occasionally, in particularly sensitive or scandalous cases, only the first initials of a prisoner's first and last names would be printed (e.g., "A_____ B______"), in which case it was usually (but not always) possible to obtain an indication of gender in the textual description of the case. There were a few ambiguous names that were not clarified by the text, and these were assumed to be male.

[c] In the report of the sessions for April 1680, twenty-four prisoners were sentenced to death. The report

indicates that, of the twenty-four, "Three Women (one a [Coin] Clipper) were, by a Jury of Matrons, after they were Attainted found to be quick with Child, so that as to them Execution must be respited."

[d] In the February 1691 sessions report appears the following statement: "After Sentence of Death had passed upon these 25 Criminals, the Women were all called over again and [eight of the ten women] ordered to be set by. . . ." No reason is indicated; presumably they were reprieved.

e Incomplete reports for December 1691, March 1703, September 1712, and May 1714 are held by the British Library and the Guildhall Library, but the sections that show the sentencing are missing. The December 1691 sentencing report is, however, presented in the Hitchcock and Shoemaker online compilation.

[f] From February 1793 through October 1795, and consistently after 1800, the summaries of sentences received by prisoners at the sessions disappeared, each prisoner's sentence being given instead at the end of the textual description of his case. By the 1790s, the reports had increased substantially in size from the pattern of the early eighteenth century and before. The report for each sessions was printed in multiple installments—sometimes as many as ten. Since the appearance of the jury of matrons was, by the end of the century, a rarity, the tabular presentation was closed with the year 1800.

Appendix 2

Additional English Criminal Cases in Which Juries of Matrons were Impanelled[a]

Prisoner	Date[b]	Whether Found With Quick Child	Source[c]
Elizabeth Walton[a]	1387	Yes	Richardson & Sayles, n. 10
Katherine Newport[a]	1458	Yes	NA, Just 3/213, m. 16d. *Northern History* 19 (1983): 57–58
Conania Surbye[a]	1611	Not indicated	King, n. 17
Mary Bolton[a]	1662	Yes	G.D. Books (Middlesex)
Mary Carleton[a]	Jan. 1673	No	Capt. Smith, n. 129
Martha Huckle	1682	Yes	G. D. Books (London)
Elizabeth Scott	1682	Yes	G. D. Books (London)
Anne Stubbs, otherwise Ditcher	1682	No	G. D. Books (Middlesex)
Elizabeth Hunt	1682	Yes	G. D. Books (London)
Anne Fawcett	1682	Yes	G. D. Books (London)
Mary Gilbert	1682	No	G. D. Books (London)
Sarah Browne, otherwise Bowen	1682	Yes	G. D. Books (Middlesex)
Margaret Ford	Mar. 1683	Yes	Assize Report, bound into OBSP
Elizabeth Ford	Mar. 1683	No	Assize Report, bound into OBSP
Moll Hawkins, otherwise Fudge[a]	Mar. 1702	Yes	Capt. Smith, n. 129
Nan (Anne) Harris, alias Sarah Davis, alias Thorn, alias Gotham[a]	Oct. 1704	Yes	Capt. Smith, n. 129
Deborah Churchill[a]	June 1708	Jury uncertain	Knapp & Baldwin, n. 83
Mary Read	Early 18th century	Yes	Capt. Johnson[c]
Ann Bonney	Early 18th century	Yes	Capt. Johnson[c]
Isabel Williams	Apr. 1725	Yes	G. D. Books (Middlesex)

Additional English Criminal Cases in Which Juries of Matrons were Impanelled[a] (Cont.)

Prisoner	Date[b]	Whether Found With Quick Child	Source[c]
Elizabeth Dole	Apr. 1725	Yes	G. D. Books (Middlesex)
Margaret Murphy	Feb. 1728	Not indicated	G. D. Books (Middlesex)
Ann Somes, otherwise Sones	Sept. 1733	No	G. D. Books (Middlesex)
Jane Smith	May 1739	No	G. D. Books (Middlesex)
Ann Beadford	Feb. 1743	No	G. D. Books (Middlesex)
Ann Boswell	Jan. 1747	No	G. D. Books (Middlesex)
Ann Boswell	Jan. 1747	No	G. D. Books (Middlesex)
Judith Butler	Apr. 1748	Yes	G. D. Books (Middlesex)
Sarah Rennigem	Oct.1748	No	G. D. Books (Middlesex)
Elizabeth Barnes, alias Dove	Dec. 1755	No	G. D. Books (Middlesex)
Margaret Larney	Jan. 1758	Yes	G. D. Books (Middlesex)
Elizabeth Tomkinson	Jan. 1758	Yes	G. D. Books (Middlesex)
Maria Groves, alias Penticross	Dec. 1755	No	G. D. Books (Middlesex)
Mary Mallet	Mar. 1794	Yes	Knapp & Baldwin, n. 83
Mary Bateman	1809	No	Ld. Birkett, n. 124
Catherine Smith	Mar. 1830	Not indicated	Kennedy, n. 115
Mary Wright	1833	No	*Medical Times and Gazette* n. 190; Kennedy, n. 115
Anne Wycherley	1838	No	8 Car. & P. 261, n. 39
Mary Ann Hunt	1847	No	*Medical Times and Gazette* n. 177
Rachael Busby	1871	No	*Medical Times and Gazette* n. 179
Christiana Edmunds	Jan. 1872	No	*Medical Times and Gazette* n. 198

[a] The information in Appendix 2 derives from a systematic review of the Newgate Calendars held by the British Library, a nonsystematic sampling of Gaol Delivery and Sessions Books at the LMA, and various other sources (e.g., a few reports of assize sessions bound in with the OBSP, and treatises on medical jurisprudence). Not included are the CAR; they are summarized in Appendix 3. I am indebted to John Baker for the NA entry and to Valerie Edwards for supplying me with the London and Middlesex G.D. entries from the years 1662 and 1682. The London Gaol Delivery Books are located in the Corporation of London Record Office, Guildhall.

Information appearing in these sources that also appears in the OBSP that I examined is not reiterated. Those entries marked with an "a" pertain to sessions for which there was no OBSP in the sources that I used. For other Old Bailey cases in this table, OBSP were located, but no indication of prisoners having pleaded their bellies to obtain a jury of matrons appeared. Why this information is missing from the OBSP is unclear. It is unlikely that preparers of the OBSP would have had regular access to G.D. or Sessions Books. Variant spellings of the names of prisoners between the OBSP and the G.D. Books, for example, suggest that the OBSP spellings were phonetic (Dimor [OBSP] vs. Dymor [GDB]; Gillfoy [OBSP] vs. Kilfoy [GDB]; Ryan [OBSP] vs. Royan [GDB]; Stanton [OBSP] vs. Staunton [GDB]). But the OBSP were not printed until after sentences were pronounced, and, since most of the juries of matrons are reflected in the OBSP, it is difficult to account for the absences. One explanation, of course, is that the request for the jury of matrons by the prisoners did not take place immediately after sentencing, but whether or why this occurred in unknown.

[b] Some of the dates indicated are approximated on the basis of information such as the date of execution and the number of months respited for pregnancy.

[c] Sources with note numbers refer to the endnotes to chapter 4. "Capt. Johnson" refers to Capt. Charles Johnson, *Lives of the Most Remarkable Female Robbers* (London, 1801).

Appendix 3

Summary of Assize Calendar Cases Involving Pleas of Pregnancy

A. Elizabeth I Calendars

Jursidiction; Date	Number of Prisoners Pleading Pregnancy	Number Found Pregnant by Jury of Matrons	Number Found Not Pregnant by Jury of Matrons	Number Remanded "Because Pregnant"; No Reference to Jury of Matrons	Number Remanded "On a Plea of Pregnancy";No Reference to Jury of Matrons	Comment
Sussex 1559–1602	45	21	15	13	0	1 prisoner "found not pregnant"; no reference to jury of matrons; 1 jury-of-matrons verdict not shown.
Hertfordshire 1580–1601	19	8	3	12	0	
Essex 1560–1601	58	16	19	24	6	3 prisoners "found pregnant" without reference to jury of matrons; 2 verdicts not shown.
Kent 1559–1603	85	22	22	23	14	2 cases: "Guilty—Pregnant, it is said"; "Not pregnant." No jury-of-matrons references in any of 3; 2 cases without verdict.
Surrey 1561–1602	88	26	9	10	43	5 cases verdict not shown. 3 cases, "verdict lost."
B. James I Calendars						
Sussex 1604–1624	11	5	3	1	1	
Hertfordshire 1603–1625	11	1	6	4	0	
Essex 1603–1621	23	4	12	0	6	1 case without verdict.
Kent 1630–1610	7	1	2	0	4	
Surrey 1605–1625	20	2	6	0	12	1 prisoner found pregnant but "not quick."

Appendix 4

Jury Qualifications Established by Parliament, Statutes of the Realm, Magna Carta (1215) to Statute of 3 Geo. 2, c.25 (1730)[1]

Statute	Year	Property Holding Requirements; Other Requirements	Limits on Applicable Cases or Juries	Jurisdictional or Geographical Limits	Comments; Other Practices Allowed; Duration (perpetual unless noted)
Magna Carta 9 Hen. 3, c.29	1225	Trial by peers			
Westminster I, 3 Edw. I, c.11	1275	Inquest by lawful men chosen by oath, of whom at least 2 to be knights.	Sherriff's murder inquests		Until statute of 28 Edw. 3, c.9 (1354)
Westminster II, 13 Edw. I, c.38	1285	20s./yr. freehold; 70+ yrs., ill, or living abroad ineligible	Petit assizes	Own shire	To remedy sheriff's abuses in returning poor or unqualified jurors (until 1293)
Westminster II, 13 Edw. I, c.38	1285	40s./yr. freehold; 70+ yrs., ill, or living abroad ineligible	Petit assizes	Other than own shire	To remedy sheriff's abuses in returning poor or unqualified jurors (until 1293)
21 Edw. 1	1293	40s./yr. freehold		Local market town and city juries excepted; own county.	To remedy sheriff's abuses in returning poor or unqualified jurors
21 Edw. 1	1293	100s./yr. freehold		Local market town and city juries excepted; other than own county.	To remedy sheriff's abuses in returning poor or unqualified jurors

Jury Qualifications Established by Parliament, Statutes of the Realm, Magna Carta (1215) to Statute of 3 Geo. 2, c.25 (1730)[1] *(Cont.)*

Statute	Year	Property Holding Requirements; Other Requirements	Limits on Applicable Cases or Juries	Jurisdictional or Geographical Limits	Comments; Other Practices Allowed; Duration (perpetual unless noted)
28 Edw., c.9	1300	"Next Neighbours, most sufficient, and least suspicious"			
27 Edw. 3, Stat. 2, c.8	1353	All jurors to be aliens if both parties foreign; half of jury to be alien if one party foreign; all jury to be denizen if neither party foreign	Merchant disputes	Staple courts	
28 Edw. 3, c.13	1354	One-half of jury to be alien if available	Disputes between aliens and denizens		
34 Edw. 3, c.4	1360–1361	"Next people, which shall not be suspect nor procured"			To keep those on juries who have knowledge of deed in question
34 Edw. 3, c.13	1360–1361	"Good People and lawful, which be sufficiently inherited and of good Fame"	Escheator inquests	Jurors from county of inquiry	
42 Edw. 3, c.11	1368	Nearest, most substantial people, not suspect, with best knowledge of truth	Inquests		

Jury Qualifications Established by Parliament, Statutes of the Realm, Magna Carta (1215) to Statute of 3 Geo. 2, c.25 (1730)[1] *(Cont.)*

Statute	Year	Property Holding Requirements; Other Requirements	Limits on Applicable Cases or Juries	Jurisdictional or Geographical Limits	Comments; Other Practices Allowed; Duration (perpetual unless noted)
2 Hen. 5, 1414 Stat. 2, c.3		40s/yr. freehold, lands or tenements	Capital criminal cases, real-property disputes, personal property disputes 40+ marks, and see *infra* statute of 8 Hen. 6, c.29 (1429); statute of 4 Hen. 8, c.3 (1512); statute of 27 Eliz. 1, c.6 (1584–85)	To allay false oaths by poor persons making living by jury service (until 1531 concerning murders and felonies in cities and towns; until 1429 concerning aliens; until 1585 in general).	
7 Hen. 5	1419	100s. freehold	Treasons and felonies	Lancaster	
8 Hen. 6, c.16	1429	People from county or Escheator or Commissioner	Escheator inquests		
8 Hen. 6, c.29	1429	40s. requirement of statute of 2 Hen. 5, Stat. 2, c.3 (1414)	*De medietate linguae* cases		To remedy harmful effect of statute of 2 Hen. 5, Stat. 2, c.3 (1414)
11 Hen. 6, c.1	1433	No persons from the Stews in Southwark to serve on juries		Surrey	To eliminate juror service by numerous criminals etc., with sufficient, often ill-gotten land, who otherwise qualify and live at the Stews.

Jury Qualifications Established by Parliament, Statutes of the Realm, Magna Carta (1215) to Statute of 3 Geo. 2, c.25 (1730)[1] *(Cont.)*

Statute	Year	Property Holding Requirements; Other Requirements	Limits on Applicable Cases or Juries	Jurisdictional or Geographical Limits	Comments; Other Practices Allowed; Duration (perpetual unless noted)
15 Hen. 6, c.5	1436–1437	£20 freehold if available, inhabitants of deeds concerning land with bailiwick	Attaints of pleas of land 40s.; attaints 40s. (detinue) or £40+ personalty	Cities and boroughs excepted	To remedy perjury by poor jurors which "horribly continueth, and daily increaseth"
18 Hen. 6, c.2	1439	£20 leasehold or non-freehold estate	Attaints as in statute of 15 Hen. 6, c.5 (1436–37)	Kent	
23 Hen. 6, c.9	1444–1445	Bailiff's or sheriff's officers not to serve	Sheriff's inquests		
33 Hen. 6, c.2	1455	100s./yr. lands and tenements, ownership or use. residents	Indictments in Lancashire or of Lancashire	Lancashire	
1 Rich. 3, c.4	1483–1484	20s. freehold or 26s. 8d. copyhold; good name and fame	Inquiries	Sheriff's turns	To remedy perjury by poor jurors
3 Hen. 7, c.1	1487	40s. land or tenements	Inquests to inquire of concealment of other inquests		
11 Hen. 7, c.21	1495	40 marks lands, tenements and chattels; 100 marks if amount in dispute above 40 marks	Inquests	London city courts	To remedy perjury by poor jurors

Jury Qualifications Established by Parliament, Statutes of the Realm, Magna Carta (1215) to Statute of 3 Geo. 2, c.25 (1730)[1] *(Cont.)*

Statute	Year	Property Holding Requirements; Other Requirements	Limits on Applicable Cases or Juries	Jurisdictional or Geographical Limits	Comments; Other Practices Allowed; Duration (perpetual unless noted)
11 Hen. 7, c.21	1495	£100; 4 indifferent, discrete persons of good fame in ward	Attaints	London city courts	To remedy perjury by poor jurors
11 Hen. 7, c.24	1495	For £40+ cases, 20 marks freehold lands and tenements; for under £40 cases, 5+ marks freehold or 100 marks goods or chattels	Attaints in cases "betwixt partie and partie" including cases concerning inheritances or freehold; no capital offenses involved.	Attaints brought only in King's Bench, Common Pleas, or at *nisi prius*	After attaint verdict, panels reformed of good and lawful men at justice's discretion. If insufficient persons qualify in own shire, may have tales in adjoining shire (until next parliament; revived in revised form by statute of 3 Hen. 8, c.12 [1512] until 1696).
11 Hen. 7, c.26	1495	10s. freehold or 13s. 4d. [1 mark] copyhold if available		Sheriff's turns, Southhampton, Surrey and Sussex	Qualifications lowered—insufficient numbers of jurors at higher amounts (until 1496)
19 Hen. 7, c.13	1503–1504	20s./yr. charterland or freehold, or 26s. 8d copyhold within shire	Jury to enquire of riots		
1 Hen. 8, c.8	1509–1510	40s. lands or tenements	Escheat inquests		

Jury Qualifications Established by Parliament, Statutes of the Realm, Magna Carta (1215) to Statute of 3 Geo. 2, c.25 (1730)[1] *(Cont.)*

Statute	Year	Property Holding Requirements; Other Requirements	Limits on Applicable Cases or Juries	Jurisdictional or Geographical Limits	Comments; Other Practices Allowed; Duration (perpetual unless noted)
3 Hen. 8, c.12	1511–1512	Good and lawful panels	Quarter-sessions criminal cases		Discretion given to justices of peace to reform panels to overcome abuses by sheriff
4 Hen. 8, c.3	1512	100+ marks in goods		London—King's Bench, Common Pleas, Exchequer	To remedy delays caused by too few jurors because of unworkable property qualification of 40s. lands or tenements.
23 Hen. 8, c.3	1531–1532	20 marks/yr. freehold	Attaints in £40+ cases; no capital offenses	London city courts have choice of this act or statute of 11 Hen. 7, c.21 (1495)	Until 1545 concerning London royal courts, see *infra* statute of 37 Hen. 8, c.5 (1545)
23 Hen. 8, c.3	1531–1532	5 marks/yr. freehold or 100 marks personalty	Attaints in underlying action less than £40	London city courts have choice of this act or statute of 11 Hen. 7, c.21 (1495)	Until 1545 concerning London royal courts, see *infra* statute of 37 Hen. 8, c.5 (1545)
23 Hen. 8, c.13	1531–1532	£40 personalty in lieu of freehold, except for knights and esquires dwelling in the city, borough, or town	Murders and felonies	Cities, boroughs and towns	
34 & 35 Hen. 8, c.26	1542–1543	Any freehold	All actions except attaint	Wales	Limited *tales de circumstantibus* authorized (until 1664 see *infra* statute of 16 & 17 Car. 2, c.3 [1664–65]; statute of 4 Will. & M., c.24 [1692])

Jury Qualifications Established by Parliament, Statutes of the Realm, Magna Carta (1215) to Statute of 3 Geo. 2, c.25 (1730)[1] *(Cont.)*

Statute	Year	Property Holding Requirements; Other Requirements	Limits on Applicable Cases or Juries	Jurisdictional or Geographical Limits	Comments; Other Practices Allowed; Duration (perpetual unless noted)
34 & 35 Hen. 8, c.26	1542–1543	40s./yr. freehold	Attaints	Wales	Limited *tales de circumstantibus* authorized. (Until 1664, see *infra* statute of 16 & 17 Car. 2, c.3 [1664–65]; statute of 4 Will. & M., c.24 [1692])
35 Hen. 8, c.6	1543–1544	6 sufficient hundredors in every panel of 40s. freeholders		*Nisi prius;* cities and towns corporate excepted	*Tales de circumstantibus* authorized for criminal cases
37 Hen. 8, c 5	1545	400 marks personalty in lieu of 20 marks freehold			
4 & 5 Phil. & M., c.7	1557–1558	Present, able persons of the county			*Tales de circumstantibus* authorized for criminal cases
5 Eliz. 1, c.25	1562–1563	Present, able persons of the county		Wales and counties palatine, cities and towns corporate excepted	*Tales de circumstantibus* authorized
14 Eliz. 1, c.9	1572				Defendants entitled to *tales* to same extent as plaintiffs

Jury Qualifications Established by Parliament, Statutes of the Realm, Magna Carta (1215) to Statute of 3 Geo. 2, c.25 (1730)[1] *(Cont.)*

Statute	Year	Property Holding Requirements; Other Requirements	Limits on Applicable Cases or Juries	Jurisdictional or Geographical Limits	Comments; Other Practices Allowed; Duration (perpetual unless noted)
18 Eliz. 1, c.12	1576			*Nisi prius*, Queen's courts, Middlesex	*Tales* available to relieve freeholders' too frequent service for trials at bar
27 Eliz. 1, c.6	1584–1585	£4 freehold, 2 hundredors sufficient in personal actions		Queen's courts and assizes; cities, towns, and Wales excepted	Until 1692, see *infra* statute of 4 Will. & M., c.24 (1692)
16 & 17 Car. 2, c.3	1664–1665	£20 freehold	Trials *de medietate linguae* excepted	England, King's courts, assizes, *nisi prius*, oyer and terminer, gaol delivery, quarter sessions	To remedy sheriff's abuses in returning poor jurors (until 1668[?])
16 & 17 Car. 2, c.3	1664–1665	£8 freehold		Wales, King's courts, assizes *nisi prius*, oyer and terminer, gaol delivery, quarter sessions	To remedy sheriff's abuses in returning poor jurors (until 1668[?])
4 Will. & M., c.24	1692	£10 freehold, £5 for talesmen	Trials *de medietate linguae* excepted	England, King's courts, assizes, *nisi prius*, oyer and terminer, gaol delivery, quarter sessions (cities and towns excepted)	Replaces expired statute of 16 & 17 Car. 2, c.3 (1664–1665)
6 & 7 Will. 3, c.4	1694	Certified practicing apothecaries exempted from jury service			

Jury Qualifications Established by Parliament, Statutes of the Realm, Magna Carta (1215) to Statute of 3 Geo. 2, c.25 (1730)[1] *(Cont.)*

Statute	Year	Property Holding Requirements; Other Requirements	Limits on Applicable Cases or Juries	Jurisdictional or Geographical Limits	Comments; Other Practices Allowed; Duration (perpetual unless noted)
7 & 8 Will. 3, c.21	1695	Registered seamen exempted from jury service			
3 Geo. 2, c.25	1730	£10 freehold, £5 for talesmen	Trials *de medietate linguae* excepted	Coverage of statute of 4 Will. & M., c.24 (1692) retained, and extended to Wales and counties palatine	To remedy corruption and sheriff's abuses in returning poor or unqualified jurors

1. Jury qualifications were further revised during the eighteenth and nineteenth centuries. See chapter 8.

Notes

Notes for Introduction

1. See Sally Lloyd-Bostock and Cheryl Thomas, "Decline of the 'Little Parliament': Juries and Jury Reform in England and Wales," *Law & Contemporary Problems* 62 (1999): 7; N. Taitt, "Outrage at Fresh Attempts to Curb Jury Trial," *Financial Times,* June 22, 2005; Jean Eaglesham and Bob Sherwood, "MPs Rebel over Move to Limit Jury Trials," *Financial Times,* May 20, 2003; Alan Pike, "Criticism of Proposals to Restrict Jury Trial," *Financial Times,* Oct. 9, 2001. Many of the proposed legislative changes originated in a seven-hundred-page report by Sir Robert Auld, a Court of Appeals judge, *Review of the Criminal Courts of England and Wales* (London: The Chancellor's Department, 2001).

Notes for Chapter 1

1. Edith Henderson, "The Background of the Seventh Amendment," *Harvard Law Review* 80 (1966): 289, 299.

2. 28 F. Cas. 745, 750 (C.C.D. Mass. 1812).

3. Ibid.

4. Thompson v. Utah, 170 U.S. 343 (1898). The Seventh Amendment applies only to federal courts, but comparable civil jury trial guarantees exist in state constitutions and statutes. See Fleming James, Jr., "Right to a Jury Trial in Civil Actions," *Yale Law Journal* 72 (1963): 655.

5. 293 U.S. 474, 476 (1935). For a recent, detailed study of applications of the historical test, see Suja A. Thomas, "The Seventh Amendment, Modern Procedure, and the English Common Law," *Washington University Law Quarterly* 82 (2004): 687.

6. Martin H. Redish, "Seventh Amendment Right to Jury Trial: A Study in the Irrationality of Rational Decision Making," *Northwestern Law Review* 70 (1975): 486, 487, citing McCulloch v. Maryland, 17 U.S. (4 Wheat.) 316, 407 (1819). See also Kenneth S. Klein, "The Myth of How to Interpret the Seventh Amendment Right to a Civil Jury Trial," *Ohio State Law Journal* 53 (1992): 1005; James, "Right to Jury Trial," *supra* n. 4, at 655. For a thorough, oft-cited study of the attitudes and circumstances surrounding the adoption of the Seventh Amendment—a study ultimately arguing for a "dynamic" rather than "static" reading—see Charles W. Wolfram, "The Constitutional History of the Seventh Amendment," *Minnesota Law Review* 75 (1973): 639.

7. See Markman v. Westview Instruments, Inc., 517 U.S. 370 (1996); Feltner v. Columbia Pictures Television, Inc., 523 U.S. 340 (1998); City of Monterey v. Del Monte Dunes at Monterey, Ltd., 526 U.S. 687 (1999).

8. I have transcribed and published many of the trial notes of Lord Mansfield, Chief Justice of the Court of King's Bench from 1756 to 1788, and I will use that published source. See James Oldham, *The Mansfield Manuscripts and the Growth of English Law in the*

Eighteenth Century, 2 vols. (Chapel Hill and London: University of North Carolina Press, 1992).

9. Jerome L. Wilson, "Dusting Off the Right to Trial by Jury," *Legal Times,* Apr. 1, 1996, at 24–25.

10. 517 U.S. at 376 (1996), citations omitted.

11. Ibid.

12. The question is whether, with English practice of 1791 in mind, the action should be viewed as one at common law or one in equity. If the latter, it would have gone to the Court of Chancery, where there would have been no jury. See chapter 2, "The Complexity Exception."

13. 517 U.S. at 377.

14. Ibid. at 379–80, footnote omitted.

15. Ibid., citing Patrick Devlin, "Jury Trial of Complex Cases: English Practice at the Time of the Seventh Amendment," *Columbia Law Review* 80 (1980): 43, 75. On the complex case question and Lord Devlin's point of view, see chapter 2.

16. 1 T.R. 602, 606, 99 Eng. Rep. 1274, 1277 (K.B. 1787).

17. Boulton v. Bull, 2 Bl. H. 463, 490, 126 Eng. Rep. 651, 665 (C.P. 1795).

18. Justice Souter referred to a total of twenty-two (reported) cases, relying on H. Dutton, *The Patent System and Inventive Activity During the Industrial Revolution, 1750–1852* (Manchester: Manchester University Press, 1984), 71. The printed reports counted by Dutton would have described only arguments on motion or questions of law before the full bench of the relevant common-law court and the judges' decisions. Unfortunately, the Supreme Court's understatement in *Markman* of the true volume of patent litigation in eighteenth-century England may be hard to set right, as is shown in commentary on the case. See J. G. Michelson, "Did the *Markman* Court Ignore Fact, Substance, and the Spirit of the Constitution in Its Rush Toward Uniformity?" *Loyola of Los Angeles Law Review* 30 (1997): 1749, 1765, where the author states, incorrectly, that "patent law in England at that time [the end of the eighteenth century] was scarcely describable; from 1750 to 1799 there were only eighteen patent decisions in England," citing Dutton.

19. See James Oldham, "Law-Making at *Nisi Prius* in the Early 1800s," *Journal of Legal History* 25 (2004): 221, 223.

20. The three common-law courts were King's Bench, Common Pleas, and Exchequer. By the late eighteenth century, King's Bench had the largest trial docket, followed by Common Pleas. The volume of civil litigation in the Court of Exchequer was comparatively small.

21. 1 T. R. 173 (K.B. 1786).

22. Ibid. at 180–82.

23. *Markman,* 517 U.S. at 388.

24. See James Oldham, *English Common Law in the Age of Mansfield* (Chapel Hill and London: University of North Carolina Press, 2004), 81–83, 277–78.

25. See generally Oldham, *The Mansfield Manuscripts, supra* n. 8. Most of the cases transcribed in the chapters on matters of commerce and contract were filed in Trespass on the Case. This was the form of action for all civil cases of defamation and libel. Other examples in Lord Mansfield's trial notes include actions for private nuisance, for damage caused during public riots, for false arrest, for damage caused by a sheriff's having let a prisoner escape, for negligence, for breach of promise of marriage, for threatening a worker boycott, and for malicious prosecution.

26. See, e.g., Robert Withey v. John Browne, Middlesex, Trinity 1770, The National Archives (formerly Public Record Office [PRO]) (hereafter "NA") NA/CP 40/3693, fol. 34 (promissory note); John Bushby v. John Carruthers, Cumberland, Trinity 1770, NA/CP

40/3694, fol. 835 (bill of exchange); William Baseley v. John Banner, Warwickshire, Trinity 1770, NA/CP 40/3693, fol. 322 (defamation); George Whiffin v. Michael Foster, Surrey, Trinity 1770, NA/CP 40/ 3693, fol. 508 (enticing away servants); Mathew Buscall & John Rose, assignees of the estate of Joseph Thickpenny, bankrupt v. George Hogg, Trinity 1770, NA/CP 40/3693, f. 366 (receiving a bankrupt's goods); Hugh Meares v. George Ansell, Surrey, Trinity 1770, NA/CP 40/3693, fol. 1121 (water rights).

27. The writ of inquiry was directed to the sheriffs of the county where the suit that instructed the sheriffs to call a jury to determine damages was brought. The inquiry juries were sometimes convened at public buildings such as the Guildhall, but as often they met at taverns or other informal venues. See chapter 4.

28. These figures were obtained by an inspection of the plea rolls and a tabulation of the entries. The comparable figures for Trinity Term 1774 are 4 cases on demurrer, compared with 197 cases sent "to the country."

29. See chapter 2, n. 37 for one special pleading alternative for trying title in a trespass case.

30. Occasionally discovery was arranged by consent. See, e.g., Martin v. Pewtress, cited in Oldham, *The Mansfield Manuscripts, supra* n. 8, at 2: 1199, 1200, n. 2 (discovery arrangements described, as entered in the King's Bench Rule Book for the plea side).

31. Even if a special verdict was requested by the judge, the jury could insist on returning a general verdict. See Giles Duncombe, *Trials per Pais,* 5th ed. (London, 1718), 233.

32. Others have done so. See Henderson, "The Background of the Seventh Amendment," *supra* n. 1, at 300–17; Austin W. Scott, "Trial by Jury and the Reform of Civil Procedure," *Harvard Law Review* 31 (1918): 669, 678–90. See also Oldham, *The Mansfield Manuscripts, supra* n. 8, at 1: 150–51, 156–60.

33. See Henderson, "The Background of the Seventh Amendment," *supra* n. 1, at 300; Scott, "The Reform of Civil Procedure," *supra* n. 32, at 687. The judgment in a "compulsory nonsuit" would be: "That the plaintiff has not prosecuted his suit . . . let the defendant depart without delay." Henderson, "The Background of the Seventh Amendment," *supra* n. 1, at 300. Examples of such entries, or close cousins, can be seen in the Common Pleas plea rolls, but they are extremely rare. See, e.g., NA/CP 40/3714, Trinity 1774, fol. 956.

34. Scott, "The Reform of Civil Procedure," *supra* n. 32, at 687.

35. Henderson, "The Background of the Seventh Amendment," *supra* n. 1, at 300–1.

36. 1 Doug. 216 (K.B. 1779).

37. Ibid.

38. 5 July 1759, Oldham, *The Mansfield Manuscripts, supra* n. 8, at 1: 256.

39. 23 Feb. 1763, ibid. at 1: 268.

40. Ibid., n. 1. Other examples of nonsuits with plaintiff's consent are Leake v. Howard, 23 Feb. 1757, ibid. at 1: 419 (Mansfield's note: "Nonsuit on the evidence [of] Calvert by their own consent"); Green v. Rucker, 8 Dec. 1759, ibid. at 1: 487 ("Plaintiff satisfied to be nonsuited"). In one case, it came out that plaintiff had sued the wrong person. Christie v. Baker, 6 Dec. 1782, ibid. at 2: 1310.

41. Williams v. Dyer, 15 Feb. 1766, ibid. at 1: 282. A similar case was Norton v. Compton, 19 Feb. 1773, ibid. at 1: 308, where the plaintiff was nonsuited in an action to recover for the sale of goods to defendant's wife, but "the evidence showed that the wife had eloped from the defendant before contracting the debt."

42. Ellis v. Galindo, 23 July 1783, ibid. at 1: 629.

43. Ibid. at 1: 630, n. 2.

44. 14 Aug. 1764, ibid. at 2: 963.

45. Ibid. For another such case, see Melchart v. Halsey, 14 June 1770, ibid. at 1: 297.

46. See Norton v. Williams, 15 July 1783, ibid. at 1: 444; Taylor v. Woodmass, 23 Feb. 1764, ibid. at 1: 503 (Mansfield wrote: "Scandalous on the part of Plaintiff"); Farquharson v. Hunter, 5 Mar. 1785, ibid. at 1: 591 (Mansfield comment: "Defendant produced the bills of sale in which there is no contract to indemnify, & put it upon the Plaintiff to prove the promise, & entered into a full argument whether this promise could be considered as an insurable interest in Plaintiff. I thought it could not. So the Plaintiff was nonsuited.").

47. Henderson, "The Background of the Seventh Amendment," *supra* n. 1, at 302.

48. Text at nn. 21–22, *supra.*

49. 23 May 1782, Oldham, *The Mansfield Manuscripts, supra* n. 8, at 1: 368.

50. Thus, in Rigard v. Wright, 25 July 1763, ibid. at 1: 264, Mansfield wrote, "I am much dissatisfied with the verdict & I certified," which meant that he certified the case as proper for a motion for new trial. See also the cases discussed ibid. at 1: 89–90.

51. The first trial was 24 July 1781, ibid. at 1: 563; the second, 20 Dec. 1781, ibid. at 1: 569.

52. 4 Aug. 1783, ibid. at 1: 354.

53. 26 July 1773, ibid. at 2: 1239.

54. For example, after the third trial of Bruckshaw v. Hopkins, 13 June 1776, ibid. at 2: 994, Mansfield wrote: "A wrong verdict, but [it] should not be set aside."

55. 3 Dec. 1776, ibid. at 1: 316.

56. Henderson, "The Background of the Seventh Amendment," *supra* n. 1, at 305–6.

57. On Mansfield's use of the "case stated," see Oldham, *The Mansfield Manuscripts, supra* n. 8, at 1: 101, n. 179. In Vallejo v. Wheeler, 1 Cowp. 143, 153, 98 Eng. Rep. 1012, 1017 (K.B. 1774), Lord Mansfield observed that "it is not easy to collect with certainty from a general verdict, or from notes taken at Nisi Prius, what was the true ground of decision," so that in the case before him, "as in all doubtful cases," he "wished a case to be made for the opinion of the Court."

58. 10 Aug. 1759, Oldham, *The Mansfield Manuscripts, supra* n. 8, at 1: 251.

59. 11 Feb. 1760, ibid. at 1: 258.

60. Barzillai v. Lewis, 5 Mar. 1782, ibid. at 1: 576.

61. 10 July 1781, ibid. at 2: 1171.

62. Mansfield ceased being an active judge in 1786, although he did not resign until 1788. He died in 1793.

63. 21 Feb. 1778, Oldham, *The Mansfield Manuscripts, supra* n. 8, at 1: 748.

64. Ibid. at 1: 756. The argument was held on May 8, 1778, the day after Buller took his seat as a judge on King's Bench.

65. *Markman,* 517 U.S. at 380, n. 5.

66. See chapter 3, "Law versus Fact."

67. 517 U.S. at 384.

68. 526 U.S. 687 (1999).

69. Ibid. at 718–21. On the *City of Monterey* case, see also chapter 4, text following n. 4.

70. On the extensive history of the special jury, see chapters 6, 7, and 8.

71. Compare P. J. McCabe and P. M. Smith, "Courts Order 'Markman' Hearings Early in Cases," *National Law Journal,* Oct. 19, 1998, at C42, with S. Z. Szczepanski and F. R. Nation, "A 'Markman' Hearing Can Determine Case Outcome," ibid., May 24, 1999, at C26.

72. Phillips v. AWH Corporation, dissenting from order vacating opinion reported at 363 F.3d 1207 (Fed. Cir. 2004) and granting rehearing *en banc* (case 03-1269, -1286, order entered July 21, 2004).

Notes for Chapter 2

1. 52 F.3d 967, 993 (concurring in the judgment) (1995).

2. 396 U.S. 531 (1970).

3. 517 U.S. 370 (1996). See generally the discussion of the case in chapter 1. In n. 10 to his *Markman* opinion, Justice Souter wrote:

> Because we conclude that our precedent supports classifying the question as one for the court, we need not decide either the extent to which the Seventh Amendment can be said to have crystallized a law/fact distinction . . . or whether post-1791 precedent classifying an issue as one of fact would trigger the protections of the Seventh Amendment if (unlike this case) there were no more specific reason for decision.

Ibid. at 385.

4. The leading Supreme Court case on this aspect of the historical test is Beacon Theaters, Inc. v. Westover, 359 U.S. 500 (1959). For representative scholarly commentary and criticism, see Martin H. Redish, "Seventh Amendment Right to Jury Trial: A Study in the Irrationality of Rational Decision Making," *Northwestern Law Review* 70 (1975): 488–508, 514–30; D. L. Shapiro and D. R. Coquillette, "The Fetish of Jury Trial in Civil Cases: A Comment on *Rachal v. Hill,*" *Harvard Law Review* 85 (1971): 442.

5. 396 U.S. at 538.

6. In addition to the Devlin-Arnold dialogue (see nn. 8–11, *infra,* and accompanying text), the question of what to do about the jury-trial guarantee in complex civil litigation has provoked substantial scholarly output in the law journals, much of it in student notes. See, e.g., Note, "The Right to a Jury Trial in Complex Civil Litigation," *Harvard Law Review* 92 (1979): 898; Joel B. Harris and Lenore Liberman, "Can the Jury Survive the Complex Antitrust Case?" *New York Law School Law Review* 24 (1979): 611; Montgomery Kersten, Note, "Preserving the Right to Jury Trial in Complex Civil Cases," *Stanford Law Review* 32 (1979): 99; Note, "The Case for Special Juries in Complex Civil Litigation," *Yale Law Journal* 89 (1980): 1155; Richard O. Lempert, "Civil Juries and Complex Cases: Let's Not Rush to Judgment," *Michigan Law Review* 80 (1981): 68; Peter W. Sperlich, "The Case for Preserving Trial by Jury in Complex Civil Litigation," *Judicature* 65 (1982): 394; Douglas King, Note, "Complex Civil Litigation and the Seventh Amendment Right to a Jury Trial," *University of Chicago Law Review* 51 (1984): 581; James S. Campbell, "The Current Understanding of the Seventh Amendment: Jury Trials in Modern Complex Litigation," *Washington University Law Quarterly* 66 (1988): 63; Joseph C. Wilkinson, Jr., Frank D. Zielinski, and George M. Curtis III, "A Bicentennial Transition: Modern Alternatives to Seventh Amendment Jury Trial in Complex Cases," *Kansas Law Review* 37 (1988): 61; Rita Sutton, Note, "A More Rational Approach to Complex Civil Litigation in the Federal Courts: The Special Jury," *University of Chicago Legal Forum* 1990: 575; Richard Lempert, "Civil Juries and Complex Cases: Taking Stock After Twelve Years," in Robert E. Litan, ed., *Verdict: Assessing the Civil Jury System* (Washington, DC: The Brookings Institution, 1993); Keith Broyles, Note, "Taking the Courtroom into the Classroom: A Proposal for Educating the Lay Juror in Complex Litigation Cases," *George Washington University Law Review* 64 (1996): 714; Franklin Strier, "The Educated Jury: A Proposal for Complex Litigation," *De Paul Law Review* 47 (1997): 49; Joseph A. Miron, Jr., Note, "The Constitutionality of a Complexity Exception to the Seventh Amendment," *Chicago-Kent Law Review* 73 (1998): 865.

7. 631 F.2d 1069 (3d. Cir. 1980).

8. Patrick Devlin, "Jury Trial of Complex Cases: English Practice at the Time of the Seventh Amendment," *Columbia Law Review* 80 (1980): 43; Morris Arnold, "A Historical

Inquiry into the Right to Trial by Jury in Complex Civil Litigation," *Pennsylvania Law Review* 128 (1980): 829.

9. P. Devlin, "Equity, Due Process and the Seventh Amendment: A Commentary on the *Zenith* Case," *Michigan Law Review* 81 (1983): 1571.

10. Clench v. Tomley, Cary 23, 21 Eng. Rep. 13 (Ch. 1603); Blad v. Bamfield, 3 Swans. App. 604, 36 Eng. Rep. 992 (Ch. 1674). Morris Arnold points out that the proper name and spelling of the first of these two cases is Towneley v. Clench. Arnold, "A Historical Inquiry," *supra* n. 8, at 840, n. 63.

11. Arnold, "A Historical Inquiry," *supra* n. 8, at 846. The debate was expanded by two lawyers who had worked with Lord Devlin on behalf of IBM. See J. S. Campbell and N. Le Poidevin, "Complex Cases and Jury Trials: A Reply to Professor Arnold," *Pennsylvania Law Review* 128: (1980): 966; M. S. Arnold, "A Modest Replication to a Lengthy Discourse," *Pennsylvania Law Review* 128 (1980): 986.

12. 631 F.2d at 1083.

13. Ibid. at 1080.

14. Ibid. at 1081. The court explained that "The Chancellor's authority to direct an issue to a jury derived from his control over the method of finding facts in suits already within his jurisdiction," citing an article by John Langbein, "Fact Finding in the English Court of Chancery: A Rebuttal," *Yale Law Journal* 83 (1974): 1620.

15. 631 F.2d at 1083.

16. Ibid.

17. Ibid. at 1084.

18. 1 Sch. & Lef. 305 (Ch. Ire. 1804).

19. See Devlin, "Equity, Due Process and the Seventh Amendment," *supra* n. 9, at 1571, n. 3.

20. John Mitford, *A Treatise on the Pleadings in Suits in the Court of Chancery* (Dublin, 1789), 111, quoted by Devlin, "Equity, Due Process and the Seventh Amendment," *supra* n. 9, at 1629.

21. 1 Sch. & Lef. at 309, quoted by Devlin, "Equity, Due Process and the Seventh Amendment," *supra* n. 9, at 1628.

22. 2 Atk. 141, 26 Eng. Rep. 489; Barn. C. 368, 27 Eng. Rep. 682 (Ch. 1740); further proceedings reported at 3 Atk. 269 (*sub. nom.* Gyles v. Wilcocks), 26 Eng. Rep. 957 (Ch. 1745).

23. See Devlin, "Jury Trial of Complex Cases," *supra* n. 8, at 73.

24. Devlin discusses the arbitration features of the Common Law Procedure Act of 1854 and subsequent reform legislation, mainly as they related to actions of account. Ibid. at 77–80.

25. 8 Anne, c.19 (1709).

26. 2 Atk. at 144; 26 Eng. Rep. at 491.

27. In a brief note at 3 Atk. 269, 26 Eng. Rep. 957 (Ch. 1740), the agreement to arbitrate is indicated. With consent of the parties, Lord Hardwicke issued an order referring all matters in dispute to the award and determination of Mr. Cay and Mr. Thomas Stephens, with the customary terms of such an order set out. On this procedure, see Henry Horwitz and James Oldham, "John Locke, Lord Mansfield, and Arbitration During the Eighteenth Century," *The Historical Journal* 36 (1993): 137.

28. O'Connor v. Cook, 8 Ves. Jr. 535, 536, 32 Eng. Rep. 463 (Ch. 1803). Relying on this case and others, Harold Chesnin and Geoffrey Hazard attempted, in a 1974 article, to show that "the rule that a court of equity may decide fact issues . . . was not firmly established in England until some time after 1800, at least a decade after the effective date of the Seventh Amendment." H. Chesnin and G. C. Hazard, Jr., "Chancery Procedure and the

Seventh Amendment: Jury Trial of Issues in Equity Cases Before 1791," *Yale Law Journal* 83 (1974): 999, 1000. This proposition was thoroughly exploded by John Langbein in "Fact Finding in the English Court of Chancery: A Rebuttal," *supra* n. 14, at 1620. Langbein cited a number of Hardwicke opinions from the 1740s (not including Gyles v. Wilcox) that, with other cases, demonstrated that, throughout the eighteenth century, Chancery "had and exercised the power to resolve contested issues of fact." Ibid. at 1622. He pointed out that the tithe issue in *O'Connor* had, for special reasons, become the subject of "an automatic reference to jury trial." Ibid. at 1624, n. 26. As Lord Eldon stated in an earlier opinion in O'Connor v. Cook, "if any reasonable doubt has been raised upon [a tithe question] in the evidence, it has been of late thought wise and discreet to send the question of fact to a Jury," and "All the Judges have demonstrated their opinion in favor of that practice." O'Connor v. Cook, 6 Ves. Jr. 665, 671, 31 Eng. Rep. 1247, 1251 (Ch. 1802).

Where the factual inquiry required construction of documentary evidence, however, Chancery would keep the case, as shown in Short v. Lee, 2 Jac. & W. 463, 37 Eng. Rep. 705 (Ch. 1821). There, a lessee of an ecclesiastical corporation sued for tithes, and on being urged to send an issue to the law courts, the Master of the Rolls, Sir Thomas Plummer, said there was not "any contrariety in the evidence"; the evidence to disprove the immemorial existence of the tithes was "entirely written, contained in thirty-six ancient rolls in a dead language, embracing many terms of different kinds"; "their construction has called forth the applications of learning, critical and accurate investigation and collation, frequent and useful revision, and the assistance of glossaries and antiquarian knowledge, to form a correct judgment respecting their meaning and import." Finally, he asked, rhetorically: "Could this be done before a jury at *Nisi Prius,* with the same effect as it may in a court, assisted by the learning and industry of the bar, during a hearing of many days, devoted entirely to this one subject, and with a knowledge of the whole of the cause to which the enquiry belongs?" Ibid. at 502, 719.

29. The Master of the Rolls in the late eighteenth century was a sort of deputy Lord Chancellor. He was chief of the twelve Masters in Chancery, sat in his own court, and heard a variety of cases and petitions, including technical matters referred to him by the Chancellor. See Joseph Harrison, *The Practice of the Court of Chancery,* 2 vols., 8th ed. (London, 1794), 1: 56–58.

30. Barn. C. 368, 27 Eng. Rep. 682 (Ch. 1740).

31. Arnold, "A Modest Replication to a Lengthy Discourse," *supra* n. 11, at 988 (footnote omitted).

32. In English practice, the plaintiff's complaint was termed the Declaration and the defendant's answer was called the Plea.

33. See chapter 1, text at n. 28.

34. According to [Anon.], *The Practising Attorney: Or, New King's Bench Guide* (London, 1779), 95:

> The General Issue or General Plea, is what traverses, thwarts and denies at once the whole Declaration, without offering any special Matter whereby to evade it. . . . Formerly, the General Issue was seldom pleaded, except when the Party meant wholly to deny the charge alledged against him; but when he meant to distinguish away or palliate the charge, it was always usual to set forth the particular Facts in what is called a Special Plea, which was originally intended to apprize the Court and the adverse Party, of the Nature and Circumstances of the Defence, and to keep the Law and Fact distinct . . . but the Science of Special Pleading having been frequently perverted for the Purposes of Chicane and Delay; the Courts have of late in some instances, and the Legislature in many more, permitted the General Issue to be

> pleaded, which leaves every thing open, the Fact and the Law, and the Equity of the Case, and have allowed Special Matter to be given in Evidence at the Trial.

35. As noted earlier (see chapter 1, text following n. 27), the stock expression for jury trial was to "put oneself upon the country." Thus,

> if the Traverse or Denial comes from the Defendant, the Issue is tendered in this Manner: "And of this he puts himself upon the country," thereby submitting himself to the Judgment of his Peers; but if the Traverse lies upon the Plaintiff, he tenders the Issue, or prays the Judgment of the Peers against the Defendant, in another Form thus: "And this he prays may be enquired of by the Country."

Ibid. at 102.

36. The required steps were laid out in the standard practice books, such as in [Anon.], *The Attorney's Compleat Guide In the Court of King's Bench* (London, 1773) ("By an Attorney of the Court"). The copy of this book held by the Georgetown University Law Library is a commonplace version, signed by Edward Grave, January 1778, and filled with interleaved manuscript additions. One manuscript addition that illustrates the role of plaintiff's attorney in getting the case to trial is a "Form of Notice of Trial where there [are] issues in Fact & in Law, to be indorsed on the back of Paper Book," which reads as follows (at 116a):

> Messrs. G & P
>
> Take Notice that the several Issues joined in the Cause to be tried by a Jury of the Country will be tried at the Sittings after the present Michaelmas Term at Guildhall London. And that the Jurors of that Jury will at the Trial of those Issues inquire what Damages the plaintiff has sustained on Occasion of the premises whereof the said parties have put themselves upon the Judgment of the Court in Case Judgment shall be given thereof for the said plaintiffs.
>
> Yours &c

37. Special pleading was an arcane art form, and no doubt there were maneuvers that are no longer appreciated or understood. Some techniques may have have avoided a jury without going to Chancery or filing a demurrer. [Anon.], *The Practising Attorney* (*supra*, n. 34) gives one example (at 98):

> If the Defendant in an Action of Trespass be desirous to refer the validity of his Title to the Court rather than the Jury, he may state his Title specially, and at the same time *give colour* to the Plaintiff, or suppose him to have an Appearance or colour of Title bad indeed in Point of Law, but of which the Jury are not competent Judges.

38. See Horwitz and Oldham, "John Locke," *supra* n. 27, at 147–48, 154–55.

39. See, e.g., James Oldham, *The Mansfield Manuscripts and the Growth of English Law in the Eighteenth Century*, 2 vols. (Chapel Hill and London: University of North Carolina Press, 1992), 1: 154.

40. Devlin cites a comment by Lord Campbell in an 1847 case, Taff Vale Railway Co. v. Nixon, 1 H.L. Cas. 111, 9 Eng. Rep. 695 (H.L. 1847), that the judge's recommendations of references to arbitration would be accepted ninety-nine out of one hundred times. Devlin, "Jury Trial of Complex Cases," *supra* n. 8, at 77. I am certain that the same was true of Lord Mansfield's time on the Court of King's Bench in the late eighteenth century.

41. Examples abound among the references to arbitration from the Court of King's Bench when Lord Mansfield was presiding as the trial judge. See Oldham, *The Mansfield Manuscripts, supra* n. 39, at 1: 151–54, and 2: 1540–1665 (Appendix E).

42. See chapter 8.

43. 3 Geo. 2, c.25, s.15.

44. B. J. Sellon, *The Practice of the Courts of King's Bench and Common Pleas*, 2 vols. (Dublin, 1793, 1795), 2: 444. Sellon adds that, by a 1751 enactment, the party requesting

the special jury became responsible for the costs, unless the judge certified otherwise. He also spells out the steps to be taken by counsel to move for a special jury, which "is a matter of course," such that "no notice of the motion or affidavit of the facts is necessary." Ibid.

45. For a forceful demonstration of this point using reported cases, see King, "Complex Civil Litigation and the Seventh Amendment," *supra* n. 6, at 581. One example of a nineteenth-century case that seemed to the Master of the Rolls to be formidably complex was Short v. Lee, 2 Jac. & W. 463, 37 Eng. Rep. 705 (Ch. 1821), discussed at n. 28, *supra.* Yet even this case falls far short of the complex civil litigation of the late twentieth century.

46. 631 F.2d 1069 (3d Cir. 1980).

47. Ibid. at 1079.

48. 494 U.S. 558 (1990).

49. Ibid. at 565, n. 4., quoting Tull v. United States, 481 U.S. 412, 418 n. 4 (1987).

50. 517 U.S. at 384.

51. Ibid. at 388.

52. Ibid.

53. Ibid. at 389.

54. Ibid. at 389–90.

Notes for Chapter 3

1. 293 U.S. 474 (1935). See chapter 1, text at n. 5; chapter 4, text at nn. 79–81, 91–95.

2. Ibid. at 486.

3. 3 Dallas 1 (1794). For the full context of the case and for transcriptions of surviving documents, see Maeva Marcus, ed., *The Documentary History of the Supreme Court of the United States, 1789–1800,* 7 vols. (New York: Columbia University Press, 1998), 6: 73–175.

4. 3 Dallas at 4.

5. Ibid.

6. William E. Nelson, *Americanization of the Common Law: The Impact of Legal Change on Massachusetts Society, 1760–1830* (Cambridge, MA, and London: Harvard University Press, 1975), 28.

7. For a contrasting study, see James D. Rice, "The Criminal Trial Before and After the Lawyers: Authority, Law, and Culture in Maryland Jury Trials, 1681–1837," *The American Journal of Legal History* 40 (1996): 455. Rice concludes that in Maryland in the colonial and post-Revolutionary era, "Judges possessed tremendous power over the outcome of criminal trials" and that his interpretation of the Maryland documentary sources "differs significantly from the one offered by many legal historians," most notably William E. Nelson. Ibid. at 473. See, generally, Shannon C. Stimson, *The American Revolution and the Law: Anglo-American Jurisprudence Before John Marshall* (Princeton: Princeton University Press, 1990); David Millon, "Juries, Judges, and Democracy," *Law and Social Inquiry* 18 (1993): 135.

8. Stimson, *The American Revolution and the Law, supra* n. 7, at 49.

9. Vaugh. 135, 124 Eng. Rep. 1006 (C.P. 1670).

10. Thomas A. Green, *Verdict According to Conscience: Perspectives on the English Criminal Trial Jury, 1200–1899* (Chicago: University of Chicago Press, 1985).

11. See chapter 6.

12. Green, *Verdict According to Conscience, supra* n. 10, at 94.

13. Ibid. at 239–64.

14. Ibid. at 328.

15. See, generally, Phillip Hamburger, "The Development of the Law of Seditious Libel and the Control of the Press," *Stanford Law Review* 37 (1985): 661.

16. For details, see James Oldham, *The Mansfield Manuscripts and the Growth of English Law in the Eighteenth Century*, 2 vols. (Chapel Hill and London: University of North Carolina Press, 1991), 2: 775–805, 814–22.

17. *Lloyd's Evening Post*, 22 Dec. 1770.

18. 1 T.R. 73, 94, 99 Eng. Rep. 774, 785 (K.B. 1784).

19. Ibid. at n. [1].

20. *The London Chronicle*, 13–16 Nov. 1784.

21. Green, *Verdict According to Conscience, supra* n. 10, at 338.

22. *Lloyd's Evening Post*, 20 July 1770. See also the report of the trial at T. B. Howell, ed., *Cobbett's Complete Collection of State Trials and Proceedings for High Treason*, 33 vols. (London, 1809–26) (*State Trials* hereafter) 20: 869, 894–95 (1770). Years earlier, in connection with the trial of Wilkes, *The London Chronicle* (3–6 Mar.1764) reported:

> To the honour of a great Personage in the law, the jury, on a late trial, were told by him from the bench, that, if they pleased to take it upon themselves, they were judges as well of Law as Fact; and farther, that they were not answerable to any person whatever for the verdict they might bring in, but God and their conscience.

See, in this connection, Green, *Verdict According to Conscience, supra* n. 10, at 238, nn. 101–2, and accompanying text.

23. James Alexander, *A Brief Narrative of the Case and Trial of John Peter Zenger, Printer of The New York Weekly Journal*, Stanley N. Katz, ed. (Cambridge, MA: The Belknap Press, 1972).

24. Ibid. at 15.

25. Ibid. at 22.

26. Ibid. at 100.

27. Ibid. at 26.

28. Text at nn. 13–14, *supra*.

29. There is a large literature on jury nullification. See, for example, Clay S. Conrad, *Jury Nullification: The Evolution of a Doctrine* (Durham, NC: Carolina Academic Press, 1998); Nancy S. Marder, "The Myth of the Nullifying Jury," *Northwestern University Law Review* 93 (1999): 877; Lars Noah, "Civil Jury Nullification," *Iowa Law Review* 86 (2001): 1601.

30. Available at http://www.fija.org/New%20Hampshire%20Bill.htm.

31. See New Hampshire General Court, HB122 (Senate Status May 29, 2003: "Inexpedient to Legislate"). Available at http://www.gencourt.state.nh.us/index/indexstatus.asp?expbillno=h.

32. Franklin v. State, 12 Md. 236, 249 (1858), discussed in Conrad, *Jury Nullification, supra* n. 29, at 88–89.

33. Beavers v. State, 236 Ind. 549 (1957). See Conrad, *Jury Nullification, supra* n. 29, at 119–20 and, more generally, 117–24 (discussing developments in not only Maryland and Indiana but also Pennsylvania, Illinois, Georgia, Oregon, Iowa, and Kansas). For useful additional analyses of the judge-jury relationship on questions of law, see Austin W. Scott, "Trial by Jury and the Reform of Civil Procedure," *Harvard Law Review* 31 (1918): 669; Mark DeWolfe Howe, "Juries as Judges of Criminal Law," *Harvard Law Review* 52 (1939): 582; Reneé B. Lettow, "New Trial for Verdict Against Law: Judge-Jury Relations in Early Nineteenth-Century America," *Notre Dame Law Review* 71 (1996): 505.

34. 2005 U.S. App. LEXIS 9347.

35. Ibid. at 74.

36. Ibid. at 38, 40–41 (italics omitted).

37. Text at n. 22, *supra.*

38. 1 Burr. 390, 394, 97 Eng. Rep. 365, 367 (K.B. 1757).

39. Ibid. See generally John Morgan, *Essays upon the Law of Evidence, New Trials, Special Verdicts, Trials at Bar, and Repleaders,* 3 vols. (London, 1789), vols. 2–3. (All of volume 2 and three-fourths of volume 3 comprise collections of cases that illustrate the granting of new trials, arranged under nine headings.)

40. 1 Burr. at 395, 97 Eng. Rep. at 367.

41. This point was critical to Vaughan's reasoning in *Bushell's Case* (Green, *Verdict According to Conscience, supra* n. 10, at 245).

42. Harvard Law School, MS 1124, fol. 162 (n.d., K.B. circa 1701).

43. Andr. 315, 95 Eng. Rep. 414 (K.B. 1739), also briefly reported at 2 Str. 1105, 93 Eng. Rep. 1061 (K.B. 1739).

44. The quotation is from a manuscript report of Chief Justice Lee's opinion in the case that is more detailed than Andrews's report. Harvard Law School MS 2050, fols. 297, 298 (K.B. 1739).

45. Ibid. at fol. 299. The reference to the inclusion in the general verdict of matter of law does not appear in Andrews's report of the case.

46. Andr. at 316, 95 Eng. Rep. at 414.

47. Ibid. at 321, 416.

48. Harvard Law School, MS 1017, fol. 83 (K.B. 1726). Later in the century, this rule was put in practice in Lord Mansfield's *nisi prius* sittings. In Johnson v. Cawthorn, Mansfield's trial notes describe a witness named Campbell as "one of the jury sworn." Oldham, *The Mansfield Manuscripts, supra* n. 16, at 1: 577–78 (Mar. 5, 1782).

49. Text at nn. 3–5, *supra.*

50. On this doctrine, see Richard H. Helmholz, ed., *Select Cases on Defamation to 1600* (London: Selden Society, 1985), 101 Selden Society xcii–xcv.

51. Ibid. at xcvii.

52. Harvard Law School, MS 1113 (Reports by Sir Peter King), fol. 51 (K.B. 1716).

53. Several stages of the case are reported in Harvard Law School MS 1142 (Hollingshed's Reports), fols. 4, 151, 170, 313 (K.B. 1710–11). (An unrelated procedural aspect of the case is reported at 11 Mod. 234, 88 Eng. Rep. 1010 (K.B. 1709).)

54. Harvard Law School, MS 1113, fols. 316–17.

55. For comparable examples involving the jury task of ascertaining intent by way of innuendo in publications that were the subjects of seditious libel prosecutions, see Oldham, *The Mansfield Manuscripts, supra* n. 16, at 2: 800–5.

56. James Bradley Thayer, "'Law and Fact' in Jury Trials," *Harvard Law Review* 4 (1890): 147, 148–49.

57. Ibid. at 159.

58. Ibid. Cockburn's "ideal mode" would of course be complicated in America because of the Seventh Amendment.

59. Ibid. at 161.

60. Ibid.

61. Ibid. at 162.

62. 1 T.R. 167, 99 Eng. Rep. 1033 (K.B. 1786).

63. 3 Doug. 113, 99 Eng. Rep. 566 (K.B. 1782).

64. 3 Doug. 137, 99 Eng. Rep. 579 (K.B. 1782).

65. Lincoln's Inn MS 18, fols. 16, 38 (K.B. 1782).

66. 3 Doug. at 116, 99 Eng. Rep. at 568.

67. Lincoln's Inn MS 18, fol. 38 (K.B. 1782).

68. 3 Doug. at 140, 99 Eng. Rep. at 580.

69. 1 T.R. 167, 99 Eng. Rep. 1033 (K.B. 1786).

70. Ibid. at 168–69, 1034.

71. Ibid. at 169, 1035.

72. Stephen A. Weiner, "The Civil Jury Trial and the Law-Fact Distinction," *California Law Review* 54 (1966): 1867, 1896. Thus:

> Whether an offer has been accepted within a reasonable time has been called a question of fact for the jury by an Iowa and a Pennsylvania court, but a question of law for the trial judge by a New Hampshire and a Massachusetts court. Whether a contractual obligation has been performed within a reasonable time has been called a jury question by some courts, but a question of law by others. Whether an insured has reported an event to his insurer within a reasonable time has been classified as both a question of fact for the jury and a question of law for the court. Whether notice of a breach of warranty claim has been given within a reasonable time has been called both a question of fact for the jury and a question of law. Whether a party has taken sufficiently prompt action to rescind a contract has received the same dual classification in the cases. This is also true of negotiable instrument cases presenting the issue of whether a check was cashed, or a demand instrument presented for payment, within a reasonable time.

Ibid. at 1899–1900.

73. Margaret L. Moses, "The Uniform Commercial Code Meets the Seventh Amendment: The Demise of Jury Trials Under Article 5?" *Indiana Law Journal* 72 (1997): 681; Moses, "The Jury-Trial Right in the UCC: On a Slippery Slope," *Southern Methodist University Law Review* 54 (2001): 561.

74. 530 U.S. 466 (2000).

75. Ibid. at 478 (footnote omitted).

76. 124 S. Ct. 2531 (2004).

77. Ibid. at 2538–39. Once the *Blakely* decision came out, the continued validity of the federal mandatory sentencing guidelines came into question. As the force of logic of the *Blakely* decision suggested, the Court subsequently declared that *mandatory* guidelines encroached unconstitutionally on the jury's fact-finding role. United States v. Booker, 125 S. Ct. 738 (2005). The guidelines were not thrown out but were declared instead to be merely advisory.

78. O. W. Holmes, Jr., *The Common Law* (Boston: Little, Brown, 1881), 124.

79. Ibid.

80. See Thayer, "'Law and Fact,'" *supra* n. 56; Scott, "Trial by Jury," *supra* n. 33; Howe, "Juries as Judges," *supra* n. 33.

81. Scott, "Trial by Jury," *supra* n. 33, at 678–91.

82. The demurrer to the evidence would avoid the jury altogether, but, perhaps because of the strength of the tradition of trial "by the country," this was rarely invoked, the more so as the motion for new trial grew in popularity. In *The Gazeteer* for May 19, 1766, a report appeared of a trial at Guildhall before Chief Baron Parker of the Court of Exchequer and a special jury of merchants. After the jury returned a verdict for the plaintiffs, counsel for the defendant (an insurance underwriter) "thought it proper to demur to the evidence," which the report described as "a method of preventing a determination of a jury of merchants not at all expected, and [one that] has not, as we hear, been practiced for twenty years before."

83. David Graham, *An Essay on New Trials* (New York, 1834).

84. Ibid. at v. On this treatise, and a later revision by Thomas Waterman, see Lettow, "New Trial for Verdict Against Law," *supra* n. 33, at 507.

85. See chapter 1, text at nn. 47–55.

86. Lettow, "New Trial for Verdict Against Law," *supra* n. 33, at 522. For an illustration, see the *Scrimshire* case discussed *infra,* chapter 8, text at nn. 63–64.

87. See text following n. 71, *supra.*

88. Lettow, "New Trial for Verdict Against Law," *supra* n. 33, at 521.

89. William E. Nelson, "The Province of the Judiciary," *The John Marshall Law Review* 37 (2004): 335.

90. See chapter 2, text at nn. 20–30.

91. 253 U.S. 300 (1920).

92. Ibid. at 312–13.

93. Ibid. at 313.

94. Ibid. at 305.

95. Ibid. at 310–11.

96. On the history of the special master and the extent to which the practice derived from English Chancery practice, see Amalia Kessler, "Our Inquisitorial Tradition: Equity Procedure, Due Process, and the Search for an Alternative to the Adversarial," *Cornell Law Review* 90 (2005): 1181. In describing early-nineteenth-century New York practice with special masters, Kessler points out that, "unlike what the common-law jury had long since become, the master was not simply a passive audience for whatever evidence the parties chose to present, but instead played an active, inquisitorial role in determining what evidence should be heard and which questions asked." Ibid. at 1209.

97. Fuller v. Harrison, *The Morning Chronicle,* 5 July 1777; Quince v. Whitmore, *Daily Universal Register,* 5 July 1785.

Notes for Chapter 4

1. 526 U.S. 687 (1999).

2. 532 U.S. 424 (2001).

3. 526 U.S. at 743 (dissenting).

4. 532 U.S. at 437, 432.

5. Ibid. at 720, citing, among other sources, Coke's *Institutes* (Edward Coke, *The First Part of the Institutes of the Lawes of England, or a Commentarie Upon Littleton* [London, 1628]).

6. 526 U.S. at 720.

7. Ibid.

8. See chapter 3.

9. Lord Townsend v. Hughes, 2 Mod. 150, 151, 86 Eng. Rep. 994, 995 (C.P. 1677), quoted by Justice Thomas in his opinion for the Court in Feltner v. Columbia Pictures Television, Inc., 523 U.S. 340, 353 (1998). See also Barker v. Dixie, Cas. t. Hardwicke 279, 281, 95 Eng. Rep. 180, 181 (K.B. 1736), discussed at text accompanying nn. 101–6, *infra.*

10. U.S. Constitution, Amendment VII.

11. 532 U.S. at 437, n. 11. In explaining this evolution, Justice Stevens stated,

> Until well into the nineteenth century, punitive damages frequently operated to compensate for intangible injuries, compensation which was not otherwise available under the narrow conception of compensatory damages prevalent at the time. . . . As the types of compensatory damages available to plaintiffs have broadened, . . . the theory behind punitive damages has shifted towards a more purely punitive (and therefore less factual) understanding.

Ibid. There is a view, nevertheless, that punitive damages continue to encompass compensation for intangible injuries. See Victor E. Schwartz and Leah Lorber, "Twisting the Purpose of Pain and Suffering Awards: Turning Compensation into 'Punishment,'" *South Carolina Law Review* 54 (2002): 47.

12. See also *Feltner*, 523 U.S. at 353 ("there is overwhelming evidence that the consistent practice at common law was for juries to award damages") (Justice Thomas, speaking for the Court).

13. 517 U.S. 559 (1996). See Justice Stevens' reference to *BMW* in *Cooper*, 532 U.S. 431, n. 4.

14. 538 U.S. 408 (2003).

15. 517 U.S. at 574–75.

16. Ordinarily the trial judge will be asked by the defendant to order a *remittitur*, that is, an order instructing the plaintiff to accept a smaller amount of damages, or to elect a new trial. See text at nn. 176–84, *infra*.

17. See Gasperini v. Center for Humanities, Inc., 518 U.S. 415 (1996).

18. 532 U.S. at 433, quoting from Browning-Ferris Industries of Vt., Inc. v. Kelco Disposal, Inc., 492 U.S. 257, 279 (1989). It is unclear how a court could conclude that punitive damages awarded by a jury, although constitutional, are nevertheless so high that a trial judge would abuse his or her discretion in allowing the jury award to stand.

19. 526 U.S. at 711, quoting from United States v. Reynolds, 397 U.S. 14, 18 (1970), citing also Bauman v. Ross 167 U.S. 548, 593 (1897).

20. Ibid. at 743. See also Eric Grant, "A Revolutionary View of the Seventh Amendment and the Just Compensation Clause," *Northwestern Law Review* 91 (1996): 144.

21. 526 U.S. at 740–43.

22. See discussion *infra*, text accompanying nn. 23–32.

23. John Impey, *The New Instructor Clericalis, Stating the Authority, Jurisdiction, and Modern Practice of the Court of Kings Bench* (London, 1791), 399. In this passage, Impey "borrows" almost verbatim from Blackstone's *Commentaries* (William Blackstone, *Commentaries on the Laws of England*, 4 vols. [Oxford, 1765–69], 3: 397–98 [1768]).

24. A third context, although quite rare, occurred when a plaintiff obtained a jury verdict at trial but the jury, for whatever reason, failed to ascertain damages.

25. George Crompton, *Practice Common-placed: or, The Rules of Cases of Practice in the Courts of King's Bench and Common Pleas, Methodically Arranged*, 2 vols. (London, 1780), 1: 283.

26. Barnes 235, 94 Eng. Rep. 892 (K.B. 1751).

27. *"Rules and Orders on the Plea Side of the Court of Kings Bench," Easter Term, 1731—Trinity Term, 1795, compiled by Charles Abbot, Clerk of the Rules on the Plea Side of the Court of Kings Bench* (Rule Office: Trinity Term, 1795), 25. Subsequently, the notice period was reduced to one day. Ibid.

28. See, e.g., East India Company v. Ellis, 8 Mod. 240, 88 Eng. Rep. 172 (K.B. 1724) ("After a judgment by default for the plaintiff, and a writ of enquiry brought, it was moved that it might be executed before the Chief Justice at the sittings in Guildhall in London, the action being brought for Twenty Thousand Pounds: and a rule was made accordingly").

29. Impey, *New Instructor Clericalis, supra* n. 23, at 407. Impey adds that, "in case of success, the rule will be for the sheriff to summon a good jury." On "good juries," see chapter 7, text at nn. 263–83.

30. 2 Str. 1065, 93 Eng. Rep. 1035 (K.B. 1736).

31. Harvard Law School, Long Notebooks, MS 4055(b) Mich., 10 G. 2 (1736), fol. 40.

32. Crompton, *Practice Common-placed, supra* n. 25, at, 1: 283.

33. 3 Wils. 61, 95 Eng. Rep. 934 (C.P. 1770).

34. The court expressed astonishment at the defendants' unlawful entry into plaintiff's

house ("which is his castle"); "they know the risk they run by such conduct, and must take the consequence." Ibid. at 63, 934.

35. Ibid. at 62, 934. Two years earlier, Wilmot made a similar observation in Hewit v. Mantell, 2 Wils. 372, 95 Eng. Rep. 868 (C.P. 1768).

36. 2 Wils. 244, 95 Eng. Rep. 790 (C.P. 1764), discussed *infra,* text accompany nn. 112–19.

37. See generally the discussion *infra,* text at nn. 112–28.

38. 2 Wils. at 248; 95 Eng. Rep. at 792.

39. John Archbold, *Practice of the Court of King's Bench in Personal Actions, and Ejectment,* 2 vols. (London, 1823), 2: 20 (emphasis added), citing Bruce v. Rawlins, among other cases.

40. In Dimick v. Schiedt, 293 U.S. 474 (1935), Justice Sutherland, in the majority opinion, referred to the fact that in English common law, the power to increase or diminish damages assessed upon a writ of inquiry had been upheld, "but this upon the ground that the justices might themselves have awarded damages without the writ, and the inquisition, therefore, was nothing more than an inquest for their information," citing, among other sources, Beardmore v. Carrington. See 293 U.S. at 478–79. More recently, in an article entitled, "Why Judges, Not Juries, Should Determine Punitive Damages," *Chicago Law Review* 65 (1998): 179, Paul Mogin describes the writ of inquiry and then states that when juries determined damages after a default judgment, this was "a matter of convenience, rather than because a party was deemed to have a right to have a jury assess them." Ibid. at 201–2.

41. 2 Wms. Saund. 106, 85 Eng. Rep. 808 (K.B. 1670).

42. The Prothonotaries were the principal clerks in the Court of Common Pleas.

43. 2 Wms. Saund. at 107; 85 Eng. Rep. at 809.

44. Ibid. Implicit as to the defendant in this formulation is something like estoppel or waiver—by allowing judgment to go by default, the defendant gave up his right to "put himself upon the country," that is, to have a trial by jury.

45. 3 Leon. 213, 74 Eng. Rep. 640 (K.B. 1588).

46. Noy 96, 74 Eng. Rep. 1062 (K.B. 1626).

47. Ibid.

48. Yelv. 151, 80 Eng. Rep. 102 (K.B. 1609).

49. Alternatively, "I have no instructions to defend."

50. Yelv. at 152, 80 Eng. Rep. at 102.

51. 1 H. Bl. 541, 126 Eng. Rep. 311 (C.P. 1791). For a like case, see also Rashleigh v. Salmon, 1 H. Bl. 252, 126 Eng. Rep. 147 (C.P. 1789).

52. 1 H. Bl. at 542, 126 Eng. Rep. at 311.

53. 1 Doug. 315, 99 Eng. Rep. 203 (K.B. 1780).

54. Ibid. at 316, 204–5.

55. 4 T.R. 493, 100 Eng. Rep. 1137 (K.B. 1791).

56. In the Court of King's Bench, the Master was also called the Secondary and was deputy to the chief clerk, the Prothonotary. See chapter 7 n. 189.

57. 8 T.R. 395, 101 Eng. Rep. 1452 (K.B. 1799).

58. 1 Anst. 249, 145 Eng. Rep. 863 (Ex. 1793).

59. Ibid. at 251.

60. Ibid. at 254.

61. Barker v. Dixie, Cas. t. Hardwicke 279, 281, 95 Eng. Rep. 180, 181 (K.B. 1736) (per Hardwicke, C.J.).

62. 3 U.S. 344 (1797).

63. *Supra,* text at nn. 33–35.

64. 3 U.S. at 354
65. Ibid. at 356.
66. 14 U.S. 215 (1816).
67. Ibid. at 218.
68. Ibid.
69. Ibid., citing 2 Wms. Saund. 107, 85 Eng. Rep. 809 (K.B. 1797).
70. See text at nn. 41–44, *supra.*
71. 3 U.S. at 354. Regarding Rhode Island, an early-twentieth-century decision of the state Supreme Court is worth passing comment. In Dyson v. Rhode Island Company, 57 A. 771 (R.I. 1904), the question was whether the trial court erred in giving the job of determining negligence damages after a default judgment to a jury, rather than (as the defendant requested) doing so itself. The trial court procedure was affirmed, since in Rhode Island the matter is left to the discretion of the trial judge (see text at n. 64, *supra*), but Justice Blodgett took the occasion to discourse for more than twenty-five printed pages on the writ of inquiry. The justice flaunted his learning by displaying Year Book cases from the fourteenth and fifteenth centuries, quoting extensively (without translation) in both Latin and Law French, in order to establish, as bedrock, the proposition that the writ-of-inquiry jury verdict was from the beginning (for example, as in the *Registrum Brevium*) for the benefit of the court, not the parties. He also noted that the court could adjust the amount of damages up or down at its discretion. Although he shored up his views with a few seventeenth- and eighteenth-century cases, he said nothing about the English decisions in which the plaintiff's request to dispense with the writ of inquiry was rejected because the damages were uncertain (as they would have been in a negligence case, such as that before the *Dyson* court). Nor did he recognize that the plaintiff's consent might have been present, indeed necessary, whenever the writ of inquiry was omitted.
72. Raymond v. Danbury & N.R. Co., 20 F. Cas. 332, 333 (Cir. Ct. Conn. 1877).
73. Ibid. See also text accompanying nn. 112–19, *infra.*
74. 20 F. Cas. at 334.
75. Ibid.
76. Seeley v. City of Bridgeport, 22 A. 1017 (Conn. 1885).
77. 19 A. 334 (Conn. 1889).
78. Ibid. at 335. The quotation is from Zephaniah Swift, *A System of the Laws of the State of Connecticut,* 2 vols. (Windham, 1796), 2: 268. The same passage was quoted by Judge Shipman in the *Raymond* case, text at n. 72, *supra,* 20 F. Cas. at 333.
79. 293 U.S. 474 (1935).
80. The second clause states that "no fact tried by a jury shall be otherwise re-examined in any Court of the United States, than according to the rules of the common law."
81. 293 U.S. at 486. It is important to note, however, that in a large majority of the states, *additur* remains valid, although in varying circumstances. The procedure is authorized in some states by statute, in some by court rule, and in others by court decision. For representative examples, see Fisch v. Manger, 24 N.J. 66 (1957); Va. Code Ann. §8.01-383.1(B) (2005); Bowers v. Sprouse, 254 Va. 428 (1997); Galloway v. Kuhl, 346 Ill. App. 3d 844 (2004); Walker v. Copopett, 808 N.E.2d 85 (Ind. 2004) (applying Indiana Rules of Trial Procedure, Rule 59(a)(2)(2005). Three states allow *additur* on punitive-damage awards. See Bankers Life and Casualty Co. v. Crenshaw, 483 So.2d 254 (Miss. 1985); Crookston v. Fire Insurance Exchange, 819 P.2d 811 (Utah 1991); Tennessee Code Annotated §20-10-101 (2005). In one state, Alabama, the use of *additur* in punitive-damage situations has been declared unconstitutional. See Boseman v. Busby, 639 So.2d 501 (Ala. 1994).
82. For excellent scholarly studies of the English common-law background of jury awards of damages, see George T. Washington, "Damages in Contract at Common Law,"

Law Quarterly Review 47 (Part I, 1931): 345 and *Law Quarterly Review* 48 (Part II, 1932): 90; Richard H. Helmholz, "Damages in Actions for Slander at Common Law," *Law Quarterly Review* 103 (1987): 624.

83. G. O. Sayles, ed., *Select Cases in the Court of King's Bench Under Richard II, Henry IV, and Henry V (Vol. VII)* (London: Selden Society, 1971), 88 Selden Society ("SS" hereafter), 134–35.

84. Ibid. at 162–63.

85. Ibid. at 199–200.

86. Ibid. at 144–49.

87. J. H. Baker, ed., *The Reports of Sir John Spelman* (London: Selden Society, 1977), 94 SS 115. By "mayhem" was meant a physical assault that resulted in the maiming of the victim.

88. Ibid. Baker notes that "The same principle (as to increasing the damages) may have extended to battery," citing a case from 3 Hen. IV. He also states that "the court itself could assess the damages in such an appeal, without the need for a writ of enquiry."

89. Style 310, 82 Eng. Rep. 735 (K.B. 1651).

90. The jury had awarded £200 damages upon a writ of inquiry. In an earlier case, Hooper v. Pope, Latch 223, 82 Eng. Rep. 357 (K.B. 1628), the Court of King's Bench increased damages for a "mayhem" to plaintiff's hand, but first the court required sworn testimony from a surgeon that it was a "mayhem" and also a certificate from the Justices of Assize who had tried the case "that it is the same wounding on which the action is brought."

91. 298 U.S. at 477.

92. 1 Wils. 5, 95 Eng. Rep. 461 (K.B. 1742).

93. Easter 1782, Gibbs MSS, Middle Temple Library, London, 22 G. III (Hilary-Trinity), fol. 25.

94. 293 U.S. at 477.

95. Having explained away the mayhem cases, the Court concluded that *additur* was unconstitutional under the Seventh Amendment's historical test. Here the Court was applying the first clause of the Seventh Amendment, as is evident in the following rhetorical question put by Justice Sutherland:

> When . . . the trial court here found that the damages awarded by the jury were so inadequate as to entitle plaintiff to a new trial, how can it be held, with any semblance of reason, that that court, with the consent of the defendant only, may, by assessing an additional amount of damages, bring the constitutional right of the plaintiff to a jury trial to an end in respect of a matter of fact which no jury has ever passed upon either explicitly or by implication?

Ibid. at 486–87. Since *additur* fell under the first clause of the Seventh Amendment, we can safely conclude that *Cooper* (decided under the re-examination clause) does not resuscitate *additur* for purposes of punitive damages. *Remittitur,* by contrast, implicates the re-examination clause of the Seventh Amendment. Justice Sutherland in *Dimick* described an earlier Supreme Court case—Arkansas Land and Cattle Co. v. Mann, 130 U.S. 642 (1889)—as the "nearest approach to a reasoned opinion on the subject in any of the decisions." 293 U.S. at 484. In *Arkansas Land and Cattle,* according to Justice Sutherland, the contention was made "that to make the motion for new trial depend upon a remission of part of the verdict is in effect a reexamination by the court in a mode not known at the common law of facts tried by the jury, and therefore a violation of the Seventh Amendment," but the Court rejected this contention on the basis of Justice Story's opinion in Blunt v. Little, 3 Mason 102 (C.C.D. Mass. 1822), among other authorities.

Remittitur was not at issue in *Dimick,* though the Court discussed *remittitur* cases and observed in passing that "it . . . may be that if the question of remittitur were now before us for the first time, it would be decided otherwise." 293 U.S. at 484. For a recent revisitation of the question, in which the author argues thoroughly and persuasively that, like *additur, remittitur* is unconstitutional under the Seventh Amendment historical test, see Suja A. Thomas, "Judges over Juries: Re-Examining the Constitutionality of Remittitur," *Ohio State Law Journal* 64 (2003): 731. Justice Sutherland, in *Dimick,* rationalized *remittitur* as "not without plausible support in the view that what remains is included in the verdict along with the unlawful excess—in that sense that it has been found by the jury—and that the remittitur has the effect of merely lopping off an excrescence." 293 U.S. at 486.

96. Anon., 2 Leon. 214, 74 Eng. Rep. 489 (K.B. 1588). In this case, a poor woman brought a successful action of trespass and received a jury verdict for only ten shillings; she argued that this should be increased because the trespass had continued for six years and the land was worth £4 per annum rent. The court noted that sometimes at the prayer of the defendant a new writ of inquiry had been issued because the first verdict was excessive, but this was never done for the plaintiff because of inadequate damages, "because the suing forth of the writ is his own act."

97. 12 Mod. 347, 88 Eng. Rep. 1371 (K.B. 1700).

98. 8 Mod. 196, 88 Eng. Rep. 142 (K.B. 1723).

99. 1 Str. 425, 93 Eng. Rep. 612 (K.B. 1721).

100. 2 Barn. K.B. 177, 94 Eng. Rep. 432 (K.B. 1732). There might, however, be strategic alternatives. Justice Page in *Hayward* recollected a case that he had tried in the Court of Exchequer in which the jury gave but six pence damages and the judge directed the jury to retire and consider its verdict again; when the jury came in the second time, Page advised his client to be nonsuited, and afterward, another action was brought and the plaintiff recovered £80. Another possibility was for the plaintiff "to abstain from praying judgment and to commence a fresh action, because he was not allowed an attaint." J. H. Baker, *The Oxford History of the Laws of England (Volume VI), 1483–1558* (Oxford: Oxford University Press, 2003), 380. (On attaint, see text at and following n. 104, *infra.*)

101. Cas. t. Hardwicke 279, 95 Eng. Rep. 180 (K.B. 1736). The dispute was evidently one of some notoriety, given the numerous reports of the case that survive. In addition to the cited report, a brief note of the case appears at 2 Str. 1051, 93 Eng. Rep. 1027 (K.B. 1736), and three different manuscript versions are held by the Harvard Law Library. See Harvard Law School MS 2050, fol. 114; MS 4055(5), fol. 23b; Long Notebooks, NB 80*, fol. 32b.

102. Cas. t. Hardwicke at 281, 95 Eng. Rep. at 181. Hardwicke noted that in the cases of Woodford v. Eades and Parr v. Purbeck the court "did in some measure depart from this distinction," but those cases involved "plain contracts, of which the Court could judge, and the finding less damages than appeared due upon the contracts, must have been a mistake of the jury." The case before Hardwicke, however, was "merely for a tort," and "in torts the damages are uncertain always, and the language of the law is, that the jury are judges of damages."

103. Harvard Law School Long Notebooks, NB 80*, fol. 34 (K.B. 1736).

104. Ibid.

105. Harvard Law School MS 4055(5), fol. 25 (K.B. 1736).

106. Ibid.

107. For an example of an attaint for excessive damages, see Gaynesford v. Guldeford (K.B. Easter 1506), reported in J. H. Baker, ed., *Reports of Cases by John Caryll, Part II, 1501–1522* (London: Selden Society, 2000), 116 SS 517–18. Although the jurors were ultimately pardoned, the attaint jury had issued the standard punishment against the attainted jurors, namely that they could be jurors never again, and "that they do forfeit all their

goods and chattels to the Lord King, and that their lands and tenements be taken into the Lord King's hands, wasted and uprooted, and their wives and children therefrom expelled." Ibid. at 518.

108. Vaugh. 135, 124 Eng. Rep. 1006 (C.P. 1671). See generally Thomas A. Green, *Verdict According to Conscience* (Chicago: University of Chicago Press, 1985), chapter 6.

109. 1 Burr. 390, 97 Eng. Rep. 365 (K.B. 1757).

110. Ibid. at 393, 366.

111. These cases could be viewed as ones in which the court is determining the amount of damages as a matter of law. This is the approach taken in modern American practice. See Colleen P. Murphy, "Judgment as a Matter of Law on Punitive Damages," *Tulane Law Review* 75 (2000): 459, 467.

112. 2 Wils. at 250, 95 Eng. Rep. at 793.

113. 2 Wils. 275, 95 Eng. Rep. 807 (C.P. 1765).

114. For an enumeration of many of the verdicts, including a number of unreported cases, see James Oldham, *The Mansfield Manuscripts and the Growth of English Law in the Eighteenth Century,* 2 vols. (Chapel Hill and London: University of North Carolina Press, 1992), 2: 821, n. 17.

115. See, e.g., J. Sayer, *The Law of Damages* (London, 1770), 222–27.

116. 2 Wils. at 248, 95 Eng. Rep. at 792.

117. Ibid. at 247, 792.

118. See text at n. 38, *supra.*

119. 2 Wils. at 248; 95 Eng. Rep. at 792. Pratt's observations in *Beardmore* were fully quoted by Justice Sutherland in Dimick v. Schiedt, 293 U.S. at 479–80.

120. Ibid. at 249, 793, distinguishing Wood v. Gunston, Style 462, 82 Eng. Rep. 863 (K.B.1655), and Ash v. Lady Ash, Comb. 357, 90 Eng. Rep. 526 (K.B. 1696).

121. 2 Str. 691, 93 Eng. Rep. 787 (K.B. 1726).

122. 2 Wils. at 249; 95 Eng. Rep. at 793.

123. Ibid.

124. Ibid.

125. Barnes 233, 94 Eng. Rep. 891 (K.B. 1741).

126. Ibid.

127. 4 T.R. 651, 100 Eng. Rep. 1226 (K.B. 1792).

128. Ibid. at 655, 1228. Justices Ashhurst and Grose concurred. Justice Buller, however, would have sent the case back for a new trial because of excessive damages. In a later case, Jones v. Sparrow, 5 T.R. 257, 101 Eng. Rep. 144 (K.B. 1793), a motion for new trial on the ground of excessive damages was opposed on the authority of *Duberley.* A new trial was nevertheless granted, and Chief Justice Kenyon stated: "It must be remembered that although the case of *Duberley v. Gunning* was decided after a very full discussion of the subject, the Court were not unanimous in the determination. But, whether rightly or wrongly decided, that is a case sui generis, and cannot govern the present." In *Jones,* a servant sued his master for assault and recovered a verdict of £40 despite the fact that, according to the printed report at least, the servant had "received a slight blow from his master for impertinent behaviour," after which the servant "violently beat him." Clearly, Kenyon thought the verdict outrageous.

129. See, e.g., Schwartz and Lorber, "Twisting the Purpose of Pain and Suffering Awards," *supra* n. 11, at 47.

130. *Chicago Law Review* 65 (1988): 179, referenced also at n. 40, *supra.* See also Murphy, "Judgment as a Matter of Law," *supra* n. 111.

131. 481 U.S. 412 (1987). See Mogin, "Why Judges, Not Juries," *supra* n. 40, at 197–99.

132. Ibid. at 426, n. 9.

133. For a well-argued anticipation of this development, see Alan H. Schneider, Note, "Judicial Assessment of Punitive Damages, the Seventh Amendment, and the Politics of Jury Power," *Columbia Law Review* 91 (1991): 142 (presenting, among much more, "several reasons to believe that Tull cannot be the last word on the jury and determination of damages under the seventh amendment," ibid. at 205). See also in general Colleen P. Murphy, "Judicial Assessment of Legal Remedies," *Northwestern Law Review* 94 (1999): 153.

134. 523 U.S. at 353. The Court was unanimous in the judgment, although Justice Scalia wrote a separate opinion stating the reasons why he thought the Seventh Amendment question need not be reached.

135. Ibid. at 354.

136. Ibid. See the quotation from the Court's opinion in *Dimick,* n. 199, *infra.*

137. 481 U.S. at 423.

138. Ibid. at 425–26.

139. Ibid. at 426, quoting from Colgrove v. Battin, 413 U.S. 149, 157 (1973), and in turn from Austin Scott, "Trial by Jury and the Reform of Civil Procedure," *Harvard Law Review* 21 (1918): 669, 671. Brennan added that "Congress' authority to fix the penalty by statute has not been questioned, and it was also the British practice, see e.g., *Atcheson v. Everitt,*" 1 Cowp. 382, 98 Eng. Rep. 1142 (K.B. 1776). The reference to Atcheson v. Everitt was sleight of hand. The issue there was whether a jury trial had to be invalidated because the trial judge had allowed a Quaker to testify on his affirmation rather than on the customary oath. A statute allowed this, but not in criminal cases, and the question was whether the action of debt on a statute against bribery was civil or criminal. The Quaker's testimony was upheld since the court concluded that the action to recover a civil penalty was not encompassed by the exception disallowing Quakers' testimony in criminal cases. Nothing in *Atcheson* dealt with whether "the assessment of civil penalties" was properly a jury function. Countless statutes in England in the late eighteenth century provided for penalties that could be recovered in *qui tam* actions. No one questioned the power of Parliament to set the amount of the penalty, but the amounts were fixed sums, and no one supposed that a jury could be invited to return a verdict of a different amount.

140. 481 U.S. at 426–27.

141. 523 U.S. at 353. Justice Thomas did comment that "the awarding of civil penalties to the Government [in *Tull*] could be viewed as analogous to sentencing in a criminal proceeding," which could not be said of the setting of the amount of damages in general or in copyright cases. There was, moreover, one context in eighteenth-century English law in which Parliament had removed from juries the possibility of assessing punitive damages, and this line of cases might be invoked in support of Justice Brennan's legislative power theory in *Tull.* The context was that of the conditional bond. Historically, this was a technique used to ensure performance of contracts for services. The contracting party promising the services would take out a bond in the face amount of two or three times the value of the services contracted for, promising that if he did not perform the services specified in the contract, the other party could collect the face amount of the bond in court. Recovery of the face amount of the bond would have a penal effect whenever the actual damages were significantly less than the face amount, as was typically the case. In the late seventeenth century, the Court of Chancery began to relieve parties from penalties due on conditional bonds, and, in 1697, Parliament passed a statute that required juries "to assess the Damages that the Plaintiff shall have sustained" by any breach that gave rise to an action on such a bond. 8 & 9 W. 3, c.11. See generally A. W. B. Simpson, "The Penal Bond with Conditional Defeasance," *Law Quarterly Review* 82 (1966): 392. Conditional bonds continued to be used throughout the eighteenth century, but, in a case that went to jury trial,

the jury would be instructed to return only actual damages. The procedure was a little different when there was a default judgment on the bond and a writ of inquiry issued. Although the default judgment was for the face value of the bond, the writ of inquiry directed the jury to ascertain actual damages. If the inquiry jury returned damages in the amount of the face value of the bond, that award would be set aside. See William Tidd, *The Practice of the Courts of King's Bench, and Common Pleas, in Personal Actions; and Ejectment,* 1st Amer. ed. from 8th London ed., 2 vols. (Philadelphia, 1828), 1: 631–33.

142. Mogin, "Why Judges, Not Juries," *supra* n. 40 at 199. For an interesting example of a recent federal case in which the court emphatically thought the question closed, see Hartford Fire Insurance Co. v. First National Bank of Atmore, 198 F.Supp. 2d 1308 (S.D. Ala. 2002). Relying on Cooper Industries, Inc. v. Leatherman Tool Group, Inc. and Justice Stevens's adoption of Justice Scalia's earlier remark that "the level of punitive damages is not really a 'fact' 'tried' by the jury," Hartford argued that "punitive damages involve the application of law to the facts, which is a function of the trial court, not the jury." Ibid. at 1309. Magistrate Judge Steele ruled that the argument was fatally flawed because it assumed that the first clause of the Seventh Amendment was at issue in *Cooper,* when in fact only the second clause (the "re-examination" clause) was relevant. Quoting from the *City of Monterey* case, and in turn from Markman v. Westview Instruments, Inc., 517 U.S. 370 (1996), Judge Steele said that "whether the right to trial by jury attaches to a particular issue depends on whether the issue was historically decided by juries, not on whether it constitutes a 'fact.'" 198 F.Supp. 2d at 1311. Citing *Feltner* and many other cases, he concluded that, "Because history proves, and precedent confirms, that the right to trial by jury attaches to the determination of the amount of punitive damages, it is irrelevant whether functional considerations also weigh in favor of the jury," though in fact "these considerations also point toward the jury as the appropriate decisionmaker." Ibid. at 1312. (Referring to the *Markman* case, the court pointed out that "The fact/law boundary becomes relevant only when functional considerations must be considered due to the absence of clear historical evidence." Ibid. at 1311.)

143. Mogin, "Why Judges, Not Juries, *supra* n. 40, at 204, citing Wilkes v. Wood, Lofft 1, 98 Eng. Rep. 489 (C.P. 1763), and Huckle v. Money, 2 Wils. 205, 95 Eng. Rep. 768 (C.P. 1763) (although identified by Mogin as a King's Bench case, *Huckle* was decided by Common Pleas).

144. Ibid.

145. 4 T.R. 651, 100 Eng. Rep. 1226 (K.B. 1792). See text accompanying nn. 127–28, *supra.*

146. 2 Mod. 150, 86 Eng. Rep. 994 (C.P. 1677) (see n. 9 *supra,* and accompanying text).

147. Ibid. at 151, 994–95.

148. 2 W. Bl. 1327, 96 Eng. Rep. 777 (K.B. 1779).

149. Ibid. at 1328, 778.

150. Ibid. The court added that it could not "enter into stories of private scandal, which have been liberally propagated on both sides."

151. Ibid.

152. Ibid. at 1329, 778.

153. Ibid. One of the judges participating in the case was William Blackstone; in his *Commentaries,* he wrote that conspirators who indict an innocent man of felony, falsely and maliciously,

> may be indicted at the suit of the King, and were by the antient common law to receive what is called the *villenous* judgment; *viz.* to lose their *liberam legem,* whereby they are discredited and disabled to be jurors or witnesses; to forfeit their goods and

chattels, and lands for life; to have those lands wasted, their houses rased, their trees rooted up, and their own bodies committed to prison.

Blackstone, *Commentaries, supra* n. 23, at 4: 136. Blackstone added that this judgment had become obsolete, "not having been pronounced for some ages." Ibid.

154. See text at nn. 112–19, *supra.*

155. 2 Wils. 205, 95 Eng. Rep. 768 (C.P. 1763).

156. Ibid.

157. Ibid. at 206–7, 768–69.

158. 2 Wils. 252, 95 Eng. Rep. 794 (C.P. 1764).

159. Ibid. at 253, 794.

160. 3 Wils. 18, 95 Eng. Rep. 909 (C.P. 1768).

161. Ibid.

162. Ibid. at 19, 909.

163. Perkin v. Proctor, 2 Wils. 382, 386, 95 Eng. Rep. 874, 877 (C.P. 1768).

164. Many of the decisions of the Court of Common Pleas went unreported; indeed in the decade before the Seventh Amendment was adopted, that court is almost entirely absent in the printed record—no printed case reports whatever for Common Pleas exist for the years 1780–1788. See James Oldham, "Underreported and Underrated: The Court of Common Pleas in the Eighteenth Century," in Hendrik Hartog, William E. Nelson, and Barbara Wilcie Kern, eds., *Law as Culture and Culture as Law* (Madison, WI: Madison House, 2000), 119.

165. 1 Burr. 609, 97 Eng. Rep. 472 (K.B. 1758).

166. Ibid.

167. Ibid.

168. Misc. MS 195, Inner Temple Library, fol. 250, Trinity Term, 31 G. 2, 1758 (emphasis added). On Barker v. Dixie, see *supra,* text at nn. 101–6. Cibber v. Sloper was a notorious 1737 case in which Mansfield (then a young barrister, William Murray) was junior counsel for the defendant. See Oldham, *The Mansfield Manuscripts, supra* n. 114, at 1: 11–12. I have not located a report of Pennington's Case.

169. 3 Burr. 1845, 97 Eng. Rep. 1130 (K.B. 1766).

170. Ibid. at 1846, 1130. For another King's Bench case rejecting an excessive-damages argument, see Gilbert v. Burtenshaw, 1 Cowp. 230, 98 Eng. Rep. 1059 (K.B. 1774), in which a jury gave £400 for a malicious perjury indictment. In upholding the verdict, Lord Mansfield declined to say "that in cases of personal torts, no new trial should ever be granted for damages which manifestly shew the jury to have been actuated by passion, partiality, or prejudice," but "it is not to be done without very strong grounds indeed"—"unless it appears that the damages are flagrantly outrageous and extravagant, it is difficult for the Court to draw the line." Ibid. at 231, 1060.

In Feltner v. Columbia Pictures Television, Inc. (*supra,* n. 12), Justice Thomas cites the King's Bench decision of Duke of York v. Pilkington, 2 Show. 246, 89 Eng. Rep. 918 (K.B. 1682), but mistakenly dates it 1760, in which case it would have been decided under Mansfield's chief justiceship. 523 U.S. at 353. In fact decided in 1682, the brief printed report indicates that the only question was whether the words upon which the *scandalum magnatum* was based were actionable; no claim of excessive damages appears.

171. The case is unreported and was tried during a term for which Lord Mansfield's trial notes do not survive. The quotation is from *The London Chronicle,* 6–9 Mar. 1779. According to the newspaper report, the jury stayed out for only fifteen minutes, then returned a verdict of £300. For further details about the case, see Oldham, *The Mansfield Manuscripts, supra* n. 114, at 2: 1237–38.

172. 5 Taun. 442, 128 Eng. Rep. 761 (C.P. 1814).

173. Ibid. at 443, 761.

174. Ibid.

175. An example is Goldsmith v. Lord Sefton, 3 Anst. 808, 145 Eng. Rep. 1046 (Ex. 1796). There, plaintiff, a sheriff's officer, had arrested a man who escaped into defendant's house, where plaintiff pursued him, yet the fugitive escaped again. Later, defendant found the plaintiff and demanded to see his warrant for having entered his house; an argument ensued, defendant threatened the plaintiff with his horse whip, plaintiff raised his officer's stick, and defendant took the stick out of plaintiff's hand and threw it away. For having done so, plaintiff brought an action of assault, and a writ of inquiry jury gave a verdict of £200 damages. The judges of the Court of Exchequer stated that jury verdicts in tort cases should never be overturned for excessive damages except where the awards were outrageous (citing, among other cases, Huckle v. Money and Gilbert v. Burtenshaw). They viewed the facts before them as such a case and ordered a new trial, Chief Baron Macdonald declaring that "we are bound to protect a party where, by the improper warmth or worst passions of a jury, damages glaringly and outrageously great have been given against him." Ibid. at 810, 1046.

176. 523 U.S. 208 (1998).

177. Ibid. at 211.

178. Helmholz, "Damages in Actions for Slander," *supra* n. 82, at 629–30. Helmholz's analysis remedies this omission for slander cases, invoking a variety of manuscript sources.

179. In Harper v. Eyles, 3 Doug. 399, 99 Eng. Rep. 717 (K.B. 1784), the *remittitur* of damages was described as "commonly entered to accelerate the judgment, and prevent a writ of error."

180. In Pickwood v. Wright, 1 H. Bl. 643, 126 Eng. Rep. 367 (C.P. 1791), the reporter's headnote summary of the decision by the Court of Common Pleas was as follows: "Where a verdict is given for a greater sum than the amount of the damages laid in the declaration, and for that cause a writ of error is brought, the Court will permit the plaintiff to enter a remittitur of the excess above the sum laid in the declaration, on payment of the costs of the writ of error." For a comparable case in the Court of King's Bench, see Strawn v. Fletter, 2 Barn. K.B. 344, 94 Eng. Rep. 542 (K.B. 1733). For a full discussion of the English *remittitur* usage, see Thomas, "Judges over Juries," *supra* n. 95 at 739–46.

181. See Helmholz, "Damages in Actions for Slander," *supra* n. 82, at 631.

182. Ibid. at 631–32.

183. Ibid. at 635, citing Hawkins v. Sciet, reported *sub nom.* Scutt v. Hawkins, 2 Rolle 243, 81 Eng. Rep. 775 (K.B. 1676).

184. Ibid. at 637.

185. 4 T.R. 651, 100 Eng. Rep. 1226 (K.B. 1792).

186. Ibid. at 657, 1229. Accord: Goldsmith v. Lord Sefton, 3 Anst. 808, 145 Eng. Rep. 1046 (Ex. 1796) ("We cannot say what the damages ought to be, but can only send it for the investigation of another jury").

187. See Chambers v. Robinson, 2 Str. 691, 93 Eng. Rep. 787 (K.B. 1726); Clerk v. Udall, 2 Salk. 649, 91 Eng. Rep. 552 (K.B. 1702). (*Chambers* was the case disapproved of by Chief Justice Pratt in his decision in *Beardmore.* See text accompanying nn. 121–22, *supra.*) It was occasionally acknowledged that a third new trial was at least a theoretical possibility (see, e.g., Goodwin v. Gibbons, 4 Burr. 2108, 98 Eng. Rep. 100 (K.B. 1767)), but I have located no instance of this having been done because of excessive damages.

188. 170 F.3d 1320 (11th Cir. 1999). *Johansen* has received vigorous academic criticism. See Murphy, "Judgment as a Matter of Law on Punitive Damages," *supra* n. 111, at 468–71, 473–78.

189. 170 F.3d at 1331.

190. Ibid.

191. 839 A.2d 682 (D.C. App. 2003).

192. Ibid. at 700.

193. Ibid. at 701 (footnote omitted).

194. The Fifth and the Tenth Circuits have ruled that a new trial is required. See Rubinstein v. Administrators, 218 F.3d 392 (5th Cir. 2000); Continental Trend Resources, Inc. v. OXY USA, Inc., 101 F.3d 634 (10th Cir. 1996). The Eighth and Eleventh Circuits hold that a new trial need not be ordered. See Ross v. Kansas City Power & Light Company, 293 F.3d 1041, 1049 (8th Cir. 2002); *Johansen, supra* n. 118. The Ninth Circuit on remand in *Cooper* reduced the punitive damages award from $4.5 million to $500,000, citing *Johansen.* Leatherman Tool Group, Inc. v. Cooper Industries, Inc., 285 F.3d 1146, 1152 (9th Cir. 2002). See also, in general, Murphy, "Judgment as a Matter of Law," *supra* n. 111, at 460–61; Mark R. Kravitz, "Handling Remittiturs," *National Law Journal* (Nov. 6, 2000): 18.

195. 538 U.S. at 425.

196. Ibid.

197. See Samuel A. Thumma, "Punitive Damages: Post-'Campbell' Cases," *National Law Journal* (June 7, 2004), 13.

198. 293 F.3d at 1050.

199. 4 T.R. at 657, 100 Eng. Rep. at 1229. See also Dimick v. Schiedt, 293 U.S. 474, 486 (1935), where the Court stated the following:

> Where the verdict returned by the jury is palpably and grossly inadequate or excessive, it should not be permitted to stand; but, in that event, both parties remain entitled, as they were entitled in the first instance, to have a jury properly determine the question of liability and the extent of the injury by an assessment of damages. Both are questions of fact.

Admittedly the Court was dealing here with compensatory damages, but, as we have seen, the determination of constitutionally permissible punitive damages remains a jury responsibility even after *Cooper.* See text at n. 12, *supra.*

200. 293 F.3d at 1050.

201. For a thorough analysis supporting a like conclusion, see Murphy, "Judgment as a Matter of Law," *supra* n. 111, at 472–78.

202. 101 F.3d at 642.

203. Ibid.

204. Ibid. at 642–43, quoting from Morgan v. Woessner, 997 F.2d 1244, 1258 (9th Cir. 1993).

205. See Murphy, "Judgment as a Matter of Law," *supra* n. 111, at 474–75. See also Thomas, "Judges over Juries," *supra* n. 95, at 765–67.

206. 170 F.3d at 1332.

207. 517 U.S. at 585. See also Murphy, "Judgment as a Matter of Law," *supra* n. 111 at 476–77.

208. Bruce v. Rawlins, 3 Wils. at 61, 95 Eng. Rep. at 934 (C.P. 1770), text at nn. 33–35, *supra.*

209. Indeed, as has been shown, a plaintiff's request to dispense with the jury would ordinarily be denied if there was any doubt about the amount of the damages.

210. 526 U.S. 687 (1999).

211. In fact, this has already happened. See Hartford Fire Insurance Co. v. First National Bank of Atmore, 198 F. Supp. 2d 1308 (S.D. Ala. 2002), discussed at n. 142, *supra.*

Notes for Chapter 5

1. Daniel Defoe, *The Fortunes and Misfortunes of the Famous Moll Flanders* (London, 1722).

2. Not until the twentieth century were women regularly eligible for jury service in England and America. See *Halsbury's Laws of England,* 3d ed., 43 vols. (London: Butterworth's, 1952–64), 23:21, s.34 (1958); Linda K. Kerber, *No Constitutional Right to be Ladies* (New York: Hill and Wang, 1998), 136–40. Blackstone observed that jurymen were to be *liber et legalist homo* and that "Under the *homo* also, though a name common to both sexes, the female is however excluded." William Blackstone, *Commentaries on the Laws of England,* 4 vols. (Oxford, 1765–69), 3: 362 (1768).

3. The phrase is taken from [Anon.], *The Office of the Clerk of Assize,* rev. ed. (London, 1681).

4. The phrase was applicable to criminal cases. In civil cases, the writ *de ventre inspiciendo*—"to inspect the belly"—was employed: Blackstone, *Commentaries, supra* n. 2, at 3: 362.

5. The term "quickening" described the state of pregnancy at which the movement of the child was first discernible. The two phrases "with quick child" and "quick with child" appear to have been used interchangeably, both satisfying the requirement that "quickening" had taken place (see text at n. 137 *infra*). The double formulation of the *Clerk of Assize* ("quick with child of a quick child") is not usually encountered in the court records and did not consistently appear in other editions of that work.

6. Because no question would ordinarily arise concerning the jury of matrons at the appellate stage in either a criminal or a civil proceeding, evidence of the use of the jury of matrons must be drawn from trial court records. There was very little reporting in England of trial-court proceedings prior to the nineteenth century. One notable exception was the Old Bailey Session Papers (hereafter "OBSP"), which began in the 1670s. As is later indicated, the OBSP are generally reliable, and I have made extensive use of them in preparing this study. In order to spot-check the accuracy of the OBSP, I have also sampled original court records held by what was formerly (until 1997) known as the Greater London Record Office, now part of the London Metropolitan Archives (hereafter "LMA"). All of these records deal with criminal trials and account for the extent to which this study is skewed toward criminal usage of the jury of matrons. It is unlikely that comparable undiscovered patterns of use in civil cases occurred, but it is certain that, from the Middle Ages through the eighteenth century, the jury of matrons was a feature of some number of unreported cases. Jury lists might appear in the plea rolls, just as they do on occasion in the Gaol Delivery Books, but, without any guide to the civil cases in which juries of matrons were impaneled, a search of the plea rolls would be random and altogether impracticable. None was attempted.

7. S. P. Scott, trans., *The Civil Law,* 17 vols. (Cincinnati: The Central Trust Company, 1932), 3: 43. If all, or only two, of the midwives confirmed the pregnancy, a custodian for the wife would be appointed.

8. Ibid. at 45.

9. *Pauli Sententiaei* 1.12.4; *Digest* 1.5.18 and 48.19.3. I am indebted to Professor Alan Watson for directing me to these sources.

10. H. G. Richardson and G. O. Sayles, eds., *Select Cases of Procedure Without Writ Under Henry III* (London: B. Quaritch, 1941), 60 Selden Society ("SS" herafter) clii.

11. Ibid.

12. Ibid. at cliii, n. 11. The "close roll," or "Letters Close," contained enrollments of writs and other documents that had the potential to affect the financial interests of the

Crown. See Percy H. Winfield, *The Chief Sources of English Legal History* (Cambridge, MA: Harvard University Press, 1925), 137–38.

13. Richardson and Sayles, eds., *Select Cases, supra* n. 10, at cliv–clv.

14. G. O. Sayles, ed., *Select Cases in the Court of King's Bench (Vol. VII), Richard II, Henry IV, and Henry V* (London: B. Quaritch, 1971), 88 Selden Society 56 (Plea 30, Pasch. 1388). In 1388, Elizabeth was called down to her former sentence and ordered to be executed.

15. See Appendixes 1 and 3.

16. William W. Hening and William Munford, *Reports of Cases Argued & Determined in the Supreme Court of Appeals of Virginia, 1619–1660,* 4 vols. (Flatbush, NY, 1809–11).

17. Peter S. King, "The Middlesex Justices 1590–1640, The Commissions of the Peace, Oyer and Terminer and Gaol Delivery for Middlesex," Master's Thesis, University of Durham, 1972, 66. On file with the LMA.

18. Edward Coke, *The Third Part of the Institutes* (London, 1648), 17. The subject is treated in both of Matthew Hale's works on criminal law: *A Methodical Summary of the Law Relating to the Pleas of the Crown,* 6th ed. (London, 1759), 272, and *Historia Placitorum Coronae* (London, 1736; London, 1778), 368–70. William Staunford, *Les Pleas del Coron* (London, 1557; reprint, Guildford, 1971), 198. Henry Finch, *Law, Or, a Discourse Thereof; in Four Books* (London, 1627; London, Garland reprint of Pickering ed. of 1759, London: Henry Lintot, 1978), 478. William Lambard, *Eirenarcha or of the Office of the Justices of Peace* (London, 1581; London, 1614), 555. Ferdinand Pulton, *De Pace Regis et Regni* (London, 1609; London: Garland, 1978), 225–26. References to these and to some of the previously cited authorities are collected by William Hawkins, *A Treatise of the Pleas of the Crown* (London, 1721, London: Garland, 1978), 464. The three abridgments cited by Hawkins with regard to the jury of matrons are the *Abridgment of the Book of Assizes* (anon.), Fitzherbert and Brooke.

19. Blackstone, *Commentaries, supra* n. 2, at 3: 362 and 1: 444. In a nineteenth-century case in Chancery, counsel for the widow who claimed to be pregnant argued that the writ *de ventre* presumed the existence of fraud on the part of the female and was not appropriate absent some grounds for suspicion. See *Medical Gazette,* 15 Aug. 1835, at 698 (the argument was rejected).

20. See n. 175, *infra.*

21. Ibid. See also text at n. 201.

22. See Willoughby's Case, Cro. Eliz. 566, 78 Eng. Rep. 811 (C.P. 1597); Theaker's Case, Cro. Jac. 686, 687, 79 Eng. Rep. 595 (C.P. 1625); Ex parte Aiscough 2, P. Wms. 591, 594, 24 Eng. Rep. 873, 874 (Ch. 1730). In *Willoughby's Case* a new writ was issued naming ten matrons (who may or may not have been on the original jury), some of whom were to view of the pregnant woman every day until the birth and were to be present at the delivery.

23. Francis N. Rogers, *A Practical Arrangement of Ecclesiastical Law* (London, 1840), 563.

24. Ibid.

25. Joel P. Bishop, *Commentaries on the Law of Marriage and Divorce,* 4th ed., 2 vols. (Boston, 1864), 2: 473. An illustrative case is treated in *The Cases of Impotency and Virginity Fully Discuss'd,* published by John Crawfurd, L.L.D. (London, 1732), 31, where one of Elizabeth Weld's six depositions against her husband, Edward, gave the following as the certificate of "Three experienced Midwives":

> The Honourable *Catherine Elizabeth Weld* to be, *Virgo intacta,* A pure and untouched Virgin. That her Parts of Generation are in such a State as render her capable of *Conjugal Embraces* no Defect in their Formation, or otherwise, appearing.

> And, that on their Inspection they are full convinced, That *it is impossible she can have had any* Carnal Conversation *with a man.*

I am indebted to Catherine Crawford for this reference.

26. Richard. H. Helmholz, *Marriage Litigation in Medieval England* (London: Cambridge University Press, 1974), 88.

27. In the following translation, Prof. Helmholz reveals another, rather different use of women in medieval England:

> The same witness exposed her naked breasts, and with her hands warmed at the said fire, she held and rubbed the penis and testicles of the said John. And she embraced and frequently kissed the same John, and stirred him up in so far as she could do to show her virility and potency, admonishing him that for shame he should then and there prove and render himself a man. And she says, examined and diligently questioned, that the whole aforesaid, the said penis was scarcely three inches long, . . . remaining without any increase or decrease.

Ibid. at 89. The case quoted arose in the year 1433. Other cases are identified in the years 1292, 1370, 1380, 1430, and 1432.

28. Accorded to the printed memorials of the Archbishop of Canterbury, the Commissioners were the Archbishop of Canterbury; the Bishops of Winchester, Ely, Litchfield, Coventry, and Rochester; Doctors of Law Sir Julius Caesar, Sir Thomas Parry, Sir Daniel Dunn, Sir John Bennet, Francis James, and Thomas Edwards. *The Case of Impotency, &c. Debated,* 2 vols. (London, 1715), 1: 163. The report in the *State Trials* erroneously omits the Bishop of Winchester: T. B. Howell, ed., *Cobbett's Complete Collection of State Trials and Proceedings for High Treason,* 33 vols. (London, 1809–26) (*State Trials* hereafter), 2: 785 (1809).

29. Ibid. at 2: 802–3.

30. 2 *State Trials* 803 (1809). The Register was the officer who wrote and kept the Registry in which the proceedings of spiritual courts were recorded. Giles Jacob, *A New Law Dictionary,* 10th ed. (London, 1782).

31. B. L. Harl. MS 39, fol. 420v. The quotations are taken from a transcription of the manuscript by Prof. L. A. Knafla, of the University of Calgary. I am indebted to Prof. Knafla for making his transcription available to me and directing me to the printed memorials of the Archbishop of Canterbury.

32. *The Case of Impotency, supra* n. 28, at 1: 163.

33. Ibid. at 1: 9.

34. Wilson was a close acquaintance of the Earl of Essex and cannot be considered to have been objective. Nevertheless, his assertion was as follows: "The Countess being ashamed, and bashful, to come to such a Trial, would not expose her Face to the Light; but being to appear before Matrons under a Veil, another young Gentlewoman, that had less offended, was fobbed into the Place; and she passed, in the Opinion, both of Jury and Judges, to be a Virgin." Arthur Wilson, "*An Account of the Intrigue between* Robert Carr, Earl of Somerset, *Viscount* Rochester, &c. *and the Lady* Frances Howard, An. Reg. 10. An. Christi, 1612," quoted in *The Case of Impotency, supra* n. 28, at 1: 166, 184. A similar account was given by Sir Anthony Weldon in his *The Court and Character of King James* (London, 1651), 81, which was quoted at 2 *State Trials* 803, n.* (1809). See also Victor MacClure, *She Stands Accused* (London: George G. Harrap & Co., 1935), 73–74.

35. Capt. J. Buchan Tefler, *The Strange Career of the Chevalier D'Eon de Beaumont* (London, 1885), 284. One account put the figure at £200,000. See Gary Kates, *Monsieur d'Eon Is a Woman* (New York: Basic Books, 1995), xiii.

36. Tefler, *The Strange Career, supra* n. 35, at 285 ff.; see also Ernest A. Vizetelly, *The*

True Story of the Chevalier D'Eon (London, 1895), 282, 303; Kates, *Monsieur d'Eon Is a Woman, supra* n. 35, ch. 46.

37. *Town & Country* (1771), 248. The venue for the trial was "Medmenham Abbey," the well-known gathering place of the "Medmenham Monks." This group was organized by Sir Francis Dashwood, reputedly included such notables as the Earl of Sandwich and John Wilkes, and was famous for evenings that constituted "a direct inversion of all traditional monastic behavior." Adrian Hamilton, *The Infamous Essay on Woman* (London: André Deutsch, 1972), 15–16, 29.

38. A sequel was published in *Town & Country* (1771), 305, being an account by the matron who had been appointed the inspectress. Probably the notion of an "inspectress" was a literary invention, although the forematron of the jury may have typically played a leading part in the inspection process.

39. Regina v. Wycherley, 8 Car. & P. 262, 264, 173 Eng. Rep. 486, 487 (Ex. 1838).

40. One writer asserts that with Baron Gurney's explanation, "arguably, the distinction of quickening in law ceased to have any real meaning." Shelley Gavigan, "The Criminal Sanction as It Relates to Human Reproduction: The Genesis of the Statutory Prohibition of Abortion," *Journal of Legal History* 5 (1984): 20, 35. But Gurney was merely attempting to explain the jury charge; as is later indicated, the quickening requirement persisted.

41. Historically, the notion of "quickening" has had a variety of interpretations. See Gavigan, "Criminal Sanction," *supra* n. 40, at 33–36; also the discussion by the U.S. Supreme Court in Roe v. Wade, 410 U.S. 113, 132–36 (1972).

42. Roe v. Wade, 410 U.S. at 132–38. According to the Court: "It is undisputed that at common law, abortion performed *before* 'quickening'—the first recognizable movement of the fetus *in utero*, appearing usually from sixteenth to the eighteenth week of pregnancy—was not an indictable offense." See also Gavigan, "Criminal Sanction," *supra* n. 40, at 21–26. Interestingly, there was theoretical writing in the late seventeenth century that the embryo was "a complete child," even as early as a few days after conception. See Eve Keller, "Embryonic Individuals: The Rhetoric of Seventeenth Century Embryology and the Construction of Early Modern Identity," *Eighteenth-Century Studies* 33 (2000): 321, 322, 336 (describing in particular the work of Theodore Kerckring).

43. Blackstone, *Commentaries, supra* n. 2, at 3: 388. Blackstone explained that "she may now be executed before the child is quick in the womb" (4: 388), thus (as was then thought) preceding the point at which the infant would become a human life.

44. Archives of Maryland, *Provincial Court Proceedings* 1649–1657 (Baltimore, 1891), 10: 456.

45. Ibid. at 457.

46. Archives of Maryland, *Proceedings of the County Courts of Kent (1656–1676), Talbot (1662–1674), and Somerset (1665–1668) Counties* (Baltimore: Maryland Historical Society, 1936), 54: xxix.

47. *Records of the Suffolk County Court, 1671–1680* (Boston: The Colonial Society of Massachusetts, 1933), 128, 149–50, 185–86.

48. See J. Paris and J. Fonblanque, *Medical Jurisprudence*, 2 vols. (London, 1823), 1: 248–54. In addition to marks on the body, it would be possible to ascertain a recent pregnancy by the presence of milk in the breasts, as the following example illustrates: "[The elders] got together some grave and skilful Women, in order to draw her breasts." [Anon.], *A Trophy of Christ's Victory* (Dumfries, 1719), 2. I am indebted to Catherine Crawford for this reference.

49. Savin is an evergreen shrub, the dried tops of which were once used as a drug; it is "strongly poisonous; it possesses emmenagogic properties, and hence was a common means of procuring abortion." *The Oxford English Dictionary*, compact ed., 2 vols. (Ox-

ford: Oxford University Press, 1971), 2: 2647. See also Theodric R. Beck, *Elements of Medical Jurisprudence*, two vols. (Albany, NY, 1823), 1: 214; Paris and Fonblanque, *Medical Jurisprudence, supra* n. 48 at 2: 378–79, and idem. 3: 86–89, 94; Anon., 3 Camp. 73, 170 Eng. Rep. 1310 (K.B. 1811).

50. Archives of Maryland, *Provincial Court Proceedings, 1658–1662* (Baltimore, 1922), 41: 20 (1657–58).

51. R. W. Malcolmson, "Infanticide in the Eighteenth Century," in James S. Cockburn, ed., *Crime in England 1550–1800* (Princeton: Princeton University Press, 1977), 187–209, also Appendix 1, n. b; Leon Radzinowicz, *A History of English Criminal Law and Its Administration from 1750*, 5 vols. (London: Stevens, 1948–86), 1: 430–36 (1948); Beck, *Medical Jurisprudence, supra* n. 49, at 1: 281–82.

52. Edgar Peel, *The Trials of the Lancashire Witches* (New York: Taplinger, 1969), 111. According to Peel, *The Malleus* was written by two Dominican inquisitors (with the Pope's blessing), went through fourteen editions between 1486 and 1520, "and, starting in 1584, at least six editions were put out in English." It was said that "The Malleus lay on the bench of every judge and on the desk of every magistrate—it was the ultimate, irrefutable, unarguable authority." Keith Thomas has pointed out, however, that "The *Malleus Maleficarum* was slow to impinge upon England. It was found in the library of the learned, for English intellectuals were used to buying and reading the publications of foreign presses; but the total absence of an English edition is striking by the side of the thirteen editions on the Continent by 1520." Keith Thomas, *Religion and the Decline of Magic* (New York: Scribner, 1971), 440. I am indebted to Douglas Hay for the Thomas reference.

53. Montague Summers, trans., *Malleus Maleficarum* (1489; Bungay, Suffolk, 1928), 225. Without identifying his source, Peel quotes a very different translation of this passage, viz.: "The accused should be stripped, if a woman by a jury of matrons, the purpose of this stripping is to discover whether she should have hidden upon her body some charm which would enable her to withstand the torture. Some hide them in their hair, others in more secret parts of their bodies." Peel, *Trials, supra* n. 52, at 115. The reference to the "jury of matrons" in the foregoing passage was undoubtedly a liberty taken by the translator, drawing upon the English experience.

54. John Demos, *Entertaining Satan* (New York: Oxford University Press, 1982), 179.

55. Peel, *Trials, supra* n. 52, at 23.

56. Montague Summers, *A Popular History of Witchcraft* (London: Dover, 1937), 67.

57. See Peel, *Trials, supra* n. 52, at 23, 135–36; C. L'Estrange Ewen, ed., *Witch Hunting and Witch Trials* (London: Frank Muller, 1929), 62; Wallace Notestein, *A History of Witchcraft in England from 1558 to 1718* (New York: Thomas Y. Crowell, 1911), 45, 108; Christina Hole, *Witchcraft in England* (London: B. T. Batsford, 1945), 75; Alan Macfarlane, *Witchcraft in Tudor and Stuart England* (New York: Routledge & Kegan Paul, 1970), 85, 276.

58. Peel gives the following account "from Webster's time" (Peel, *Trials, supra* n. 52, at 136): "One Katherine Walkden . . . was examined by a jury of matrons who discovered a private teat, and upon this and other evidence was convicted." (Webster was the author of *Displaying of Supposed Witchcraft*, 1677.) See also Summers, *Maleficarum, supra* n. 56; Notestein, *Witchcraft, supra* n. 57, at 45; Macfarlane, *Witchcraft, supra* n. 57, at 55.

59. Notestein, *Witchcraft, supra* n. 57, at 108. Notestein is in error if he is suggesting that the jury of matrons as a method for ascertaining pregnancy (rather than guilt) was not then accepted in the courts. Indeed, Notestein earlier refers to the appointment of "juries of women" by the judge at Chelmsford trials in 1582 to make examination of the accused (ibid. at 45). Presumably this information was taken from the 1582 pamphlet of the examining magistrate, Brian Darcey, entitled "A True and Juste Recorde of the Information, Ex-

amination and Confession of All the Witches taken in S. Oses in the countie of Essex by W. W.," quoted ibid. at 85.

60. Ibid. at 276, case 843 (1650). See also Montague Summers's description of the discovery of a witchmark of Isabell LeMoigne "by women appointed for that purpose" in a case on the Channel Island of Guernsey in 1617 (Summers, *Popular History, supra* n. 56, at 68).

61. I am indebted to Clive Holmes for calling my attention to this point. Professor Holmes has noted one case in which an inspection of a defendant at the Old Bailey was ordered by the justices after the regular jury had hesitated to convict. An examination was ordered and conducted by three women, one the Keeper of the Sessions house, the other two "brought in by the officers out of the street, passing there by chance." Henry Goodcole, *The Wonderful Discoverie of Elizabeth Sawyer* (London, 1621), sig. A2v–A3. Further, Holmes's examination of detailed accounts of trials leads him to discount the suggestion by "witch-finder" Matthew Hopkins that *twelve* "ancient skillful matrons or midwives" were used for the searches. Matthew Hopkins, *The Discovery of Witches* (London, 1647), 2–3; see also John Stearns, *A Confirmation and Discovery of Witchcraft* (London, 1648), 49.

62. Ewen, *Witch Hunting, supra* n. 57, at 61.

63. Hole, *Witchcraft in England, supra* n. 57, at 75. Fox identifies the composition of the inspection team as "ten midwives, six surgeons, and no less a figure than William Harvey, then physician to Charles I." Sanford J. Fox, *Science and Justice—The Massachusetts Witchcraft Trials* (Baltimore: Johns Hopkins Press, 1968), 88–89.

64. Demos, *Satan, supra* n. 54, at 180.

65. *Records of Salem Witchcraft copied from the Original Documents,* reissue of Woodward's *Historical Series* 1–2 (New York: B. Franklin, 1969), 146–47.

66. Marion L. Starkey, *The Devil in Massachusetts* (New York: Knopf, 1949), 163.

67. Paul Boyer and Stephen Nissenbaum, *Salem Possessed* (Cambridge, MA: Harvard University Press, 1974), 13.

68. Starkey, *The Devil, supra* n. 66, at 163. The full text of Rebecca Nurse's petition is set out in Fox, *Science and Justice, supra* n. 62, at 80–81. Nurse requested a new inquiry by "some other women . . . that are Moast Grand wise and skillful," and she nominated four, "two of them being Midwives."

69. Convictions for murder by witchcraft occurred in Essex on July 21, 1564; July 3, 1589; and in July 1609. James S. Cockburn, ed., *Calendar of Assize of Records: Essex Indictments, Elizabeth I* (London: Her Majesty's Stationery Office [hereafter "HMSO"], 1975); idem., *Calendar of Assize Records: Essex Indictments, James I* (London: HMSO, 1982). This was also true in Kent in March 1674 and in Surrey on Feb. 21, 1675, and in March 1682. James S. Cockburn, ed., *Calendar of Assize Records: Kent Indictments, Elizabeth I* (London: HMSO, 1980); idem., *Calendar of Assize Records: Surrey Indictments, Elizabeth I* (London: HMSO, 1980) (hereafter "CAR," together with the relevant county and monarch).

70. The Elizabeth I calendars were published in the following years: Sussex and Hertfordshire, 1975; Essex, 1978; Kent and Surrey, 1980; and the James I calendars: Sussex and Hertfordshire, 1975; Kent, 1981; Surrey and Essex, 1982.

71. James S. Cockburn, *Calendar of Assize Records: Home Circuit Indictments Elizabeth I and James I: Introduction* (London, HMSO, 1985) ("Introduction" hereafter).

72. Ibid. at 22.

73. Ibid.

74. Ibid. at 123.

75. See *infra,* text at nn. 170–76.

76. See John H. Langbein, The Criminal Trial Before the Lawyers," *University of Chicago Law Review* 45 (1978): 263; idem. "Shaping the Eighteenth-Century Criminal Trial: A View from the Ryder Sources," *University of Chicago Law Review* 50 (1983): 1.

77. Langbein, "Ryder Sources," *supra* n. 76, at 4.

78. Ibid. at 4, 3.

79. Ibid. at 25. Langbein's conclusion is based on his study of mid-eighteenth-century sessions papers and a comparison of them with the trial notes of Sir Dudley Ryder, Chief Justice of King's Bench from 1754 to 1756. As is later indicated, there are cases in which the juries of matrons noted in the OBSP are not shown in the "Goal Delivery" Books, but this is probably attributable to inconsistencies in the record-keeping habits of the clerks keeping them. On the whole, Langbein's generalization can be extended to the earlier period.

80. The Old Bailey Sessions were held eight times per year. Until 1732, each sessions was covered in its entirety by a single paper. Because of the increased volume of business and a fuller reporting style, most of the sessions papers from 1732 on were published in several parts and sold sequentially on the streets a few days apart. By the end of the eighteenth century, the number of parts per sessions reached as high as ten, and the combined total for sessions could easily number one hundred to two hundred pages. In the seventeenth and early eighteenth centuries, the papers typically ranged from two to twelve pages each.

81. OBSP, Apr. 1715.

82. Surviving long runs of the OBSP are not always identical; some years may be incomplete, some sets have supplementary material bound in, and some have handwritten notes and annotations. For the years addressed by this chapter (1677–1833), I initially used the OBSP held by the British Library, the Guildhall Library for the City of London, and the Harvard Law School Library. Subsequently these OBSP sets were supplemented by Old Bailey Proceedings Online, compiled by Tim Hitchcock and Robert Shoemaker, at http://www.oldbaileyonline.org.

83. One source describes the plea of pregnancy as having been granted by a very old statute, giving no citation. Andrew Knapp and William Baldwin, *Criminal Chronology, or the New Newgate Calendar,* 5 vols. (London, 1809), 4: 83. A search of the statute books did not make this reference intelligible.

84. For a review of all the statutory property holding requirements for jurymen from Magna Carta to 1730, see Appendix 4.

85. See ibid. for the traditional residence requirements.

86. The procedure of returning twenty-four names applied to civil cases. See Michael Dalton, *The Office and Authority of Sheriffs* (London, 1682), 316. Larger panels were returned in serious criminal cases in order to preserve to the prisoner his rights to exercise peremptory challenges. Since peremptory challenges would have no application to juries of matrons, the civil-jury pattern would presumably apply, if any of the trial jury procedures did. The only examples I have found of lists of juries of matrons that exceed twelve names are those few examples from the CAR, described at n. 121, *infra.* There are, nevertheless, fleeting references in legal literature to the use of a *venire facias tot matrones* for juries of matrons. For example, "Justices of Peace cannot award a *venire facias tot matrones,* to know whether a Felon be with child or no." Richard Chamberlain, *The Complete Justice* (London, 1681), 430.

87. "Talesmen" were jurymen procured by the sheriff to fill up a jury when fewer than twelve jurors appeared or proved acceptable from the original jury panel. For the rules with regard to talesmen, see Joseph Chitty, *A Practical Treatise on the Criminal Law,* 2 vols. (London, 1816; New York: Garland, 1978), 2: 517–21.

88. *Registrum Brevium* (London, 1553), fol. 227.

89. Richardson and Sayles, eds., *Select Cases, supra* n. 10, at cliii.

90. *Medical Gazette,* 15 Aug. 1835, at 698–99.

91. Cro. Eliz. 566, 78 Eng. Rep. 811 (C.P. 1597) (emphasis added).

92. Cro. Jac. 686, 79 Eng. Rep. 595 (C.P. 1625).

93. Edward Coke, *The First Part of the Institutes of the Laws of England,* 1st Amer. ed. from 19th London ed. (Philadelphia, 1853), 123b. Francis Hargrave published separately his views on the theme in "Two Notes on the Legal Time for Human Birth," *Jurisconsult Exercitations* (London, 1813). I am indebted to Catherine Crawford for these references.

94. 2 P. Wms. 591, 592, 24 Eng. Rep. 873, 874 (Ch. 1730).

95. Ibid. at 593–94, 874. The "register" was the *Registrum Brevium* (London, 1553).

96. Mos. 391, 393, 25 Eng. Rep. 458, 459 (*sub. nom.* Ex Parte Ayscoughe).

97. Ibid.

98. Cooke 62–63, 125 Eng. Rep. 958–59 (C.P. 1730) (*sub. nom.* Ascough v. Lady Chaplin).

99. Ibid. at 63, 959.

100. 4 Bro. C. C. 90, 99, 29 Eng. Rep. 794, 798 (Ch. 1792).

101. 1 Cox 297, 300, 29 Eng. Rep. 1174 (Ch., at the Rolls 1786).

102. Kenyon would succeed Lord Mansfield in 1788 as Chief Justice of the Court of King's Bench.

103. 1 Cox at 299, 29 Eng. Rep. at 1175.

104. Inner Temple Library, Mitford MS 54, fols. 267–68 (1786). John Mitford (later Lord Redesdale) was called to the bar in 1777, and three years later, he published *A Treatise on Pleadings in Suits in the Court of Chancery by English Bill* (London, 1780), which quickly became accepted as authoritative and helped Mitford acquire a large Chancery practice. Mitford served as Solicitor General from 1793 to 1799 and as Attorney General from 1799 to1802; he subsequently served as Lord Chancellor of Ireland.

105. Ibid. at fols. 352–53.

106. Ibid. at fol. 353.

107. Ibid. at fol. 356.

108. 1 Holt Eq. 328, 71 Eng. Rep. 769 (V.C. 1845).

109. See Blackstone, *Commentaries, supra* n. 2, at 4: 388. Hale refers simply to the "jury of women." Hale, *Placitorum Coronae, supra* n. 18, at 1:368–69.

110. OBSP, Dec. 1688.

111. In some traditions, the term "matron" was viewed as synonymous with midwife. See E. Ackerknecht, "Midwives as Experts in Court," *Bulletin of the New York Academy of Medicine* 52, No. 10 (Dec. 1976), 1224.

112. *The Oxford English Dictionary,* compact ed., 2 vols. (New York: Oxford University Press, 1971).

113. Samuel Johnson, *A Dictionary of the English Language,* 6th ed. (London, 1786).

114. John Kersey, *Dictionarium Anglo-Britanicum* (1708; Menston [Yorke], Scolar, 1969).

115. Thus, in E. Kennedy, *Observations on Obstetric Ausculation* (New York, 1843), 217, the author describes the indignation of a physician over a jury of matrons impaneled in Ireland in 1830: "Some of them were *unmarried,* and not one of them ever attended a lying-in case during her life." See also Knapp and Baldwin, *Criminal Chronology, supra* n. 83, at 4: 83 ("a jury of women, called by the law, Matrons, that is, females who have themselves borne children"). Interesting in this connection is a short case in Foster's mid-eighteenth-century book on crown law. While on trial for stealing out of a dwelling house, the prisoner, Elizabeth Meadow, screamed out in pain and appeared to some of the jury to

be in labor, whereupon the court designated (in Foster's words) "two *matron-like* women" to consult privately with the prisoner. Sir Michael Foster, *A Report of Some Proceedings on the Commission for the Trial of the Rebels in the Year 1746, in the County of Surrey; and of other Crown Cases,* 2d ed. (London, 1776), 76 (emphasis added). One of the women volunteered her qualifications when she returned to the court, explaining that in her opinion, having herself borne twelve children, the prisoner was in labor "though much before her time."

116. See [Anon.], *The Compleat Midwife's Practice* (London, 1656), 75: "Although in these dayes there are many unskilful women that take upon them the knowledge of Midwifry, barely upon the priviledge of their age: yet there are many things which ought to be observed in a Midwife, that they are utterly wanting of."

117. Ackerknecht, "Midwives," *supra* n. 111, at 1224.

118. Lisa Forman Cody, "The Politics of Reproduction: From Midwives' Alternative Public Sphere to the Public Spectacle of Man-Midwifery," *Eighteenth-Century Studies* 32 (1999): 477, 484.

119. There is, moreover, some basis to reject the idea of such a practice. It would be supposed that the population of available midwives would be relatively small, and that if juries regularly returned midwives, some pattern of repeated jury service by midwives would be discernible. While I have not discovered records sufficient to discard this possibility, it is worth noting that in Gaol Delivery Books in which juries of matrons were shown impaneled in a series of successive or near-successive months, not a single instance of repeat service by a matron is evident. See LMA/MJ/GBB/299–305 (Dec. 1715 and Jan. 1716); LMA/MJ/GBB/312–314 (Apr., June, Sept., Oct., Dec. 1733; Feb., July 1734); LMA/MJ/GBB/315–317 (Apr., Sept., and Dec. 1738).

120. For a description of the customary jury forms and procedures, see Chitty, *Criminal Law, supra* n. 87, at 2: ch. 13.

121. [Anon.], *Clerk of Assize, supra* n. 3, at 61. Interestingly, the CAR reveal several instances of juries of matrons with more than twelve members: CAR Herts. Eliz. (Mar. 1, 1591, fourteen jurors); CAR Essex Eliz. (July 17, 1570, and July 29, 1583, thirteen jurors).

122. Where the Assize Calendars indicate a jury of matrons determination, the jury was ordinarily impaneled the same day as conviction; delayed examinations were the exceptions.

123. The only scintilla of evidence I have discovered that might bear on this point comes from the LMA. Apart from the Gaol Delivery Books, the records office holds four lists of the names of juries of matrons from the second half of the eighteenth century. Each of these lists is a single sheet of paper; a representative caption at the top is "Names of the jury to try whether Mary Baxter otherwise Jones be with Quick Child or not" LMA/OBSP/1757/17. In all four cases, one or two names are entered in the list, crossed out, and other names added to reach the required twelve. Also, in all four cases, the verdict by the jury is set out at the bottom of the page.

Lists of the names that made up juries of matrons are also set out on the front or reverse side of the first folio of the MS record kept for each sessions in the Gaol Delivery Books. I have examined more than fifty of these lists, all eighteenth-century save one (1687). In all cases, these lists immediately follow the lists of the regular Middlesex trial jurors impaneled for the sessions. Most of the lists of juries of matrons in the Gaol Delivery Books are entered in an orderly manner in what appears to be the same ink and hand as the regular jury lists, but occasionally the matron list is squeezed into cramped space in what is clearly different ink. These jury-of-matrons entries do not reflect the pattern of deletions and additions shown on the four separate lists. One possibility that these few facts might signify is that the separate sheets were the papers filled out by the sheriff in the impaneling process, resulting in the lists that would be transferred to the Gaol Delivery Book by a clerk, who would not copy over the names that had been deleted.

There is little doubt that Gaol Delivery records depended upon the individual habits of the clerk in office; no fixed pattern over the decades is apparent. Occasionally, for example, the summoning of a jury of matrons is shown by a notation opposite the entry for an individual prisoner, even though no separate list of the names of the jurors is set out. See LMA/MJ/GBB/318–320 (Sept. 1751). More often, no indication whatever is given of a jury of matrons for prisoners who are specifically shown in the OBSP to have pleaded their bellies. See LMA/MJ/GBB/299–305 (Jan. 1712); LMA/MJ/GBB/306–309 (Aug. 1726); LMA/MJ/GBB/315–317 (Apr. 1737).

124. Lord Birkett, ed., *The New Newgate Calendar* (London: Folio Society, 1960), 44.

125. 8 Car. & P. 262, 173 Eng. Rep. 487 (Ex. 1838).

126. Ibid. at n.(a)[1]. Similarly, in the report of Regina v. Edmunds in the *Medical Times and Gazette,* 27 Jan. 1872, 98, the jury was said to be filled by a dozen "respectably dressed women" who were obtained by "a raid . . . made by the Under-Sheriffs upon the matrons present in Court."

127. One feature of the numerous jury of matrons cases in the Assize Calendars lends support to the *de circumstantibus* theory; while some cases reflect a deferred jury of matrons examination as late as nine to twelve months after conviction, with subsequent imprisonment and eventual pardon, many of the deferred examination cases involve a much shorter delay, with the jury of matrons examination taking place in the summer assizes following the conviction at Lent, or comparable examples. Often the delayed cases were joined with another conviction or two arising out of the later assizes, and the combined group of prisoners would be examined by a single jury of matrons. It is well known that the courts were often plagued by the appearance of an insufficient number of jurors to fill the required juries, and the *circumstantibus* device was fashioned to avoid the systematic delay of these cases to another term or session (see chapter 7, text at nn. 256–61). Ordinarily, the vicinity of the courtroom supplied enough male jurors to get on with the regular cases. But there likely were occasions on assize when an insufficient number of matrons was found in the courtroom or its environs to fill a jury of matrons. Probably no steps were taken to have women in attendance at the court to be in readiness in case a female felon were to be convicted and were to plead pregnancy. If too few women were available to fill the jury, the court may have decided to put the cases involving pregnancy pleas over to the next sessions, remanding the women to prison in the meantime.

128. Intermittently, from the early eighteenth century well into the twentieth century, these works appeared. They were compilations of allegedly true accounts of famous criminals drawn from a variety of records, such as shorthand accounts of trials or the OBSP. Sometimes the accounts were embellished by editorial comment by the author or authors. Later compilations often "borrowed" liberally from the earlier ones. The best known of the early works was published under the name of Capt. Alexander Smith (n. 129, *infra*). Perhaps the best nineteenth-century compilation was that by Knapp and Baldwin (n. 83, *supra*). The original Newgate Calendar was a "large sheet of parchment, up to 3 ft. long, on which the Deputy Keeper drew up a list of all admissions during the previous month, a day or two before the Sessions." Gerald Howson, *Thief-Taker General, The Rise and Fall of Jonathan Wild* (New York: St. Martin's, 1970), 163 n. *

129. Capt. Alexander Smith, *The History of the Lives of the Most Noted Highwaymen, Foot-pads, House-breakers, Shop-lifts and Cheats, of Both Sexes, etc.*, 2d ed., 2 vols. (London, 1714), 2: 185.

130. Howson, *Thief-Taker, supra* n. 128, at Appendix IV. The Sessions House where the Old Bailey trials were conducted was completed in 1673 and stood in its open-air condi-

tion for sixty-six years, thus encompassing the earliest and the peak years in which the juries of matrons appear in the OBSP (see Appendix 1, *infra*). Prior to the Great Fire of 1666, the judges at the Old Bailey heard cases under an open-sided roof in the Sessions House garden, while from 1666 to 1673 trials were conducted in a wooden shed "erected amidst the rubble." Ibid. at 315.

131. Ibid. at 27, and opposite 51 (illustrations 2 and 3).

132. OBSP, Dec. 1688.

133. In the seventeenth and eighteenth centuries, and earlier, it was not uncommon for babies to be stillborn. See Harvey Graham [pseud.], *"Eternal Eve," The History of Gynaecology and Obstetrics* (New York: Doubleday, 1951), 369. But it was not necessarily true that the absence of the "quickening" in a relatively advanced state of pregnancy signified that the baby would be stillborn. Consider, for example, the seventeenth-century memoir of Madame Louyse Bourgioes, midwife to the Queen of France, in which she describes a case in 1630 of a pregnant woman who came to her frightened by the lack of movement by the child in her womb: "I advised her to be patient, and to wait Nature's leisure, which is provident enough of itself; telling her that I had seen an infant which had lain a long time in the womb without budging, which for all that was not dead, although you could not perceive in the woman any thing, but the signs of a dead Child." [Anon.], *Compleat Midwife's Practice,* John Pechey, ed., 5th ed. (London, 1698), 328.

134. But see Keller, "Embryonic Individuals," *supra* n. 42; also, for a closely reasoned argument by a mid-nineteenth-century writer endeavoring to show that the quickening requirement was not present in the older authorities and grew out of a misreading of those authorities by Coke, see J. Smith, Esq., in Kennedy, *Observations, supra* n. 115, at Appendix 293–301. Smith's argument neatly interpreted the older authorities to render them receptive to modern medical evidence, but most medical views of the mid-eighteenth century and earlier did not suggest the need for any such interpretation, and quickening was unquestionably a required part of the jury of matrons' task in criminal cases in England.

135. Blackstone, *Commentaries, supra* n. 2, at 4: 388. That Blackstone equated "alive in the womb" with "quickening" is apparent from his explanation of why a prisoner could not gain another respite if she became pregnant a second time before being executed: "For she may now be executed before the child is quick in the womb."

136. For example, OBSP for Apr. 1680; June 1685; Sept. 1716; LMA/MJ/GBB 313 (Apr., Sept. 1733); LMA/OBSB/2 (Apr. 1759).

137. All four of the separate jury of matrons lists at the LMA are expressed in this way, and so are most of the Gaol Delivery Book entries and the OBSP reports.

138. OBSP, Apr. 1714. The jury of matrons examined three prisoners; one was found not with quick child, one was with quick child, and one was with child but not quick. In one case from Surrey, a prisoner was remanded "because the child [was] tho't not quick." CAR Surrey James (July 1, 1613). This truly was a case of judicial discretion, since the accepted principles allowed a reprieve only after the quickening had taken place. Much later (in 1831), Kennedy reports a case in Limerick, Ireland, in which the doctor called upon to examine the prisoner allowed that the prisoner might be young with child, but "she had not quickened" (Kennedy, *Observations, supra* n. 115, at 213). The prisoner was executed, and the doctor awaited the *post mortem* with great anxiety. The prisoner was found not to have been pregnant.

139. See generally Radzinowicz, *Criminal Law, supra* n. 51, at 1: ch. 4.

140. Ibid. at 113.

141. Cockburn, *Introduction, supra* n. 71.

142. John M. Beattie, *Crime and the Courts in England 1660–1800* (Oxford: Clarendon, 1986), 431. Overall, the records examined by Beattie from ninety-six of the years be-

tween 1660 and 1800 show that, except for a very small number of murder cases, that "women convicted of capital crimes had a very good chance of escaping the gallows." Ibid. at 439.

143. King, "Middlesex Justices," *supra* n. 17, at 98.

144. OBSP, Dec. 1684.

145. OBSP, July 1698 (three females); Oct. 1703 (five females); Dec. 1711 (one female); Jan. 1712 (one female); Nov. 1716 (two females).

146. This was reported of Moll Hawkins (1703) and Nan (Anne) Harris (alias Sarah Davis, alias Thom, alias Gotham, 1705) by Capt. Smith, *History, supra* n. 129, at 2: 192, 185, respectively. See also Knapp and Baldwin, *Criminal Chronology, supra* n. 83 (Deborah Churchill, 1708 [OBSP, Dec. 1708], 1: 76; Margaret Harvey, 1750, 2: 35; Catherine Nairn, 1766, 3: 184 [who, though called down to her former sentence, escaped in men's clothing]; Mary Mallet, 1794, 4: 83).

147. OBSP, Apr. 1686. Interestingly, also in the second category were Ellinor Rogers and Mary Lush, who had pleaded their bellies in May 1686 and had been found not with quick child.

148. OBSP, Apr., July 1688. Other examples of transportation being allowed to women after they pleaded their bellies are shown in OBSP for June 1690 (Margaret Jones); Apr. 1740 (Elizabeth Davis, Margaret Newel, and Mary Nash); Sept. 1743 (Mary Stansbury); Oct. 1761 (Mary Bulger); and Apr. 1789 (Eleanor Kirwin).

149. LMA/OBSB/1758/01.

150. I was not able to determine whether either, or both, ultimately escaped execution.

151. The extent to which witness testimony and other aspects of criminal trials were manipulated in the early eighteenth century by the thief-takers and comparable characters is graphically revealed in Howson's study of Jonathan Wild. See Howson, *Thief-Taker, supra* n. 128, especially chapters 14–16.

152. I have not discovered evidence to suggest the packing of juries of matrons in civil cases. Of the three types of abuses, the third abuse would have no application to the civil context; with regard to the second, it became harder for the jury of matrons in a civil case to ascertain pregnancy than in the criminal case because, in the civil context, "quickening" was not a requisite finding.

153. M. Misson, *Travels over England,* quoted in Radzinowicz, *Criminal Law, supra* n. 51, at 1: 12, n. 35. Cockburn quotes Misson, as well, and states that several cases in the CAR "point to pregnancies initiated in gaol" (*Introduction, supra* n. 71). Further, Sheehan observes that "in 1702 a group from the Society for Promoting Christian Knowledge visited the gaol [Newgate] several times and was scandalized to see female prisoners openly soliciting in hope of becoming pregnant so that they could 'plead their belly' and be pardoned by the justices at Sessions." W. J. Sheehan, "Finding Solace in Eighteenth-Century Newgate," in Cockburn, ed., *Crime in England, supra* n. 51, at 243.

154. Howson, *Thief-Taker, supra* n. 128, at chapters 1, 19.

155. William H. Irving, *John Gay Favorite of the Wits* (Durham, NC: Duke University Press, 1940), 235.

156. As noted at the outset of this article, Moll Flanders described herself has having been born while her mother was respired on a pregnancy plea. Howson persuasively identified an actual criminal—Moll King—as the model used by Defoe for Moll Flanders. Howson, *Thief-Taker, supra* n. 128, at 156–61. Moll King, shown in the OBSP under the alias "Mary Gouldston," successfully pleaded her belly in Dec. 1718.

157. Defoe, *Moll Flanders, supra* n. 1, at 260.

158. As *The Beggar's Opera* demonstrates, Gay "knew the Newgate World and its denizens intimately." Chester F. Burgess, "The Genesis of the Beggar's Opera," *Clithara* 2

(Nov. 1962): 6, 10. In 1716, Gay's *Trivia* (subtitled "On the Art of Walking the Streets of London") was published, which, as Burgess notes (10), "Reveals not only an astonishing knowledge of the city but also of Gay's continued interest in the affairs of the demi-monde." Burgess asserts that Gay was influenced by the trials, in the 1720s, of Jonathan Wild, Jonathan Blake, and Jack Sheppard. Indeed, Herbert states that Gay must be given "new credit for understatement and artistic restraint" in his depiction of London's criminal underworld. A. P. Herbert, *Mr. Gay's London* (London: E. Benn, 1948), 10.

159. John Gay, *The Beggar's Opera,* Edgar Roberts, ed. (Lincoln: University of Nebraska Press, 1968), 7. Again, no explanation of the phrase "pleading the belly" was thought necessary.

160. Ibid. at 62.

161. Howson observes (*Thief-Taker, supra* n. 128, at 157, n.*) that "Any young man with money enough to buy himself a good pair of gloves, some lace, and a sword, could call himself 'Captain' and assume this gave him a license to riot round the town. Thus the title was adopted by authors of picaresque books: 'Capt. Alexander Smith', 'Capt. Charles Johnson', 'Capt. Charles Walker', etc."

162. Smith, *History, supra* n. 129, at 2: 46. She was found not quick with child. On the other hand, Smith asserts that Moll Hawkins in 1703 was reprieved for nine months for pregnancy "tho' she was not." Ibid. at 2: 192.

163. Ibid. at 2: 184–85.

164. See text at n. 153 *supra.*

165. For example, in the OBSP for Dec. 1692, Mary Bamford, "an old Woman," claimed to be with child, but the jury found otherwise.

166. [Anon.], *Compleat Midwife's Practice, supra* n. 133, at 51.

167. Ibid.

168. Ibid. at 49, 51–52. The "false moles" are described as "windie," "watrie," "Humorous," and "Membranous."

169. Ibid. at 48–49. Later, the term "mole" often described only a false conception. See Michael Ryan, *A Manual of Medical Jurisprudence* (Philadelphia 1832), 126; and W. Kendrick, *A New Dictionary of the English Language* (London, 1773). Confusion over the terminology persisted. In his mid-eighteenth-century medical dictionary, James wrote: "La Motte says, that a Mole, and a false conception, seem to be the same thing, except that, if it is excluded before the second or third month, it is called a false Conception; if after that time a Mole. And thus it is distinguished by Mauriceau." R. James, *Medicinal Dictionary* (London, 1745), 2. See also H. Power and L. Sedgwick, *Lexicon of Medicine and the Allied Sciences* (London, 1889), 4 (the "true mole" is "[a] mole which is the result of conception").

170. John Jones, *Medical, Philosophical and Vulgar Errors* (London, 1797), 65–66; I am indebted to Catherine Crawford for referring me to this work.

171. Beck, *Medical Jurisprudence, supra* n. 49, at 1: 200.

172. Ibid.

173. This view may have been a derivative of the Aristotelean "three-stage theory of life: vegetable, animal, rational." Roe v. Wade, 410 U.S. at 133, n. 22.

174. Beck, *Medical Jurisprudence, supra* n. 49, at 1: 202 (emphasis deleted). See also Paris and Fonblanque, *Medical Jurisprudence, supra* n. 49, at 1: 239–40; Alfred S. Taylor, *Elements of Medical Jurisprudence,* 5th Am. ed. from 7th rev. London ed. (London, 1861), 404; T. Madden, *On Spurious, Feigned, and Concealed Pregnancy,* (Dublin, 1872), 15; *Medical Times and Gazette,* 27 Jan. 1872, at 98. Compare also the seventeenth-century theorizing by Theodore Kerckring, (n. 42 *supra*).

175. There is evidence that, by the nineteenth century, "quickening" was not a required

finding in civil cases. See the Massachusetts case of Hall v. Hancock, 15 Pick. 255, 257–58 (Mass. 1834), where the court, after arguments of counsel drawing upon English authorities, stated its opinion that "quick with child" was a finding "applicable mainly if not exclusively to criminal cases; and that it does not apply to cases of descents, devises and other gifts; and that, generally, a child will be considered in being, from conception to the time of its birth, in all cases where it will be for the benefit of such child to be so considered." This fact provoked the following observation by Dr. Paris: "it is a strange anomaly that by the law of real property, an infant *in ventre sa mere* may take an estate from the moment of its conception, and yet be hanged four months afterwards for the crime of its mother." Paris and Fonblanque, *Medical Jurisprudence, supra* n. 48, at 3: 141, n.(a). For the same point, see *Medical Gazette,* 6 Apr. 1833, at 25.

176. Ryan, *Medical Jurisprudence, supra* n. 169, at 128.

177. *Medical Times and Gazette* 27 Jan. 1872, at 98.

178. Ibid. Wright's case is described in detail in Kennedy, *Observations, supra* n. 115, at, 220–23, and in *Medical Gazette,* 6 Apr. 1833 at 22–26.

179. *Medical Times and Gazette,* 16 Mar. 1872, at 317.

180. Montgomery gives one seventeenth-century example from Paris in which a woman was hanged, dissected, and found to be four months pregnant "Notwithstanding the report of the persons who had visited and examined her by order of the judge before her execution, and pronounced that she was not pregnant, *being deceived by the fact of her continuing to menstruate.*" William F. H. Montgomery, *An Exposition of the Signs and Symptoms of Pregnancy, the Period of Human Gestation, and the Signs of Delivery* (Philadelphia, 1839), 23.

181. A. Hayward, *Lives of the Most Remarkable Criminals Who have been Condemned and Executed for Murder, the Highway, Housebreaking, Street Robberies, Coining or Other Offenses* (London, 1735; London: Reeves and Turner, 1927), 379.

182. Pierre Cazeaux, *A Theoretical and Practical Treatise on Midwifery,* 5th Amer. from the 7th French ed. (1871), 251.

183. Taylor, *Elements, supra* n. 174, at 404. See also Montgomery, *Exposition, supra* n. 180, at 57.

184. Madden, *Pregnancy, supra* n. 174, at 15. For like assertions, see Kennedy, *Observations, supra* n. 115, at Appendix, 299; and text at n. 199 *infra.*

185. Text at n. 162, *supra.*

186. Her case is described in J. H. Aveling, *English Midwives Their History and Prospects* (London, 1872), 63. Sophisticated trickery was not limited to the common-law cases under discussion. Richard Helmholz referred me to cynical commentaries on the subject among the canonists. Hostiensis, for example, speaks of the need for a particularly expert panel of women to test for virginity "propter diversas medicinas mulierum, quae corruptionem sophisticant, ita quod corrupta virgo appareat" ("because of various effeminating medicines that conceal depravity, giving the appearance of virginity"). Hostiensis, *Lectura in Libros Decretalium* (Venice, 1581), X 2.19.14 (*Causam matrimonii*), no. 4 (fol. 58). He suggests that the woman being inspected be placed first in a bath of hot water and kept there long enough "quod si aliquod glutinum appositurn est liquefiat" ("that if anything is put in with adhesive it will melt").

187. "Mr. Prance's Answer to Mrs. Cellier's Libel, &c.; to which is added the Adventures of the Bloody Bladder: a tragi-comical farce, acted with much applause at Newgate by the said Mme. Cellier, on Saturday, September 18th. Faithfully related by an eye-and-ear witness" (1680), quoted in Aveling, *Midwives, supra* n. 186, at 70. Dr. Aveling notes that the incident was "frequently referred to in the broadsides of the times," giving some examples (70–71).

188. In civil cases, life-or-death stakes were not involved, but the jury determination was nevertheless weighty. Blackstone notes (*Commentaries, supra* n. 2, at 1: 444), for example, that "if the widow be upon due examination found not pregnant, any issue she may afterwards produce, though within nine months, will be bastard."

189. See William Forsyth, *History of Trial by Jury* (New York, 1875), 203–15. An 1838 case reports the following oath being administered to the bailiff: "You shall well and truly keep this jury of matrons without meat, drink, or fire, candle light excepted; you shall suffer no person but the prisoner to speak to them; neither shall you speak to them yourself, unless it be to ask them if they are agreed on their verdict, without leave of the Court. So help your [*sic*] God." Regina v. Wycherley, 8 Car. & P. 262, 263, 173 Eng. Rep. 486, 487 (Ex. 1838). Nevertheless, as the cases in the text indicate, juries of matrons were allowed to be undecided. The forematron and the eleven other members of the jury were also administered oaths in *Wycherley* almost exactly in the form set out in the *Clerk of Assize,* first published in 1660. After the oaths are set out, the following appears:

> When they be all sworn, one of the Bailiffs, shall convey the jury and the Prisoner to a chamber, where they shall search and try whether she be quick with Child of a quick Child, or not; and when they be all agreed of their Verdict, and be returned to the Court, the Clerk of Assize shall call them severally by their names; and ask them whether they be all agreed of their Verdict, and who shall speak for them.

[Anon.], *Clerk of Assize, supra* n. 3, at 61–62. No bailiff's oath is there given, nor is there any reference to a duty to keep the matrons "without meat, drink, or fire."

190. Knapp and Baldwin, *Criminal Chronology, supra* n. 83, at 1: 77. An early, analogous bastardy case is found in the Maryland archives, as is shown in the following description:

> At the June 7, 1662, court a jury of nine women proceeded "to search" a servant woman who declared she had become pregnant by a certain man on "Candlemuse Day last in the night," and brought in a verdict that they could not decide whether or not she was pregnant, but the court took no chances and bound over the man by a bond of 5000 pounds of tobacco "to save the county harmless . . . if in case it be proved to be his."

Archives of Maryland, *Proceedings of the County Courts of Kent, supra* n. 46, at 54: xxiv, 233.

191. Jury traditions in Scotland were different from those in England. The regular use of a jury in civil cases was not established until the nineteenth century. The tradition of jury trial in criminal cases was venerable, but verdicts were not required to be unanimous. Further, a compromise verdict of "not proven" was permitted in criminal cases. See generally Forsyth, *Trial by Jury, supra* n. 189, at 249–88.

192. 19 *State Trials* 1327–30 (Justiciary Court 1765). Mrs. Nairn was, in fact, pregnant and was delivered of a daughter, after which she contrived to escape (ibid. at 1338). As earlier noted (n. 146), Knapp and Baldwin asserted that she fled the country in men's clothing.

193. Knapp and Baldwin, *Criminal Chronology, supra* n. 83, at 4: 241. Interestingly, the OBSP say nothing of the jury of matrons, despite a comparatively lengthy report of Ann Hurle's trial (OBSP, Jan. 1804). The report merely notes that "the prisoner left her defense to her counsel."

194. John L. Raynor and G. T. Crook, eds., *The Complete Newgate Calendar,* 5 vols. (London: Navarre Society, 1926), 5: 39. After fifteen minutes, the jury returned a verdict that the prisoner was not quick with child.

195. 8 Car. & P. at 263, 173 Eng. Rep. at 487 (see n. 39, *supra*).

196. Ibid. at 264, 487. According to the reporters, the prisoner was nevertheless respited

"in order that it might be ascertained with certainty whether she was with child or not." Ibid., n. (a)[3].

197. Ibid. at n. (a)[2].

198. *Medical Times and Gazette,* 27 Jan. 1872, at 98. The author then alluded to further delay in the case, reporting the wonderful rumor that a policeman, on being sent out of court to fetch a stethoscope, returned with a telescope.

199. Ibid. Whether Mr. Ryley retired with the jury, thus raising the evidentiary question posed in Regina v. Wycherley, is not known.

200. *The Law Times* (July 19, 1879): 67: 212.

201. Ibid.

202. *The Times* (July 11, 1879): 7, col. e.

203. *The Times* (Dec. 12, 1913): 4, col. c.

204. Ibid.

205. *The Times* (July 19, 1917): 3, col. c.

206. Great Britain, *House of Commons Sessional Papers* (London, 1878–79), vol. 2, title 7, part 43 (s. 531).

207. Laws of New York, *Code of Criminal Procedure* (New York, 1881), 2: 122–23.

208. In discussing the murder trial of Mary Wright at Norwich, the editors of the *Medical Gazette,* 6 Apr. 1833, wrote that "there are cases in which the jury of matrons has been dispensed with, in favour of a professional jury consisting of two surgeons and two physicians: let us hope that the discretionary power of such a dispensation may always be exercised by the bench in the future." Two years later, in an account in the same publication of a civil case in which the writ *de ventre inspiciendo* was requested, the editors wrote that "in latter times, there has been an understanding the writ may be carried into execution . . . by substituting, for the four-and-twenty discreet men and women, a jury of medical referees, with power to investigate and determine." *Medical Gazette,* 15 Aug. 1835, 699. I have found no other report of any such cases; presumably the substitution procedure, if it existed, was ad hoc and never became formalized or widespread.

209. See, e.g., G. Collinson, *A Treatise on the Law, Concerning Idiots, Lunatics and Other Persons Non Compos Mentis,* 130–31, quoted in Alan Dershowitz, "The Origins of Preventive Confinement in Anglo-American Law—Part I: The English Experience," *University of Cincinnati Law Review* 43 (1974): 1, 35. Also, for nineteenth-century commentary on proposed New York legislation, see Ralph Lyman Parsons, "Jury Trial of the Insane," *The Medico-Legal Journal* 1 (1883–84): 327.

210. OBSP, Feb. 1818. The jury concluded that the defendant's silence was the result of a visitation from God.

211. The number of females sentenced to death at the Old Bailey declined during the mid-1700s but increased again temporarily during the 1780s. See Appendix 1.

212. Sheehan's study of Newgate in the eighteenth century indicates that sporadic efforts were made to eliminate corruption in the management of the prisoners, but the efforts were ineffective or short-lived. Sheehan, "Finding Solace," in Cockburn, ed., *Crime in England, supra* n. 153.

213. See Langbein, "Ryder Sources," *supra* n. 76, at 40–41; Radzinowicz, *Criminal Law, supra* n. 51, at 1: 94–97; see also chapter 3, text at nn. 2–36.

214. There may have been some judicial manipulation for the same purpose in some eras, as Cockburn has suggested. See text at n. 72, *supra.*

215. Langbein, *"Criminal Trial," supra* n. 76, at 60–76.

216. From 1727 through 1800, only 40 percent of the females who pleaded their bellies were found to be quick with child. See Appendix 1.

Notes for Chapter 6

1. See *An Index and Paraphrase of Printed Year Book Reports, 1268–1535,* David J. Seipp, comp., at http://www.bu.edu/law/seipp/. Since the database is an ongoing project, it is ever-expanding. When I used the database for this chapter (Summer 2004), it contained approximately 18,000 record numbers.

2. John P. Dawson, *A History of Lay Judges* (Cambridge, MA: Harvard University Press, 1960) 123, citing Frederick Pollock and Frederic W. Maitland, *The History of English Law Before the Time of Edward I,* 2d. ed., 2 vols. (Cambridge and Boston, 1899) 2: 622 ("*HEL*" hereafter).

3. Pollock and Maitland, *HEL,* 2: 622–23.

4. Ibid.

5. Ibid. at 1: 628 (footnote omitted).

6. Maureen Mulholland and Brian Pullan, eds., *Judicial Tribunals in England and Europe, 1200–1700: The Trial in History,* 2 vols. (Manchester: Manchester University Press, 2003).

7. Daniel Klerman, "Was the Jury Ever Self-Informing?" ibid. at 1: 58. (The chapter was subsequently reprinted at *University of Southern California Law Review* 77 (2003): 123.)

8. Ibid. at 1: 59, referring to chapters by B. W. McLane, J. B. Post, and E. Powell in James S. Cockburn and Thomas A. Green, eds., *Twelve Good Men and True: The Criminal Trial Jury in England 1200–1800* (Princeton: Princeton University Press, 1988).

9. Klerman searched for witnesses in thirteenth-century plea rolls containing 1,300 crown cases from different parts of England. Mulholland and Pullan, eds., *The Trial in History, supra* n. 6, at 1: 70.

10. Ibid. at 1: 76. In a recent review of *The Trial in History,* John Langbein calls Daniel Klerman's chapter "perhaps the standout contribution to the collection," stating that, "Klerman's account gives us confidence that the received understanding of the self-informing character of the medieval jury is sound, while helping us to see more of how that institution ultimately unravelled." John H. Langbein, "The Trial in History," review in *The English Historical Review* 119 (2004): 192, 193–94.

11. Also that by Roger D. Groot.

12. Cockburn and Green, eds., *Twelve Good Men and True, supra* n. 8, at 370.

13. David J. Seipp, "Jurors, Evidences and the Tempest of 1499," in John W. Cairns and Grant McLeod, eds., "*The Dearest Birth Right of the People of England": The Jury in the History of the Common Law* (Oxford and Portland, OR: Hart, 2002), 75, 81.

14. Ibid. at 82.

15. I limit this revisitation of the classic model to the period from the thirteenth to the late fifteenth centuries. There was a later transitional phase when jurors were told to take the witness stand and to testify in open court about any knowledge they had of the case. See, e.g., Constable v. Nichols, Harvard Law School MS 1017, fol. 83 (1726), discussed in James Oldham, "The Jury: Perspectives on Thomas Andrew Green's *Verdict According to Conscience," Criminal Justice History* VIII (1987): 163, 169, and J. M. Mitnick, "From Neighbor-Witness to Judge of Proofs: The Transformation of the English Civil Juror," *American Journal of Legal History* XXXII (1988): 201, 222–23. Mitnick discusses some of the transitional developments, especially those occurring in the seventeenth and eighteenth centuries.

16. Y.B., 1 Edw. 3, fols. 2a–2b, lib. ass. 16 (Seipp, 1327.142 ass).

17. Y.B., Mich. 9 Edw. 3, fols. 37b–38a, pl. 43 (Seipp, 1335.22).

18. W. P. Baildon, ed., *Select Civil Pleas (1200–1203)* (London: B. Quaritch, 1889), 3 Selden Society ("SS" hereafter) 50, Case 126 (1202). See also G. O. Sayles, ed., *Select Cases in the Court of King's Bench Under Edward I (Vol. I)* (London: B. Quaritch, 1936),

55 SS 93, Coram Rege Roll 64 (1281) ("totally insufficient jury" in a plea of trespass, with a new jury to be impaneled of "twelve, of whom eight at least should be knights girt with the sword, excepting coroners of the aforesaid neighbourhood, to make the aforesaid inquisition").

19. Sayles, ed., *Select Cases (Vol. I), supra* n. 18, at 32, Coram Rege Roll 30 (1277).

20. F. W. Maitland, L. W. V. Harcourt, and W. C. Bolland, eds., *Year Book of the Eyre of Kent, 6 & 7 Edward II (1313–1314)* (London: B. Quaritch, 1909), 24 SS cccviii–xxxix.

21. Ibid.

22. Ibid. at xli.

23. Ibid.

24. R.C. van Caenegem, ed., *Royal Writs in England from the Conquest to Glanvill* (London: B. Quaritch, 1958–59), 77 SS 90, citing M. M. Bigelow, *History of Procedure in England from the Norman Conquest: The Norman Period, 1066–1204* (London, 1880), 336.

25. Ibid. at 91.

26. C. T. Flower, ed., *Introduction to the Curia Regis Rolls, 1199–1230* (London: B. Quaritch, 1943), 62 SS.

27. Ibid. at 42.

28. Ibid. at 446–47.

29. Sayles, ed., *Select Cases (Vol. I), supra* n. 18, at 120, 126, Coram Rege Roll 79 (1283).

30. G. O. Sayles, ed., *Select Cases in the Court of King's Bench Under Edward I (Vol. III)* (London: B. Quaritch, 1939), 58 SS.

31. Ibid. at lxxxii, citing Coram Rege Roll 290 (1332), Appendix XVIII(d). Another assault that occurred at Westminster in the presence of the justices in 1345 resulted in an order to the serjeant criers "to empanel thereon twelve of those in whose presence etc. and of others most qualified and least suspect." G. O. Sayles, ed., *Select Cases in the Court of King's Bench (vol. VI), Edward III* (London: B. Quaritch, 1965), 82 SS 39, 40, Coram Rege Roll 341 (1345).

32. G. O. Sayles, ed., *Select Cases in the Court of King's Bench Under Edward III (Vol. V)* (London: B. Quaritch, 1957), 76 SS 93, 95, Coram Rege Roll 306 (1336). For other "eyewitness" cases, see Helen M. Cam, ed., *The Eyre of London, 14 Edward II (A.D. 1321)* (London: B. Quaritch, 1969), 86 SS 227, 228 (1321) (defendant called plaintiff a traitor in the hall of pleas in the presence of the justices; jury was collected from those who were present and heard what was said); Sayles, ed., *Select Cases (Vol. VI), supra* n. 31, at 30, Coram Rege Roll 336 (1344) (defendant was prosecuted for contempt for wearing body armour in the king's court, but a jury of attorneys and ministers of the court (with others) acquitted, deciding that the man was protecting himself from plotters against him).

33. Daniel Klerman makes this same point about records in the plea rolls. Mulholland and Pullan, eds., *The Trial in History, supra* n. 6, at 1: 67–68.

34. Sayles, ed., *Select Cases (Vol. I), supra* n. 18, at 27, 28, Coram Rege Roll 24 (1276).

35. Cockburn and Green, eds., *Twelve Good Men and True, supra* n. 8, at 366.

36. F. W. Maitland, ed., *Select Pleas of the Crown (A.D. 1200–1225)* (London: B. Quaritch, 1887), 1 SS 1 (1201).

37. Ibid. at 17 (1201).

38. Ibid.

39. See Klerman in Mulholland and Pullan, eds., *The Trial in History, supra* n. 6, at 1: 74.

40. Y.B., K.B. Trin. 15 Edw. 2, fols. 469–70, pl. 9 (Seipp, 1322.033).

41. Maitland, ed., *Select Pleas (1200–1225), supra* n. 36, at 123–27, Case 192 (1220).

42. Ibid. at 6, Case 16 (1201).

43. Sayles, ed., *Select Pleas (Vol. III), supra* n. 30, at 106, Coram Rege Roll 164 (1306).

44. Ibid. at lxvii. In a late-thirteenth-century King's Bench case, a wife who gave birth more than forty weeks after her husband's death claimed that the child was her late husband's, but the jury said that the husband, Robert, had been ill for a month before his death and had seen his wife only on the evening before he died and "questioned whether they believed that during this time he carnally knew [his wife], they say that they do not believe it because he was in the grip of so serious and grave an illness . . . that the dissolution of his body was clearly imminent and he was altogether impotent." Ibid. at 28, 31, Coram Rege Roll 142 (1294).

45. See text at nn. 27–28, *supra.*

46. See David J. Seipp, "The Mirror of Justices," in *Learning the Law: Teaching and the Transmission of Law in England 1150–1900* (London and Rio Grande, TX: Hambledon Press, 1999), 85. Seipp begins his chapter by quoting Plucknett's remark that *The Mirror of Justices* is "certainly the most fantastic work in our legal literature." Heaped upon this remark are those of Frederick Pollock ("It is quite impossible to take this production seriously"), William Holdsworth ("A joke"—"Wholly unworthy of credit"), and Percy Winfield ("Rubbish"), among others. Ibid. at 85–86. Seipp attempts a modest rehabilitation, providing a reasoned analysis of what Andrew Horne was up to in his book and why Maitland's reaction was so fiercely negative. In the end, Seipp calls the *Mirror* "a reformist textbook on law," one that states "general propositions with remarkable clarity and insight." Ibid. at 112.

47. W. J. Whittaker, ed., *The Mirror of Justices* (London: B. Quaritch, 1893), 7 SS 116 (treatise written circa 1285).

48. Van Caenegem, ed., *Royal Writs, supra* n. 20, at xli.

49. Ibid. at xlvii–xlix. See Klerman in Mulholland and Pullan, eds., *The Trial in History, supra* n. 6, at 1: 75–76.

50. G. O. Sayles, ed., *Select Cases in the Court of King's Bench Under Edward I (Vol. II)* (London: B. Quaritch, 1957), 57 SS 82, 83, Coram Rege Roll 130 (1292).

51. F. W. Maitland and G. J. Turner, eds., *Year Books 3 & 4 Edward II (1310),* 22 SS 4, Case 3 (1310).

52. Ibid. at 5. Presumably the espousals were thought by the Chief Justice to be an ecclesiastical matter beyond his authority, and he thought it improper for him or his court to intervene.

53. Y.B., C.B. Mich. 21 Hen. 6, fol. 22a, pl. 46 (Seipp, 1442.142).

54. Y.B., C.B. Mich. 34 Hen. 6, fols. 15b–16a, pl. 29 (Seipp, 1455.095).

55. For examples, see F. W. Maitland, ed., *Year Books 1 & 2 Edward II (1307–9)* (London: B. Quaritch, 1903), 17 SS 115, Case 56 (1309) (Common Pleas Justice Staunton "ordered that half the jury should come from the place where the espousals occurred and half from the place where the lands lay, for the folk of both places may have cognizance of the matter"); ibid. at 95, Case 42 (1309) (bastardy; Staunton ordered a mixed jury from two counties, one where the tenements were and the other where the claimant was born); Donald W. Sutherland, ed., *The Eyre of Northamptonshire, 3–4 Edward III (A.D. 1329–1330) (Vol. II)* (London: Selden Society, 1982), 98 SS 793 (Ropet v. Anon., Common Pleas, probably from 1310–20) (dower; wife left husband to live with her lover in another county, and a jury was awarded from both counties); Y.B., C.B. Trin. 11 Hen. 6, fol. 54a, pl. 22 (Seipp 1433.03) (jury ordered from two counties where two manors were located).

56. See, e.g., Y.B., Mich. 28 Hen. 6, fol. 1b, pl. 6 (Seipp, 1449.027), where a dispute among remaindermen produced a claim by the defendant that an intermediate remainderman in fee tail had married in another county and had issue yet alive. The question was

whether the *venire facias* should come from the county where the land was or from the county where the birth of issue was alleged. The report of the case says that the justices were of different opinions, "but the better opinion was that it (the jury) would come from the county where the land was."

57. Occasionally this was pinpointed, as in Y.B., Mich. 22 Hen. 6, fols. 35a–35b, pl. 55 (Seipp, 1443.114). There, defendant was accused of trespass but pleaded justification in another place in another county. The court allowed the plea but ordered that the jury should come from the vill where the trespass was supposed, and not from the body of the county.

58. See the discussion by Klerman in Mulholland and Pullan, eds., *The Trial in History, supra* n. 6, at 1: 68–72.

59. Paul Vinogradoff and Ludwik Ehrlich, eds., *Year Book 6 Edward II (1312–1313)* (London: B. Quaritch, 1917), 34 SS xlix.

60. Ibid. at 197, 198, Case 58. The editors state that "'In evidence' probably means that each party had to give to the assize his version of the facts." Ibid. at n. 1.

61. Ibid. at 199, Case 59 (Anon.).

62. Morris Arnold, ed., *Select Cases of Trespass from the King's Courts 1307–1399 (Vol. I)* (London: Selden Society, 1985), 100 SS.

63. Ibid. at 37, Coram Rege Roll (Trinity 1318).

64. Ibid. at 39.

65. Ibid. at 40–41.

66. Seipp, "Jurors, Evidences and the Tempest of 1499," in Cairns and McLeod, eds., "*The Dearest Birth Right*", *supra* n. 13.

67. Ibid. at 81.

68. Ibid. at 81–82.

69. Ibid. at 83. Seipp gives examples from Year Book cases that involved prosecutions for maintenance. For instance, it was considered maintenance, thus wrongful, for "someone not in the party's camp to 'show the truth of the matter' to prospective jurors before trial, or to sworn jurors in court," but parties or those close to them (e.g., relatives, servants) could "inform prospective jurors of the truth of the matter, to show the party's title deeds and other evidences, and thus to 'labour' them by trying to persuade them that the party had the right or the better matter." Ibid. (citations omitted).

70. G. O. Sayles, ed., *Select Cases in the Court of King's Bench Under Edward II (Vol. IV)* (London: B. Quaritch, 1955), 74 SS 68, Coram Rege Roll 222 (1315).

71. Ibid. at 69.

72. G. O. Sayles, ed., *Select Cases in the Court of King's Bench (Vol. VII), Richard II, Henry IV and Henry V* (London: B. Quaritch, 1971), 88 SS 80, Coram Rege Roll 522 (1391).

73. Ibid. at 81–82.

74. Ibid. at 82.

75. Ibid. A comparable case arose in 1402 in an attaint in which only four knights of the forty-eight summoned to form the attaint jury were left unchallenged by the litigating parties. After the four knights had reached their conclusions, the justices learned that they had used a certain roll as evidence when trying each of the trial jurors. When the knights were questioned, it came out that one of them had received the roll from a man whose name he did not know, and although the four knights swore under oath that they did not take any evidence from the roll in trying the jurors, they were nevertheless removed from the jury and delivered to the sheriff, after which they eventually "made fine with the King." Ibid. at 126, Coram Rege Roll 565 (1402).

76. Sayles, ed., *Select Cases (Vol. VII), supra* n. 72, at 14, 15, Coram Rege Roll 476 (1380).

77. Ibid. at 16.

78. Ibid. at 64, Coram Rege Roll 515 (1390).

79. David Seipp mentions this case in his chapter in Cairns and McLeod, eds., "*The Dearest Birth Right*", *supra* n. 13, at 81.

80. Mary Bateson, ed., *Borough Customs (Vol. I)* (London: B. Quaritch, 1904), 18 SS; idem., *Borough Customs (Vol. II)* (London: B. Quaritch, 1906), 21 SS. Some of the customs are startling to the modern reader, such as the finding that in Wycomb in 1275, as soon as a young man turned twelve, "he can give, sell, or bequeath his land according to the custom of the town, and also can be put on the assizes and juries before any justices or bailiffs." 21 SS 158.

81. F. W. Maitland, ed., *Select Pleas in Manorial Courts (Reigns of Henry III and Edward I)* (London: B. Quaritch, 1888), 2 SS; see, e.g., cases at 39, 88, 125. Maitland also includes cases decided by juries of "merchants and neighbors" at the Abbot of Ramsey's Court at the Fair of St. Ives. Ibid. at 141, 143, 144, 154.

82. Sayles, ed., *Select Cases (Vol. I), supra* n. 18, at 120, 128 (1283), Coram Rege Roll 79.

83. Ibid.

Notes for Chapter 7

1. *The Case of Libel, The King v. John Lambert and Others, Printer and Proprietors of the Morning Chronicle*, 2d ed. (London, 1794), 16. A trial at bar was a trial conducted in London before all of the judges of a particular court, contrasted with a trial at *nisi prius* conducted before a single judge in the country on assize or at special sittings in London and Westminster.

2. The special jury was used on the criminal side for misdemeanors, especially in seditious libel cases (see chapter 8, n. 67), but civil usage was much more frequent than criminal usage by the mid-1700s.

3. This chapter does not address the "special verdict." For a discussion of the special verdict, see William Blackstone, *Commentaries on the Laws of England*, 4 vols. (Oxford, 1765–69), 3:377–78 (1768). Except in the loose sense that a special verdict might be requested as a way of getting a meaningful jury response to complicated facts, the concepts of special verdict and special jury are unrelated.

4. Many of the standard works on the history of the jury contain useful sketches of the special jury. See, e.g., [Anon.], *The Complete Juryman: Or, a Compendium of the Laws Relating to Jurors* (Dublin, 1774), 69–72, 92–93, 126–28 [hereafter *The Complete Juryman*]; William Forsyth, *History of Trial by Jury* (London, 1852), 173–75; James Kennedy, *A Treatise on the Law and Practice of Juries* (London, 1826), 80–89; Richard R. Phillips, *On the Powers and Duties of Juries, and on the Criminal Laws of England* (London, 1811), 28–38, 66–68; James B. Thayer, *A Preliminary Treatise on Evidence at the Common Law* (Boston, 1898), 94–97, 419, n. 1.

Standard eighteenth- and nineteenth-century practice books contain passages on the special jury, although they do not ordinarily discuss the special jury in historical terms. See, e.g., John F. Archbold, *The Practice of the Court of King's Bench in Personal Actions, and Ejectment*, 2d ed. (London, 1826) (1st ed., 2 vols. London, 1819), 1: 180–91, 203–5; John Impey, *The New Instructor Clericalis*, 4th ed. (London, 1788) (1st ed. London, 1784),

281–82; [Robert Richardson], *The Attorney's Practice in the Court of King's Bench* (London, 1739), 123; B. J. Sellon, *The Practice of the Courts of King's Bench and Common Pleas,* 2 vols. (Dublin, 1793, 1795),1: 442–47, 455–57; John Sheridan, *The Present Practice of the Court of King's Bench* (Dublin, 1792), 261–65; William Tidd, *The Practice of the Courts of King's Bench, and Common Pleas, in Personal Actions, and Ejectment,* 3d Amer. ed. from 9th London ed., 2 vols. (London, 1828; Philadelphia, 1840), 2: 787–94.

Occasional twentieth-century articles have advocated the revival of the special jury, and these pieces contain some historical discussion. See, e.g., R. C. Baker, "In Defense of the 'Blue Ribbon' Jury," *Iowa Law Review* 35 (1950): 409; Jeannette. E Thatcher, "Why Not Use the Special Jury?" *Minnesota Law Review* 31 (1947): 232; see also sources cited in chapter 2, n. 6.

5. The struck-jury procedure was associated early with trials at bar. See text at nn. 185, 206–30.

6. See text at nn. 105–14, *infra.*

7. See n. 68, *infra.*

8. See text at n. 171, *infra.*

9. See chapter 4.

10. An Act for the better Regulation of Juries, 3 Geo. 2, c.25 (1730).

11. See, e.g., Edward Coke, *The First Part of the Institutes of the Lawes of England. Or, a Commentarie upon Littleton,* 2d ed. (London, 1629), § 234, at 155a–56b; William Walwin, *Juries Justified* (London, 1651), 4; E. Waterhous, *Fortescutus Illustratus* (London, 1663), 252, 342.

12. John Hawles, *The Englishman's Right: A Dialogue Between a Barrister at Law and a Juryman* (London, 1680).

13. Ibid. at 39. On the Petition of Right and the Habeas Corpus Act of 1679, see R. J. Sharpe, *The Law of Habeas Corpus,* 2d ed. (Oxford: Oxford University Press, 1989), 13–14, 18–20.

14. On Horne's *Mirror of Justices,* see chapter 6, n. 46. Coke's *Institutes* were dense and forbidding; even Lord Mansfield called Coke a "crabbed author, who has disappointed and disheartened many a tyro." John Holliday, *The Life of William Late Earl of Mansfield* (London, 1797), 89. *Vaughan's Reports* were the case notes of Sir John Vaughan, who was Chief Justice of the Court of Common Pleas, 1668–74. See John W. Wallace, *The Reporters,* 4th ed. (Boston, 1882), 334–37.

15. A Proclamation for Jurors, by James I (Oct. 5, 1607). A copy of this proclamation printed later that year by Robert Barker in London is held in the Rare Book Room of the University of Michigan Law Library.

16. John March, *The Commonwealth's Friend* (London, 1651), 102. According to another tract writer, "In ordinary Cases, the Jurors are of the meanest of Free-holders, both in Understanding, Credit, and Estate; and, for the most part, such as will give the Bailiffs nothing to excuse them." [A. Booth], *Examen Legum Angliae* (London, 1656), 77. The first of Henry Robinson's well-known seven objections to trial by jury was that "There is not a competent number of understanding and fit men to be had in the lesser Divisions of a County, for trial of all Causes upon all occasions." Henry Robinson, *Certain Considerations in Order to a More Speedy, Cheap, and Equal Distribution of Justice Throughout the Nation* (London, 1651), 2 (emphasis omitted). Robinson added in his fourth objection that "Most commonly one or two active & nimble-pated men over-sway all the rest of the Jury, and too often for the worst."

17. See *infra* nn. 37–40 and accompanying text. Consider also Duncombe's allegation about sheriffs' abuses and jury service as a means of sustenance, quoted *infra* text accompanying n. 27.

18. 3 Hen. 8, c.12 (1511–12).

19. Ibid. This statute reenacted an earlier version that had expired, 11 Hen. 7, c.24 (1495). Sixteenth- and seventeenth-century local practice manuals faithfully described the 1512 statute. See, e.g., Michael Dalton, *The Office and Authority of Sheriffs* (London, 1682), 310 (Dalton or the printer mistakenly identified the statute as "33 H. 8. c.12" instead of 3 Hen. 8, c.12 (1511–12)); [Anthony Fitzherbert], *The New Boke of Justices of the Peas,* R. Redman, comp. (London, 1538), fol. 129. Much later the statute was dusted off to illustrate how official sanction historically had been given to jury-packing. See Lysander Spooner, *An Essay On the Trial by Jury* (Boston, 1852), 149.

20. James Cockburn, *A History of English Assizes 1558–1714* (Cambridge: Cambridge University Press, 1972), 112 (footnote omitted).

21. The term "*tales de circumstantibus*" refers to people who are drawn from among the bystanders at the court to fill up a jury in circumstances where insufficient prospective jurors named on the panel have appeared or where the number of jurors has been reduced below twelve by virtue of challenges. See Blackstone, *Commentaries, supra* n. 3, at 3: 364–65. See also text at nn. 256–61, *infra.*

22. Cockburn, *History of English Assizes, supra* n. 20, at 118 (footnotes omitted).

23. John Morrill, *The Cheshire Grand Jury 1625–1659* (Leicester: Leicester University Press, 1976), 19.

24. Ibid.

25. The reference is to legislation requiring jurors to own a specified amount of freehold—probably the four-pound freehold requirement of An Act for the Returning of Sufficient Jurors and for the Better Expedition of Trials, 27 Eliz. 1, c.6 (1584–85). See *infra* Appendix 4.

26. Eight pence was the customary fee earned by a common juror at *nisi prius* at Guildhall for his service during the seventeenth and eighteenth centuries. Jurors at Westminster Hall earned more—one shilling apiece. See, e.g., [Anon.], *The Practick Part of the Law,* 4th ed. (London, 1711), 53–54, appendix.

27. S. E., *Tryals Per Pais* (London, 1665), 72. Later editions were claimed by Giles Duncombe, suggesting that Duncombe authored this book. See, e.g., G. D. [G. Duncombe), *Tryals Per Pais,* 2d ed. (London, 1682). The "S.E." in the first edition refers to Samson Euer, but whether Euer or Duncombe is the original author is unclear. See *British Museum Catalogue of Printed Books* (London: Trustees of British Museum, 1961), 57: 376–77; ibid. at 58: 512 (1960); *Catalogue of the Library of the Law School of Harvard University,* 2 vols. (Cambridge, MA: Harvard Law School, 1909), 1: 581; W. Spilsbury, *Catalogue of Printed Books in the Library of Hon. Society of Lincoln's Inn* (London, 1849), 843; Donald G. Wing, *Short-Title Catalogue of Books Printed In England, Scotland, Ireland, Wales, and British America and of English Books Printed in Other Countries 1641–1700,* rev. 2d ed., 3 vols. (New York: Index Society, 1982), 2: 19. To avoid unnecessary confusion, further citations to the 1665 edition will be designated G. Duncombe, 1665 edition.

28. J. H. Baker, ed., *The Reports of Sir John Spelman (Vol. II)* (London: Selden Society ["SS" hereafter], 1978), 94 SS 107.

29. An Act for the Returning of Sufficient Jurors and for the Better Expedition of Trials, 27 Eliz. 1, c.6 (1584–85).

30. An Act for the Returning of Able and Sufficient Jurors, 16 & 17 Car. 2, c.3, s.1 (1664–65). The quoted language is virtually identical to the preamble of the Elizabethan statute cited *supra* n. 29.

31. An Act for the Returning of Able and Sufficient Jurors, 16 & 17 Car. 2, c.3, s.6 (1664–65).

32. Statute of 4 Will. & M., c.24, s.16 (1692).

33. Statute of 4 Will. & M., c.24, s.8 (1692).

34. See Criminal Justice Act, 1972, c.71, s.25; *Halsbury's Laws of England,* 3d ed., 43 vols. (London: Butterworth's, 1952–64) 42: 774, general note.

35. For example, leasehold worth £20 was declared in 1730 to be the equivalent of a £10 freehold. See An Act for the Better Regulation of Juries, 3 Geo. 2, c.25, s.18 (1730).

36. Although the point is disputed, legal authorities have asserted that even when statutes did not specifically mention freeholding as a qualification for jury duty, common law required some freehold, however small. See Joseph Chitty, *A Practical Treatise on the Criminal Law,* 2 vols. (London, 1816), 1: 502; Coke, *Institutes, supra* n. 11, § 234, at 155b–57a; William Hawkins, *A Treatise on the Pleas of the Crown,* 2 vols. (London, 1721), 2: 415; "Remarks on Lord Russell's Trial," by Sir John Hawles, Solicitor General in the Reign of William III, in T. Howell, ed., *Cobbett's Complete Collection of State Trials and Proceedings for High Treason and Other Crimes and Misdemeanors from the Earliest Period to the Present Time* (hereafter "*State Trials*"), 33 vols. (London, 1809–26) 9: 793, 795 (1683). There are occasional indications that such a freeholding requirement was applied, for example, in city courts, which were exempted from the statutes requiring jurors to be freeholders, and in noncapital criminal trials, but no consistent pattern appears.

37. Baker, ed., *The Reports of Sir John Spelman (Vol. II), supra* n. 28, at 107.

38. Baker cites as an example the statute *Per le Juries infra Civitatem London,* 4 Hen. 8, c.3 (1512), substituting personalty valued at one hundred marks for freehold worth forty shillings for the City of London, a development that Baker terms "a sensible adaptation to the realities of urban life." Ibid.

39. See *supra* n. 29 and accompanying text.

40. I. S. Leadam and J. Baldwin, eds., *Select Cases Before the King's Council (1243–1482)* (Cambridge, MA: Harvard University Press, 1918), 35 SS 10 (Citizens of London v. The Bishop of Bath (1295)) (footnote omitted). See also Frederick Pollock and Frederic W. Maitland, *The History of English Law,* 2d ed., 2 vols. (London, 1898), 2: 631 ("The poorer freeholders groaned under [jury] duty which consumed their time"); G. O. Sayles, ed., *Select Cases in the Court of King's Bench Under Edward III, Vol. V* (London: B. Quaritch, 1958) (plea 28, Mich. 1331), 76 SS 66.

41. See, e.g., Rex v. Fitz-Patrick & Broadway, 3 *State Trials* 419 (K.B. 1631), in which the defendants were brought to the King's Bench at Westminster "where was a jury of sufficient and able Wiltshire men, impannelled to go upon and try them."

42. G. O. Sayles, ed., *Select Cases in the Court of King's Bench Under Edward I (Vol. II)* (London: B. Quaritch, 1938), 57 SS ciii.

43. Ibid. (footnote omitted).

44. For allegations of jury-packing by sheriffs, see *supra* nn. 18–22 and accompanying text.

45. In his study of the Old Bailey Sessions Papers, John Langbein notes the infrequency of challenges and asserts that, "although the vast medieval law of challenge was preserved in the law books of the time [mid-1670s to mid-1730s], this book learning was virtually dead letter in the ordinary courts." John H. Langbein, "The Criminal Trial before the Lawyers," *University of Chicago Law Review* 45 (1978): 263, 275–76 (footnote omitted). For early examples of the law writers who acknowledged the validity of a challenge for want of freehold, see Coke, *Institutes, supra* n. 11, § 234, at 155b–57a; John Fortescue in S. B. Chrimes, ed., *De Laudibus Legum Angliae* (New York: Garland, 1942 [1st ed. London, 1545]), 59.

46. Frederic W. Maitland in L. Alston, ed., Thomas Smith, comp., *De Republica Anglorum* (Cambridge: Cambridge University Press, 1906 [1st ed. London, 1583]), x.

47. Thomas Smith in ibid., 42.

48. Ibid.

49. The forty-shilling requirement originated in the thirteenth century. See *Statutu de illis q' debent poni in Jura' & Assis'* (The Statute of Persons to be Put in Assises and Juries), 21 Edw. 1 (1293). I know of no assessment of the change in the value of forty shillings from 1293 to 1414, although some fluctuation must have occurred.

50. See An Act for the Returning of Sufficient Jurors and for the Better Expedition of Trials, 27 Eliz. 1, c.6 (1584–85).

51. Michael Dalton, *The Office And Authority of Sheriffs* (London, 1625), 201b. Later editors annotated the statement in the text with a citation to Smith's work. See, e.g., Dalton, *Office and Authority of Sheriffs, supra* n. 19, at 318.

52. Waterhous, *Fortescutus Illustratus, supra* n. 11, at 342.

53. Ibid.

54. Some evidence supports these figures. Waterhous buttressed his assertion with many comparisons of wages, rents, commodity prices, and other fundamental components of the cost of living over the previous two centuries. Ibid. Writing in the early eighteenth century, James Astry observed that "in Hen. the Third's Time One Shilling was as much as Forty Shillings now." James Astry, *A General Charge to all Grand Juries, And Other Juries,* 2d ed. (London, 1725) (1st. ed. London, 1703), 7. See also Richard Boote, *An Historical Treatise of an Action or Suit at Law* (London, 1766), 143 n. // ("But quaere, if 20 s. the 13 E. I was not more than 10 l. now?"). Further corroboration can be found in E. H. Phelps Brown and Sheila V. Hopkins, "Wage-rates and Prices: Evidence for Population Pressure in the Sixteenth Century," *Economica* 24 (1957): 289. The authors present in Table 4, ibid. at 306, a composite foodstuff price index for southern England running from 1400 to 1700. Applying the authors' figures to the Waterhous example would yield an increase in prices from 1470 to 1663 of approximately 700%, translating forty shillings of 1470 money into £14 of 1663 money. This is considerably below Waterhous's estimate, but it is a far greater change than the nominal increases in statutory property qualifications for jurors.

55. An Act for the Returning of Sufficient Jurors and for the Better Expedition of Trials, 27 Eliz. 1, c.6 (1584–85).

56. Statute of 4 Will. & M., c.24, s.16 (1692).

57. As an example, a £50 freehold requirement was advanced in an early-eighteenth-century reform pamphlet that ran through numerous editions. See [Anon.], *Proposals Humbly offer'd to the Parliament, for Remedying the Great Charge and Delay of Suits at Law, and in Equity,* 4th ed. (London, 1724), 34.

58. Waterhous, *Fortescutus Illustratus, supra* n. 11, at 252.

59. Coke, *Institutes, supra* n. 11, at § 234, at 155b. Citing "Glanvill lib. 2. c.14." and "Bract[on] fol. 116", Zachary Babington noted that "In ancient time the Jury, as well in Common Pleas as in Pleas of the Crown, were twelve knights." Z. Babington, *Advice to Grand Jurors in Cases of Blood* (London, 1677) (emphasis omitted), 13 n. (o). See Samuel Thorne, ed., *Bracton on the Laws and Customs of England,* 2 vols. (Cambridge, MA: Belknap Press of Harvard University Press, 1968 [1st ed. ca. 1240]), 2: 329 (fol. 116; "oath of the twelve knights chosen to speak the truth in a plea of the crown") (emphasis omitted). In referring to "Common Pleas," Babington referred not to the Court of Common Pleas but to disputes between private individuals. The discussion in Glanvill concerns knights' service on one important type of private dispute—the grand assize. See G. D. G. Hall, ed., *The Treatise on the Laws and Customs of the Realm of England Commonly Called Glanvill* (London: Nelson, 1965 [1st ed. ca. 1188]), 33 (hereafter "Glanvill").

60. See *infra* nn. 90–95 and accompanying text.

61. C. T. Flower, ed., *Introduction to the Curia Regis Rolls, 1199–1230* (London: B. Quaritch, 1944), 62 SS 434. See R. C. van Caenegem, *Royal Writs in England from the*

Conquest to Glanvill (London: B. Quaritch, 1959), 77 SS 86, for a discussion of the various assizes.

62. Doris Stenton, ed., *Pleas Before the King or His Justices 1198–1202 (Vol. I)* (London: B. Quaritch, 1953), 67 SS 93 n.3.

63. See Flower, ed., *Introduction to the Curia Regis Rolls, supra* n. 61, at 435; Doris Stenton, ed., *Rolls of the Justices in Eyre Being the Rolls of Pleas and Assizes for Lincolnshire 1218–9 and Worcestershire 1221* (London: B. Quaritch, 1934), 53 SS lxx; idem., *Rolls of the Justices in Eyre Being the Rolls of Pleas and Assizes for Gloucestershire, Warwickshire and Staffordshire, 1221, 1222* (London: B. Quaritch, 1940), 59 SS lix.

64. The most infamous technique was *peine forte et dure*. Leon Radzinowicz describes this as follows: "A prisoner who upon arraignment 'stood mute,' which meant that he refused to plead so as to evade conviction, might be laid naked on his back in a dark room, while weights of stone or iron were put on his chest. If he continued to maintain silence, he was pressed until he died." Leon Radzinowicz, *A History of English Criminal Law and Its Administration from 1750*, 5 vols. (London: Stevens, 1948–86), 1: 26, n. 82 (1948) (citing A. Andrews, *The Eighteenth Century* [London, 1856], 285–86). This form of torture was not abolished by statute in England until 1772, although it was used infrequently during the eighteenth century. See An Act for the More Effectual Proceeding Against Persons Standing Mute on Their Arraignment for Felony, or Piracy, 12 Geo. 3, c.20 (1772) (*peine forte et dure* eliminated, but willful refusal to plead became equivalent to conviction). In 1827, Parliament adopted the "modern rule," which treated refusal to plead as though it were a plea of not guilty. See An Act for Further Improving the Administration of Justice in Criminal Cases in England, 7 & 8 Geo. 4, c.28, s.2 (1827). For an informative discussion of *peine forte et dure*, see John H. Langbein, *Torture and the Law of Proof*, (Chicago: University of Chicago Press, 1977), 74–77, 184, n. 20.

65. As was noted in chapter 1 (text following n. 27) and chapter 2 (n. 35), the expression "put himself on the country" is a standard reference to trial by jury. See Blackstone, *Commentaries, supra* n. 3, at 3: 349, 352; Pollock and Maitland, *History of English Law, supra* n. 40, at 2: 623.

66. See Stenton, ed., *Gloucestershire Eyre Rolls, supra,* n. 63, at lix; Stenton, ed., *Lincolnshire Eyre Rolls, supra* n. 63, at lxix. Lady Stenton states that "The empanelling of a jury of twenty-four knights was an exceptional measure to secure convictions in what the bench clearly regarded as particularly flagrant cases." *Gloucestershire Eyre Rolls, supra* n. 63, at lx.

67. H. G. Richardson and G. O. Sayles, eds., *Select Cases of Procedure Without Writ Under Henry III* (London: B. Quaritch, 1941), 60 SS clxv. For a description of the case, see ibid. at 122 (entry no. 123).

68. Although not necessarily an exhaustive list, a thoroughly representative selection of cases follows: Rex v. de Berkele, 1 *State Trials* 55, 56 (Parliament 1331) (murder of King Edward II; jury of knights); Rex v. Fisher, ibid. at 395, 399 (Oyer & Terminer [O. & T.] at Westminster 1535) (high treason; jury of knights and esquires); Regina v. Abington, ibid. at 1141, 1143 (O. & T. at Westminster 1586) (high treason; jury of esquires and gentlemen); Regina v. Blunt, ibid. at 1409 (O. & T. at Westminster 1600) (high treason; jury of Aldermen of London and gentlemen); Rex v. Raleigh, 2 *State Trials* 1, 4 (O. & T. at Westminster 1603) (high treason; jury of knights and gentlemen); Rex v. Drewrie, ibid. at 357, 360–61 (Old Bailey [O.B.] 1607) (high treason; a "very sufficient Jury"); Rex v. Turner, ibid. at 929, 931 (King's Bench [K.B.] 1615) (aiding and assisting a murderer; jury of knights, esquires, and freeholders); Rex v. Franklin, ibid. at 947 (K.B. 1615) (murder; jury of esquires and gentlemen); Sindercome's Case, 5 *State Trials* 841, 844 (Upper Bench 1657) (high treason; jury of "gentlemen of worth and quality," separately described as "a

very substantial company of men, most of them being justices of the peace," ibid. at 843 n. *); Rex v. Coleman, 7 *State Trials* 1, 3 (K.B. 1678) (high treason; jury of one baronet and esquires); Rex v. Ireland, ibid. at 79, 81 (O.B. 1678) (high treason; jury of baronets, one knight, esquires, and one gentleman); Rex v. Green, ibid. at 159, 161 (K.B. 1679) (murder; jury of baronets, knights, and esquires); Rex v. Wakeman, ibid. at 591, 595 (O.B. 1679) (high treason; jury of esquires and gentlemen); Rex v. Gascoigne, ibid. at 959, 966 (K.B. 1680) (high treason; jury of one knight and eleven esquires); Rex v. Palmer, ibid. at 1067 (K.B. 1680) (high treason; jury of baronets, esquires, and one gentleman); Rex v. Thwing & Pressicks, ibid. at 1161, 1163 (York assizes 1680) (high treason; jury of one baronet and gentlemen); Rex v. Stapleton, 8 *State Trials* 501, 503 (York assizes 1681) (high treason; jury of knights and esquires); Rex v. Bushby, ibid. at 525, 528 (Derby assizes 1681) (high treason; ten of the twelve jurors designated gentlemen); Rex v. Borosky, 9 *State Trials* 1, 14 (O.B. 1682) (murder; jury of one baronet, esquires, and gentlemen); Rex v. Grey, ibid. at 127 (K.B. 1682) (debauchery; jury of gentlemen); Rex. v. Sidney, ibid. at 817, 823 n. * (K.B. 1683) (high treason; entire panel of eighty-nine names enumerated, all baronets, knights, esquires, or gentlemen); Rex v. Hampden, ibid. at 1053, 1061 (K.B. 1684) (high misdemeanor; jury of one baronet and esquires); Rex v. Rosewell, 10 *State Trials* 147, 157 (K.B. 1684) (high treason; jury of one baronet, knights, and esquires); Mossam v. Ivy, ibid. at 555 (K.B. 1684) (title to tenements; a "special jury of the county of Middlesex" made up of baronets, knights, and esquires); Rex v. Johnson, 11 *State Trials* 1339, 1339–40 (K.B. 1686) (seditious libel; jury of knights and gentlemen); Duke of Norfolk v. Germaine, 12 *State Trials* 927 (K.B. 1692) (trespass on the case for adultery; jury of knights and esquires); Rex v. Anderton, ibid. at 1245 (O.B. 1693) (high treason; jury of gentlemen); Rex v. Charnock, ibid. at 1377, 1379 (O.B. 1696) (high treason; panel called by sheriff of "above eight-score, and consisting of baronets, knights, esquires, and gentlemen"); Regina v. Baynton, 14 *State Trials* 597 (Q.B. 1702) (forcible taking; jury of gentlemen); Regina v. Lindsay, ibid. at 987, 990 (O.B. 1704) (high treason; jury of esquires); Regina v. Dammaree, 15 *State Trials* 521, 548 (O.B. 1710) (high treason; knight and five esquires among the twelve jurors); Rex v. Hendley, ibid. at 1407, 1411 (Rochester assizes 1719) (unlicensed preaching; one baronet and ten esquires among the twelve jurors); Rex v. Francklin, 17 *State Trials* 625 (K.B. 1731) (seditious libel; jury of esquires); Craig v. Earl of Anglesea, ibid. at 1139 n. * (Ire. Ex. 1743) (ejectment; "the jury (most of them) gentlemen of the greatest property in Ireland, and almost all members of parliament").

It does not necessarily follow, of course, that merely because jurors are designated "knights, esquires, or gentlemen," they were in fact men of quality or of substantial property. There may have been considerable looseness in the use of the terms, especially "esquires" and "gentlemen." See, e.g., Rex v. Gascoigne, 7 *State Trials* 959, 966 (K.B. 1680) (high treason), where the jury consisted of one knight and eleven esquires despite the fact that "the best gentlemen stay at home." (On this case, see also text at n. 133, *infra.*) Nonetheless, most of the cases reported in *State Trials* were sufficiently consequential to allow weight to be given to the designations of juror quality.

69. This was Lord Chief Justice Jeffreys, who never hesitated to speak his mind. He has been described as "this very worst judge that ever disgraced Westminster Hall." Edward Foss, *Biographia Juridica* (London, 1870), 369 (quoting Justice Foster). Foss called "truly disgusting" Jeffreys' "brutality in the examination of the witnesses in Lady Lisle's case, the blasphemy of his imprecations, his unjust insinuations against the unfortunate prisoner in his summing up, the ferocious anxiety he evinced for her conviction, and the threats to the jury by which he enforced it." Ibid. at 372.

70. Rex v. Lisle, 11 *State Trials* 297, 311 (O. & T. at Winchester 1685).

71. Regina v. Udall, 1 *State Trials* 1271, 1277 (Croydon assizes 1590). See also the 1303

Year Book case discussed by Sir James Stephen, in which a defendant unsuccessfully protested "that he was a knight, and his jurors were not his equals, not being knights." James Stephen, *A History of the Criminal Law of England,* 3 vols. (London, 1883), 1: 261.

72. Rex v. Acton, 17 *State Trials* 511 (Surrey assizes 1729).

73. Ibid. Acton was the deputy keeper of the Marshalsea Prison. The crown prosecuted Acton for the alleged murders of four prisoners. Acton was found not guilty in each case. Rex v. Acton, ibid. at 545, 562 (Surrey assizes 1729); Rex v. Acton, ibid. at 525, 544 (Surrey assizes 1729); Rex v. Acton, ibid. at 511, 524 (Surrey assizes 1729); Rex v. Acton, ibid. at 461, 510 (Surrey assizes 1729).

74. Presumably, the different panel sought by the solicitor for the crown.

75. Rex v. Acton, 17 *State Trials* at 511.

76. Rex v. Gascoigne, 7 *State Trials* 959, 963 (K.B. 1680).

77. Ibid.

78. Ibid. at 966.

79. Ibid. The Attorney General was Sir Creswell Levinz, who later became a judge of the Court of Common Pleas, where he was "respected for his legal knowledge and upright conduct." Foss, *Biographia Juridica, supra* n. 69, at 406.

80. In civil cases, the regular jury panel consisted of twenty-four names. See Dalton, *Office and Authority of Sheriffs, supra* n. 51, at 316. But because of the large number of potential challenges, much larger panels were returned in criminal cases. See, e.g., Rex v. Charnock, 12 *State Trials* 1377, 1390 (O.B. 1696) (defendants exercised thirty-three challenges before jury impaneled); Rex v. Sidney, 9 *State Trials* 817, 823 n. * (K.B. 1683) (eighty-nine-man panel).

81. This attitude finds support across several centuries. Defending himself against a libel charge, John Horne cast many aspersions on special-jury practice, including:

> The best men and the worst men are sure to attend upon a special jury where the crown is concerned; the best men, from a nice sense of their duty; the worst men, from a sense of their interest. The best men are known by the Solicitor of the Treasury: such an one cannot be in above one or two verdicts; he tries no more causes for the crown. There is a good sort of a man, who is indeed the most proper to try all this kind of causes; an impartial, moderate, prudent man, who meddles with no opinions. That man will not attend; for why should he get into a scrape? He need not attend; he is sure not to be censured; why should he attend? The consequence follows, that frequently only four or five men attend, and those such as particularly ought not to attend in a crown cause.

Rex v. Horne, 20 *State Trials* 651, 691–92 (K.B. 1777).

82. Cockburn notes one report that a conviction at the Somerset assizes in 1615 was ensured "by drafting seven knights, all apparently local magistrates, to serve on the petty jury." Cockburn, *History of English Assizes, supra* n. 20, at 115 (footnote omitted).

83. There is evidence, however, that, in the sixteenth and seventeenth centuries, grand juries tended to be made up of respected local freeholders and not necessarily the most prominent citizens within the county. See *infra,* text accompanying nn. 113–14.

84. For example, in Rex v. James, 6 *State Trials* 67 (K.B. 1661), a report of the trial written by James's friends states that "John James received a letter from a person of note, to advertise him that there was such a jury of life and death impannelled to proceed upon him, as had not been for many years before, being all picked men, and most of them knights and gentlemen; and that if he did not except against them, or most of the chief of them, he was a dead man." Ibid. at 75–76.

85. Cockburn asserts that "From the 1640s onwards assizes increasingly came to resemble a political forum in which judges and local factions lobbied for support and competed

openly for control of the grand jury" and that "In this environment jury packing became a standard political tool." Cockburn, *History of English Assizes, supra* n. 20, at 116 (footnote omitted).

86. For representative examples, see Regina v. Tutchin, 14 *State Trials* 1095, 1099 (Guildhall 1704); Rex. v. Lewis, 7 *State Trials* 249, 249–50 (Monmouth assizes 1679); The Trials of Twenty-Nine Regicides, 5 *State Trials* 947, 985 n. * (O.B. 1660); Rex v. Penruddock, ibid. at 767, 773 (O. & T. Exon Castle 1655); Regina v. Throckmorton, 1 *State Trials* 869, 871 (Guildhall 1554); Astry, *A General Charge, supra* n. 54, at 27; [Booth], *Examen Legum Angliae, supra* n. 16, at 77; W. P. Baildon, ed., *Select Cases in the Court of Chancery (1364–1471)* (London: B. Quaritch, 1896), 10 SS 21 (entry no. 19); Spooner, *Trial By Jury, supra* n. 19, at 148–49; M. D. Legge & William Holdsworth, eds., *Year Book 10 Edward II (1316–17)* (London: B. Quaritch, 1934), 52 SS 152 (entry 56, Anon., 1316); *Remarks of Sir John Hawles, Solicitor General to William III on the Trials of Fitzharris et al,* 8 *State Trials* 425, 435–36 (1681).

87. The best-known category hardly requires mention—trials of peers. *Magna Carta* secured to every free man the right not to be deprived of liberty or property "but by the lawful Judgment of his Peers." 9 Hen. 3, c.29 (1225). This principle was already in place under Henry I, see Francis B. Palmer, *Peerage Law in England* (London: Stevens, 1907), 146; Pollock and Maitland, *History of English Law, supra* n. 40, at 1: 409, but it did not necessarily guarantee to earls and barons trial by a jury of earls and barons since the king's judges also could be viewed as peers, ibid. at 409–10. Bracton, however, pointed out that in cases of high treason and felony, the king was the prosecutor, and a baron or earl should not be judged by the king's own representatives, his justices. Thorne, ed., *Bracton on The Laws And Customs of England, supra* n. 59, at 2: 337. In this way, trial by other barons and earls came to be established for these cases. Pollock and Maitland, *History of English Law, supra* n. 40, at 1: 410.

88. "A grand assize is composed of twelve lawful knights of the district in which the disputed tenement lies, who have been chosen in the presence of the justices by four knights, who have been chosen by the sheriff." Pollock and Maitland, *History of English Law, supra* n. 40, at 2: 621 (footnote omitted). For additional descriptions of the grand assize, see William Holdsworth, *A History of English Law,* 17 vols. (London: Methuen: Sweet and Maxwell, 1903–72), 1: 327–29 (7th ed., 1956); W. F. Finlason, ed., *Reeves' History of the English Law,* 5 vols. (Philadelphia, 1880), 1: 394–401.

89. Henry II created the grand assize and made it available to a tenant-defendant sued under a writ of right. See William Dugdale, *Origines Juridiciales* (London, 1666), 73; Pollock and Maitland, *History of English Law, supra* n. 40, at 1: 147. See generally M.J. Russell, "Trial by Battle and the Writ of Right," *Journal of Legal History* 1(1980): 111.

90. Flower, ed., *Curia Regis Rolls, supra* n. 61, at 130. Flower was speaking of the early part of the thirteenth century; thus, the property qualification of the Statute of Westminster II, 13 Edw. 1, c.38 (1285), had not yet become a requirement for common jurors in the possessory assizes.

91. Pollock and Maitland, *History of English Law, supra* n. 40, at 2: 621 n. 1. See *supra* n. 88.

92. Glanvill, *supra* n. 59, at 32. In Glanvill, it is recommended that six or more knights be summoned for safety, and in general it is urged that "it is far better to rely on the discretion of the court than to insist on the settled law and custom of the court." Ibid. Later writers adopted this passage from Glanvill. See, e.g., Dugdale, *Origines Juridiciales, supra* n. 89, at 73.

93. William Hughes, *The Commentaries Upon Original Writs* (London, 1655), 67.

94. Ibid. That is, by or with the consent of the parties.

95. Ibid.

96. Holdsworth, *A History of English Law, supra* n. 88, at 1: 329. The statute abolishing real actions eliminated the grand assize. An Act for the Limitation of Actions and Suits Relating to Real Property, and for Simplifying the Remedies for Trying the Rights Thereto, 3 & 4 Will. 4, c.27, s.36 (1833).

97. T. F. T. Plucknett, *A Concise History of the Common Law* (Boston: Little, Brown, 1956), 131.

98. Holdsworth, *A History of English Law, supra* n. 88, at 1: 341.

99. It is not necessary for my purposes to trace the history of the writ or its scope. Suffice it to say that the writ was largely obsolete by the late sixteenth century, and by the mid-eighteenth century Lord Mansfield described it as "a mere sound." Bright v. Eynon, 1 Burr. 390, 393, 97 Eng. Rep. 365, 366 (K.B. 1757). The writ was formally abolished in 1825. See An Act for Consolidating and Amending the Laws Relative to Jurors and Juries, 6 Geo. 4, c.50, s.60 (1825). See generally Holdsworth, *A History of English Law, supra* n. 88, at 1: 337. The writ was never applicable to criminal actions, and authorities differ about the types of civil actions to which the writ attached. See Glanvill, *supra* n. 59, at 36, n.1; Holdsworth, *A History of English Law, supra* n. 88, at 1: 337; Richardson and Sayles, eds., *Select Cases of Procedure Without Writ Under Henry III, supra* n. 67, at lxxxvii–lxxxix.

100. Fortescue, *De Laudibus Legum Angliae, supra* n. 45, at 61. In early cases, attaint jurors were knights. For an example of a distringas of twenty-four knights in an attaint, see Richard Brownlow, *Writs Judiciall* (London, 1653), 30. William Sheppard, however, described the attaint jurors merely as "twenty four sufficient Gentlemen of the Countrey." William Sheppard, *An Epitome of All the Common & Statute Laws of this Nation, Now in Force* (London, 1656), 121. This is corroborated by Hughes's statement that "the Writ of Attaint is 24 Milites [knights], and yet if the Return be Generosos [gentlemen], it is good." Hughes, *The Commentaries, supra* n. 93, at 67.

101. Statute of 15 Hen. 6, c.5 (1436–37). Three years later, Parliament enacted a special rule for Kent, allowing a £20 leasehold or nonfreehold to qualify. Statute of 18 Hen. 6, c.2 (1439).

102. Statute of 15 Hen. 6, c.5 (1436–37).

103. An Act Against Perjury, 11 Hen. 7, c.21, s.1 (1495).

104. As of 1531, an attaint juror was qualified by freehold worth twenty marks per year for cases that involved neither a capital offense nor less than £40 in dispute. See An Act Concerning Perjury & Punishment of Untrue Verdicts, 23 Hen. 8, c.3, s.1(o) (1531–32). For disputes concerning amounts in controversy less than £40, the qualification was freehold worth five marks per year or personalty worth one hundred marks. Ibid. at s.3. The old (higher) standard remained in effect for capital offenses. In 1545, four hundred marks personalty were made equivalent to twenty marks freehold for jurors serving in the royal courts while sitting in London. An Act That Such as Have Goods to CCCC Marks May Pass in Attaints, 37 Hen. 8, c.5 (1545).

105. [Anon.], *A Guide to English Juries* (London, 1682), 143.

106. [Anon.], *The Office of the Clerk of the Assize* (London, 1682) (1st ed. London 1660), 30.

107. Babington, *Advice to Grand Jurors, supra* n. 59, at 5 (emphasis in original). See also Astry, *A General Charge, supra* n. 54, at 5 (echoing Babington's observation); [John. Hawles], *The Grand-jury-man's Oath and Office Explained* (London, 1680), 2 (describing grand jurors as men who "ought to be Persons of more than ordinary Account, Estates, Understanding"); [John Somers], *The Security of English-mens Lives* (London, 1681), 14

(describing grand jurors as "of the most honest, and most sufficient for Knowledge, and Ability of Mind and Estate").

108. 6 *State Trials* 879 (O.B. 1668).

109. Ibid.

110. If the grand jury found the evidence insufficient to indict, the accepted practice of the time was to return the bill of indictment marked "ignoramus," meaning "we know nothing of it." Chitty, *A Practical Treatise on The Criminal Law, supra* n. 36, at 1: 324.

111. Rex v. Shaftesbury, 8 *State Trials* 759 (O.B. 1681).

112. G. Burnet, *Bishop Burnet's History of His Own Time,* 2 vols. (London, 1724–34), 1: 508.

113. Cockburn, *History of English Assizes, supra* n. 20, at 112–13 (footnotes omitted).

114. See Morrill, *The Cheshire Grand Jury, supra* n. 23, at 18–19; Cynthia Herrup, *The Common Peace: Participation and the Criminal Law in Seventeenth-Century England* (Cambridge: Cambridge University Press, 1987), 97.

115. See chapter 8, text at nn. 10–64.

116. Thayer, *A Preliminary Treatise, supra* n. 4, at 94.

117. *Articuli super Cartas* (Articles upon the Charters), 28 Edw. 1, c.9 (1300).

118. Statute of 42 Edw. 3, c.11 (1368).

119. See Blackstone, *Commentaries, supra* n. 3, at 3: 360; Coke, *Institutes, supra* n. 11, § 234, at 157a.

120. According to Sir Thomas Smith, shires were at first divided into geographical units each containing one hundred towns and villages, and these divisions continued to be called hundreds even if the number of towns and villages grew smaller. Alternatively, the term "hundred" may have described an area that could supply for the King's wars "an hundred able men." Smith, *De Republica Anglorum, supra* n. 47, at 81.

121. Dalton, *Office And Authority of Sheriffs, supra* n. 51, at 315.

122. Coke, *Institutes, supra* n. 11, § 234, at 157a.

123. An Act Concerning the Appearance of Jurors in the Nisi Prius, 35 Hen. 8, c.6 (1543–44).

124. Ibid. at s.1.

125. An Act for the Returning of Sufficient Jurors and for the Better Expedition of Trials, 27 Eliz. 1, c.6, s.5 (1584–85).

126. An Act for the Amendment of the Law and the Better Advancement of Justice, 4 & 5 Anne, c.3, s.6 (1705) (citing "great Delays . . . by reason of Challenges to the Arrays of Panels of Jurors and to the Polls for Default of Hundredors").

127. Rex v. Kiffin, 3 Keb. 740, 84 Eng. Rep. 984 (K.B. 1677); Mich. 1649 Banc. sup., Style 233, 82 Eng. Rep. 672 (Upper Bench 1650).

128. Attorney General v. Pickering, Hardres 228, 145 Eng. Rep. 465, 466 (Ex. 1662).

129. 2 Ld. Raym. 1364, 92 Eng. Rep. 389 (K.B. 1724), also reported at 8 Mod. 245, 88 Eng. Rep. 175 (K.B. 1724); 1 Str. 593, 93 Eng. Rep. 720 (K.B. 1724).

130. 2 Ld. Raym. at 1366, 92 Eng. Rep. at 390. Counsel for Burridge cited the practice in Common Pleas to issue a rule for a special jury only after the parties had agreed not to challenge for want of hundredors, arguing that, by negative inference, the Common Pleas admitted a right in the parties to challenge whenever that right had not been expressly waived. Ibid. at 1365, 389. The King's Bench rejected this theory, expressing annoyance at the defendant's challenge as "a concerted contrivance, only to put off the trial." Ibid. at 1366, 390. One report recited that the defendant had advanced this challenge "with an air of insolence" and that the court "was of the opinion, that the defendant was guilty of a premeditated contempt." 8 Mod. at 246–47, 88 Eng. Rep. at 176. Strange reported the

court's blunt response to the defendant's challenge as: "This is a plain contempt." 1 Str. at 593, 93 Eng. Rep. at 720.

131. Trials *de medietate linguae* were trials "of the half tongue," or trials in which one party was an alien whose native language was not English. The statutory property qualifications for jurors were not applicable to alien jurors who served in such cases, because aliens would not be freeholders. See statute of 8 Hen. 6, c.29 (1429); [Anon.], *The Complete Juryman, supra* n. 4, at 146–47.

132. Thayer, *A Preliminary Treatise, supra* n. 4, at 94, n. 4.

133. Rex v. Gascoigne, 7 *State Trials* 959, 963 (K.B. 1680); see *supra,* text accompanying nn. 76–77.

134. Statute of 28 Edw. 3, c.13 (1354) (brackets are contained in *Statutes of The Realm,* 12 vols. (London, 1810–22) at 1: 348 (1816), where compilers direct readers to omit bracketed words, ibid. at n. 10). For representative early cases of such trials, see G. O. Sayles, ed., *Select Cases in the Court of King's Bench (Vol. VII)* (London: B. Quaritch, 1971) (plea 46, Hil. 1397), 88 SS 90; Mary Hemmant, ed., *Select Cases in The Exchequer Chamber Before All The Justices of England (Vol. II), 1461–1501* (London: B. Quaritch, 1945) (entry 29, Lombards v. Taillour, Pasch. 1485), 64 SS 96, 100. The form of the *venire facias* in use during the early seventeenth century is shown in Brownlow, *Writs Judiciall, supra* nn. 100, at 155.

135. One year earlier, Parliament had enacted a series of provisions applying aspects of the law merchant to staple towns, including the *medietate linguae* principle. See *Ordinacio Stapularum* (The Ordinance of the Staples), 27 Edw. 3, Stat. 2, c.8 (1353). Forsyth pointed out that the commonly held view that the origin of trial *de medietate* dates to the reign of Edward III is mistaken; evidence of the concept exists in a charter of Edward I. Forsyth, *History of Trial by Jury, supra* n. 4, at 228. Forsyth was referring to the *Carta Mercatoria* of Edward I, discussed in Pollock and Maitland, *History of English Law, supra* n. 40, at 2: 624, n. 3; see *infra* n. 163 and accompanying text. Charles Gross indicates that trial *de medietate* was followed as well in the temporary piepowder courts associated with trade fairs. Charles Gross, "The Court of Piepowder," *Quarterly Journal of Economics* 20 (1996): 231, 243.

136. Charles Gross, ed., *Select Cases Concerning the Law Merchant (Vol. I), Local Courts, 1270–1638* (London: B. Quaritch, 1908), 23 SS xxvii; see Thayer, *A Preliminary Treatise, supra* n. 4, at 94, n. 4.

137. Hubert Hall, ed., *Select Cases Concerning the Law Merchant (Vol. II), Central Courts, including Assizes, 1239–1633* (London: B. Quaritch, 1929), 46 SS xx.

138. J. M. Rigg, ed., *Select Pleas, Starrs, and Other Records from the Rolls of the Exchequer of the Jews (1220–1284)* (London: B. Quaritch, 1901), 15 SS .

139. Ibid. at xxiii. For examples of this procedural right, see Articles Touching the Jewry, ibid. appendix V, at lxi, and various cases, ibid. at 63, 64, 78, 79, 83, 84, 103, 104, 116.

140. Mary Bateson, ed., *Borough Customs (Vol. I)* (London: B. Quaritch, 1904), 18 SS 10.

141. Ibid. at 10, n. 3; Dugdale, *Origines Juridiciales, supra* n. 89, at 64. Even before An Act for an Union of the Two Kingdoms of England and Scotland, 6 Anne, c.11 (1706), Scotsmen were not considered aliens. See [Anon.], *The Complete Juryman, supra* n. 4, at 145–46; Hawkins, *Pleas of The Crown, supra* n. 36, at 2: 420. The reason was simple—they "speaketh our language." William Lambard, *Eirenarcha* (London, 1614), 555.

142. Blackstone, *Commentaries, supra* n. 3, at 4: 275.

143. John Mallory, *Quare Impedit* (London, 1737), 169.

144. See, e.g., Richard Burn in John King, ed., *The Justice of the Peace, and Parish Offi-*

cer, 22d ed., 5 vols. (London, 1814), 3: 104; John Herne, *The Pleader* (London, 1657), 462.

145. See Marianne Constable, *The Law of the Other: The Mixed Jury and Changing Conceptions of Citizenship, Law, and Knowledge* (Chicago: University of Chicago Press, 1994).

146. See *supra* text accompanying n. 132.

147. Hall, in describing a mercantile case involving a Lombard plaintiff relying on ledger accounts, states that "it was clearly essential (if justice was not to become a farce) that not only half the jurors, but also some at least of the auditors . . . and of the arbitrators . . . should speak the language that was before them in a written form." Hall, ed., *Select Cases, supra* n. 137, at xx. See Lambard, *Eirenarcha, supra* n. 141, at 554–55.

148. See, e.g., Herne, *Pleader, supra* n. 144, at 462, where the plaintiff alleged that he was an alien born at Antwerp and requested a party jury, half to be aliens born at Antwerp. Five such alien jurors were returned. A sixth foreigner, who was also from Antwerp according to the pleadings, was added as a talesman from the bystanders in court.

149. Ferdinando Pulton, *De Pace Regis et Regni* (London, 1610), 193a.

150. *Ordinacio Stapularum* (The Ordinance of Staples), 27 Edw. 3, Stat. 2 (1353).

151. Ibid.

152. Pulton, *De Pace, supra* n. 149, at 193a.

153. Ibid. See also Giles Duncombe, *Trials Per Pais,* 5th ed. (London, 1718), 195; Hawkins, *Pleas of the Crown, supra* n. 36, at 2: 420.

154. John Lilly, *The Practical Register,* 2 vols. (London, 1719), 2: 125.

155. An Act Concerning Egyptians, 22 Hen. 8, c.10, s.1 (1530–31); An Act for the Punishment of Vagabonds Calling Themselves Egyptians, 5 Eliz. 1, c.20, s.2 (1562–63). For discussion of these statutes, see Hawkins, *A Treatise on the Pleas of the Crown, supra* n. 36, at 2: 420; Pulton, *De Pace, supra* n. 149, at 193a.

156. See An Act Whereby Certain Offences Be Made Treasons; and also for the Government of the Kings and Queens Majesties Issue, 1 & 2 Phil. & M., c.10, s.6 (1554 & 1554–55); [Anon.], *The Complete Juryman, supra* n. 4, at 145.

157. See, e.g., An Act for Preventing Frauds and Regulating Abuses in His Majesties Customs, 14 Car. 2, c.11, s.13 (1662).

158. [Anon.], *The Complete Juryman, supra* n. 4, at 146.

159. Ibid.; Hawkins, *A Treatise on the Pleas of the Crown, supra* n. 36, at 2: 419.

160. Kennedy, *Law and Practice of Juries, supra* n. 4, at 87.

161. See, e.g., Rex v. Borosky, 9 *State Trials* 1 (O.B. 1682). Count Conigsmark, one of the defendants on trial for murder, was an alien. Speaking through an interpreter, he requested a trial *de medietate,* a jury composed of "half foreigners and half English . . . [who were] persons of some quality, as they use to treat persons of his quality, and strangers." Ibid. at 9. Chief Justice Pemberton responded: "There shall be such strangers, tell him." He then addressed the undersheriff: "You have merchants of good account, I suppose, upon this pannel?" The undersheriff replied: "Yes, my Lord, they are all such." Ibid. (Bishop Burnet's comments on Rex v. Hayes, 10 *State Trials* 307 (K.B. 1684)).

162. Henry Finch, *Law: Or, a Discourse Thereof, in Four Books* (London, 1636), 412. In the staple towns, merchants joined judges to form lay tribunals. See William Mitchell, *An Essay on the Early History of the Law Merchant* (New York: B. Franklin, 1904), 72–73.

163. See Pollock and Maitland, *History of English Law, supra* n. 40, at 2: 624 n. 3 (discussing the *Carta Mercatoria*).

164. See, e.g., Gross, ed., *Cases Concerning the Law Merchant, supra* n. 136, at xxvii, 17. The role of the merchants was not limited to the customary medieval jury function of

being witnesses to the facts; often the merchants "declared the law." Mitchell, *Early History of the Law Merchant, supra* n. 162, at 73. In other contexts the merchant jury was closer to common-law traditions. Mitchell refers, for example, to a case in the maritime court in Padstow in which the mayor and burgesses were assisted by "a jury of mariners and merchants." Ibid. (footnote omitted).

165. Matthew Hale, *Treatise of the Admiralty Jurisdiction* (unpublished manuscript), quoted in J. H. Baker, "Ascertainment of Foreign Law: Certification to and by English Courts Prior to 1861," *International and Comparative Law Quarterly* 28 (1979): 141, 144.

166. It should be emphasized again that most of the analysis in this chapter is derived from printed sources, which do not necessarily contain data about jury composition or characteristics. The absence of any but scattered evidence in printed sources about seventeenth-century merchant juries does not prove that they were not frequently used. Original source work from the plea rolls and elsewhere might tell a different or more complete story, but even this is uncertain. For example, in Filks v. Newman, Harvard MS 4055(4), fol. 4 (K.B. 1734), Chief Justice Hardwicke noted that "on Trials at Bar the names of the Jury are never entered on [the] Record and [it] is in no case necessary but where [there] is a Tales, and there 'tis to show how many are of the original pannel and how many [are] of the Tales."

167. William Style, *Regestrum Practicale* (London, 1657).

168. Ibid. at 161 (emphasis deleted).

169. Style 132, 82 Eng. Rep. 587 (Upper Bench 1649).

170. Ibid. at 132, 588.

171. Thayer, *A Preliminary Treatise, supra* n. 4, at 94 & n. 4.

172. Rex v. Twyn, 6 *State Trials* 513 (O.B. 1663).

173. Ibid. at 519.

174. Ibid.

175. Anon., Holt 703, 90 Eng. Rep. 1288 (K.B. 1700).

176. Ibid.

177. Ibid.

178. 88 SS 90, *supra* n. 134, at 47 (plea 18, Pasch. 1330).

179. Ibid. at xx.

180. Ibid. at 83–84 (plea 38, 1336). See also G. O Sayles, ed., *Select Cases in the Court of King's Bench (Vol. VI), Edward II* (London: B. Quaritch, 1965), 82 SS 30–31 (plea 15, Pasch. 1344), reporting the lively case of a man arrested for insisting on walking about Westminster Hall in a full suit of armor. A jury of attorneys and ministers of the court confirmed that the defendant had been spoken to in "coarse and wicked language" by unknown men and that he was genuinely in fear of his life. Ibid. at 31.

181. J. H. Baker, "The Attorneys and Officers of the Common Law in 1480," *Journal of Legal History* 1 (1980): 182, 184.

182. [Anon.], *Praxis Utriusque Banci* (London, 1674), 40–41.

183. [William Bohun], *The Practising Attorney* (London, 1724), 39.

184. 3 Geo. 2, c.25 (1730).

185. Blackstone, *Commentaries, supra* n. 3, at 3: 357–58.

186. Ibid.

187. See, e.g., ibid., at 3: 359 ("challenges to the array . . . may be made upon account of partiality . . . in the sheriff"); Coke, *Institutes, supra* n. 11, § 234, at 156a ("there is a principal cause of challenge . . . if the sheriff . . . be of . . . kindred or affinity to the plaintiff or defendant"); Duncombe, *Trials Per Pais,* 1665 ed., *supra* n. 153, at 29 (if the plaintiff "surmise . . . that the Sheriff is his Cozen," he may pray that the "Venire be directed to the Coroners"); Finch, *Law: Or, a Discourse Thereof, supra* n. 162, at 401 ("Cousinage in

the Sheriff is a good principal challenge to the array"); William Greenwood, *A Practical Demonstration of County-judicatures,* 5th ed. (London, 1675) (1st ed. London, 1654), 21 ("Challenge is said to be, where . . . the Sheriff or Bailiff which make the Panel, is of the Plaintiff's kindred"); Herne, *Pleader, supra* n. 144, at 256–57 ("Challenge for that Sheriff is father to the Wife of the Plaintiff"); John Kitchin, *Jurisdictions* (London, 1651), 180 ("the Plaintiff may quash the array though the Sherif is of consanguinity or affinity of the Defendant"), 587 (if the sheriff is "cozen to the Plaintiff," the defendant "may have his challenge and quash the Jury"); T. Powell, *The Attorneys Academy* (London, 1623), 118 (if either party believes "the Jury to be favourable, and not indifferently returned by the Sheriff," he may challenge); [Anon.], *The Practick Part of The Law* (London, 1654), 30 ("where the Defendant is of kindred to the Sheriff . . . the Plaintiff may pray the Venire Facias directed to the Coroners"); Baker, ed., *Reports of Sir John Spelman, supra* n. 28, at 2: 104 (a party may challenge a jury impaneled by a sheriff who is a party or related to a party); R. Vaughn, *Practica Walliae* (London 1672), 38 (the plaintiff may challenge the array if "there be any kindred, affinity, or alliance between [the defendant] or his Wife; and the Sheriff or his Wife"); J. Wilkinson, *A Treatise Concerning the Office and Authorities of Coroners and Sheriffs* (London, 1657), 377 (plaintiff may challenge the array if the "Sheriff is Cousin" to the defendant).

If the coroner was also suspected of bias, process issued to two electors or elizors, "two whom the Court shall choose and deem fit to return the Jury; And to the return of these [Electors] . . . no challenge will be admitted." Duncombe, *Trials Per Pais,* 1665 ed., *supra* n. 153, at 28. See also Herne, *Pleader, supra* n. 144, at 257 ("coroners challenged for the cause of consanguinity"); Vaughn, *Practica Walliae, supra,* at 39 (the defendant may "put in a challenge to both coroners, if there be cause, and pray process to Elizors").

188. See James Oldham, "The Origins of the Special Jury," *University of Chicago Law Review* 50 (1983): 137, 176.

189. Duncombe, *Trials Per Pais,* 1665 ed., *supra* n. 153, at 73. The chief clerk of King's Bench on the plea side was the Prothonotary. His deputy was the Secondary, who was also called "the Master." William Bohun, *Institutio Legalis,* 3d ed. (London, 1724) (1st ed. London, 1708), 16. On the crown side, the principal officer was the Clerk of the Crown Side, who in turn was attended by a Secondary. See generally [Anon.], *The Clerk's English Tutor,* 2 vols. (London, 1733), 1: 42, 47–48.

190. Style, *Regestrum Practicale, supra* n. 167, at 163.

191. William Style, *Practical Register,* 3d ed. (London, 1694) (1st ed. London, 1657), 288–89. Lilly published, in 1710, a two-volume work entitled *A Continuation of the Practical Register.* In the preface, Lilly states:

> There having come to my Hands a little Book, entitled, Style's Practical Register, wherein I thought were many Things well worth Observation, and some others which wanted some Correction and Amendment . . . I did in the year 1694, make such Alterations, Corrections and Additions thereunto . . . as I though necessary and fit for my own Private Use, without any Intention of making it Public.

John Lilly, *A Continuation of The Practical Register,* 2 vols. (London, 1710), 1: iii–iv. He added that the bookseller who held an interest in Style persuaded him to allow one impression of the 1694 revised version as a trial run, after which Lilly would do a more complete job if the trial succeeded. But the bookseller died, and his executors published several impressions of the 1694 edition "with such Additions as they could get; and what they are, let the World judge." Ibid. at v. The two-volume "continuation" in 1710 was largely a compilation of new and revised material, but, in 1719, Lilly incorporated this material into the 1694 edition of Style and published *The Practical Register* under his own name. The revised passage from the 1694 edition quoted in the text was repeated unchanged in the 1719 edition, ibid. at 2: 123, and therefore seems properly attributable to Lilly as of 1694.

192. 12 *State Trials* 183 (K.B. 1688). The charge was publishing a libel.

193. Ibid. at 247.

194. Ibid. at 242 (Mr. Finch). Heneage Finch was Lord Nottingham's son and a former Solicitor General. See Foss, *Biographia Juridica, supra* n. 69, at 254. Pollexfen, also counsel for the defendants (and later Chief Justice of Common Pleas), acknowledged that it was "customary for the court to ask what is the course of the court in doubtful cases, and to receive the information from the officers of the court on both sides," even though what they reported was not to be taken as "final and conclusive." 12 *State Trials* at 243. Chief Justice Wright stated that the certificate of court practice from Sir Samuel Astry "truly weighs a great deal with me." Ibid. at 255. (According to Holdsworth, Jeffreys had engineered Wright's elevation to the bench, and, before that time, Wright had been "a notoriously incompetent lawyer." Holdsworth, *A History of English Law, supra* n. 88, at 6: 507.)

195. Trial of the Seven Bishops, 12 *State Trials* at 276 (Sir Robert Sawyer).

196. The Attorney General was Sir Thomas Powys. Ibid. at 191.

197. Ibid. at 276.

198. Ibid. (Sir. Robert Sawyer).

199. Ibid.

200. Ibid.

201. Ibid.

202. Ibid.

203. An Act for the Ease of Jurors and Better Regulating of Juries, 7 & 8 Will. 3, c.32, s.8 (1695–96), specified the size and number of the jury panels for civil cases at the York assizes "except only where Special Juries are directed to be returned by Rule of Court."

204. Anon., 1 Salk. 405, 91 Eng. Rep. 352 (K.B. 1696). These rules are discussed *infra* nn. 239–40 and accompanying text.

205. See [Bohun], *Institutio Legalis, supra* n. 189, at 37; [Anon.], *Law Quibbles,* 2d ed. (London, 1726), 76–77; Thomas Wood, *An Institute of The Laws of England,* 4th ed. (London, 1728), 591. Continued attention to the concept was, of course, reflected in updated editions of *Tryals per Pais.* See, e.g., Duncombe, *Trials Per Pais, supra* n. 153, at 84, 90.

206. Blackstone, *Commentaries, supra* n. 3, at 3: 357–58; see *supra* text at n. 185.

207. [Richardson], *The Attorney's Practice, supra* n. 4, at 123. Although Richardson's generalization was too broad when written, the close correspondence between trials at bar and special juries continued into the nineteenth century. Thus Archbold states: "The jury is almost invariably special; and the rule for the special jury, forms a part of the rule for the trial at bar." Archbold, *Practice of the Court of King's Bench, supra* n. 4, at 1: 188.

208. See J. Morgan, *Essays,* 3 vols. (Dublin, 1789), 3: 369–98 (collecting many of the cases).

209. Style, *Regestrum Practicale, supra* n. 167, at 310. Practice books trace this basic formula to the Statute of Westminster II, 13 Edw. 1 (1285). See Philip Burton, *Practice of the Office of Pleas, in the Court of Exchequer,* 2 vols. (London, 1791), 1: 245; Tidd, *Practice of the Courts of King's Bench, supra* n. 4, at 2: 747. Before the Statute of Westminster II, all civil trials were at the bar except those decided in eyre, the procedure for itinerant justices that existed before the circuits of assize. Ibid.

210. Style, *Regestrum Practicale, supra* n. 167, at 310. In the 1670 edition, Style added the caution that "otherwise this Court is not to be troubled with Trial Causes, because the Court is thereby hindered in their proceedings in matters of Law, and not matters of fact."

Ibid. at 510. Neither the 1694 edition, Style, *Practical Register, supra* n. 191, at 513, nor Lilly's 1719 continuation, see Lilly, *The Practical Register, supra* n. 191, at 2: 604, changed this passage.

211. Style, *Regestrum Practicale, supra* n. 167, at 314.

212. Ibid. at 315. By the early 1700s, the court could take up "extraordinary Cases" in any term if necessary to avoid prejudicial delay. Lilly, *The Practical Register, supra* n. 191, at 2: 615. Rules limiting the number of trials at bar pertained to King's Bench; I have located no comparable rules for Common Pleas.

213. Style, *Practical Register, supra* n. 191, at 517.

214. 2 Salk. 648, 91 Eng. Rep. 550 (K.B. 1699).

215. Ibid.

216. Ibid.

217. Harvard NB 163 (unpaginated) (K.B. 1701).

218. Ibid.

219. *Reports of Cases Adjudged Between Trinity Term 13 Anne: & Trinity Term 1 Georgii inclus' in the King's Bench,* Harvard MS 1019 [hereafter *King's Bench Reports, 1714–1715,* Harvard MS 1019], 14 (K.B. 1714).

220. Ibid. This general rule was reiterated as an accepted principle in Wynn v. Middleton, Harvard MS 4055(7), fol. 32 (K.B. 1743).

221. See Mead v. Constable, *King's Bench Reports, 1714–1715*, Harvard MS 1019, at 102 (K.B. 1715).

222. Rex v. Johnson, 1 Str. 644, 93 Eng. Rep. 754 (K.B. 1725).

223. 1 Barn. K.B. 141, 94 Eng. Rep. 98 (K.B. 1728).

224. Ibid. In a *per curiam* ruling in 1762, the King's Bench belatedly noted that the phrase "value or difficulty" in Lord Sandwich's Case, 2 Salk. 648, 91 Eng. Rep. 550 (K.B. 1699), should be changed to value "and" difficulty. (The *per curiam* ruling is shown as a footnote to the report of Lord Sandwich's Case in the fifth ed. of Salkeld, published in 1773 by Serjeant George Wilson.)

225. Barnes 447, 94 Eng. Rep. 997 (C.P. 1741).

226. Ibid.

227. Ibid. William Tidd remarked in the 1820s that "the courts are extremely unwilling to grant a trial at bar, except in cases where it appears to be absolutely necessary." Tidd, *Practice of the Courts of King's Bench, supra* n. 4, at 2: 749.

228. See Castell v. Bambridge, 2 Str. 854, 856, 93 Eng. Rep. 894, 895 (K.B. 1730); Anon., 2 Salk. 644, 91 Eng. Rep. 543 (K.B. 1693). Style's version of the limitation referred to disputes over houses within the City of London and was based on a 1648 King's Bench rule. Style, *Regestrum Practicale, supra* n. 167, at 313. The general limitation in the London charter was added to the 1694 edition. See Style, *Regestrum Practicale, supra* n. 191, at 517.

229. Ibid. at 317 (emphasis in original). Later, the various geographic limitations were said to be waivable by the parties in a case otherwise appropriate for trial at bar. Archbold, *Practice of the Court of King's Bench, supra* n. 4, at 1: 187.

230. Edward Coke, *The Fourth Part of the Institutes of the Laws of England: Concerning the Jurisdiction of Courts* (London, 1644), 212. See Rex v. Amery, 1 T.R. 363, 99 Eng. Rep. 1141 (K.B. 1786).

231. Jones T. 222, 84 Eng. Rep. 1227 (K.B. 1682).

232. Ibid. at 222, 1227–28.

233. Ibid. at 222, 1228.

234. This rationale is articulated in Rex v. Duncombe, 12 Mod. 224, 88 Eng. Rep. 1278 (K.B. 1698). See also Charles Viner, *A General Abridgement of Law and Equity,* 2d ed., 24

vols. (London, 1793), 21: 301 (description of a manuscript report of Rex v. Makartney (K.B. 1716)). For a description of the criminal defendant's peremptory challenges, see Blackstone, *Commentaries, supra* n. 3, at 4: 347.

235. For representative cases shown as trials at bar, see Philips v. Crab, 12 Mod. 94, 88 Eng. Rep. 1187 (K.B. 1696); Mr. Farington's Case, Jones T. 222, 84 Eng. Rep. 1227 (K.B. 1682); Rex v. Kiffin, 3 Keb. 740, 84 Eng. Rep. 984 (K.B. 1677). For representative cases silent about whether the trial was at bar, see Rex v. Duncombe, 12 Mod. 224, 88 Eng. Rep. 1278 (K.B. 1698); Anon., 1 Salk. 405, 91 Eng. Rep. 352 (K.B. 1696).

236. Style, *Practical Register, supra* n. 191, at 286.

237. 8 Mod. 245, 88 Eng. Rep. 175 (K.B. 1724).

238. Ibid. at 247, 177. See also Regina v. Banks, 2 Ld. Raym. 1082, 92 Eng. Rep. 217 (Q.B. 1704) (special jury granted for trial on assize after complex procedural dispute between prosecutor requesting a trial at bar and defendant seeking to have the case heard at *nisi prius*).

239. Anon., 1 Salk. 405, 91 Eng. Rep. 352 (K.B. 1696). The events leading to the issuance of the rule are described in Lilly, *The Practical Register, supra* n. 191, at 2: 25–26. The case was to be tried at bar, but the defendant's attorney did not appear to participate in striking the jury. The court was irked, stating that if the rule for a trial at bar had been obtained by consent of counsel for both sides, then defendant's attorney was in contempt for not attending the striking of the jury, or at least "it was the Defendant's Attorney's Fault, and a Trick in him." Ibid. at 25. The court, however, grudgingly accepted defendant's attorney's excuse of having been too busy to attend and allowed the striking of a new jury, issuing at the same time the general rule to govern future cases. Ibid. at 25–26. Lilly does not identify the case, but a manuscript report shows that the case was Earl of Bath v. Earl of Montague (K.B. 1696). See James Wright, *A Collection of Certain Cases and Proceedings at Law, From the Death of King Charles 2, to the End of the Reign of King William* 3, Harvard MS 1071, fol. 50. Interestingly, Wright notes elsewhere that an earlier phase of the dispute between the parties was "so very long and tedious" that it kept the court and jury sitting for an uninterrupted 24 hours, during which "refreshments were brought into Court to the Jury, once or twice." Ibid., fol. 39.

240. Anon., 1 Salk. 405, 91 Eng. Rep. 352 (K.B. 1696).

241. For a sampling of conflicting views of the judges in both reported and unreported cases from the late 1600s and early 1700s, see Oldham, "Origins of the Special Jury," *supra* n. 188, at 197–200.

242. "It . . . has always been the course of the court, that when either party will suggest any special matter about awarding the venire out of the common course, a copy must be given to the opposite party, and they must have a reasonable time to consider it." Brocas v. Civit' London, 1 Str. 235, 93 Eng. Rep. 493 (K.B. 1719).

243. This was not likely to be done in a crown case if the attorney general withheld his consent. See Rex v. Chipping-Norton, 1 Barnard. K.B. 41, 94 Eng. Rep. 29 (K.B. 1727). But, in Pyle v. Grant, 1 Barn. K.B. 260, 94 Eng. Rep. 177 (K.B. 1729), the court ordered a special jury as an automatic part of a trial at bar, despite the appellant's protest that he was too poor to bear the expense of a trial at bar. See also Wilks v. Eames, Andr. 51, 52, 95 Eng. Rep. 293, 294 (K.B. 1737), where the court stated that "though it was not usual, before the said act [An Act for the Better Regulation of Juries, 3 Geo. 2, c.25 (1730)], to grant special juries without consent, yet in some instances, and for special causes, it was and might be done."

244. Anon., *Hollinshed's Reports*, Harvard MS 1142, at 190 (Q.B. 1710).

245. 3 Geo. 2, c.25, s.15, quoted *supra,* text following n. 184.

246. Wilks v. Eames, Andr. at 52, 95 Eng. Rep. at 294.

247. An Act for the Better Regulation of Juries, 3 Geo. 2, c.25, s.16 (1730).

248. See *Lists of the Officers and Their Deputies, Belonging to the Several Courts in Westminster-hall, and Elsewhere* (London, 1731) (presented to the House of Commons pursuant to an order of Mar. 4, 1730), 66, where an entry for a proceeding in the Exchequer indicated that "for striking a special Jury . . . half was paid by the Plaintiff, and half by the Defendant, before the Act of Parliament [An Act for the Better Regulation of Juries, 3 Geo. 2, c.25 (1730)], to the Master."

249. [Anon.], *An Exact Table of Fees, of All the Courts at Westminster* (London, 1694), 53. See also [Anon.], *The Practick Part of the Law, supra* n. 26, at 38 appendix (noting that no authentic tables of ancient fees on the plea side of King's Bench were known to exist, such tables reputedly having been burned in the great fire of London). The fees given, ibid. at 39 appendix, appear to be identical to those in the 1694 table; they were compiled from responses received to inquiries sent to the "several Offices and Clerks" of King's Bench. For trials at bar, special fees were due to other officers—for example, the Clerk of the Papers, the Deputy Marshall, the Crier—but these were not incidents of the special jury.

250. Robert Richardson, *The Attorney's Practice in the Court of King's Bench,* 2d ed. (London, 1743), 217.

251. *Lists of the Officers and Their Deputies, supra* n. 248, at 22.

252. Wilks v. Eames, Harvard MS 2050, 2 vols., at 1: 60 (K.B. 1737).

253. Wilks v. Eames, Andr. 51, 52, 95 Eng. Rep. 293, 293–94 (K.B. 1737) (emphasis deleted).

254. Ibid. Indeed Duncombe in his fifth edition, published in 1718, asserted that Middlesex juries "court the Bailiffs to return them, especially to Trials at Bar, where five Pounds a Man is frequent Gratuity, sometimes more." Duncombe, *Trials Per Pais, supra* n. 153, at 218.

255. Wilks v. Eames, Andr. at 53, 95 Eng. Rep. at 294 (Probyn, J.).

256. For useful summaries of the rules pertaining to talesmen, see Chitty, *Treatise on the Criminal Law, supra* n. 36, at 2: 517–21; [Anon.], *The Complete Juryman, supra* n. 4, at 90–99.

257. See also the statute of 4 Will. & M., c.24, ss.18–20 (1692).

258. For an example of a trial put off four times because a full jury was not produced by the original panel and four decem tales (four successive orders for the return of ten new jurors as talesmen), see the pleadings in Regina v. Watson, 2 Ld. Raym. 856, 92 Eng. Rep. 72 (Q.B. 1703), reprinted in George Wilson, *Entries or Pleadings,* 3d ed. (Dublin, 1785), 18–25.

259. See Appendix 4.

260. See [Anon.], *The Complete Juryman, supra* n. 4, at 93. Lilly noted that if a jury was not filled for a trial at bar from the original panel, "the Court will order the Sheriff to return a Decem Tales, which he usually doth of Gentlemen in London having Estates in his County. Pas. 23 Car. B.R." Lilly, *The Practical Register, supra* n. 191, at 2: 357.

261. It is highly improbable that, despite the 1692 requirement, talesmen impaneled *de circumstantibus* in ordinary cases would be freeholders.

262. 1 Barn. K.B. 41, 94 Eng. Rep. 29 (K.B. 1727).

263. Ibid.

264. Tidd, *Practice of the Courts of King's Bench, supra* n. 4, at 72: 87.

265. For more on the writ of inquiry, see chapter 4, text at nn. 23–78.

266. See, e.g., Wilkinson v. Malin, 1 Cr. & M. 237, 238, 149 Eng. Rep. 388, 389 (Ex. 1832) (stating that the granting of a good jury is at the court's discretion); [Anon.], *The Practick Part of the Law, supra* n. 187, at 137.

267. E.g., Anon., 3 Mod. 112, 87 Eng. Rep. 71, 72 (K.B. 1686). Another common form of the writ in English called for twelve "honest and lawful" men. See, e.g., Brownlow, *Writs Judiciall, supra* n. 100, at 50, 64, 66, 68; Daniel Reading, *The English Clerk's Instructor in the Practice of the Court of King's Bench and Common Pleas,* 2 vols. (London, 1733), 1: 119; Tidd, *Practice of the Courts of King's Bench, supra* n. 4, at 1: 573.

268. John Lilly, *A Collection of Modern Entries* (London, 1771), 675–76. By contrast, Lilly's examples of the venires in writs of inquiry specify a jury of "good and lawful" men. Ibid. at 8, 102. Accord, Poole v. Longuevill, 2 Wms. Saund. 282, 286, 85 Eng. Rep. 1063, 1072 (K.B. 1670–71) (venire in writ of inquiry specified a jury of "good and lawful men").

269. See, e.g., John Impey, *The Office of Sheriff* (London, 1786); idem., *The Undersheriff* (London, 1766).

270. Rex v. Smith, 1 Str. 265, 93 Eng. Rep. 513 (K.B. 1720).

271. Vickery v. London, B. & S. Coast Ry., 5 L.R.-C.P. 165, 167 (1870).

272. Tidd, *Practice of the Courts of King's Bench, supra* n. 4, at 2: 787 (citing Rex v. Smith, 1 Str. 265, 93 Eng. Rep. 513 (K.B. 1720)).

273. Later cases suggest that after the 1730 statute, the special jury largely supplanted the good jury except in connection with the writ of inquiry.

274. In Enquest, 1 Keb. 864, 83 Eng. Rep. 1288, (K.B. 1665).

275. Ibid.

276. Pocklington v. Hatton, 8 Mod. 220, 221, 88 Eng. Rep. 158, 159 (K.B. 1724). See also Rex v. Chipping-Norton, 1 Barn. K.B. 41, 94 Eng. Rep. 29 (K.B. 1727)

277. Anon., *Hollinshed's Reports,* Harvard MS 1142, at 291 (Q.B. 1710).

278. Rex v. Burridge, 8 Mod. 229, 88 Eng. Rep. 165 (K.B. 1724).

279. Gilb. Cas. 130, 93 Eng. Rep. 283 (Q.B. 1714).

280. Ibid.

281. Later practices are illuminated somewhat by Vickery v. London, B. & S. Coast Ry., 5 L.R.-C.P. 165 (1870) (indicating that good jurors were usually chosen from the special-jury list).

282. Anon., *King's Bench Reports, 1714–1715,* Harvard MS 1019, at 20. In Dormer v. Jones, *King's Bench Reports, 1714–1715,* Harvard MS 1019, at 87, the court granted a motion for a good jury in Middlesex, "this being upon a Special occasion and otherwise all are presumed good as in London." In Rex v. Makartney (K.B. 1716), however, the unpublished case discussed in *Viner's Abridgement, supra* n. 234, at 21: 301, Chief Justice Parker denied a similar motion, stating that "they are all good juries in Middlesex, and so in all cases of jurors at the bar."

283. Rex v. Smith, 1 Str. 265, 93 Eng. Rep. at 513 (K.B. 1720).

284. Anon., *Hollinshed's Reports,* Harvard MS 1142, at 187 (Eyre, J.).

285. See chapter 8, text at nn. 77–88.

Notes for Chapter 8

1. *The Fullest Reports of the Trial Before a Special Jury, Saturday, June 27, 1816, Lord Geo. T. Beresford against The Earl of Bective, . . . for Crim. Con.* (London, 1816).

2. *Report of the Proceedings Upon an Inquisition of Damages, in a Cause Between the Rev. George Markham, Plaintiff, and John Fawcett, Esq., Defendant, for Criminal Conversation . . . on Tuesday, May 4, 1802, Before Joseph Burchell, Esq., Deputy Sheriff of the County of Middlesex, and a Special Jury* (London, 1802).

3. *Clayton v. Davis, Before Sir J. Wilde and a Special Jury, December 9, 1863* (London, 1863).

4. *Report from the Select Committee on the Juries Bill* (London: House of Commons, 27 June 1870), 7 (testimony of Mr. J. Rayner, Town Clerk of Liverpool).

5. *Report of the Trial of the Cause, "Lawton vs. Tarratt et al.," at the Circuit Court, at the City of St. John, New Brunswick, May 26th to June 13th, 1857, Before His Honor Chief Justice Carter and a Special Jury* (Boston, 1857).

6. The Acts of the General Assembly of Prince Edward Island (1851) 1: 657 [5 Vict., c.6, s.5 (1842)].

7. *The Whole Proceedings on the Trial of an Information . . . against Robert Henshaw, Esq, Custom-Master of Bombay . . . Tried by a Special Jury, in the Court of the Recorder of Bombay, on Tuesday, Nov. 5, 1805, and the Three Following Days* (Edinburgh, 1807).

8. Georgia v Brailsford, 3 Dallas 1 (1794).

9. John Campbell, *Lives of the Chief Justices,* 3 vols. (London, 1849), 2: 407. Fifoot wryly notes that this experience occurred at a time when Lord Campbell "was yet young enough to indulge admiration." C. H. S. Fifoot, *Lord Mansfield* (Oxford: Clarendon Press, 1936), 105.

10. 2 Burr. 1167, 1168, 97 Eng. Rep. 769, 770 (K.B. 1761).

11. See. James Oldham, *The Mansfield Manuscripts and the Growth of English Law in the Eighteenth Century,* 2 vols. (Chapel Hill and London: University of North Carolina Press, 1992), 1: 93–99. Since only about half of Lord Mansfield's trial notes survive, and since he did not invariably record the presence of a special jury in the notes that do survive, the figure of six hundred cases is far below the actual number of cases that were tried by special juries. See text following n. 68, *infra.*

12. 1 Barn. & Ald. 193, 203, 106 Eng. Rep. 71, 75 (K.B. 1817). Parliament later required that special jurors fall within one of three categories: merchant, esquire, or banker. See text at n. 89, *infra.*

13. Corporation of London Records Office, Misc. MS 89.16.

14. *Minutes of the Proceedings of the Court of Common Council* (London, 1817), 210–11.

15. See 3 Geo. 2, c.25 (1730). Special juries were ordered by the court in response to a motion from one party or by the consent of both parties.

16. According to Chitty: "The usual practice is for the solicitor of the applicant to draw up a motion paper for the rule signed by counsel, procure the Master's appointment for the time of naming the jury, and serve copies of both on the adverse party's clerk in court, and at the sheriff's office." Joseph Chitty, *A Practical Treatise on Criminal Law,* 2 vols. (London, 1816), 2: 523. This seems to have been true by 1792. Sheridan wrote, in his practice book issued that year: "If either of the parties wish to have a special jury, a brief is given to counsel for that purpose, which is done on a slip of paper, and signed by him, Fee, 10 shillings and sixpence; this brief is to be carried to the clerk of the rules, who draws up the rule." John Sheridan, *The Present Practice of the Court of King's Bench* (Dublin, 1792), 261, n. 4.

17. Oldham, *The Mansfield Manuscripts, supra* n. 11, at 1: 95.

18. Ibid.

19. Anon., 2 P.Wms. 68, 24 Eng. Rep. 643 (Ch. 1722). The only printed report of Attorney General v. Snow is of a case in Exchequer, noted briefly at Bunb. 96, 145 Eng. Rep. 608 (Ex. 1721), but there is no mention of proceedings in Chancery or of a special-jury order. Other cases where the Court of Chancery specified in its order referring a question to law for a jury trial that the jury should be special include Lord Falmouth v. Innys, Mos. 87, 25 Eng. Rep. 287 (Ch. 1729); Earl of Thanet v. Pattison, Cas. t. Hard. 454, 25 Eng. Rep. 1029 (Ch. 1738).

20. In the nineteenth century, there was much statutory attention to special juries, and,

in an 1841 case, it was argued that one section of the County Juries Act of 1825 (6 Geo. 4, c.50) removed the power of the Court of Chancery to order a special jury. The Master of the Rolls observed that "though the direction for a special jury was thought imperative on the parties, it was only an intimation to the Judge at common law, of the course considered expedient, and that this Court would not feel satisfied with the finding of any other jury than that specified in the order." Fowler v. Wood, reported in n. (1) to Ellis v. Bowman, 13 Beav. 318, 51 Eng. Rep. 122 (M.R. 1851).

21. 1 Cowp. 143, 98 Eng. Rep. 1012 (K.B. 1774), Lofft 631, 98 Eng. Rep. 836 (K.B. 1774).

22. 1 Cowp. at 153, 98 Eng. Rep. at 1017.

23. 2 Burr. 1167, 97 Eng. Rep. 769 (K.B. 1761). See text at n. 10, *supra*. See also Capel Lofft's version of Vallejo (styled "Vallezjo") v. Wheeler, Lofft 631, 640, 98 Eng. Rep. 836, 841 (K.B. 1774), where Mansfield is reported to have remarked, "I should pay great respect to the gentlemen of the special jury who were considerable merchants, the proper judges of a cause of this nature."

24. 2 Str. 1211, 93 Eng. Rep. 1134 (K.B. 1744).

25. Ibid. at 1212, 1135.

26. Thompson v. Williamson, 7 Bligh NS 432, 443–44, 5 Eng. Rep. 833, 837 (H.L. 1831).

27. 11 East 265, 102 Eng. Rep. 1006 (K.B. 1809).

28. Ibid. at 267, 1007.

29. 9 Bing. 19, 131 Eng. Rep. 521 (C.P. 1832).

30. 3 El. & Bl. 48, 118 Eng. Rep. 1058 (Q.B. 1852).

31. Ibid. at 82–83, 1072.

32. Middlewood v. Blakes, 7 T.R. 162, 168, 101 Eng. Rep. 911, 914 (K.B. 1797).

33. Driscol v. Passmore, 1 B. & P. 200, 203, 126 Eng. Rep. 858, 860 (C.P. 1798).

34. Langhorn v. Allnutt, 4 Taunt. 511, 518–19, 128 Eng. Rep. 429, 432 (C.P. 1812).

35. Stewart v. Aberdein, 4 M. & W. 211, 227, 150 Eng. Rep. 1406, 1413 (Ex. 1838).

36. Bonzi v. Stewart, 4 Man. & G. 295, 325–26, 134 Eng. Rep. 121, 133 (C.P. 1842).

37. Malcolm v. Scott, 2 H. & Tw. 440, 443, 47 Eng. Rep. 1755, 1757 (Ch. 1849).

38. Fletcher v. Tayleur, 17 C.B. 21, 28–29, 139 Eng. Rep. 973, 976 (C.P. 1855).

39. Pole v. Cetcovich, 9 C.B. N.S. 430, 440, 142 Eng. Rep. 169, 173 (C.P. 1860).

40. Unreported, but discussed by Lord Kenyon in Burnett v. Kensington, 7 T.R. 210, 222, 101 Eng. Rep. 937, 943 (K.B. 1797).

41. 7 C.B. 164, 137 Eng. Rep. 67 (C.P. 1849).

42. Ibid. at 167, 68.

43. 3 F.& F. 960, 176 Eng. Rep. 437 (Ex. 1863).

44. An interesting variation is shown in Poingdestre v. Royal Exchange, Ry. & Moody 378, 379, 171 Eng. Rep. 1055, 1056 (C.P. 1826), when Serjeant Bosanquet proposed to call merchants and insurers to prove an insurance usage applicable to the facts, but "Best, C.J. interposed and said that it would scarcely be insisted upon by the plaintiff, that witnesses should be called to establish that usage before a special jury of London, every one of whom must be perfectly cognizant of the fact of the usage. The jury assented to this." The verdict, therefore, went for defendants.

45. 4 T.R. 206, 100 Eng. Rep. 976 (K.B. 1791).

46. 2 Camp. 247, 249, 170 Eng. Rep. 1145, 1146 (K.B. 1809).

47. 3 Camp. 51, 170 Eng. Rep. 1303 (K.B. 1811).

48. 4 Camp. 251, 252–53, 171 Eng. Rep. 80, 81 (C.P. 1815).

49. See, for example, Baring v. Vaux, 2 Camp. 541, 543, 170 Eng. Rep. 1245 (K.B. 1810) ("The gentlemen of the special jury said, they were clearly of opinion the ship was

not to be considered as in port when she was captured, and immediately found a verdict for the plaintiff"); Pearce v. Cowie, 4 Camp. 363, 365, 171 Eng. Rep. 116 (K.B. 1814) ("The gentlemen of the special jury corroborated this statement, and observed that many cargoes of cotton from Amelia Island had been allowed to be imported both into London and Liverpool, in neutral vessels of European build"); Levi v. Barnes, Holt 412, 415, 171 Eng. Rep. 288, 289 (C.P. 1816) ("The jury (which was a special jury of merchants) found a verdict for the plaintiffs, and stated that it was their unanimous opinion that the allowance was a gratuity merely"); Friere v. Woodhouse, Holt 572, 574, 171 Eng. Rep. 345, 345–56 (C.P 1817) ("The jury, which was a special jury of merchants, said, that inasmuch as the arrival of the 'Victorioso,' and of the other vessels was noticed in Lloyd's List at the time the insurance was effected, and as these Lists were in the hands of the underwriters, they were of opinion that there was no concealment").

50. 5 Car. & P. 385, 172 Eng. Rep. 1020 (C.P. 1832).

51. Ibid. at 390, 1023.

52. 4 T.R. at 206, 100 Eng. Rep. at 976 (K.B. 1791), *supra* n. 45.

53. Ibid. at 208, 977.

54. 7 Taunt. 278, 129 Eng. Rep. 112 (C.P. 1816).

55. *Supra* text at nn. 48–49.

56. 7 Taunt. at 287, 129 Eng. Rep. at 115.

57. Ibid. at 290, 117.

58. As noted in *Arnould on Marine Insurance,* 2d ed., 1:50–51, quoted in Parry v. Great Ship Company, 4 B. & S. 556, 122 Eng. Rep. 568 (Q.B. 1864).

59. 2 Camp. 537, 170 Eng. Rep. 1243 (K.B. 1810).

60. Ibid. at 539, 1244.

61. See the discussion of Medcalf v. Hall, Appleton v. Sweetapple, and Tindal v. Brown, chapter 3, text at nn. 62–71. Interestingly, in *Medcalf,* Lord Mansfield noted that there was evidence of different customs east and west of Mansion House.

62. Tindal v. Brown, 1 T.R. 167, 169, 99 Eng. Rep. 1033, 1035 (K.B. 1786). See chapter 3, text at n. 71.

63. 2 Str. 1182, 93 Eng. Rep. 1114 (K.B. 1743).

64. Ibid. at 1183, 1115.

65. *Minutes of Evidence, Select Committee on Special and Common Juries* (London, 1868), 47.

66. See text following n. 11, *supra.*

67. Alleged seditious libel could be serious enough to be pursued under a theory of high treason, which would be a capital case. Special juries were not available in such cases, in order not to deprive the prisoner of his thirty-five peremptory challenges. Seditious libel ordinarily, however, was a misdemeanor, and special juries were customary in such cases. See Oldham, *The Mansfield Manuscripts, supra* n. 11, at 1: 807 and libel cases transcribed at 1: 810–62.

68. This is known because many of these cases were sufficiently salacious to make it worthwhile to print reports of the trials in pamphlet form. The pamphlets customarily indicated whether the jury was special or common, and often named the jurors.

69. *Parliamentary Papers,* House of Commons (London, 1854), 53: 507.

70. *Minutes of Evidence, supra* n. 65, at 211.

71. *Report from the Select Committee on Special and Common Juries* (London,1867), 2. John Campbell, in his autobiography, claimed that in the early 1800s, "the Guildhall business was ten times greater than when Lord Mansfield was Chief Justice" since Lord Mansfield "never appointed more than one special jury cause in a day and finishing his paper within a week after term, whereas the sittings now continued from the end of term

for a week after the commencement of the circuits, and eight or ten special jury causes were appointed for a single day." M. S. Hardcastle, ed., *Life of John, Lord Campbell,* 2 vols. (London, 1881), 1: 214–15. As was often true, Campbell exaggerated. Lord Mansfield's notebooks prove that he many times heard more than one special-jury case on a single day, sometimes as many as five to seven. But Lord Campbell is surely correct in the general proposition that the special-jury business had increased significantly by 1807.

72. See text at n. 65, *supra.*

73. See text at and preceding n. 14, *supra.*

74. 7 & 8 Will. 3, c.32, s.8 (1696). See chapter 7, n. 203.

75. 3 Geo. 2, c.25 (1730). See chapter 7, text following n. 184. This provision was expressly made applicable to the counties palatine (Chester, Lancaster and Durham) in 1733. 6 Geo 2, c.37 (1733).

76. 24 Geo. 2, c.18 (1751).

77. For earlier jury-packing complaints, see Rex v. Throckmorton, in T. Howell, ed., *Cobbett's Complete Collection of State Trials and Proceedings for High Treason and Other Crimes and Misdemeanors from the Earliest Period to the Present Time* (hereafter "*State Trials*"), 33 vols. (London, 1809–26) 1: 869, 871 (Sp. Comm. 1554); Rex v. Penruddock, 5 *State Trials* 767, 773 (O. & T. Exon Castle 1655); Rex v. Lewis, 7 *State Trials* 249, 250 (Monmouth Ass. 1679); *Remarks of Sir John Hawles, Solicitor General to William III on the Trials of Fitzharris et al.,* 8 *State Trials* 425, 435 (1681); Rex v. Tutchin, 14 *State Trials* 1095, 1099 (Q.B. 1704).

78. Rex v. Horne, 20 *State Trials* 651, 687 (K.B. 1777).

79. *The Craftsman,* 23 Nov. 1771.

80. Jeremy Bentham, *The Elements of the Art of Packing, as Applied to Special Juries, Particularly in Cases of Libel Law* (London, 1821).

81. Sir Samuel Romilly wrote to Bentham on 31 Jan. 1810 as follows:

> I have read a good deal of "Elements of Packing," and I most sincerely and anxiously entreat you not to publish it,—I have not the least doubt that [Attorney General] Gibbs would prosecute both the author and the printer. . . . [He] would say that not to prosecute such an attack upon the whole administration of justice, would be a dereliction of his duty.

J. Bowring ed., *Bentham's Collected Works,* 11 vols. (New York, 1843), 10: 450–55.

82. Bentham, *Elements of the Art of Packing, supra* n. 80, at 28.

83. Ibid.

84. See n. 76, *supra* and accompanying text.

85. See n. 12, *supra.*

86. T. J. Wooler, *An Appeal to the Citizens of London Against the Alledged Lawful Mode of Packing Special Juries* (London, 1817).

87. The manuscript report is in the Corporation Records Office of the City of London. The quotations are taken from pp. 14–15.

88. 6 Geo. 4, c.50, ss.31–32 (1825). The old method of selection of a special jury from the freeholders book was allowed to continue whenever both parties to a case chose it. 6 Geo. 4, c.30, s.33 (1825). A jury formed in the old manner after the County Juries Act became known as a "special special jury." See testimony of Fredrick Deacon, *Minutes of Evidence, 1867–68 Select Committee on Special Juries,* (London, 1868), 31, 37.

89. 6 Geo. 4, c.50, s.31 (1825).

90. British Library, Add. MS 40,383, fols. 148–49 (7 Apr. 1827). In an earlier draft of this letter, held by the University College Library, University of London, Bentham began more bluntly: "Yes Sir: instead of being *abolished,* (which as far as I can learn is the general wish) the practice of packing Juries has been *established:* established by Act of Parliament:

passed in conformity to the Bill brought in by you." University College London, MS Add. 175, Bentham MSS, UC, Box 11b (Dec. 1826).

91. British Library, Add. MS 40,393, f. 156 (9 Apr. 1827).

92. *Minutes of Evidence, supra* n. 65, at 47.

93. Testimony of H. S. Mitchell, vestry clerk of Whitechapel, ibid., at 6.

94. Testimony of W. E. Greenwell, vestry clerk at St. Marylebone, ibid. at 11.

95. Ibid.

96. Ibid.

97. Testimony of Richard Nicholson, Middlesex Clerk of the Peace, ibid. at 31.

98. Ibid.

99. Testimony of W. E. Greenwell, ibid. at 7.

100. T. R. P., "On the Law of Libel," *The Newgate Monthly Magazine,* vol. 1, no. 8 (1 Apr. 1825): 340.

101. *Report, supra* n. 71, at 15.

102. The legal definition of the term "esquire" is "The younger sons of noblemen, and the eldest sons of such younger sons; the eldest sons of knights, and their eldest sons; the officers of the King's courts and of the King's household; Counsellors at law; justices of peace." Giles Jacob, *A New Law Dictionary,* 10th ed. (London, 1782).

103. *Minutes of Evidence, supra* n. 65, at 8.

104. Ibid. at 9; see also testimony of Henry Avory, Esq., Clerk of Arraigns at the Central Criminal Court, ibid. at 68.

105. Ibid. at 4 (testimony of H. S. Mitchell).

106. Ibid. at 7 (testimony of W. E. Greenwell).

107. Ibid. at 41 (testimony of Charles Bull).

108. See, e.g., ibid. at 3 (testimony of H. S. Mitchell); ibid. at 61 (testimony of David Meredith); 1867 *Report, supra* n. 71, at 13 (testimony of Serjeant Alexander Pulling).

109. Mr. J. Rayner, Town Clerk of Liverpool, testified in 1870 that "Some men would rather be on the special jury, than not when trade is not particularly good; they make perhaps four or five guineas a day." *Report from the Select Committee on the Juries Bill* (London, 1870), 10.

110. See text at n. 83, *supra.*

111. *Minutes of Evidence, supra* n. 65, at 5 (testimony of H. S. Mitchell), and 56 (testimony of Sir William Erle); *Report, supra* n. 71, at 10 (testimony of William Erle).

112. See text at n. 78, *supra.*

113. *Report from the Select Committee on Administration of Justice in Wales,* 38, *Parliamentary Papers,* House of Commons (London, 1820) (273), ii, 45; *Minutes of Evidence, supra* n. 65, at 56, 38, 16; *Report, supra* n. 71, at 1. As was noted in chapter 7, talesmen put on the jury from among bystanders in court were called "tales *de circumstantibus,*" a concept legitimized in the mid-1550s. See chapter 7, text at nn. 256–61. The device was not available in trials at bar, but by the nineteenth century few special jury cases were of this type.

114. *Minutes of the Court of Common Council, supra* n. 14, at 211.

115. *Parliamentary Papers,* House of Commons, (London, 1824) [paper no. 147], 19: 1.

116. These figures and the others given in the text are computations drawn from 125 pages of reports contained in *Parliamentary Papers,* n. 115, *supra.*

117. Ibid. at 97.

118. Ibid. at 125. See also, to the same effect, remarks of retired Chief Justice Erle in testimony given in 1867. *Report, supra* n. 71, at 56.

119. *Parliamentary Papers, supra* n. 115, at 97.

120. *First Report of Her Majesty's Commissioners for Inquiring into the Process, Prac-*

tice and System of Pleading the Superior Courts of Common Law, 44, *Parliamentary Papers,* House of Commons (London, 1851) [paper no. 1389], 22: 567.

121. *Minutes of Evidence, supra* n. 65, at 52.

122. See the description of the "special special jury," *supra* n. 88.

123. 33 & 34 Vict., c.77, ss.11–15, 17, 19 (1870).

124. Ibid., s.6.

125. Testimony of J. Whitwell, *Third Report of the Judicature Commissioners,* 181, *Parliamentary Papers,* House of Commons (London, 1874) [paper no. 957], 24: 1.

126. Ibid.; *Minutes of Evidence, supra* n. 65, at 148.

127. See Juries Act, 1949, *Halsbury's Laws of England,* 3rd ed., 43 vols. (London: Butterworth's, 1952–64), 23: 4 (1958); Courts Act, 1971, *Halsbury's Laws of England,* 4th ed., 56 vols. (London: Butterworth's, 1973–), 26: 213 (1979).

128. *Fraud Trials Committee Report* (London: HMSO [Her Majesty's Stationery Office], 1986), 145. The proposal envisioned "a panel of people with an above average standard of education, training and experience," such as academics, lay magistrates or persons versed in trade and finance. Ibid. at 144. Compare the experience in the United States in the State of Delaware. See chapter 9, text at nn. 205–9.

Notes for Chapter 9

1. This requirement is now a widespread feature of state and federal law. For a thoughtful and thorough discussion of this jurisprudential "sea change," see Jeffrey Abramson, *We, the Jury: The Jury System and the Ideal of Democracy* (New York: Basic Books, 1994), ch. 3.

2. *In re* Tiffany Green, No. 96-0222, 1996 WL 660949, at *1 (E.D. Pa. Nov. 13, 1996). Judge Hutton then quoted language from a 1918 Arizona case about "the blood and treasure it has cost to get and keep this birthright" and the "evils tyranny and the lust of power have visited upon the weak and helpless who were without its protecting aegis," after which he presented a remarkable one-page history of trial by jury across four thousand years. Ibid. at *2–3 (citing Priestly v. Arizona, 171 P. 137, 138 (Ariz. 1918)).

3. Duncan v. Louisiana, 391 U.S. 145, 156 (1968).

4. See Kathryn Wexler and William Claiborne, "Rep. Tucker Convicted of Extortion," *Washington Post,* Dec. 9, 1995, at A1.

5. Greg Pierce, "Inside Politics: Tucker Resigns," *Washington Times,* Dec. 14, 1995, at A6. The news story was distributed by United Press International on Dec. 12, 1995. See "California Rep. Tucker Resigns," United Press International, Dec. 12, 1995, available in LEXIS, News Library, ARCNWS File.

6. See "Tucker," City News Service, Dec. 12, 1995, available in LEXIS, News Library, ARCNWS File. Former congressman Walter Tucker probably was alluding to the racial composition of the jury (which consisted of seven whites, four Asian-Americans, and one African-American), suggesting that, as an African-American, his race was unfairly underrepresented. Ibid.

7. Harry Toulmin, *The Magistrate's Assistant* (Natchez, 1807), 140; see also Lewis H. LaRue, "A Jury of One's Peers," *Washington and Lee Law Review* 33 (1976): 841.

8. In Strauder v. West Virginia, 100 U.S. 303 (1880), Justice Strong, writing the majority opinion, stated: "The very idea of a jury is a body of men composed of the peers or equals of the person whose rights it is selected or summoned to determine; that is, of his neighbors, fellows, associates, persons having the same legal status in society as that which he holds." Ibid. at 308. In Ex parte Virginia, 100 U.S. 339 (1879), dissenting, Justice Field re-

marked that "no one will contend that equal protection to women, to children, to the aged, to aliens, can only be secured by allowing persons of the class to which they belong to act as jurors in cases affecting their interests." Ibid. at 367 (Field, J., dissenting); see also LaRue, "A Jury of One's Peers," *supra* n. 7, at 846–47.

9. In People v. Ruppert, 279 N.Y.S.2d 895 (Westchester County Ct. 1967), the court upheld a New York statute that stated that jurors must own at least $250 worth of real or personal property. According to the court:

> It does not seem unreasonable in our "free society" to have a minimal ownership in something real or personal to invest a person with the privilege of performing a vital public function, such as being a member of the Grand Jury or Trial Jury, to whom the free rights of individuals, as well as great public interests are committed for resolution in the respective spheres granted to these bodies by custom and statute.

Ibid. at 989–99. The New York Supreme Court reached the same result in People v. Cohen, 283 N.Y.S.2d 817 (Sup. Ct. 1967). The *Cohen* court quoted an earlier opinion by U.S. District Judge Medina that called a challenge to the property qualification under the Fifth and Sixth Amendments "frivolous." Ibid. at 824, quoting United States v. Foster, 83 F. Supp. 197, 207 (S.D.N.Y. 1949).

10. See Toulmin, *The Magistrate's Assistant, supra* n. 7, at 140.

11. See chapter 7, text at nn. 131–60.

12. For a thoughtful analytical treatment of the half-and-half jury, see Marianne Constable, *The Law of the Other: The Mixed Jury and Changing Conceptions of Citizenship, Law, and Knowledge* (Chicago: University of Chicago Press, 1994). For good reviews of eighteenth- and nineteenth-century applications of the procedure in American cases, see LaRue, "A Jury of One's Peers," *supra* n. 7, at 850–63, and Deborah A. Ramirez, "The Mixed Jury and the Ancient Custom of Trial by Jury *De Medietate Linguae:* A History and a Proposal for Change," *Boston University Law Review* 74 (1994): 777, 783–89; see also Hiroshi Fukurai and Darryl Davies, "Affirmative Action in Jury Selection: Racially Representative Juries, Racial Quotas, and Affirmative Juries of the Hennepin Model and the Jury De Medietate Linguae," *Virginia Journal of Social Policy and Law* 4 (1997): 645; Daniel W. Van Ness, "Preserving a Community Voice: The Case for Half-and-Half Juries in Racially Charged Criminal Cases," *John Marshall Law Review* 28 (1994): 1.

13. Rex v. Gascoigne, T. B. Howell, ed., *Cobbett's Complete Collection of State Trials and Proceedings for High Treason,* 33 vols. (London, 1809–26) (*State Trials* hereafter) 7: 959, 963 (K.B. 1680) (see *supra,* chapter 7, text at n. 133). According to LaRue, Justice Field understood the jury *de medietate* as a mode of trial made available in England for an alien "probably as much because of the difference of language and customs between him and Englishmen, and the greater probability of his defense being more fully understood, as because it would be heard in a more friendly spirit by jurors of his own country and language." LaRue, "A Jury of One's Peers," *supra* n. 7, at 847, quoting Ex parte Virginia, 100 U.S. 339, 369 (1879) (Field, J., dissenting). For an elaboration of the several rationales supporting the jury *de medietate,* see Constable, *The Law of the Other, supra* n. 12, ch. 6; LaRue, "A Jury of One's Peers," *supra* n. 7, at 852–63; Van Ness, "Preserving a Community Voice," *supra* n. 12, at 37–39.

14. See Fukurai and Davies, "Affirmative Action," *supra* n. 12; Van Ness, "Preserving a Community Voice," *supra* n. 12. These articles make the explicit argument for adapting the historical *de medietate* practice to modern trials that promise to be racially charged. Others argue for racial quotas in order to give reality to the "jury of peers" and thereby to secure a fair trial. See Albert W. Alschuler, "Racial Quotas and the Jury," *Duke Law Journal* 44 (1995): 704; Sheri Lynn Johnson, "Black Innocence and the White Jury," *Michigan Law Review* 83 (1985): 1611; Diane Potash, "Mandatory Inclusion of Racial Minorities

on Jury Panels," *Black Law Journal* 3 (1973): 80; Note, "The Case for Black Juries," *Yale Law Journal* 79 (1970): 531; see also Constable, *The Law of the Other, supra* n. 12, at 41–48. Ramirez uses the history of the mixed jury to argue for what she terms "affirmative peremptories." Ramirez, "The Mixed Jury," *supra* n. 12, at 806–17; see also *infra* nn. 235–44 and accompanying text.

15. See *infra* n. 249 and accompanying text.

16. See *infra,* text at nn. 167–81.

17. See chapter 8, text at nn. 10–64.

18. See *infra* nn. 250–56 and accompanying text.

19. See *infra,* text at nn. 26–90.

20. See Rita Sutton, "A More Rational Approach to Complex Civil Litigation in the Federal Courts: The Special Jury," *University of Chicago Legal Forum* 1990: 575; Note, "The Case for Special Juries in Complex Civil Litigation," *Yale Law Journal* 89 (1980): 1155.

21. See *infra* nn. 263–68 and accompanying text.

22. An Act for the Better Regulation of Juries, 3 Geo. 2, c.25, s.15 (1730).

23. See chapter 7, text at nn. 185, 206–38.

24. Act of Nov. 27, 1741, ch. DCCXX, N.Y. Colonial Laws (encouraging the return of able and sufficient jurors, as well as the better regulation of juries).

25. See text at nn. 103–10, 187–94, *infra.*

26. I refer to states in which the struck jury originated by statute. As is noted later, there are states in which trial judges adopted the struck-jury method without statutory authorization. See *infra* text accompanying nn. 89–90. There are also instances of the adoption of the method by court rules. I have not attempted to canvas federal, state, and local trial courts to discover struck-jury usages in states in which there is no statutory history supporting the practice. For a description of the adoption of the struck-jury method by court rule, see State v. Enno, 807 P.2d 610, 614 (Idaho 1991). After referring to a 1961 case in which a new trial was granted because the struck-jury method used by the trial court was at odds with statutory requirements, the Idaho Supreme Court noted that the struck-jury procedure followed by the trial court had been made available by court rule.

27. See *infra,* text at nn. 151–52.

28. Act of Feb. 2, 1793, Del. Laws ch. VIII (1793).

29. Ibid.

30. Act of Jan. 30, 1810, Del. Laws ch. CXX (1810).

31. 161 A.2d 795 (Del. 1960).

32. Ibid. at 799.

33. 491 A.2d 439 (Del. 1985).

34. Ibid. at 443. The Delaware Supreme Court quoted the trial judge in pointing out that special juries originally had been authorized only for courts of civil jurisdiction—the Supreme Court and the Court of Common Pleas—and not for the criminal courts (the court of Oyer and Terminer and General Gaol Delivery and the court of General Quarter Sessions of the Peace and Gaol Delivery). See ibid. at 443 n. 3.

35. Act of Jan. 30, 1810, Del. Laws ch. CXX (1810). The statute also provided that in civil cases in which the jury was impaneled according to the 1793 statute, each side was to be allowed three peremptory challenges.

36. 66 Del. Laws, ch. 5, § 4506 (1987), Del. Code Ann., tit. 10 § 4506 (1987).

37. See Ramada Inns, Inc. v. Dow Jones & Co., No. C.A. 83C-AU-56, 1987 WL 28311 (Del. Super. Ct. Oct. 22, 1987) (granting part of the motion for summary judgment in the libel action); see also *infra,* text preceding n. 229.

38. See *infra,* n. 206 and accompanying text.

39. Act of December 22, 1788, 1788 Virginia Acts ch. 67, § 128 (establishing district courts and regulating the general court).

40. See Va. Code of 1849, ch. 162, § 8.

41. Va. Code of 1887, ch. 152, § 3158.

42. The current statutory references are, for civil cases, Va. Code Ann. § 8.01-362 (2005) ("Any court in a civil case in which a jury is required may allow a special jury, in which event . . . a jury shall be made in accordance with the provisions of § 8.01-359A.") and, for criminal cases, Va. Code Ann. § 19.2-262(c) (2005) ("The parties or their counsel . . . shall alternately strike off one name from the panel until the number remaining shall be reduced to the number required for a jury.").

43. Va. Code of 1950, § 8-208.21.

44. Va. Code Ann. § 8.01-359A (2005).

45. In an early case, Atlantic & Danville R.R. Co. v. Peake, 87 Va. 130 (1890), the court disallowed a special jury because there was nothing in the case to suggest prejudice or exceptional difficulty. This case suggests that cases of exceptional difficulty qualify for special juries and, further, that the jurors would be specially qualified. I have not investigated whether such a practice in Virginia courts is called for in court rules or is followed informally.

46. 44 Va. Code Ann. § 8.01-359D (2005).

47. During the eighteenth century in England, it was common to refer pending court cases to arbitration, and one or some number of jurors would at times be chosen to be the arbitrators. More commonly, arbitrators with expertise in the subject matter in dispute would be selected. If the number of arbitrators chosen was an even number, there would customarily be a provision for the named arbitrators to select an umpire for tiebreaking purposes. See James Oldham, *The Mansfield Manuscripts and the Growth of English Law in the Eighteenth Century*, 2 vols. (Chapel Hill and London: University of North Carolina Press, 1992), 1: 151–55; 2: Appendix E. There are examples of naming two arbitrators with instructions to them to choose a third. See, e.g., Hotchkin v. Cotes (Trinity Feb. 15, 1758) (Radford and Sweet, Arbitrators), ibid. at 2: 1544. These practices became common in American colonies and states in the eighteenth and nineteenth centuries. The experience with arbitration in colonial America and in the early republic was extensive. For an excellent study of arbitration in colonial Connecticut, see Bruce Mann, "The Formalization of Informal Law: Arbitration Before the American Revolution," *New York University Law Review* 59 (1984): 443.

48. Ala. Code of 1841, ch. 10, § 52.

49. Ibid.

50. Ala. Code of 1932, Ex. Sess., 34.

51. See Ala. Code § 12-16-140 (2005); see also Wallace v. Alabama Power Co., 497 So.2d 450 (Ala. 1986).

52. See Ala. Rules of Civil Procedure 47(b) (2005).

53. See Holman v. Baker, 169 So.2d 429 (Ala. 1964).

54. Act of Sept. 29, 1919, 1919 Alabama Acts No. 715. For current statutory provisions, see Ala. Code § 12-16-100 (2005) and Rule 18.4(f) of the Alabama Rules of Criminal Procedure.

55. See Brown v. State, 231 So.2d 167 (Ala. App. 1970).

56. See Dixon v. State, 167 So. 340 (Ala. App. 1936).

57. See *supra* n. 26 for the method I followed in identifying states with current special jury practices.

58. See text at nn. 84–85, *infra.*

59. See text at nn. 86–90, *infra.*

60. See *infra* nn. 188–94 and accompanying text.

61. See Act of July 29, 1769, 1769 S.C. Acts, No. 1095, sec. XXIII ("establishing courts, building gaols, and appointing sheriffs and other officers, and for the more convenient administration of justice in this province").

62. Ibid.

63. See Act of Dec. 20, 1791, 1791 S.C. Acts, No. 1526 ("to alter and amend the Law Respecting Juries and to make some additional regulation to the Acts for establishing and regulating the Circuit Courts").

64. Ibid.

65. Act of Dec.16, 1797, 1797 S.C. Acts No. 1665.

66. S. C. Code Ann. § 14-7-1050 (2004).

67. 1 Indiana R.S. 1896, Frank A. Horner, comp., § 522. The 1896 compilation is the earliest set of Indiana statutes to which I have had access. Later historical annotations show that the special-jury provisions originated in "An Act Concerning Proceedings in Civil Cases," 1881 Ind. Acts 240, ch. 38, §§ 357–362.

68. 1 Indiana R.S. 1896, Horner, § 523.

69. Ibid. § 524.

70. Ibid. § 525.

71. 1913 Ind. Acts ch. 15, § 1.

72. The repealing authority was 1988 Ind. Acts, P.L.180-1988, § 2. For the retained provisions in the current statutes, see Ind. Code Ann. § 34-36-2-2 (2005) ("Special jury by agreement") and ibid. at § 34-36-2-3 (2005) (struck jury by consent).

73. See Ark. Code Ann. § 16-32-203 (2005).

74. Ibid. at § 16-33-203 (2005).

75. See Ark. Rev. Statutes ch. 85, §§ 20–21 (1837). The statute had an interesting, pragmatic twist: If the request came outside of term time, the clerk of the circuit court was authorized to order the struck jury if "satisfied that a struck jury ought to be granted." Ibid. at § 18. The statute did not indicate the criteria to be applied in deciding whether to grant the request.

76. See 1797 Md. Laws ch. 87, § 9.

77. See 1802 Md. Laws ch. 69.

78. Md. R. 2-512(g) & (h) (2005).

79. Ibid., 4-313(a) (2005).

80. Ibid., 4-313(b)(2) (2005).

81. W. Va. Code § 56-6-13 (1966).

82. See W. Va. Code § 56-6-13 (a) (2005)

83. Ibid., § 56-6-13(b) (2005). For eminent-domain cases, the twenty names are to be qualified freeholders of the county where the land being condemned is located. See *infra* nn. 230–31 and accompanying text.

84. See Ariz. Rules of Civil Procedure 47(a) (2005). In criminal cases, the number of jurors to serve in the case is to be drawn and then augmented by the number of alternates plus the number of peremptories allowed each party. See Ariz. Rules of Criminal Procedure18.5(b) (2005).

85. Tex. Code Crim. Proc. art. 35.25 (2005).

86. 631 N.E.2d 1002 (Mass. 1994).

87. Ibid. at 1004, 1007–8.

88. Ibid. at 1007 n. 7.

89. 835 P.2d 1181 (Alaska 1992).

90. See People v. Wright, 802 P.2d 221, 240–41 (Cal. 1990); State v. Echineque, 828

P.2d 276 (Haw. 1992); State v. Corpuz, 880 P.2d 213 (Haw. Ct. App. 1994); State v. Shiroma, 855 P.2d 34 (Haw. Ct. App. 1993).

91. See N.Y. Laws of 1965, ch. 778, § 3.

92. Act of Apr. 23, 1896, ch. 378, 1896 N.Y. Laws 354.

93. Ibid., § 13. Here we see an echo of the English trial at bar and of Blackstone's reference to cases that were "of too great nicety for the discussion of ordinary freeholders." William Blackstone, *Commentaries on the Laws of England,* 4 vols. (Oxford, 1765–69), 3: 357 (1768).

94. 1896 N. Y. Laws 354, ch.778, § 9.

95. Ibid., § 8.

96. Benjamin Tucker, *A Blow at Trial by Jury* (New York: Benjamin Tucker, 1889).

97. Ibid. at 3–4.

98. 205 N.Y.S.2d 190 (Sup. Ct. 1960).

99. Ibid. at 197.

100. Ibid. at 200–3 (quoting Moore v. New York, 333 U.S. 565, 570 (1948) (Murphy, J., dissenting)).

101. Ibid. at 196–97. The 1901 statute amended the 1896 act to make it applicable to both criminal and civil cases in counties with a population of over one million (New York and Kings). 1901 N.Y. Laws ch.602, s.2, 1464.

102. Morton Horwitz, *The Transformation of American Law 1780–1860* (Cambridge, MA: Harvard University Press, 1977), 155–58.

103. Ibid. at 155. For the 1741 statute, see *supra* n. 24 and accompanying text.

104. Ibid. (citing 1801 New York Laws ch. 98).

105. See George Caines, *A Summary of the Practice of the Supreme Court of the State of New York* (New York, 1808), ch. 43.

106. Ibid. at 456.

107. Schuster v. City of New York, *supra* n. 98, at 197.

108. Ibid. at 203.

109. See Horwitz, *The Transformation of American Law, supra* n. 102, at 155–56.

110. Ibid. at 157–58.

111. *Supra,* n. 98, at 193–96. One case involved the valuation of railroad bonds, which called for "a jury equipped with practical business experience"; two were libel cases; one was a quo warranto to test the validity of the mayor's election; and two were probate contests. Ibid.

112. Ibid. at 205.

113. Ibid.

114. See, e.g., Abramson, *We, the Jury, supra* n. 1.

115. See People v. Willis, 257 N.E.2d 650 (N.Y. 1970) (upholding a murder conviction and finding that the defendant was not deprived of due process by having been tried before a special jury); People v. Jackson, 231 N.E.2d 722 (N.Y. 1967) (rejecting a challenge to a special jury under the Sixth and Fourteenth Amendments to the United States Constitution); People v. Horton, 241 N.Y.S.2d 224, 227 (App. Div. 1963) (upholding a special-jury conviction, despite the claim that the special-jury list excluded Puerto Ricans: "In a county such as New York, composed of a vast number of minority groups, it will be almost inevitable that the small number of prospective jurors called for Special Jury service will not conform in proportion to the percentage of each minority group in the population."), aff'd, 221 N.E.2d 909 (N.Y. 1966), cert. denied, 387 U.S. 934 (1967); People v. Follette, 306 N.Y.S.2d 789 (Sup. Ct. 1970) (upholding the use of a special jury drawn from the 1964 New York County Special Jury panels).

116. Laws of New Jersey, An Act relative to juries and verdicts, 10 Nov. 1797, §§ 14–15.

117. Ibid.

118. Ibid.

119. New Jersey Public Laws 1851, 92.

120. See chapter eight, text at nn. 120–21.

121. New Jersey Public Laws 1851, 92.

122. Act of June 14, 1898, ch. 237, § 76, 1898 N.J. Laws 866, 895, quoted and discussed in United States v. Ricks, 802 F.2d 731, 735 n. 2 (4th Cir. 1986), quoting Brown v. State, 42 A. 811, 812 (N.J. 1899).

123. See N.J. Stat. Ann. § 2A: 75-1 (1971).

124. Ibid. at §§ 2A: 75-2, 2A: 75-5 (1971).

125. 34 A. 682 (N.J. Sup. Ct. 1896), aff'd, 39 A. 1113 (N.J. Ct. of Errors, 1896).

126. 34 A. at 682.

127. 42 A. 811 (N.J. 1899), aff'd, 175 U.S. 172 (1899).

128. 42 A. at 813.

129. Ibid. at 818.

130. Ibid.

131. See *infra,* n. 153 and accompanying text.

132. See State v. Gilmore, 489 A.2d 1175 (N.J. Super. Ct. App. Div. 1985) (holding that the assistant prosecutor's use of peremptory challenges to exclude all black jurors violated the defendant's constitutional right to an impartial jury), aff'd, 511 A.2d 1150 (N.J. 1986).

133. Act of Apr. 9, 1991, ch. 91, § 533, 1991 N.J. Laws 329, 610.

134. The two statutes are akin to the procedures later discussed for state condemnation of land or other property rights. See *infra* text accompanying nn. 230–33. The first of the two New Jersey statutes in question provides for payments to riparian owners for uses of or improvements to land under water, and it provides that if the riparian owner "is dissatisfied with said award he may apply to the Superior Court for a struck jury to try the question in such place as may be designated by said court." N.J. Stat. Ann. § 12: 3-9 (2005). The second statute relates to payments for encroachments upon cemeteries and provides that, if an objection is raised, "The court may hear any such objection or proceed in the action in a summary manner or otherwise and with a struck jury if any party demands a jury." Ibid. § 40: 60-25.45 (2005).

135. See Mich. Rev. Stat. tit. XXII, ch. 103, §§ 36, 38 (1846) (requiring that a special jury be ordered by a circuit court when it appears "that a fair and impartial trial will be more likely to be obtained in any cause pending therein, by having a struck jury" and that a panel of forty-eight deemed "most indifferent" and "best qualified" be returned and reduced to twenty-four by twelve strikes by each party). In 1929, the numbers were changed to a panel of thirty-six, with six strikes per party. See Mich. Comp. Laws § 13856 (1929). This method was authorized until 1963. See People v. Miller, 276 N.W.2d 558, 561 n. 1 (Mich. Ct. App. 1979), rev'd, 307 N.W.2d 335 (Mich. 1981). As has been true elsewhere, however, the struck-jury method continued to have appeal because of perceived voir dire advantages. See *infra* nn. 151–52 and accompanying text. In *Miller*, a trial judge's use of the procedure in a murder trial, although violative of the Michigan jury selection rules, was held by the court of appeals to be a nonprejudicial error, insufficient to overturn the convictions. See 276 N.W.2d at 561. The Supreme Court of Michigan, however, held that failure to follow the Michigan jury-selection rules, coupled with an appropriate challenge before the jury-selection process had begun, required reversal. See 307 N.W.2d at 337. The court further stated that "the 'struck jury method' or any system patterned thereafter is disapproved and may not be used in the future." Ibid.

In Georgia, a colonial statute provided "that all special juries that shall hereafter be moved for and allowed by the court shall be struck in the manner now used in the Courts of Westminster." Act of Dec. 13, 1756. After independence, however, special juries were tied to grand juries. Special jurors were to be taken from the grand-jury list, and, when a special jury was needed, the clerk was to supply the names of grand jurors then impaneled, which would be reduced to twelve by alternate strikes by the parties. Judiciary Act, § 27 (1796). This method remained in place until the special jury disappeared in Georgia around 1930. Special juries appear in the 1926 Code but are absent in the 1933 Code.

In Vermont the standard formula (forty-eight names, reduced to twenty-four by alternate strikes) was followed from 1884 to 1968 whenever it appeared to a county court judge that a struck jury was needed to obtain a fair and impartial trial of an issue of fact or because of the intricacy, importance, or special circumstances of a case. See "An Act Providing for Summoning Special Juries in Extraordinary Cases in the County Courts," Public Act No. 117 (1884); Vt. Stat. Ann. §§ 1471, 1474 (1958); Act of Mar. 14, 1968, § 3, 1967 Adj. Sess.

136. In 1816, Ohio adopted a struck-jury statute calling for a panel of forty to be reduced by striking to sixteen; of the sixteen, the first twelve to appear in court and not be challenged became the jury. See Ohio Stat. § 17 (1816). In 1824, this statute was made inapplicable to criminal cases in which more than two peremptory challenges were made on either side. See An Act Relating to Juries, c.580, § 19 (1823–24). This scheme remained in place until its repeal in 1894. See 91 Ohio Stat. 290 (1894). In 1880, an amendment for counties with a population greater than 200,000 was passed calling for the presiding judge in the court where a jury was to be struck to select the names of the special jurors "personally, and without suggestion from anyone." Act of Feb. 26, 1880, 1880 Ohio Laws 12, 13. Apart from the large-county feature, Minnesota followed the "forty-to-sixteen-to-twelve" formula (reportedly copied from Ohio) from 1864 until its repeal in 1891, see Minn. Stat. ch. XXXI, §§ 1, 5 (1864), as did Wisconsin (reportedly copied, in turn, from Minnesota) from 1898 to 1913. See Wis. Stat. Ann. § 2544a (1898); Wis. Stat. § 2544a (1913). Wisconsin, however, had a simpler struck jury (panel of thirty-six, reduced to twelve by alternate strikes) from 1858 to 1898. See Rev. Stat. Wis. ch. 115, § 9 (1858). Missouri utilized a formula calling for a much smaller jury panel—eighteen, reduced to twelve by alternate strikes of three on each side. See Act of Mar. 17, 1835, § 14, *repealed by* Mo. Rev. Stat. § 3791 (1899).

137. See Nev. Gen. Stat. § 3183 (1861–1885) (1875 amended statute). This statute disappears from the books in the early 1900s, but I have not located the specific point of repeal.

138. See Iowa Code ch. 96, § 1776 (1851). The struck jury was granted at the request of both parties, and, when chosen, it supplanted the parties' right to five peremptories each. Ibid. at § 1774.

139. Ibid. at § 2778 (1873).

140. Ibid. at ch. 496, § 11484 (1927), *repealed by* Act of Mar. 31, 1927, ch. 221, § 1, 1927 Iowa Acts 193.

141. Okla. Code (Terr.) ch. 70, § 7 (1890).

142. Ibid. Compare the Oklahoma Territory statute with the like provision in Indiana, *supra* n. 67 and accompanying text.

143. Okla. Code (Terr.) ch. 70, § 7 (1890). The Oklahoma statute did not last long; it does not appear in the 1893 Code. I have not been able to mark its exact disappearance.

144. Act of June 25, 1937, No. 419, § 1, 1937 Pa. Laws 2093.

145. Pa. Code ch. IX, Juries, § 81 n. 3 (1894).

146. 151 U.S. 396 (1884) (approving a struck-jury system).

147. Ibid. at 408–9.

148. 802 F.2d 731 (4th Cir. 1986).

149. Ibid. at 734.

150. Ibid. at 735.

151. 666 F.2d 796 (2d Cir. 1981) (footnotes omitted).

152. Ibid. at 798.

153. For representative cases from New Jersey, see State v. Bey, 548 A.2d 887 (N.J. 1988) and State v. Ramseur, 524 A.2d 188 (N.J. 1987). Sometimes the challenge on appeal is that the use of the struck-jury method somehow deprived a defendant of the full effect of his peremptories. In Van Huff v. Sohio Alaska Petroleum Co., 835 P.2d 1181 (Alaska 1992), the Supreme Court of Alaska rejected a defendant's protest that "the struck jury method is inconsistent with the Alaska Rule of Civil Procedure 47(d) because that rule provides for the exercise of peremptory challenges as to jurors in the box, and under the struck jury method peremptory challenges are exercised before jurors are seated in the box.." Ibid. at 1184–85. But see People v. Miller, 307 N.W.2d 335 (Mich. 1981), discussed at n. 135, *supra,* where a similar protest was successful.

154. See *Blouin, supra* n. 151, at 799.

155. *Supra,* n. 148.

156. Ibid. at 736–37.

157. Ibid. at 737–39 (Wilkinson, J., dissenting). In state courts, struck-jury panels often have been qualified that were larger than the number that would be produced by the Fourth Circuit's formula. New Jersey cases are again illustrative. See State v. Perry, 590 A.2d 624, 631 (N.J. 1991) (qualifying "approximately fifty-four" jurors); State v. Zola, 548 A.2d 1022, 1028 (N.J. 1988) (qualifying forty-eight potential jurors); State v. Halsey, 526 A.2d 1165, 1171 (N.J. Super. Ct. Law Div. 1987) (qualifying fifty-six potential jurors by the court before striking began). For an example of a formula that is limited in the way the Fourth Circuit describes, see the Arizona criminal procedure rule, *supra* n. 84.

158. *Ricks, supra* n. 148, at 736.

159. Ibid. at 739 (Wilkinson, J., dissenting).

160. Indeed, as was discussed in the previous chapter, the opportunities for control became, in the views of some, opportunities for improper jury packing. See chapter 8, text at nn. 77–91.

161. Some believe that this theoretical justification for peremptories has been mangled in practice beyond recognition. See Harold J. Rothwax, *Guilty: The Collapse of Criminal Justice* (New York: Random House, 1996), 203–7. Rothwax is a New York judge and former criminal defense attorney who observes that criminal defense attorneys attempt to exploit the jury selection system by seeking "jurors who will not or cannot intelligently evaluate evidence." Ibid. at 200–1.

162. See *infra* text accompanying nn. 269–88.

163. For Delaware, see n. 35, *supra,* and accompanying text; for Indiana, see n. 70, *supra,* and accompanying text.

164. See Ill. Rev. Stat. ch. 78, § 2 (1874); Kan. Comp. Laws ch. 54, § 2 (1879).

165. See the Michigan statute, *supra* n. 135, and the Indiana statute, *supra* n. 70 and accompanying text. One Indiana jury commissioner testified that he tried to make sure that jurors had been "somewhat successful in life." Shack v. State, 288 N.E.2d 155, 161 (Ind. 1972).

166. For a description of the grand jury tradition in England in the seventeenth century, see chapter 7, text at nn. 105–14.

167. Tennessee Code ch. 134, § 4 (1844) authorized the circuit courts in any civil case, on motion of either party, to empanel a special jury. In construing this statute, the Ten-

nessee Supreme Court explained that this section "contemplates the selection of men with reference to their superior competency and fitness to try and determine the particular issues involved in the case." Jackson v. Pool, 91 Tenn. 448, 453 (1892). Interestingly, the court added that the special jurors were not to be selected with reference to their relationship to the parties in nationality or color and that it was error for the trial court to select one-half of the jury from among colored persons upon the motion of a colored party litigant, solely because they were colored. Ibid.; see also Virginia v. Rives, 100 U.S. 313 (1880), discussed *infra* n. 259.

168. Act of Nov. 10, 1797, § 15.

169. See State v. Donato, 148 A. 776, 780 (N.J. Ct. Err. & App. 1930).

170. See Judiciary Act § 35 (1796). In 1914, the statute was amended to allow special jurors to be selected from either the grand or traverse jury, at the discretion of the judge. See Ga. Code Ann. art. 8, § 852 (1914).

171. Judiciary Act § 28 (1796).

172. 332 U.S. 261 (1947).

173. 333 U.S. 565 (1948).

174. 332 U.S. at 267 (citing N.Y. Judiciary Law § 749 (McKinney 1946)).

175. Ibid. at 276.

176. Ibid. at 276–77.

177. Ibid.

178. Ibid. at 298.

179. Ibid. at 299.

180. Ibid. at 299–300.

181. 333 U.S. at 570. Other challenges to the New York special-jury statute on grounds similar to those presented in the *Fay* and *Moore* cases were rejected by the Second Circuit. See United States ex rel. Torres v. Mancusi, 427 F.2d 168 (2d Cir. 1970). The juries in these cases were impaneled before the repeal of the New York blue-ribbon-jury statute in 1965. The argument in *Mancusi* was interesting. The defendant claimed that the jury had a large number of educated and well-to-do people on it and "was less well equipped than a general jury would have been to pass judgment upon his offense, which he represents was a crime of passion committed by a man of underprivileged background, frail in health, of low intelligence, and who had been working at poorly paid menial jobs." Ibid. at 169.

182. Louisiana, for example, once formed a commercial court. See *infra* n. 199 and accompanying text.

183. Patent appeals are now part of the responsibilities of the U.S. Court of Appeals for the Federal Circuit.

184. See chapter 2, text at nn. 12–16; text following n. 47.

185. See *supra* n. 20 and accompanying text.

186. For the English experience, see chapter 8, text at nn. 10–64.

187. See *supra* text at nn. 102–10. One twentieth-century example cited by Judge Martuscello in Schuster v. City of New York, 205 N.Y.S.2d 190 (Sup. Ct. 1960) (*supra* n. 98), was the case of Industrial & Gen. Trust, Ltd. v. Tod, 46 Misc. 492 (N.Y. Sup. Ct. 1905). The case involved valuation of railroad bonds, and the trial court granted a motion for a special jury on the ground that the issue should be determined by a jury "of intelligence and of practical business experience . . . the best which any established method of selection may secure." Ibid. at 493. Indeed, the court stated that "each juror should have much of the capacity for financial analysis which a successful reorganizer of railroad properties may be deemed to possess." Ibid. at 494.

188. Horwitz, *The Transformation of American Law, supra* n. 102.

189. Ibid. at 158.

190. The statute allowed special juries, on consent of both parties or motion of one willing to pay the cost, in cases involving much money or "concerning trade, and disputes with merchants." Ibid.

191. Act of Dec. 20, 1791, No. 1526 (altering and amending the South Carolina law respecting juries of 1769 and instituting additional regulations to the Acts for establishing and regulating the circuit courts).

192. Gelee Corley Hendrix and Morn McCoy Lindsay, *The Jury Lists of South Carolina 1778–1779* (privately printed n.d.).

193. See Horwitz, *The Transformation of American Law, supra* n. 102, at 159; Act of Dec. 16, 1797, No. 1665 (abolishing the right of trial by special jury, except by consent of both parties).

194. See Horwitz, *supra* n. 102, at 159. As Horwitz noted, standard printed sources show no special juries in use in South Carolina after 1796, but they likely were used with the consent of both parties in cases with no printed record, or in cases that were reported but in which there was no occasion for the reporter to note the fact that the jury was special. See [Anon.], *The South Carolina Justice of the Peace* (New York, 1810), 257 (describing how the special-jury lists in Charleston and other districts are to be fashioned, even though the description that had been in the 1788 edition (at page 291) of the empaneling of special juries pursuant to the 1769 statute no longer appears).

195. Act of 1807, ch. 23.

196. Richard Kilbourne, *Louisiana Commercial Law: The Antebellum Period* (Baton Rouge: Paul M. Herbert Law Center, 1980), 101–5.

197. Ibid. at 101.

198. Ibid. at 102.

199. This court lasted in New Orleans from 1839 to 1846. Ibid. at 85.

200. Ibid. at 102–3.

201. Ibid. at 102–3, 106–7.

202. Ibid. at 26–28, 102–5; see also chapter 8, text at nn. 10–16.

203. Ibid. at 103–4.

204. Ibid. at 102–4.

205. Del. Code Ann. tit. 10, § 4506 (1987).

206. 551 A.2d 1296 (Del. Super. Ct. 1988). In reaching its conclusions, the Superior Court relied on the 1982 decision of the Delaware Supreme Court that upheld the constitutionality of the special-jury statute then in effect. Ibid. at 1298 (citing Haas v. United Techs. Corp., 450 A.2d 1173 (Del. 1982)).

207. Ibid. at 1297.

208. Ibid. at 1297, 1300.

209. Ibid. at 1297; see also chapter 7, text at nn. 185, 206.

210. Ibid. at 1298.

211. Ibid.

212. In re. Asbestos Litigation, 551 A.2d at 1298. The later requirement ended when the special-jury law in Delaware changed in 1987. Ibid. Del. Code Ann. tit. 10, § 4506 (1987).

213. No. C.A. 86C-MY-189, 1987 WL 26911 (Del. Super. Ct. Dec. 4, 1987).

214. See Bradley v. A. C. & S. Co., Inc., Nos. 84C-MY-145, 85C-FE-10, 1989 WL 70834 (Del. Super. Ct. May 23, 1989).

215. Ibid. at *1.

216. Ibid. at *3.

217. Dan Drazan, "The Case for Special Juries in Toxic Tort Litigation," *Judicature* 72 (1989): 292.

218. Bradley, *supra* n. 214, at *3.

219. Ibid. One prior statutory authorization in the United States came close to the proposed scheme—the 1807 Louisiana statute. See text at n. 195, *supra.*

220. No. C.A. 85C-MY-54, 1990 WL 199509 (Del. Super. Ct. Oct. 22, 1990).

221. Ibid. at *1.

222. Ibid. The court also wondered why the parties had not followed a common path in the case by seeking expertise through arbitration, adding that "The application for a special jury here may result in having 'expertise' the parties did not freely contract for." Ibid.

223. No. C.A. 83C-AU-56, 1987 WL 28311 (Del. Super. Ct. Oct. 22, 1987).

224. Ibid. at *1.

225. Ibid.

226. Ibid. (quoting Wheat v. State, 527 A.2d 269 (Del. 1987)).

227. Ibid.

228. In addition to the cases that have been discussed, a product-liability case against General Motors in 1990 also used the special jury. See McLain v. General Motors Corp., 569 A.2d 579 (Del. 1990).

229. Ramada Inns, Inc. v. Dow Jones & Co., No. C.A. 83C-AU-56, 1987 WL 28311 (Del. Super. Ct. Oct. 22, 1987).

230. W. Va. Code § 56-6-13(b) (2005).

231. Ibid.

232. Wash. Rev. Code Ann. § 8.04.080 (2005). The parties to such a dispute in Washington can consent to a jury of fewer than twelve, but no fewer than three. Ibid.; also ibid., § 85.06.120 (2005) (setting forth procedures for juries to resolve disputes about diking district assessments).

233. Colorado Rev. Stat. Ann. § 37-23-104 (2005). The continued statutory reference to "men" is obviously obsolete.

234. See *supra,* nn. 11–14 and accompanying text.

235. See Kentucky Revised Statute ch. 55, art. III, § 5 (1852); Virginia, Act of Dec. 22, 1788, ch. 67, § 44, reprinted in W. W. Hening, ed., *The Statutes at Large; Being a Collection of All the Laws of Virginia, from the First Session of the Legislature in the Year 1619,* 13 vols. (New York, Philadelphia, and Richmond, 1819–23) 12: 746 (1823); Respublica v. Mesca, 1 Dallas 73 (Phila. O. & T. Sept. Sess. 1783).

236. Toulmin, *The Magistrate's Assistant, supra* n. 7, at 140.

237. [Anon.], *A New Conductor Generalis* (Albany, 1803), 257.

238. *South Carolina Justice of the Peace, supra* n. 194, at 252. The passage in the 1810 edition is the same as that in the 1788 edition (Philadelphia, 1788) at 288.

239. See n. 14, *supra,* and accompanying text.

240. *The Royal Commission on Criminal Justice Report* (London: HMSO [Her Majesty's Stationery Office], 1993): 133.

241. See Rex v. McCalla, 1986 *Criminal Law Review* 335 (Stoke-on-Trent Crown Ct. 1985); Rex v. Bansal, Bir, Mahio and Singh, 1985 *Criminal Law Review* 151 (Maidstone Crown Ct. 1984); Rex v. Danvers, 1982 *Criminal Law Review* 680 (Nottingham Crown Ct. 1982); A. Dashwood, "Juries in a Multi-Racial Society," 1972 *Criminal Law Review* (1972): 85. In one case in 1981, a judge on the Bristol Crown Court ruled that, notwithstanding the apparently preclusive wording of the Juries Act 1974, he had discretion to manipulate jury selection to achieve racial balance when it appeared that this would not be achieved through the use of peremptory challenges. See Rex v. Binns, 1982 *Criminal Law Review* 522 (Bristol Crown Ct. 1981).

242. Regina v. Ford, 1 Q.B. 868, 873 (C.A. 1989); see also Dashwood, "Juries in a Multi-Racial Society," *supra* n. 241, at 828.

243. Frances Gibb, "Lord Chief Justice Rejects Jury Race Quota as Insidious," *The Times,* July 1, 1995 (quoting Chief Justice Taylor).

244. Ibid.

245. Abramson, *We, the Jury, supra* n. 1, at 99.

246. 419 U.S. 522 (1975).

247. See Abramson, *We, the Jury, supra* n. 1, at 99–125.

248. Ibid. at 100.

249. Ibid. at 100–1.

250. 476 U.S. 79 (1986).

251. 499 U.S. 400 (1991).

252. 500 U.S. 614 (1991).

253. 505 U.S. 42 (1992).

254. 511 U.S. 127 (1994).

255. See *Batson, supra* n. 250, at 103–8; Rodger L. Hochman, Note, "Abolishing the Peremptory Challenge: The Verdict of Emerging Caselaw," *Nova Law Review* 17 (1993): 1367; Jeffrey S. Jubera, Note, "The Peremptory Challenge at the Federal Level and in Maryland: Its Uncertain Future After *Georgia v. McCollum," University of Baltimore Law Review* 23 (1993): 225; Antony Page, "Batson's Blind Spot: Unconscious Stereotyping and the Peremptory Challenge," *Boston University Law Review* 85 (2005): 155; Edward P. Schwartz and Warren F. Schwartz, "The Challenge of Peremptory Challenges," *Journal of Law, Economics, and Organization* 12 (1996): 325.

256. 493 U.S. 474 (1990).

257. Abramson, *We, the Jury, supra* n. 1, at 139.

258. Ibid. In Willis v. Zant, 720 F.2d 1212 (11th Cir. 1983), the court noted: "Although the distinctiveness of a group for sixth amendment purposes is a question of fact, . . . a court can determine as a matter of law that a group is not cognizable or distinct. For example, no evidentiary hearing would be needed to determine that redheads or vegetarians are not distinctive classes within the sixth amendment fair cross-section analysis." Ibid. at 1217. Despite the assurance of the Eleventh Circuit, the lines are ever moving. For example, one can imagine a future argument, in litigation involving animal-rights protests, that vegetarians should represent a cognizable class.

259. The Supreme Court considered and rejected the quota idea in 1880 in Virginia v. Rives, 100 U.S. 313 (1880). As Abramson explains, "the defendants moved prior to their trial to have the panel of available jurors modified so that it would be one-third black," a motion "premised on the existence of an affirmative right to have blacks actually included on the jury (that is, to have blacks represented in rough proportion to their population in the county)." Abramson, *We, the Jury, supra* n. 1, at 106. Thus, "the Virginia defendants' motion . . . was a claim that society was so cleaved along racial lines that the jury had to be also." Ibid. Although the Supreme Court rejected this notion in 1880, the idea is not far from the rationale commonly given for the cross-section requirement. See *supra* n. 249 and accompanying text.

260. See, e.g., Lemley v. State, 599 So.2d 64 (Ala. Crim. App. 1992).

261. See Ramirez, "The Mixed Jury," *supra* nn. 12, 14.

262. See *supra,* text accompanying n. 233.

263. See *supra,* text preceding n. 229.

264. See Hernandez v. New York, 500 U.S. 352, 359 (1991) (comparing a neutral selection process in the use of peremptory strikes to employment discrimination).

265. 450 A.2d 1173 (Del. 1982).

266. Ibid. at 1185 (citation omitted).

267. Ibid.

268. Ibid.

269. 489 A.2d 1175, 1180 (N.J. Super. Ct. App. Div. 1985), aff'd, 511 A.2d 1150 (N.J. 1986).

270. People v. Wheeler, 583 P.2d 748, 762 (Cal. 1978), cited and quoted by the New Jersey Appellate Court in State v. Gilmore, *supra* n. 132, at 1182.

271. Ibid. at 762.

272. See Barbara D. Underwood, "Ending Race Discrimination in Jury Selection: Whose Right Is It, Anyway?" *Columbia Law Review* 92 (1992): 725.

273. In addition to race and sex, claims have been made based on age, education, economic status, and religion. See generally Foster v. Sparks, 506 F.2d 805 (5th Cir. 1975); United States ex rel. Chestnut v. Criminal Court, 442 F.2d 611 (2d Cir. 1971); United States v. Butera, 420 F.2d 564 (1st Cir. 1970); Rabinowitz v. United States, 366 F.2d 34 (5th Cir. 1966); Brooks v. Beto, 366 F.2d 1 (5th Cir. 1966); State v. Davis, 504 N.W.2d 767 (Minn. 1993); Casarez v. Texas, 913 S.W.2d 468 (Tex. Crim. App. 1995). See also Purkett v. Elem, 514 U.S. 765 (1995), where the Supreme Court reveals how a *prima facie* case of improper use of peremptories can be overcome by a race-neutral explanation.

274. *Rabinowitz,* 366 F.2d at 55. The court quoted from the recommendations of the September 1960 Judicial Conference, as follows: "Any attempt to gain competent jurors that would result in a less representative cross-section than a choice from the statutorily qualified pool destroys the 'right' Congress intended to confer." Ibid. at 55 n. 53 (referring to the amendments to 28 U.S.C. § 1861, "Qualifications of Federal Jurors;" effected by the Civil Rights Act of 1957 [71 Stat. 637, 42 U.S.C. 1971]).

275. People v. Brandenberg, 75 N.Y.S.2d 851, 853 (Bronx County Ct. 1947); see also *supra* n. 181 and accompanying text (discussing Justice Murphy's dissent in the *Moore* case); *supra* nn. 214–19 and accompanying text (discussing the Delaware Superior Court in the *Bradley* case).

276. See *supra* n. 274.

277. Stuart Taylor, Jr., "Making Juries Look Like America," *Legal Times,* Aug. 7, 1995, at 19. The author comments on the case of State v. Harris, 660 A.2d 539 (N.J. Super. Ct. App. Div. 1995), in which the court held that, just as constitutional policies limit a prosecutor's use of peremptory challenges to exclude members of a particular race from a jury, these policies "also require a trial court to consider racial demographics in exercising its authority . . . to change the venue of a criminal trial or to impanel a foreign jury." 660 A.2d at 543. The court explained:

> If a trial court disregards racial demographics in selecting a county for a change of venue or as the source for impanelling a foreign jury, resulting in a jury pool with a significantly smaller percentage of a racial minority than would be generated in the county where the crime was committed, it will reduce the likelihood that the jurors ultimately selected will be members of different groups whose "respective biases . . . will tend to cancel each other out" in the course of jury deliberations.

Ibid. at 543, quoting State v. Gilmore, 511 A.2d 1150, 1158 (N.J. 1986). According to Taylor, the holding in *Harris* "should not be seen as a first step toward racializing jury selection in general. It can and should be cabined to the context of venue changes and foreign juries." Taylor, *supra,* at 19.

278. *Supra* n. 12; see also *supra* text accompanying n. 240 (quoting the 1993 recommendation of the Royal Commission on Criminal Justice).

279. 552 N.E.2d 621 (N.Y. 1990), aff'd, 500 U.S. 352 (1991) (n. 264, *supra*). *Hernandez* has been the subject of extensive legal commentary. For interesting early examples, see Deborah A. Ramirez, "Excluded Voices: The Disenfranchisement of Ethnic Groups from Jury Service," *Wisconsin Law Review* 1993: 761; Note, "Peremptory Exclusion of Span-

ish-Speaking Jurors: Could *Hernandez v. New York* Happen Here?" *New Mexico Law Review* 23 (1993): 467.

280. *Hernandez*, *supra* n. 264, at 375.

281. Ibid. The theory of the prosecution in striking Spanish-speaking prospective jurors was to eliminate those jurors who might disregard translations introduced into evidence of testimony or documents given or written in Spanish, favoring instead their own translations.

282. Ibid. at 371.

283. 19 F.3d 857 (3rd Cir. 1994).

284. Ibid. at 870.

285. Ibid. at 872.

286. See Ramirez, "Excluded Voices," *supra* n. 279, at 789–90.

287. State v. Rochester, 253 A.2d. 558, 571 (N.J. Super. Ct. Law. Div. 1967).

288. See *supra* n. 274 and accompanying text.

Table of Statutes

United States

Federal

State

Alabama

Texas

Vermont

Virginia

Washington

West Virginia

Wisconsin

Table of Cases

Note: Citations in the following table are only to cases that appear in the standard reports. For England, these are the nominative reports (with parallel citations to the *English Reports* reprints), plus *State Trials*. For the United States, they include the federal and regional state reports of West Publishing Company, Westlaw, LEXIS, and a few original state and federal reporters. Citations to cases found only in manuscript or printed sources other than the standard reports are given in the endnotes to the pages where the case are discussed or referenced.

Index

About the Author

James Oldham is St. Thomas More Professor of Law and Legal History at Georgetown University Law Center. He is the author of *The Mansfield Manuscripts and the Growth of English Law in the Eighteenth Century* and *English Common Law in the Age of Mansfield.*

www.ingramcontent.com/pod-product-compliance
Lightning Source LLC
LaVergne TN
LVHW101439200926
848483LV00004B/406